SEVENTH EDITION

GRAMMAR IN CONTEXT 3

SANDRA N. ELBAUM

NATIONAL GEOGRAPHIC
LEARNING

Australia · Brazil · Mexico · Singapore · United Kingdom · United States

National Geographic Learning,
a Cengage Company

***Grammar in Context 3,* Seventh Edition**
Sandra N. Elbaum

Publisher: Sherrise Roehr

Executive Editor: Laura Le Dréan

Senior Development Editor: Eve Einselen Yu

Director of Global Marketing: Ian Martin

Heads of Regional Marketing:

  Joy MacFarland (United States and Canada)

  Charlotte Ellis (Europe, Middle East and Africa)

  Kiel Hamm (Asia)

  Irina Pereyra (Latin America)

Product Marketing Manager: Tracy Bailie

Content Project Manager: Beth F. Houston

Media Researcher: Leila Hishmeh

Art Director: Brenda Carmichael

Senior Designer: Lisa Trager

Operations Support: Rebecca G. Barbush, Hayley Chwazik-Gee

Manufacturing Planner: Mary Beth Hennebury

Composition: MPS North America LLC

For permission to use material from this text or product,
submit all requests online at **cengage.com/permissions**
Further permissions questions can be emailed to
permissionrequest@cengage.com

Grammar in Context 3 ISBN: 978-0-357-14025-3
Grammar in Context 3 + OLP ISBN: 978-0-357-14051-2

National Geographic Learning
200 Pier 4 Boulevard
Boston, MA 02210
USA

Locate your local office at **international.cengage.com/region**

Visit National Geographic Learning online at **ELTNGL.com**
Visit our corporate website at www.cengage.com

Printed in China
Print Number: 01 Print Year: 2019

CONTENTS

LANGUAGE   RISK

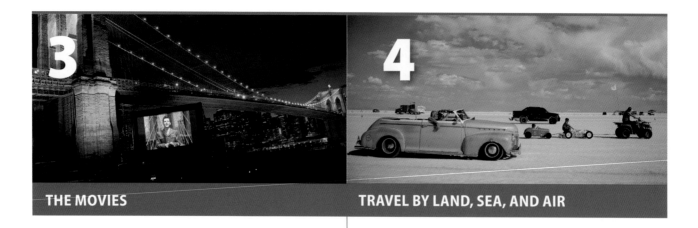

THE MOVIES · **TRAVEL BY LAND, SEA, AND AIR**

HIGH-TECH WORLD

U.S. PRESIDENTS AND ELECTIONS

ONLINE INTERACTIONS

HELPING OTHERS

COMING TO AMERICA

CHILDREN

11

SCIENCE OR SCIENCE FICTION?

A WORD FROM THE AUTHOR

My parents immigrated to the United States from Poland and learned English as a second language as adults. My sisters and I were born in the United States. My parents spoke Yiddish to us; we answered in English. In that process, my parents' English improved immeasurably. Such is the case with many immigrant parents whose children are fluent in English. They usually learn English much faster than others; they hear the language in natural ways, in the context of daily life.

Learning a language in context, whether it be from the home, from work, or from a textbook, cannot be overestimated. The challenge for me has been to find a variety of high-interest topics to engage the adult language learner. I was thrilled to work on this new edition of *Grammar in Context* for National Geographic Learning. In so doing, I have been able to combine exciting new readings with captivating photos to exemplify the grammar.

I have given more than 100 workshops at ESL programs and professional conferences around the United States, where I have gotten feedback from users of previous editions of *Grammar in Context*. Some teachers have expressed concern about trying to cover long grammar units within a limited time. While ESL is not taught in a uniform number of hours per week, I have heeded my audiences and streamlined the series so that the grammar and practice covered is more manageable. And in response to the needs of most ESL programs, I have expanded and enriched the writing component.

Whether you are a new user of *Grammar in Context* or have used this series before, I welcome you to this new edition.

Sandra N. Elbaum

For my loves
Gentille, Chimene, Joseph, and Joy

WELCOME TO *GRAMMAR IN CONTEXT*, SEVENTH EDITION

Grammar in Context, the original contextualized grammar series, brings grammar to life through engaging topics that provide a framework for meaningful practice. Students learn more, remember more, and use language more effectively when they study grammar in context.

ENHANCED IN THE SEVENTH EDITION

National Geographic photographs introduce unit themes and pull students into the context.

Unit openers include an inspirational quote to help students connect to the theme.

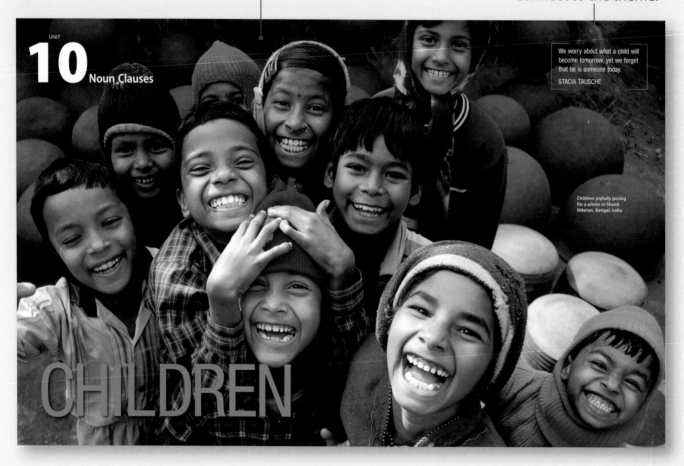

UNIT
10 Noun Clauses

We worry about what a child will become tomorrow, yet we forget that he is someone today.
STACIA TAUSCHE

Children joyfully posing for a photo in Shanti Niketan, Bengal, India

CHILDREN

New and updated readings introduce the target grammar in context and provide the springboard for explanations and practice.

New Think About It questions give students the opportunity to personalize and think critically about what they are reading.

The
TEENAGE
BRAIN

Teenagers out for a ride in a rural area of France

9243 WV 83

Read the following article. Pay special attention to the words in bold. 🔊 10.3

For many American teenagers, 16 is the magic number—the age when they can get their driver's license. But this is also the time when parents worry the most about their kids.

In the United States, one in three teen deaths is from a car crash. Parents often wonder **if kids really understand the risks they are taking when they are behind the wheel.** They warn their kids **what to do and what not to do** while driving, but they really don't know **whether their kids will follow their advice or not.** They hand over the car keys—and hope for the best.

Studies show that when teens drive alone, they take risks at the same rate as adults. But when they drive with other teens, they take more risks.

Scientists have been using scans[1] to study the teenage brain. Even though the brain is almost full size by the time a child is six years old, scientists are finding that the brain makes great changes between the ages of 12 and 25. During this time, it is natural that young people seek thrills[2]. According to Laurence Steinberg, a developmental psychologist from Temple

University, "The teenage brain is like a car with a good accelerator but a weak brake . . . . Adolescents are more impulsive,[3] thrill-seeking, drawn to the rewards of a risky decision than adults."

While new technologies can make driving more dangerous, there are other technologies that help parents keep track of their teenagers' driving habits. There are phone apps that let parents know **what their kids are doing behind the wheel.** Parents can know **if their child is texting or tweeting while driving** or **how fast their teenager is driving.**

Risky behavior is a normal stage of development in teenagers. "I can't stand riding on a roller-coaster now," said Professor Steinberg. "I liked it as a teenager. I can't stand driving fast now. I liked driving fast when I was a teenager. What has changed? I'm not as driven today by this thrill-seeking sensation[4]."

[1] scan: an examination of an inside part of the body done with a special machine
[2] thrill: a feeling of strong excitement or pleasure
[3] impulsive: done with a sudden urge
[4] sensation: a physical feeling

286   Unit 10

COMPREHENSION Based on the reading, write T for *true* or F for *false*.

1. _____ When teenagers drive with other teenagers in the car, they take more risks.
2. _____ The brain is fully developed by the age of 12.
3. _____ The majority of teen deaths are the result of car crashes.

THINK ABOUT IT Discuss the questions with a partner or in a small group.

1. Do you recognize yourself in the description of teenagers presented in this article? How are or were you similar? Different? Give examples.
2. What is your opinion of parents using technology to track their teenage children's behavior? Explain.

10.2 Noun Clauses as Included Questions

A noun clause is used to include a question in a statement or another question.

DIRECT QUESTION	INCLUDED QUESTION
Wh- questions with auxiliaries or **be**	We use statement word order. We put the subject before the verb.
How fast is my daughter driving?	I'd like to know **how fast she is driving.**
What app can I use?	Please tell me **what app I can use.**
Wh- questions with auxiliaries or **do/does/did**	We remove *do/does/did*. The verb shows -s ending for *he, she,* or *it* in the present, or use the past form.
Why does a teenager take risks?	Scientists want to know **why a teenager takes risks.**
How did the car accident happen?	I'd like to know **how the car accident happened.**
Wh- questions about the subject	There is no change in word order.
Who bought the app?	I'd like to know **who bought the app.**
What makes the teenage brain different?	Scientists want to know **what makes the teenage brain different.**
Yes/No questions with auxiliaries or **be**	We add the word *if* or *whether*. We use statement word order. We put the subject before the verb.
Is the teenager driving too fast?	The app can tell you **if the teenager is driving too fast.**
Will my teenage brother follow my advice?	I wonder **whether my teenage brother will follow my advice.**
Yes/No questions with **do**	We remove *do/does/did*. We add *if* or *whether*. The verb shows the -s ending for *he, she,* or *it,* in the present, or uses the past form.
Does my teenager follow my advice?	I want to know **if my teenager follows my advice.**
Did you do the same thing when you were my age?	My son wants to know **whether I did the same thing when I was his age.**

> **GRAMMAR IN USE**
> In social situations where perhaps someone is at fault, an included question can be less direct and, therefore, more polite.
> **Direct question:** *Who took the car keys?* (Maybe it was you!)
> **More polite:** *Do you know who took the car keys?* (I'm not suggesting it was you, but it could be you.)

17

New Grammar in Use notes highlight practical usage points to help students communicate more effectively.

New listening comprehension activities encourage students to listen for meaning through natural spoken English.

EXERCISE 17 Listen to the information about the U.S. Census. Write T for *true*, F for *false*, or NS for *not stated*. 🔊 9.6

1. _____ At first, children were not counted in the census.
2. _____ All census information is available to everyone.
3. _____ Most Americans complete the census questionnaire.

New Fun with Grammar allows the class to practice grammar in a lively game-like way.

Summary and Review sections help students revisit key points and assess their progress.

SUMMARY OF UNIT 9

The Present Perfect and the Simple Past

PRESENT PERFECT	SIMPLE PAST
The action of the sentence began in the past and includes the present.	The action of the sentence is completely past.
Sergey Brin **has been** in the U.S. since 1979.	Sergey Brin **came** to the U.S. in 1979.
Khan's videos **have been** available for many years.	Khan **created** his first math videos in 2004.
I've always **wanted** to learn more about my family's history.	When I was a child, I always **wanted** to spend time with my grandparents.
How long **have** you **been** interested in genealogy?	When **did** you **start** your family tree?

PRESENT PERFECT	SIMPLE PAST
Repetition from past to present	Repetition in a past time period
Khan Academy **has created** over 5,000 videos so far.	Khan **created** several videos for his niece in 2004.

PRESENT PERFECT	SIMPLE PAST
The action took place at an indefinite time between the past and the present.	The action took place at a definite time in the past.
Have you ever **used** Cyndi's list?	**Did** you **use** the 1940 census in 2012?
My brother **has raised** $5,000 on a crowdfunding site already.	He **put** his project on a crowdfunding site six months ago.
I'm interested in the DNA project. I've **received** my kit, but I **haven't sent** the sample back yet.	My friend **sent** her DNA sample to the Genographic Project last month.

The Present Perfect and the Present Perfect Continuous

PRESENT PERFECT	PRESENT PERFECT CONTINUOUS
A continuous action (nonaction verbs)	A continuous action (action verbs)
I **have been** interested in genealogy for five years.	I've **been working** on my family tree for five years.
A repeated action	A nonstop action
Cyndi Howell's website **has won** several awards.	The U.S. Census Bureau **has been keeping** records since the 1880s.
Question with *how many/how much*	Question with *how long*
How many times **has** Khan **been** on the cover of a magazine? How much time **has** he **spent** on Khan Academy?	How long **has** Khan **been living** in Boston?
An action that is at an indefinite time, completely in the past	An action that started in the past and is still happening
Many teachers **have started** to use Khan lectures in their classrooms.	Dr. Wells **has been collecting** DNA for several years.

254 Unit 9

REVIEW

Fill in the blanks with the simple past, the present perfect, or the present perfect continuous form of the verbs given. Include any other words you see. In some cases, more than one answer is possible.

A: What do you do for a living?

B: I _____ work _____ as a programmer. I _____ 've been working _____ as a
      1. work   2. work
programmer for five years. But my job is boring.

A: _____ about changing jobs?
      3. you/think/ever

B: Yes. Since I _____ a child, I _____ to be an actor.
                        4. be   5. always/want
When I was in college, I _____ in a few plays. But since I
                              6. be
_____, I _____ time to act. What about you?
      7. graduate   8. not/have

A: I _____ in computer security.
      9. work

B: How long _____ that?
                  10. you/do

A: For about six years.

B: I _____ the field of computer security is very important.
      11. think

A: Yes, it is. But lately I _____ the computer for other things, too. My hobby is
                              12. use
genealogy. I _____ on my family tree for about a year. Last month I
                  13. work
_____ information about my father's ancestors. My grandfather
      14. find
_____ with us now, and he likes to tell us about his past. He
      15. live
_____ born in Italy, but he _____ here when he
      16. be   17. come
was very young, so he _____ most of his life. He
                              18. live
_____ much about Italy. I _____ any information
      19. not/remember   20. not/find
about my mother's ancestors yet.

The Present Perfect, The Present Perfect Continuous 255

From Grammar to Writing gives editing advice and practice to set students up to successfully apply the grammar to writing.

FROM GRAMMAR TO WRITING

PART 1 Editing Advice

1. Don't confuse the *-ing* form and the past participle.
                taking
   I've been taken a course in genealogy.
                given
   My parents have giving me family photos.

2. Use the present perfect, not the simple present or present continuous, to describe an action or state that started in the past and continues to the present.
            had   have you been
   He has his laptop for two years.   How long are you studying math?

3. Use *for*, not *since*, with the amount of time.
                                    for
   I've been interested in my family's history since three years.

4. Use the simple past, not the present perfect, with a specific past time.
            studied
   He has studied algebra when he was in high school.
            did   study
   When have you studied algebra?

5. Use the simple past, not the present perfect, in a *since* clause.
                                        put
   He has collected $5,000 since he has put his project on a crowdfunding site.

6. Use the correct word order with adverbs.
            never studied   ever heard
   I have studied never my family history. Have you heard ever of Dr. Spencer Wells?

7. Use the correct word order in questions.
                    has your family
   How long your family has been in this country?

8. Use *yet* for negative statements; use *already* for affirmative statements.
                                        yet
   I haven't taken advanced algebra already.

9. Don't forget the verb *have* in the present perfect (continuous).
      have
   I been studying my family history for two years.

10. Don't forget the *-ed* of the past participle.
                    ed
   He's watch a math video several times.

PART 2 Editing Practice

Some of the shaded words and phrases have mistakes. Find the mistakes and correct them. If the shaded words are correct, write *C*.
                                                              have you   C
   How many changes you have made since you came to the U.S.? For our journal, our teacher
                                              1.   2.
asked us to answer this question. I have come to the U.S. two and a half years ago. Things have
                                        3.
change a lot for me since I've come here. Here are some of the changes:
      4.   5.

256 Unit 9

First, since the past two years, I am studying to be a software engineer. I knew a little about
              6.   7.   8.
this subject before I came here, but my knowledge has improve a lot. I started to work part-time
                                                              9.   10.
in a computer company three months ago. Since I have started my job, I haven't have much time
                                              11.   12.   13.   14.
for fun.

   Second, I have a driver's permit, and I'm learning how to drive. I haven't took the driver's test
                                                                          15.
yet because I'm not ready. I haven't practiced enough already.
16.   17.   18.

   Third, I've been eaten a lot of different foods like hamburgers and pizza. I never ate those in
                  19.   20.
my country. Unfortunately, I been gaining weight.
                              21.

   Fourth, I've gone to several museums in this city. But I've taken never a trip to another
                                                      22.   23.
American city. I'd like to visit New York, but I haven't saved enough money yet.
                                                    24.   25.

   Fifth, I've been living in three apartments so far. In my country, I lived in the same house
                  26.   27.
with my family all my life.

   One thing that bothers me is this: I've answered the following questions about a thousand
                                        28.
times so far: "Where do you come from?" and "How long time you have been in the U.S.?" I'm
                                                      29.   30.
getting tired of always answering the same question. But in general, I been happy since I came to
                                                                    31.   32.
the U.S.

WRITING TIP

When you write a paragraph or essay about a change in your life, start your paper with a sentence that states how the new situation (technology for example) has changed your life.

   Since I got a cell phone, my life has greatly improved.

Then use the simple past to talk about what you used to do and the simple present to talk about what you do habitually now.

   Before I got a cell phone, I went to work in the morning and only talked to my family at night. Now, I call before I go home to ask if they need anything.

PART 3 Write

Read the prompts. Choose one and write a paragraph or two about it.
1. Write about the changes that you have made since you came to this country, city, or school.
2. Write about new technology that you've started using recently. How has that made your life different?

PART 4 Edit

Reread the Summary of Unit 9 and the editing advice. Edit your writing from Part 3.

The Present Perfect, The Present Perfect Continuous 257

New Writing Tips further connect the grammar to the unit writing task.

ADDITIONAL RESOURCES

FOR STUDENTS The **Online Practice** provides a variety of interactive grammar activities for homework or flexible independent study.

GO TO ELTNGL.COM/MYELT

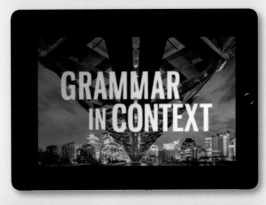

FOR TEACHERS The **Classroom Presentation Tool** allows the teacher to project the student book pages, open interactive activities with answers, and play the audio program.

The Teacher's Website hosts the teacher's guide, audio, and ExamView® Test Center, so teachers have all the materials they need in one place.

ELTNGL.COM/GRAMMARINCONTEXTSERIES

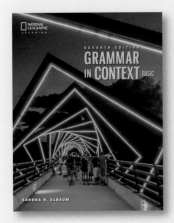
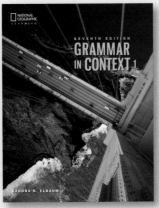
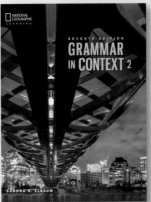
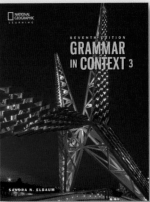

CREDITS

ACKNOWLEDGMENTS

The Author and Publisher would like to acknowledge and thank the teachers who participated in the development of the seventh edition of *Grammar in Context*.

A special thanks to our Advisory Board for their valuable input during the development of this series.

ADVISORY BOARD

Andrea Gonzalez, BYU English Language Center, Provo, UT, USA

Ellen Rosen, Fullerton College, Fullerton, CA, USA

Erin Pak, Schoolcraft College, Livonia, MI, USA

Holly Gray, Prince George's Community College, Largo, MD, USA

John Halliwell, Moraine Valley Community College, Palos Hills, IL, USA

Katherine Sieradzki, FLS Boston, Boston, MA, USA

Maria Schirta, Hudson County Community College, Jersey City, NJ, USA

Oranit Limmaneeprasert, American River College, Sacramento, CA, USA

Susan Niemeyer, Los Angeles City College, Los Angeles, CA, USA

REVIEWERS

Adriana García, Institut Nord-America, Barcelona, Spain

Alena Widows, Institut Nord-America, Barcelona, Spain

Augustine Triantafyllides, So Easy, Athens, Greece

Bilal Aslam, GTCC, High Point, NC, USA

Carmen Díez, CFA Les Corts, Barcelona, Spain

David Finfrock, QU, Doha, Qatar

Deanna Henderson, LCI, Denver, CO, USA

Ellen Barrett, Wayne State University, Detroit, MI, USA

Francis Bandin, UAB, Barcelona, Spain

Jonathan Lathers, Macomb Community College, Warren, MI, USA

Karen Vallejo, University of California, Irvine, CA, USA

Kathy Najafi, Houston Community College, Houston, TX, USA

Katie Windahl, Cuyahoga Community College, Cleveland, OH, USA

Laura Jacob, Mt. San Antonio College, Walnut, CA, USA

Leah Carmona, Bergen Community College, Paramus, NJ, USA

Luba Nesterova, Bilingual Education Institute, Houston, TX, USA

Marcos Valle, Edmonds Community College, Lynnwood, WA, USA

Marla Goldfine, San Diego Community College, San Diego, CA, USA

Milena Eneva, Chattahoochee Technical College, Marietta, GA, USA

Monica Farling, University of Delaware, Newark, DE, USA

Naima Sarfraz, Qatar University, Doha, Qatar

Natalia Schroeder, Long Beach City College, Long Beach, CA, USA

Paul Schmitt, Institut d'Estudis Nord-Americans, Barcelona, Spain

Paula Sanchez, Miami Dade College, Miami, FL, USA

Paulette Koubek-Yao, Pasadena City College, Pasadena, CA, USA

Robert Yáñez, Hillsborough Community College, Tampa, FL, USA

Samuel Lumbsden, Essex County College, Newark, NJ, USA

Sarah Mikulski, Harper College, Palatine, IL, USA

Steven Lund, Arizona Western College, Yuma, AZ, USA

Teresa Cheung, North Shore Community College, Lynn, MA, USA

Tim McDaniel, Green River College, Auburn, WA, USA

Tristinn Williams, Cascadia College, Seattle, WA, USA

Victoria Mullens, LCI, Denver, CO, USA

LANGUAGE

Yangzhou Zhangshuge
bookstore in Zhen
Yuan, China

The limits of my language
mean the limits of my world.

LUDWIG WITTGENSTEIN

THE AMAZING
TIMOTHY DONER

Read the following article. Pay special attention to the words in bold. 🎧 1.1

Timothy Doner **looks** like an average guy. But there **is** something very special about him. He **speaks** over 20 languages. He **doesn't speak** all of them equally well, but he **is** very comfortable in many of them. He **feels** most comfortable with Hebrew, Farsi[1], French, and Arabic. At any one time, he **is studying** three to four languages.

There are many videos of him on the Internet. In one video, he **is riding** in a taxi and **talking** to a Haitian taxi driver in French. In it, he **is telling** the driver that he **wants** to learn Creole, a language of Haiti. In another, he **is speaking** Russian with the owners of a video store in New York, where he **lives**. In another, he **is speaking** Farsi with the owner of a bookstore. He **is asking** the Farsi speaker for more information about the language. In other videos, he **is studying** Mandarin or **discussing** the similarities between Hebrew and Arabic with native speakers of these languages. He also **speaks** Urdu[2], Indonesian, Swahili[3], and Ojibwe, an American Indian language.

Doner **spends** a lot of time trying to learn languages. To learn some languages, he **takes** classes. To learn others, he **studies** on his own. He always **looks** for opportunities to practice with native speakers. Sometimes he **uses** video chats to practice with native speakers in other countries. He also **memorizes** songs and **watches** movies in other languages. He really **enjoys** learning languages. He **thinks** that language **helps** you connect to other people. When he **speaks** another language, he **feels** like a different person.

He **doesn't** only **study** languages. He also **studies** linguistics and **writes** about the history and culture of the Middle East.

---

[1] Farsi: the official language of Iran
[2] Urdu: an official language spoken in Pakistan
[3] Swahili: a language spoken in Kenya and other countries of the African Great Lakes region

COMPREHENSION Based on the reading, write T for *true* or F for *false*.

1. _____ Timothy Doner is able to communicate in over 20 languages.

2. _____ He doesn't practice with native speakers.

3. _____ It's impossible for him to practice with native speakers in other countries.

THINK ABOUT IT Discuss the questions with a partner or in a small group.

1. Do you believe that some people learn languages more easily than others? Explain.

2. What are some ways that learning a language can help you better connect with the speakers of that language?

1.1 The Present of *Be*

EXAMPLES			EXPLANATION
I	am		*Be* has three forms in the present: *am, is, are.*
He She It	is	from New York.	
You We They	are		
I'm happy to hear about Timothy. Timothy's an amazing person. They're interested in linguistics.			Subject pronouns and most singular nouns can contract with a present form of *be*. *I'm, He's, She's, It's, You're, We're, They're, Timothy's*
Timothy **is** smart. Mandarin and Cantonese **are** languages of China. Haiti **is** southeast of Florida. It **is** warm in Haiti all year. I **am** hot. Let's turn on the air-conditioning. Timothy Doner **is** from New York. How old **is** Timothy now? I **am** hungry. What time **is** it in New York now? There **are** many languages in India.			We use a form of *be* with: • a description • a classification or grouping • a location • weather • reaction to weather • place of origin • age • physical states • time • *There*

Notice these seven patterns with the verb *be*:

AFFIRMATIVE STATEMENT:	Spanish **is** the official language of Colombia.
NEGATIVE STATEMENT:	It **isn't** the language of Brazil.
YES/NO QUESTION:	**Is** Spanish easy for Italians?
SHORT ANSWER:	Yes, it **is**.
WH- QUESTION:	Why **is** Spanish easy for Italians?
NEGATIVE *WH-* QUESTION:	Why **isn't** Spanish a challenge for Timothy?
SUBJECT QUESTION:	What **is** the official language of Brazil?

Note:

We don't make a contraction with *is* if the noun ends in *s, se, ce, ge, ze, sh, ch,* or *x.*

> ***French is** one of Timothy's languages.* (NOT: *French's*)

EXERCISE 1 Listen to the first part of a conversation between two students. Fill in the blanks with the words you hear. 🎧 1.2

A: What _'s your native language_ ?
                           1.

B: My native _____ French.
                        2.

A: _____ France?
              3.

B: No. _____ from France. _____ from Cameroon.
              4.   5.

A: _____ Cameroon?
              6.

B: _____ in Africa.
              7.

A: What part of Africa _____ ?
                                   8.

B: It's in West Africa.

A: _____ the only language in Cameroon?
              9.

B: No, _____ . _____ many languages in Cameroon, but the two official
                 10.   11.

languages _____ French and English.
                  12.

EXERCISE 2 Complete the rest of the conversation from Exercise 1 on your own. Use contractions wherever possible.

A: How many languages _____ _are there_ _____ in Cameroon?
                                  1.

B: There _____ about 250 languages. French _____ my official language,
                  2.   3.

but my home language _____ Beti.
                               4.

A: _____ similar to French?
              5.

B: No, it _____ . Not at all. They _____ completely different.
                  6.   7.

A: How many speakers of Beti _____ there?
                                         8.

B: _____ about 2 million.
              9.

A: Then _____ an important language in your country.
                   10.

B: Yes, it definitely _____ .
                                  11.

A: My roommate _____ from Nigeria. _____ near Nigeria?
                            12.   13.

B: Yes. Cameroon and Nigeria _____ neighbors. Nigeria _____ north of Cameroon.
                                          14.   15.

A: I _____ interested in your country, but I _____ really hungry.
              16.   17.

_____ hungry?
       18.

B: Yes, I _____ . Let's go get something to eat. We can finish our conversation over lunch.
                  19.

1.2 The Simple Present

FORM

EXAMPLES	EXPLANATION
I **like** English. You **know** Mandarin. We **come** from China. The people of Iran **speak** Farsi.	We use the base form of the verb with *I, you, we, they,* and plural subjects. Note: *People* is plural.
Timothy **lives** in New York. He **studies** languages.	We use the *-s* form with *he, she, it,* and singular subjects.
Every language **shows** something about the culture. No one in this class **speaks** Ojibwe.	We use the *-s* form with subjects beginning with *every* and *no.*
Timothy's family **lives** in New York.	Note: *Family* is singular.
Timothy **likes to learn** languages.	We can follow many main verbs with an infinitive.

Notice these seven patterns with the base form:

AFFIRMATIVE STATEMENT:	You **speak** Urdu.
NEGATIVE STATEMENT:	You **don't speak** Hindi.
YES/NO QUESTION:	**Do** you **speak** Farsi?
SHORT ANSWER:	Yes, I **do.**
WH- QUESTION:	Where **do** people **speak** Urdu?
NEGATIVE *WH-* QUESTION:	Why **don't** you **speak** Hindi?
SUBJECT QUESTION:	How many people **speak** Hindi?

Notice these seven patterns with the *-s* form:

AFFIRMATIVE STATEMENT:	Timothy **studies** Farsi.
NEGATIVE STATEMENT:	He **doesn't study** Spanish.
YES/NO QUESTION:	**Does** he **study** French?
SHORT ANSWER:	Yes, he **does.**
WH- QUESTION:	Where **does** he **study** French?
NEGATIVE *WH-* QUESTION:	Why **doesn't** he **study** Spanish?
SUBJECT QUESTION:	Who **studies** Spanish?

Notes:

1. *Have* has an irregular *-s* form:

    I **have** *a language dictionary. Timothy* **has** *many language dictionaries.*

2. The *-s* form of *go* is *goes.* The pronunciation is /goᵂz/.

    We **go** *to college. My sister* **goes** *to high school.*

3. The *-s* form of *do* is *does.* The pronunciation is /dʌz/.

    You **do** *your homework at home. She* **does** *her homework at the library.*

GRAMMAR IN USE

A common error is to drop the helping verb *do/does* when asking about meaning, spelling, cost, and time. We use regular word order in these situations.

What **does** *"challenge"* **mean?**	*How much* **does** *the book* **cost?**
How **do** *you* **spell** *"challenge"?*	*How long* **does** *it* **take** *to learn another language?*

USE

EXAMPLES	EXPLANATION
Timothy **speaks** 20 languages. He **loves** languages, but he **doesn't like** math.	We use the simple present with facts, general truths, habits, and customs.
Timothy **often practices** with native speakers. He **always tries** to learn new things. **Does** he **ever make** videos? **How often does** he **use** a dictionary?	We use the simple present with regular activities and repeated actions.

Notes:

1. The frequency adverbs are *always, almost always, usually, generally, frequently, sometimes, occasionally, seldom, rarely, hardly ever, almost never, not ever,* and *never*. Frequency adverbs usually come after the verb *be* and before other verbs.

   Timothy is **always** interested in languages.   He **sometimes** finds native speakers to talk to.

2. We can put *sometimes* at the beginning of a sentence, too.

   Sometimes he finds native speakers to talk to.

GRAMMAR IN USE

Seldom, rarely, hardly ever, and *almost never* have similar meanings. *Seldom* and *rarely* are more formal. *Hardly ever* and *almost never* are more common in conversation and informal writing.

A: Do you **ever** speak English with your parents?
B: No, I **almost never** do. OR No, I **hardly ever** do.

EXERCISE 3 Use the underlined verbs to help you complete the sentences.

1. Timothy <u>lives</u> in New York. ___Does he live___ with his parents?

2. He <u>speaks</u> French. He __*doesn't speak*__ Spanish.

3. Timothy <u>speaks</u> a lot of languages. _____ Urdu? Yes, he _____.

4. He <u>memorizes</u> songs. _____ poems, too?

5. He _____ video chat. Does he <u>use</u> other methods, too? Yes, he _____.

6. He <u>takes</u> classes. _____ a Farsi class?

7. New York _____ people from all over the world. _____ New York <u>have</u> people

   from Indonesia? Yes, it _____.

8. Some languages _____ accent marks. _____ Hebrew <u>have</u> accent marks?

9. Timothy <u>feels</u> different when he speaks another language. Why _____ different?

10. He's <u>interested</u> in Creole, but he _____ interested in Spanish. Why _____

    interested in Spanish?

11. Farsi <u>challenges</u> him, but Spanish _____ him as much.

12. He _____ comfortable speaking Arabic. _____ <u>feel</u> comfortable speaking

   Hebrew? Yes, he _____ .

13. His parents <u>speak</u> English. _____ Hebrew?

14. He <u>is</u> very good at languages, but he _____ very good at math.

15. He <u>studies</u> languages every day. _____ only from books?

   No, he _____ .

16. He <u>practices</u> with native speakers. How _____ with native speakers?

17. Not many people <u>speak</u> Ojibwe. How many people in the U.S. _____ Ojibwe?

EXERCISE 4 Fill in the blanks to complete the conversation. Use the words given.

A: Hi. My name's Bai. I'm from China.

B: Hi Bai. My name's Khalid. __Do you speak__ Chinese?
                              1. you/speak

A: Well, a lot of people _____ our language is Chinese. But there are several dialects of
                              2. say

   Chinese. I _____ Mandarin. China _____ over 1 billion people, and most
              3. speak   4. have

   people _____ Mandarin, but not everyone does. Mandarin _____ over
          5. speak   6. have

   800 million speakers. What about you?

B: I speak Farsi. _____ anything about my language?
                     7. you/know

A: No, I _____ . Who _____ Farsi?
            8.   9. speak

B: People in Iran do. We sometimes _____ the language "Persian."
                                       10. call

A: What alphabet _____ ?
                     11. you/use

B: We _____ the Arabic alphabet, with some differences. We _____ from
         12.   13. write

   right to left. _____ my writing?
                  14. you/want/see

A: Yes, I _____ .
             15.

B: تصوير, I want to see your writing, too.

A: Here's an example of my writing. 書

B: How many letters _____ ?
                        16. Chinese/have

continued

A: Chinese _____ letters. It _____ characters. Each character
17. not/have   18. have

_____ a word or a syllable.
19. represent

B: Wow. It _____ like a hard language.
20. seem

A: Well, it isn't hard to speak it. But it _____ a long time to learn to read and write well.
21. take

B: It _____ so beautiful.
22. look

A: Your writing _____ beautiful, too.
23. look

ABOUT YOU Read the statements. Correct the statements that are not true about you. Then work with a partner and ask him or her about these statements.

A: *I'm not from Mexico. I'm from Ecuador. Are you from Mexico?*

B: *No, I'm not.*

A: *Where are you from?*

B: *I'm from the Philippines.*

       not
1. I'm ∧from Mexico.

2. I speak English with my friends from my country.

3. I speak English with my family.

4. I want to learn Urdu or Chinese.

5. I am interested in seeing Timothy Doner's videos.

6. My favorite songs are in my language.

7. Most people in my country study English.

8. Spanish is my native language.

9. I'm interested in linguistics.

10. I use video chat to communicate with my friends and family.

EXERCISE 5 Read the conversation between two new students. Fill in the blanks by using the words given and context clues.

A: Hi. My name's Marco. I come from Brazil. What 's your name and where _are you from_ ?
1.   2. you

B: My name's Ly. I'm from Vietnam.

A: How _____ your name?
3. spell

B: It's very simple: L-Y. _____ Spanish?
4.

A: No. I don't speak Spanish. Spanish _____ the official language of most countries in South
                                                  5.

America, but Brazilians _____ Portuguese. What about you?
                                  6.

B: Vietnamese _____ my native language.
                        7.

A: I _____ anything about Vietnamese. _____ the same
           8. not/know   9. Vietnamese/use

alphabet as English?

B: Yes, it _____ . But we use accent marks on our words. Look. Here's a text message in
                  10.

Vietnamese from my sister. Bạn đang ở đâu? _____ all the extra marks we use on
                                                11. you/see

our letters?

A: Yes, I _____ . Wow! It _____ very complicated. _____
              12.   13. look   14.

similar to Chinese?

B: Not at all. But there's one similarity: both Chinese and Vietnamese are tonal languages.

A: What _____ ?
              15. mean/"tonal"

B: It _____ the tone affects the meaning. There _____ six tones in
          16. mean   17.

Vietnamese. For example, "ma" _____ six different things, depending on the tone.
                                    18. mean

continued

Ha Long Bay. Vietnam

A: Really?

B: Yes. It can mean "horse," "but," or "ghost," for example. It _____ other meanings, too,
                                                        19. have

depending on the tone. Tell me about your language.

A: Portuguese _____ some accent marks, too. But it _____ tones.
                          20. have   **21. not/have**

Not everyone in Brazil _____ Portuguese. There are some other languages, too,
                                                22. speak

such as Cocama.

B: How _____ that?
                      23. you/spell

A: C-O-C-A-M-A.

B: How many people _____ Cocama?
                                    24. speak

A: I really _____ .
                      25. not/know

B: Right now I really _____ English as quickly as possible. It _____
                                  26. want/learn   **27. take**

a long time to become fluent in a foreign language.

B: Yes, it does. I have to go now. How _____ "see you later" in Portuguese?
                                              28. say

A: We say "Até mais tarde."

B: OK, ate mais tarde!

A: Ha! See you later!

ABOUT YOU Write questions to ask another student about his or her language. Then interview a partner.
(Choose a student who speaks a different language, if possible, or ask your teacher questions and he or she
will ask you questions.) Use the conversation above for ideas.

    A: What is the official language of your country?
    B: Actually, there is no official language in the U.S.

1. What is the official language of your country? _____

2. _____

3. _____

4. _____

5. _____

6. _____

1.3 The Present Continuous

FORM

EXAMPLES	EXPLANATION
We**'re watching** a video of Timothy Doner and a taxi driver. The driver **is telling** him about the Creole language.	To form the present continuous, we use a present form of be *(am, is, are)* + the present participle of the verb (base form + *–ing*).

Notice these seven forms with the present continuous:

Affirmative Statement:	We **are reading** about languages.
Negative Statement:	We **aren't reading** about animal communication.
Yes/No Question:	**Are** we **reading** about Mandarin now?
Short Answer:	No, we **aren't**.
Wh- Question:	Why **are** we **reading** about languages?
Negative Wh- Question:	Why **aren't** we **reading** about Mandarin?
Subject Question:	Who **is reading** about Mandarin?

USE

EXAMPLES	EXPLANATION
We **are practicing** English in class now. The teacher **is helping** us learn English grammar.	We use the present continuous for an action that is happening now.
Look at this video of Timothy. He**'s talking** with a taxi driver. They**'re having** a conversation in Creole.	We use the present continuous to describe what we see in a picture or video.
Timothy **is working** on a few projects. We **are reviewing** verb tenses this week.	We use the present continuous for an action that is ongoing over a longer period of time.
Mandarin **is gaining** popularity as a world language.	We can use the present continuous to describe a trend.
We're from Iran. We **are living** in the U.S. now.	*Live* in the present continuous often shows a temporary situation. It's also possible to say "We **live** in the U.S. now."
Timothy **is sitting** in the back of a taxi. He **is wearing** jeans and a T-shirt.	With certain verbs *(sit, stand, lie (down), wear, sleep)*, we can use the present continuous to describe the state even though there is no action.

EXERCISE 6 Listen to a conversation between a mother and daughter about American Sign Language. Write T for *true* or F for *false*. 🎧 1.3

1. _____ A sign language is for people who can't hear.

2. _____ American Sign Language has a sign for every word.

3. _____ Only people who can't hear learn sign language.

Friends using sign language

EXERCISE 7 Listen again. Fill in the blanks with the words you hear. 🎧 1.3

A: ___Are those people talking___ with their hands?
    _{1.}

B: Yes. They _____ sign language.
    _{2.}

A: What's that?

B: It's a language that people who can't hear well use.

A: _____ each word?
    _{3.}

B: No. They _____ symbols. Each symbol is a whole word. But sometimes
    _{4.}

they have to spell a word, such as a name.

A: How do you know so much about it?

B: A friend at work is deaf. _____ to learn American Sign Language
    _{5.}

because I want to communicate with her.

A: Where _____ it?
    _{6.}

B: At a community college near our house.

EXERCISE 8 Complete the conversation using the present continuous form of one of the verbs from the box below. Use contractions wherever possible.

get	knit	learn	take✓	wear

A: My nephew is deaf, so I <u>'m taking</u> sign language classes with my sister. It takes time and practice, but
                        1.

we _____ better every day.
        2.

B: How old is your nephew?

A: He's three years old.

B: That seems young to learn sign language.

A: It isn't. In fact, he _____ it very quickly, more quickly than we are! Here's a picture of him.
                    3.

B: He's so cute! He _____ an adorable hat.
                4.

A: It's from me. I knit. In fact, I _____ a sweater for him now.
                        5.

ABOUT YOU Read the statements. Correct the statements that are not true about you. Then work with a partner and ask him or her about these statements.

> *A: I'm reading many things in English outside of class.*
> *B: Really? Like what?*
> *A: I'm reading the news and some social media posts in English. How about you?*
> *B: No, I'm not. I'm too busy.*

1. I'm reading many things in English outside of class.

2. I'm studying another language in addition to English.

3. I'm beginning to mix English with my native language.

4. I'm living with my family.

5. I'm wearing blue jeans today.

ABOUT YOU Write sentences to tell about something you are doing at this time in your life. Use the verbs in parentheses with the present continuous.

1. (learn) <u>I'm learning to study more effectively.</u>

2. (read) _____

3. (study) _____

4. (working on) _____

5. (live) _____

6. (plan) _____

1.4 The Present Continuous vs. The Simple Present—Action and Nonaction Verbs

EXAMPLES	EXPLANATION
You don't have to speak so loud. I **hear** you. Mandarin now **has** more than 850 million speakers. I **know** something about Farsi.	Some verbs are nonaction verbs. They describe a state, condition, or feeling, not an action. We don't usually use the present continuous with these verbs, even when referring to the exact moment. See Appendix B for a list of nonaction verbs.
I **am listening** to a podcast. I **hear** some unusual sounds.	*Listen* is an action verb. *Hear* is a nonaction verb.
We **are looking** at a video. We **see** Timothy in a taxi.	*Look* is an action verb. *See* is a nonaction verb.
I'm **thinking about** a major in linguistics. I **think (that)** linguistics is interesting.	*Think about* or *of* is an action verb. *Think (that)* is a nonaction verb.
My mom **is having** a hard time with English. English **has** many irregular verbs in the past. Marco isn't in class today. He **has** a cold.	*Have* is an action verb when it means *experience*. *Have* for possession, relationship, or illness is a nonaction verb.
I **am looking** at the video.	Some verbs can describe either a sense perception or an action: *look, smell, taste, sound, feel.*
You **look** very interested in that video. Timothy Doner **looks like** an average guy.	When these verbs describe a sense perception, an adjective or the word *like* usually follows.

Notes:

1. Some common nonaction verbs are:
   - Sense perception verbs: *smell, taste, feel, look, sound, appear*
   - Feelings and desires: *like, dislike, love, hate, hope, want, need, prefer, agree, disagree, care (about), expect, matter*
   - Mental states: *believe, know, hear, see, notice, understand, remember, think (that), suppose, recognize*
   - Others: *mean, cost, spell, weigh*

2. Native speakers sometimes use *hope, understand,* and *think* as action verbs.

   I'm **hoping** I can visit Vietnam one day.

   If I'm **understanding** you correctly, you're afraid of making a mistake.

   I'm **thinking** that I need to practice English more. (This use of the present continuous often means I'm beginning to think . . .)

GRAMMAR IN USE

The verb *see* can mean *have a relationship with* (personal or professional). In this case, *see* is an action verb and can be present continuous.

I'm **seeing** someone new. (dating)

I'm **seeing** a new doctor. (visiting as a patient)

EXERCISE 9 Fill in the blanks with the simple present or present continuous to complete the conversation. In some cases, the verb is provided for you. In other cases, use context clues to find the verb.

A: What _____*are you looking*_____ at?
                 1.

B: I'm looking at a video of Timothy Doner. Listen!

A: What language _____? I _____ it.
                         2.   **3. not/recognize**

_____ it?
         4. you/understand

B: Of course. He's speaking my language, Russian! I _____ this for the second time.
                                                5. watch

I _____ very carefully now and I _____ a few small mistakes, but
         6. listen   **7. hear**

he _____ almost like a native Russian. And he _____ so much slang. He
       8. sound   **9. know**

even _____ like a Russian using Russian gestures.
       10. look

A: Who _____ to? And what _____ about?
         11. he/talk   **12. they/talk**

B: He _____ to the owners of a Russian video store. They _____
         13.   **14. introduce**

themselves. The Russians _____ surprised to hear an American speak their language so well.
                             15. look

A: Learning so many languages _____ time. I wonder if he has any fun in his life.
                               16. take

B: He _____ languages, so he _____ a great time. Listen.
         17. love   **18. have**

He _____ and _____ with the Russians.
         19. laugh   **20. joke**

A: I _____ that he's amazing. Is he good in other subjects, too?
       21. think

B: He says he _____ math.
               22. not/like

A: What _____ to do with so many languages?
           23. he/plan

B: He _____ about becoming a linguist.
         24. think

A: I _____ that's a perfect profession for him.
       25. think

ABOUT YOU Describe a video you are in or have taken.

> *In this video, my dog and cat* **are playing**. *They* **love** *playing together. My cat* **is chasing** *my dog's tail and my dog* **is jumping** *to get away from her. They* **look** *silly. They* **are having** *a good time.*

_____

_____

_____

_____

_____

TEXAS SILESIAN:
Will it Survive?

Panna Maria,
Texas

Read the following article. Pay special attention to the words in bold. 🎧 1.4

If you ask someone what the language of the United States is, they **will** probably **say** English, but in fact there is no official language in the U.S., and there are many communities that speak other languages, such as Chinese, Spanish, Korean, and so on. There are also many less widely spoken languages unique to the U.S. One example is Texas Silesian.

Silesian is a dialect[1] of the Polish language and is regarded by some linguists as a separate language. Silesian is spoken in southwestern Poland and the northeastern Czech Republic, and its vocabulary has been strongly influenced by German. However, Texas Silesian has been more heavily influenced by English. Why? The people who speak it have been living in the U.S. state of Texas for over 160 years!

With the rise of the Internet and global communication, it is becoming harder and harder for languages such as Texas Silesian to survive. It's difficult to estimate how long it and other dying languages **will last**. In the modern world, we simply don't know how technology **is going to evolve** and what effect it **will have** on languages.

So, how much longer **will** Texas Silesian **survive**? The language is already mainly spoken by the older generation. Keeping the language alive **is** no doubt **going to be** difficult. As stated, the globalization of language and culture puts such languages under great pressure, and this situation **won't go** away. Minority languages die out at the rate of about 25 per year, and they **will** no doubt **continue** to die. In some cases, losing the language **will mean** that the history and culture **will be** lost, too.

However, the Internet and global communication might also help to improve the survival chances of endangered languages. Projects such as Enduring Voices—a joint effort by the Living Tongues Institute and National Geographic—aim to preserve dying languages and their related cultures by recording living speakers and keeping the recordings online. Anyone can visit the Enduring Voices project website and hear the endangered or lost languages that they recorded. With the Internet, it's possible that these languages **won't be** lost or hidden away.

---

[1] dialect: a form of a language that is particular for a certain region or area

Sign at the entrance to a farm in Panna Maria, the oldest Polish settlement in the U.S.

COMPREHENSION Based on the reading, write T for *true* or F for *false*.

1. _____ Texas Silesian is spoken all over the U.S. state of Texas.

2. _____ The Internet and global communication are not good for dying languages.

3. _____ About two languages die every month.

THINK ABOUT IT Discuss the questions with a partner or in a small group.

1. Is it important to preserve dying languages in the modern world? Why or why not?

2. What is unique about your language? What would be lost if it disappeared?

1.5 The Future—Form

EXAMPLES	EXPLANATION
Many languages **will disappear**. English **will not disappear**. Some languages **won't survive**.	We can use *will* + the base form for the future. The contraction for *will not* is *won't*.
Some living things **are going to become** extinct. Texas Silesian **is** probably **going to disappear**.	We can use *be going to* + the base form for the future.
You **are going to hear** some strange sounds if you **visit** the Enduring Voices website. When the last speaker of Tofa Texas Silesian **dies**, the language **will die**.	Some future sentences have two clauses: a main clause and an *if* or time clause. We use the future only in the main clause. It doesn't matter which clause comes first.

Notice these seven patterns with *will*:

AFFIRMATIVE STATEMENT:	Some languages **will disappear**.
NEGATIVE STATEMENT:	My language **won't disappear**.
YES/NO QUESTION:	**Will** English **disappear** soon?
SHORT ANSWER:	No, it **won't**.
WH- QUESTION:	Why **will** some languages **disappear**?
NEGATIVE WH- QUESTION:	Why **won't** English **disappear** soon?
SUBJECT QUESTION:	Which languages **will disappear** soon?

Notice these seven patterns with *be going to*:

AFFIRMATIVE STATEMENT:	We **are going to study** English.
NEGATIVE STATEMENT:	We **aren't going to study** Mandarin.
YES/NO QUESTION:	**Are** we **going to study** French?
SHORT ANSWER:	No, we **aren't**.
WH- QUESTION:	Why **are** we **going to study** English?
NEGATIVE WH- QUESTION:	Why **aren't** we **going to study** French?
SUBJECT QUESTION:	Who **is going to study** French?

Note:

You can contract pronouns with *will*: *I'll, you'll, he'll, she'll, it'll, we'll, they'll*. In conversation, you also hear contractions with some question words: *who'll, what'll*, etc.

Pronunciation Note:

Going to of *be going to* for future is often pronounced "gonna" or /gʌnə/.

GRAMMAR IN USE

We write "gonna" only in very informal situations, such as texting.

Text message: *Are you* **gonna go** *to the library later?*

EXERCISE 10 Listen to the conversation between two students. Fill in the blanks with the words you hear. 🎧 1.5

A: What are you majoring in?

B: I'm majoring in art now, but I <u>'m going to change</u> _____ my major next semester.
1.

A: What _____?
2.

B: I _____ my master's in applied linguistics.
3.

A: What's that?

B: It's a degree that _____ me to teach English as a second language. When
4.

I _____ back to my country, I _____ an English teacher.
5.   6.

A: Why do you want to be an English teacher?

B: It _____ easy for me to find a job in China.
7.

A: Why _____ so easy?
8.

B: Because everyone there wants to learn English these days.

A: But English isn't your native language.

B: That doesn't matter. I know that if I _____ every day, I _____ fluent
9.   10.

soon. This semester, I have a Chinese roommate, and we speak Mandarin all the time. But next semester,

I _____ with an American woman from my math class.
11.

I _____ English with her every day, so my English
12.

_____ quickly. I'm sure of it.
13.

A: You're probably right. You _____ a lot of slang and natural English from her.
14.

B: That's the idea!

A: Do you have any other great plans for your future?

B: After I _____ for a few years, I _____ my own
15.   16.

language school in my hometown.

EXERCISE 11 Fill in the blanks with one of the words from the box below. Practice the future with *will*.

be able to hear	die	hear	make	visit
continue	have	learn	teach✓	

The Enduring Voices project is an important project for several reasons. It _____will teach_____
                                                                                    1.

future generations a lot about their past. After all members of a language group _____,
                                                                                              2.

future generations _____ the language of their ancestors. In addition,
                                              3.

they _____ more about the native culture of their ancestors. Also, linguistics students
        4.

and professors _____ a record of the languages. This project _____
                      5.   **6.**

linguistic research easier. I hope this project _____ for many more years so
                                                              7.

that we can preserve information about language and culture. If you _____ the
                                                                              8.

project online, you _____ many languages that are in danger of dying.
                            9.

EXERCISE 12 Fill in the blanks with the words given. Practice the future with *be going to*.

A: My wife is from Colombia. She speaks Spanish. I'm from Ukraine. I speak Ukrainian and Russian.

B: How do you communicate with your wife?

A: I speak Spanish, so we speak Spanish to each other. But we ___are going to have___ a baby in three
                                                                          1. have

months. When the baby is born, we _____ to English at home.
                                              2. switch

B: Why _____ that?
              3. you/do

A: We live in the U.S. now. The baby _____ the opportunity to speak perfect
                                              4. have

English. We're immigrants, so we _____ in our native countries anymore.
                                          5. not/live

So Spanish, Russian, and Ukrainian _____ so important in our daughter's life.
                                              6. not/be

B: Then she _____ the opportunity to become bilingual or trilingual.
                    7. lose

A: Well, we think it will confuse her if we speak three languages in the home.

B: I don't agree. I think it would open many doors for her in the future. It's so easy for small children to

learn languages.

A: When she's in high school, she _____ the chance to learn a foreign language.
                                            8. have

B: The best time to learn a foreign language is when you're young. Follow my advice. You won't be sorry.

ABOUT YOU Write about some plans you have for your future.

1. After I finish this course, *I'm going to return to my country* .

2. When/If I go back to my country, _____ .

3. After I complete class today, _____ .

4. _____ for my next vacation.

5. _____ when I finish this exercise.

6. _____ next weekend.

1.6 *Will, Be Going To*, or Present Continuous for Future

EXAMPLES	EXPLANATION
Many languages **will disappear**. Many languages **are going to disappear**. Your daughter **will have** many opportunities if she's bilingual. Your daughter **is going to have** many opportunities if she's bilingual.	For predictions, you can generally use either *will* or *be going to*. *Will* is more common in formal writing.
When the baby is born, we**'re going to switch** to English. I**'m going to start** an English language school in China.	We generally use *be going to* to describe something that was planned before it was mentioned.
I**'m studying** linguistics at the University of Illinois next year.	We sometimes use the present continuous with a future meaning when we have a definite plan. Often, a time or place is mentioned.
	We use *will* when we think of something at the time of speaking (unplanned), especially when we make:
A: You should help your kids become bilingual. **B:** Thanks for your advice. I**'ll think** about it.	• a promise
A: I'm having trouble with my English assignment. **Will** you **help** me? **B:** Of course I **will**.	• a request for help
A: I can't hear you. **B:** I**'ll speak** louder.	• an offer to help
A: I'm going to become an ESL teacher. **B:** You**'ll be** good at it.	• a comment of reassurance
My parents **won't support** me if I major in art.	We can use *won't (will not)* to mean *refuse to*.

EXERCISE 13 Fill in the blanks with the verbs given. Use *will* or *be going to*. In some cases, both *will* and *be going to* are possible.

A: Where are you going?

B: To the coffee shop around the corner.

A: I 'll go _____ with you. I need a cup of coffee, too.
         1. go

B: Well, I'm not really going there for coffee. I _____ a quiet table in the corner and
                                                        2. get

use the Wi-Fi there. I have to do research for an essay.

A: What topic _____?
                  3. you/research

B: Animal communication. I _____ those words and see what
                              4. just/google

I can find.

A: Why _____ about that?
          5. you/write

B: I read an article in *National Geographic* about it. I found it fascinating. So I _____
                                                                                        6. look

for more information about it.

A: I _____ with you anyway. I promise I _____ you.
        7. go   **8.** not/bother

I _____ a cup of coffee. I have my laptop, so I _____ my
  9. just/get   **10.** check

email while you do your research.

B: I could use your help a little. I'm not very good with spelling. After I write my first draft,

_____ me correct the spelling?
  11. you/help

A: Of course, I _____.
                  12.

B: I sometimes ask my roommate to help me, but he _____ it. He says I have to do this on
                                                      13. not/do

my own. This is my first essay for this class, and I'm afraid I _____ a good job.
                                                                14. not/do

A: I'm sure you _____ fine.
                   15. do

B: OK, then. Let's go. I _____ the coffee.
                          16. buy

A: And I _____ your spellchecker.
            17. be

An Unusual Orphan

Read the following article. Pay special attention to the words in bold. 🎧 1.6

She was born in West Africa in 1965. She **was** an orphan; her mother **died** when she was very young. She **didn't stay** in Africa long. She **came** to the United States when she **was** only ten months old. Allen and Beatrix Gardner, an American couple in Nevada, **adopted** her and named her Washoe. **Did** she **learn** to speak English with her new American family? Well, not exactly. Washoe **was** a chimpanzee. And the Gardners **were** language researchers.

The Gardners, who **were** interested in animal communication, **understood** that nonhuman primates[1] can't make human sounds. So they **taught** Washoe American Sign Language (ASL). The Gardners **avoided** using speech around her so that she could learn the way a deaf child learns. Washoe **was** the first nonhuman to acquire a human language.

Washoe **lived** at home with the Gardners. She **liked** to look through books, magazines, and catalogs. She especially **liked** shoe catalogs! Then, when she **was** five years old, language researchers

Roger and Deborah Fouts **took** her to the Primate Institute at the University of Oklahoma. There **were** other chimps there that could communicate with American Sign Language. When Washoe **met** other chimps for the first time, she **didn't like** them. She **called** them "black cats" or "black bugs." Eventually she **started** to interact and "talk" to them.

Researchers **wanted** to see if Washoe would communicate with baby chimps using ASL. Washoe **had** two baby chimps, but they **died** when they were very young. Researchers **gave** her a male baby chimp, Loulis, to take care of. Washoe quickly "adopted" him. She **started** signing to Loulis. She even **taught** him signs by taking his hands and showing him how to say "food." During her life, Washoe **learned** about 350 signs and **taught** signs to younger chimps.

Washoe **died** in 2007 at the age of 42.

---

[1] primate: a member of the highest order of animals, including humans, apes, monkeys, and lemurs

Loulis observing as Washoe looks through a trick-or-treat bag

COMPREHENSION Based on the reading, write T for *true* or F for *false*.

1. _____ Studies show that chimps can learn to speak.

2. _____ Washoe taught her own babies how to sign.

3. _____ Washoe spent time with other chimps in Oklahoma.

THINK ABOUT IT Discuss the questions with a partner or in a small group.

1. Does learning about the behavior and intelligence of animals such as the chimpanzee, Washoe, change your feelings about them or other animals? Explain.

2. What are some characteristics of an animal's behavior and/or appearance that make you like them or dislike them?

1.7 The Simple Past

FORM

EXAMPLES	EXPLANATION
Washoe **learned** about 350 signs. She **lived** with the Gardners for four years.	Many simple past verbs are regular. To form the simple past of regular verbs, add –*ed* or –*d* to the base form. learn → learned live → lived
Washoe **had** two baby chimps. She **taught** younger chimps signs.	Many simple past verbs are irregular. See Appendix B for a complete list of irregular past verbs. have → had teach → taught
Washoe **learned** to sign. She **didn't learn** to speak. **Did** the Gardners **teach** her? Who **taught** her?	We use the past form only in affirmative statements and subject questions. After *did* or *didn't*, we use the base form.
Washoe **was** an orphan. The Gardners **were** language researchers.	The past of *be* is irregular. It has two forms in the past. I, he, she, it → was we, you, they → were

Notice these seven patterns with a regular verb:

AFFIRMATIVE STATEMENT:	Washoe **learned** American Sign Language.
NEGATIVE STATEMENT:	She **didn't learn** to speak.
YES/NO QUESTION:	**Did** she **learn** 1,000 signs?
SHORT ANSWER:	No, she **didn't.**
WH- QUESTION:	When **did** she **learn** to sign?
NEGATIVE WH- QUESTION:	Why **didn't** she **learn** more than 350 signs?
SUBJECT QUESTION:	How many chimps **learned** to sign?

Notice these seven patterns with an irregular verb:

AFFIRMATIVE STATEMENT:	Researches **taught** Washoe to sign.
NEGATIVE STATEMENT:	They **didn't teach** Washoe to speak.
YES/NO QUESTION:	**Did** they **teach** her American Sign Language?
SHORT ANSWER:	Yes, they **did.**
WH- QUESTION:	Why **did** they **teach** her American Sign Language?
NEGATIVE WH- QUESTION:	Why **didn't** they **teach** her to speak?
SUBJECT QUESTION:	Who **taught** Washoe to sign?

continued

Notice these seven patterns with the verb *be*:

AFFIRMATIVE STATEMENT:	Washoe **was** an orphan.
NEGATIVE STATEMENT:	She **wasn't** successful having babies.
YES/NO QUESTION:	**Was** she a year old yet when she came to the U.S.?
SHORT ANSWER:	No, she **wasn't**.
WH- QUESTION:	Where **was** her mother?
NEGATIVE *WH-* QUESTION:	Why **wasn't** she with her mother?
SUBJECT QUESTION:	Who **were** her trainers?

USE

EXAMPLES	EXPLANATION
Washoe **met** other chimps at the Primate Institute. She **liked** to look at books. She **didn't learn** to speak. She **died** in 2007.	We use the simple past to refer to an event that started and ended at a definite time in the past. It can be a single event or a repeated event.

Note:

It is not necessary to mention when the action happened; the simple past implies a definite past time.

EXERCISE 14 Listen to the following sentences. Fill in the blanks with the words you hear. 🎧 1.7

1. **A:** Where _____ was _____ Washoe born?
      a.

   B: She _____ was _____ born in Africa. She _____ born in the United States.
         b.   c.

2. **A:** She _____ her human trainers. At first, she _____ other chimps.
         a.   b.

   B: Why _____ other chimps?
         c.

3. **A:** _____ baby chimps?
        a.

   B: Yes, she _____ . She _____ two babies but they _____ .
         b.   c.   d.

4. **A:** Who _____ her American Sign Language?
         a.

   B: The Gardners _____ her ASL.
                        b.

5. **A:** How long _____ with the Gardners?
                    a.

   B: She _____ with them for three years.
         b.

6. **A:** The Gardners _____ around Washoe.
                        a.

   B: Why _____ around her?
         b.

EXERCISE 15 Use a form of the underlined words to complete the sentences.

1. Washoe <u>lived</u> with the Gardners. She _____ didn't live _____ in a zoo.

2. The Gardners <u>took</u> care of her at home. Who _____ care of her at the Primate Institute?

3. She <u>started</u> to communicate with other chimps, but she _____ immediately.

4. She <u>felt</u> comfortable with humans. At first, she _____ comfortable with other chimps.

   Why _____ comfortable with other chimps?

5. Researchers <u>gave</u> her a baby chimp—Loulis. Why _____ her a baby chimp?

6. She <u>taught</u> Loulis to make signs. How many signs _____?

7. Washoe _____ very old when she died. She <u>was</u> only 42.

8. When _____? She <u>died</u> in 2007.

EXERCISE 16 Read the conversation and fill in the blanks with the simple past by using context clues.

A: ___<u>Did you like</u>___ the story about Washoe?
　　　　　　1.

B: Yes, I _____ . I liked it very much. Washoe was the first animal to learn human
　　　　　　　2.

communication. But she _____ the only one. There _____ many more
　　　　　　　　　　　　3.　　　　　　　　　　　　　　4.

studies with chimps and gorillas after that. I _____ a program on TV a few years ago
　　　　　　　　　　　　　　　　　　5.

about Koko, a gorilla. Like Washoe, she _____ to make about 1,000 signs using American
　　　　　　　　　　　　　　　　　　6.

Sign Language.

A: Wow! That's amazing. When _____?
　　　　　　　　　　　　　　7.

B: In 2018.

A: _____ born in Africa?
　　　　8.

B: No, she wasn't. She was born at the San Francisco Zoo.

A: When _____ to train her?
　　　　　　　9.

B: They began to train her when she _____ one year old.
　　　　　　　　　　　　　　　　10.

A: _____ anything else interesting from the TV program?
　　　11.

B: Yes, I learned a lot of interesting things. For example, when Koko wanted something, she asked for it.

One time she _____ a cat, and her trainers _____ her a stuffed cat.
　　　　　　　　12.　　　　　　　　　　　　　　　　13.

But she _____ happy with it. She didn't _____ a stuffed animal. She
　　　　　　14.　　　　　　　　　　　　　　15.

wanted a real cat.

continued

A: _____ it to her?

           16.

B: Yes, they _____ . They gave her a baby kitten. In fact, she had a choice of kittens, and she

           17.

_____ a gray male kitten. She even _____ him a name: "All Ball."

    18.   **19.**

A: That's so sweet. So she had All Ball to play with.

B: Unfortunately, not for long. One day All Ball _____ away from Koko's cage. He ran into

                                                 20.

the street, and a car hit and killed him.

A: Who _____ Koko about the death of her kitten?

            21.

B: Her trainers told her. She _____ very sad. She signed "Bad, bad, bad."

                  22.

A: What else _____ ?

            23.

B: She signed "cry, sad."

A: Did they give her another kitten?

B: Yes. They _____ her two kittens.

            24.

A: Wow! What a great story.

Koko playing with her
new pet kitten

ABOUT YOU Read the statements. If the statement is false, give the opposite (affirmative or negative) form. Then work with a partner and ask him or her about these statements.

> A: *I didn't know about language studies with animals. Did you?*
>
> B: *Yes, I did.*
>
> A: *How did you know about them?*
>
> B: *I saw a TV program about this subject a few years ago.*

1. I knew about language studies with animals.

2. I didn't know about Washoe before I read the conversation.

3. I didn't know that gorillas or chimpanzees were able to communicate with sign language.

4. I thought the story about Washoe was interesting.

5. I knew that chimpanzees could have a pet cat.

6. I didn't know animals from different species could form friendships or bonds.

7. I went to a zoo when I was a child.

8. As a child, I wasn't interested in wild animals.

FUN WITH GRAMMAR

Get to know your classmates. On the timeline, note three or four of the most important dates and events in your past (graduation, job, marriage, success in a sport or other activity). Then take turns sharing an event in a small group. Ask each other questions.

> A: I **graduated** from high school ten years ago.
>
> B: Oh, where **did** you **go** to high school?
>
> A: I **went** to Central High in Philadelphia.
>
> B: **Did** you **play** any sports?
>
> A: Yes, I **played** football.

DATE _____ _____ _____ _____ TODAY

←━━━━X━━━━━━━━━━X━━━━━━━━━━X━━━━━━━━━━X━━━━━━━X

EVENT _____ _____ _____ _____

_____ _____ _____ _____

_____ _____ _____ _____

SUMMARY OF UNIT 1

WE USE THE SIMPLE PRESENT:

With facts, general truths, habits, customs	Timothy Doner **speaks** many languages. Most Americans and Canadians **speak** English. Mandarin **is** the official language of China.
With a place of origin	Timothy Doner **is** from New York.
In a time clause or in an *if* clause when talking about the future	If children **don't practice** their native language, they will forget it. When the last speaker of a language **dies**, the language will die.
With nonaction verbs	I **think** that animal language studies are interesting. Now I **know** more about animal communication.

WE USE THE PRESENT CONTINUOUS:

With something that is happening now	We **are comparing** verb tenses now. We **are reviewing** Lesson 1 now.
To describe what we see in a movie or picture	Look at that picture of Washoe. She **is making** signs.
With an action that is ongoing over a longer period of time	Scientists **are studying** animal communication. We **are improving** our English.
With a trend	People **are using** abbreviations more and more to communicate. Letter writing **is becoming** a less popular means of communication.
With a descriptive state	Timothy Doner **is wearing** jeans in this video. He **is riding** in a taxi.
With a plan for the future	We **are finishing** this lesson tomorrow. Next semester, I **am changing** my major.

WE USE THE FUTURE:

	will	*be going to*
With predictions	Many languages **will disappear** in our lifetime.	Many languages **are going to disappear** in our lifetime.
With a request for help or with an offer to help	A: **Will** you **help** me with the experiment? B: Of course, I **will**. I**'ll help** with the research.	
When an action is unplanned and occurs to the speaker while he or she is speaking	A: I forgot my glasses and can't read the story. B: No problem. I**'ll** read it to you.	

WE USE THE SIMPLE PAST:

With events that occurred once or repeatedly at a definite past time	Washoe **was** born in Africa. She **learned** about 350 signs. She **died** at the age of 42.

REVIEW

Fill in the blanks with the correct form of the verb given. More than one verb form may be possible.

A: What ___are you reading___ ? You _____ *seem* _____ very involved in that article.
         1. you/read   2. seem

B: I am. It _____ a very interesting article about lost American Indian languages. Many of
                3. be

them _____ . The article mentions two languages that _____
         4. disappear   5. become

extinct more than 50 years ago when the last speakers _____ .
                                            6. die

A: _____ that all the members of the tribe are gone?
        7. that/mean

B: No. The tribes aren't extinct, just the languages. The older people _____ their
                                                8. not/speak

native language with their children when they were small, so the younger generation never

_____ to speak it. When the older members _____ , that was the end of
        9. learn   10. die

the language. Today's tribal members just _____ English.
                                  11. speak

A: _____ the Enduring Voices Project _____ the voices of these tribe
        12.   12. record

members before they _____ ?
            13. die

B: No. The Enduring Voices Project _____ afterward, so there _____
                        14. start   15. be

no record of their languages.

A: I wouldn't want my language to disappear. When I _____ kids,
                                          16. have

I _____ my language with them all the time.
        17. speak

B: Me too. If they _____ bilingual, they _____ more opportunities.
                18. be   19. have

A: Some of my friends already have kids. They tell me that their children only _____ to
                                              20. want

speak English. They _____ to speak their language at home anymore.
                  21. not/want

B: That's sad. Sorry, but I _____ to finish the article by noon. I have to write a paper about
                  22. need

disappearing languages for my English class tomorrow.

A: No problem. Can you _____ me the link to the article when you get a chance? I'd like
                  23. send

to read it.

B: Sure. No problem!

A: Thanks!

FROM GRAMMAR TO WRITING

PART 1 Editing Advice

1. Use the correct question formation.

   What ~~he is~~ *is he* saying?   When ~~Washoe died~~ *did Washoe die*?   What ~~means "enduring"~~ *does "enduring" mean*?

2. Don't use the present continuous with nonaction verbs.

   Now you ~~are knowing~~ *know* a lot about communication.

3. Don't use the future after a time word or *if*.

   When I ~~will~~ go back to China, I'm going to be an English teacher.

   I'll learn a lot of slang if I ~~will~~ have an English-speaking roommate next semester.

4. Don't forget *be* when using *going to*.

   We ∧ *are* going to study American Sign Language.

5. Don't forget a form of *be* with the present continuous.

   We ∧ *are* learning a lot about language.

6. Don't forget *was* or *were* with *born*.

   Washoe ∧ *was* born in Africa.   Where ~~did~~ *were* her babies born?

7. Use the base form after *do, does,* or *did*.

   At first, Washoe didn't ~~liked~~ *like* other chimps.   Does Timothy speak~~s~~ French?

8. Use the *–s* form after *he, she, it,* or a singular subject in the simple present.

   She ~~want~~ *wants* to learn American Sign Language.

9. Use the base form after *to*.

   The Gardners wanted to ~~studied~~ *study* animal communication.

10. Pay special attention to irregular verbs in the past.

    The Gardners ~~spended~~ *spent* a lot of time with Washoe.

PART 2 Editing Practice

Some of the shaded words and phrases have mistakes. Find the mistakes and correct them. If the shaded words are correct, write *C*.

My parents ~~borned~~ *were born* in Poland. Their native language was *C* Yiddish. When they came to the
    1.   2.

U.S., they didn't spoke English at all. They spoke only Yiddish and Polish. I was born in the
         3.   4.   5.

U.S. When I was a child, I heared mostly Yiddish at home. But when I went to school, I learned
                              6.   7.   8.

English and started to lost my language. Today, very few people speak Yiddish, and I'm thinking
                   9.   10.

the Yiddish language dying. I only know a few very old people who still speak the language.
                      11.   12.

Now that I'm an adult, I feel bad that I didn't tried to speak Yiddish as a child. A few years
13.   14.

ago, I become interested in Yiddish again. I go to a Yiddish conversation group once a week. One
15.   16.

of my friends asked me, "Why you want to study a dying language? Why you don't study a living
17.   18.

language, like French or Polish?" She doesn't understands that it's my native language, and this
19.

language says a lot about my culture. Sometimes, when I speak English, I throw in a Yiddish word
20.

like *schlep*. My friend asks me, "What means *schlep*? Why don't you just use the English word?" I
21.   22.

answer: There is no English word that expresses the same thing. Every language have words and
23.   24.

expressions that don't exist in other languages.

I saw the video of Timothy Doner, and I was surprised that he speak Yiddish. I'm happy that
25.   26.

he's interested in this language, too.

Right now, I don't have a lot of time to study the grammar of Yiddish. I only get conversation
27.

practice. When I will have more time, I going to take a grammar class. I want to keep this
28.   29.

language alive. It's a beautiful, rich language.

WRITING TIP

When you write about the benefits or advantages of something, write the most important benefit last.

You can use these phrases to introduce the advantages or benefits.

The first benefit of…

Another

The most significant benefit

Most important,

PART 3 Write

Read the prompts. Choose one and write one or more paragraphs about it.

1. Do you think it's important to keep a record of a dying language? What will it teach future
   generations?
2. What are the benefits of being bilingual? Give examples from your experience with two
   languages. You may also write about someone you know who is bilingual.

PART 4 Edit

Reread the Summary of Unit 1 and the Editing Advice. Edit your writing from Part 3.

The Present Perfect and the Present Perfect Continuous

RISK

Workers on a suspension bridge crossing the Yangtze River in Wuhan in China's central Hubei province

The biggest risk is not taking any risk... In a world that's changing really quickly, the only strategy that is guaranteed to fail is *not* taking risks.

MARK ZUCKERBERG

RISKY BEHAVIOR
Guppies, Like Humans, Take Risks to Impress

Read the following article. Pay special attention to the words in bold. 🔊 2.1

Imagine that your boat **has sunk** and you made it to a tiny island. You**'ve been** all over the island, and you **haven't seen** any people. You**'ve looked** for food and **found** some berries and roots. In the distance, you**'ve just noticed** what might be a bigger island, possibly with more food and a better chance of survival. You**'ve never swum** so far, but the weather is good and you are a strong swimmer. Question: Do you stay on the small island and hope for rescue, or do you swim toward a possibly better place?

Willingness to take a risk **has always been** a simple way of dividing any group of people into two separate camps: those who are comfortable taking risks and those who try to avoid them. Whether in a life-threatening situation like the island scenario or in an everyday challenge like making an expensive purchase, some are more comfortable with risk than others. But why is this the case? Why do we take risks? Why do some people take more risks than others?

Looking for the origins of risk-taking behavior in humans is not easy. Because it is not possible to study the behavior of prehistoric people, some researchers **have begun** to study risk taking and risk avoidance in animals to see if there may be any parallels with human behaviors.

Lee Dugatkin of Louisville University, for example, **has studied** the risk-taking behavior known as "predator inspection" in small fish called guppies. This is when one or more fish break away from the main group to investigate possible predators. Think of it as guard duty. The risk is obvious: These fish are more likely to be eaten by the predator. The benefits are less clear, but Dugatkin and his colleagues concluded from their experiments that risk-taking behavior makes the fish more attractive to the opposite sex. There may be some similarity here with human research, which **has demonstrated** that teenagers are more likely to take risks when in a group of their peers than when they are alone.

Research into animal behavior **has already established** some similarities in risk-taking behavior in animals and humans. Perhaps more research can further show that animals and humans behave similarly.

COMPREHENSION Based on the reading, write T for *true* or F for *false*.

1. _____ Scientists have begun to study risk taking in animals because they are more interesting than humans.

2. _____ Lee Dugatkin has studied risk-taking behavior in birds.

3. _____ Research has shown that teenagers take more risks if they are with friends.

THINK ABOUT IT Discuss the questions with a partner or in a small group.

1. How did you answer the question about swimming toward a bigger island in the first paragraph of the reading? Why did you make this choice?

2. Do you believe that animal research can help explain human behavior? Why or why not?

2.1 The Present Perfect — Form

SUBJECT	HAVE/HAS (+ *NOT*)	PAST PARTICIPLE		EXPLANATION
I	**have**	**taken**	some risks.	Use *have* with the subjects *I, you, we, they,* or *there* + a plural subject.
You	**have not**	**seen**	the photographs.	
We	**have**	**read**	about risk taking.	
Scientists	**have**	**studied**	risk in animals.	
There	**have**	**been**	interesting experiments.	
He	**has not**	**researched**	humans.	Use *has* with the subjects *he, she, it,* or *there* + a singular subject.
There	**has**	**been**	a new study.	

Notes:

1. The contraction for *have not* is *haven't*. The contraction for *has not* is *hasn't*.

   I **haven't** taken a lot of risks in my life.

   Dugatkin **hasn't** studied rats.

2. We can contract the subject pronoun with *have* or *has*: *I've, you've, we've, they've, he's, she's, it's*.

   I**'ve** read about animal behavior.

   She**'s** never taken many risks.

   The apostrophe *s* (*'s*) can mean *has* or *is*. The verb form following the contraction will tell you what the contraction means.

   He**'s studied** human behavior. = He **has studied** human behavior.

   He**'s studying** human behavior. = He **is studying** human behavior.

3. We often contract singular nouns with *has*, especially when speaking.

   The **researcher's** won many awards.

   This **article's** been downloaded by a lot of students.

4. We can contract *there* + *has*.

   There's been a study of teenage risk taking.

continued

STATEMENTS	YES/NO QUESTIONS & SHORT ANSWERS	WH- QUESTIONS
You **have taken** too many risks.	**A: Have** you **taken** an extreme risk? **B:** No, I **haven't.**	What kind of risks **have** you **taken**?
The student **has finished** the experiment.	**A: Has** he **finished** the experiment? **B:** Yes, he **has.**	How many times **has** he **done** the experiment?
Scientists **have studied** risk.	**A: Have** they **studied** teenagers? **B:** Yes, they **have.**	Why **have** they **studied** teenagers?
He **has observed** animals.	**A: Has** he **observed** birds? **B:** No, he **hasn't.**	Who **has studied** birds?

Note:

We can add a short question at the end of a statement.

I haven't read the article about risk yet. **Have you?**

EXERCISE 1 Write the base form and the simple past form of these past participles from the reading. Then write if the past participle is the same as or different from the simple past form.

BASE FORM	SIMPLE PAST FORM	PAST PARTICIPLE	SAME/DIFFERENT
be	was/were	been	different
		begun	
		demonstrated	
		established	
		found	
		looked	
		noticed	
		seen	
		studied	
		sunk	
		swum	

2.2 The Past Participle

BASE FORM	SIMPLE PAST FORM	PAST PARTICIPLE	EXPLANATION
work look notice	worked looked noticed	worked looked noticed	The past participle is the same as the simple past form for all regular verbs.
catch find hear	caught found heard	caught found heard	For some irregular verbs, the past participle is the same as the simple past form. See Appendix C for a complete list of irregular verbs with their past and past participle forms.
begin sink swim	began sank swam	begun sunk swum	For other irregular verbs, the simple past form and the past participle are different.

EXERCISE 2 Fill in the blanks with the present perfect form of one of the verbs from the box.

be	begin	do	hear	make	observe	read√	start

1. We _____*have read*_____ an interesting article about risk.

2. Jean-Guy Godin _____ experiments with guppies.

3. Scientists _____ to study risk taking in animals.

4. They _____ many interesting discoveries.

5. Lee Dugatkin _____ a scientist for many years.

6. He _____ guppies and how they take risks.

7. They _____ never _____ of this research before.

8. A new researcher _____ to study behavior in insects.

2.3 Placement of Adverbs

SUBJECT	*HAVE/HAS*	ADVERB	PAST PARTICIPLE	
You	have	**probably**	heard	about teenagers and risk taking.
I	have	**just**	read	an article about risk taking.
Scientists	have	**recently**	begun	to study risk taking in animals.
Research	has	**already**	established	links between human and animal behavior.
She	has	**even**	studied	babies.
I	have	**often**	wondered	about animal behavior.
Experiments	have	**usually**	had	interesting results.

Notes:

1. Many adverbs can come between the auxiliary (*have/has*) and the past participle.

2. *Already* can also come at the end of the verb phrase.

> They have **already** finished the experiment. OR They have finished the experiment **already**.

3. *Yet* usually comes at the end of a question or negative statement.

> A: Have you finished the experiment **yet**?
> B: No. I haven't finished it **yet**.

4. Some adverbs can also come before the subject or at the end of the verb phrase.

> Scientists have **recently** begun to learn about risk. (formal)
> **Recently**, scientists have begun to learn about risk. (informal)
> Scientists have begun to learn about risk **recently**. (informal)

5. Notice the position of *ever* in a question.

> Have you **ever** seen a guppy?

EXERCISE 3 Listen to the story and fill in the blanks with the missing words. 🎧 2.2

I _'ve never thought_ of myself as a risk taker. I _____ to make safe
         1.   **2.**

decisions in my life. I _____ out of an airplane.
                                   3.

I _____ a mountain. These things _____
              4.   **5.**

to me. But then a new friend told me, "I really admire you. You _____ a lot of risks
                                              6.

in your life." "No, I _____," I replied. "What _____ that
                           7.   **8.**

involves risk?" I _____ that risk meant doing something dangerous. My
                        9.

friend answered, "Risk means facing an unknown future. You _____ up your past
                                                 10.

life to enter a completely different world."

EXERCISE 4 Below is a continuation of the story from Exercise 3. Use the words given to form the present perfect. Use contractions wherever possible. Add the adverb given.

My friend asked, "How long _have you been_ in this country? Less than a year, right?
                                      1. you/be

_____ about how many risks you _____ since you
              2. you/ever/think   **3. take**

left your country?"

I started to think about my friend's questions, and I realized that I'm more of a risk taker than I thought.

First, of course, I _____ learn another language. Even though I studied English in my country,
                           4. have to

I never had to communicate with native speakers. My English _____ a lot.
                                          5. already/improve

But talking with strangers _____ scary for me, especially by telephone.
                                6. always/be

I _____ what Americans _____ to me,
                 7. not/always/understand   **8. say**

but people _____ very patient with me.
                    9. usually/be

Back home, I lived with my mother. She always cooked for my family and me. But here

I _____ be independent. I _____ to pay bills, rent an apartment, and make
      10. have to   **11. learn**

my own decisions. I _____ to cook for myself.
                    12. even/learn

In my hometown I walked or took the bus. But here the bus system isn't very good, and almost everyone

drives. So I took driving lessons, got my license, and bought a used car. I used to be afraid of driving, but

little by little I _____ experience, and driving _____ easier for me.
              13. gain   **14. get**

Since my friend pointed these things out to me, I realized that I _____
                                                 15. already/make

a lot of changes, and each change _____ some risk.
                       16. involve

2.4 The Present Perfect — Overview of Uses

EXAMPLES	EXPLANATION
We **have discussed** risk for a few days. He **has studied** English for a long time.	The action started in the past and continues to the present.
He **has observed** this behavior several times. He **has made** many important discoveries.	The action repeats during a period of time from the past to the present.
I**'ve learned** a lot about risk. **Have** you ever **done** anything dangerous?	The action occurred at an indefinite time in the past. It has importance to a present situation or discussion.

EXERCISE 5 Fill in the blanks with the present perfect form of the verb given to complete this paragraph.

Nik Wallenda comes from a long line of risk takers. He doesn't take risks for science or nature. He's a

circus performer; he walks a tightrope. His family, known as the Flying Wallendas, <u>has been</u> in this

1. be

business for seven generations. Nik started walking on a tightrope when he was two years old. Over time,

he _____ famous for some amazing acts of danger. He _____

2. become   **3. walk**

across Niagara Falls and over a deep canyon near the Grand Canyon on a tightrope. So far, he

_____ a serious accident.

4. never/have

Crowds watch as Nik Wallenda walks the tightrope over Niagara Falls.

Climbing
MOUNT EVEREST

Read the following article. Pay special attention to the words in bold. 🎧 2.3

Have you **ever thought** about taking a risk for the fun or excitement of it? Mount Everest, the tallest mountain in the world, **has always been** a symbol of man's greatest challenge. Located between China and Nepal, Mount Everest **has attracted** mountain climbers from all over the world. In 1953, Sir Edmund Hillary, from New Zealand, and his Nepalese guide, Sherpa Tenzing Norgay, were the first to reach the top. Since then, about 4,000 people **have reached** the summit[1]. But more than 200 climbers **have died** while trying.

Between 1953 and 1963, only six people successfully climbed to the top. But things **have changed** a lot in recent years. In 2012 alone, 500 people made it to the top.

What **has changed**? Why **has** the number of climbers **increased** so much **recently**? One reason is that there are more companies leading expeditions[2]. Now 90 percent of climbers use expedition companies. A climber pays about $100,000 to go up the mountain with a guide. But these guided expeditions **have attracted** a lot of inexperienced climbers. And the crowds **have made** it even more dangerous to make the climb. Danuru Sherpa, who **has led** 14 expeditions, **has had to carry** at least five people off the mountain to save their lives. The expedition companies might want to consider limiting the number of inexperienced climbers, both to protect people and to protect the mountain.

---

[1] summit: the top of a mountain
[2] expedition: a group journey organized for a specific purpose

Technology **has come** to Everest, too. As a result, more accurate[3] information about weather conditions at the summit **has made** it easier for expeditions to choose the safest time to make it to the top.

How **has** all of this traffic **affected** Mt. Everest? Lately, the mountain **has become** dirty as climbers leave behind garbage and equipment they no longer need. There is now a pollution control committee, and conditions **have started** to improve at the base camp[4],

but higher on the mountain, the garbage accumulates. One organization, Eco Everest Expedition, **has tried** to clean up the garbage. The members started in 2008, and **so far** they**'ve collected** over 13 tons of garbage.

According to climber Mark Jenkins, "It's not simply about reaching the summit but about showing respect for the mountain and enjoying the journey."

---

[3] accurate: exact, correct
[4] base camp: the main place from which expeditions set out

COMPREHENSION Based on the reading, write T for *true* or F for *false*.

1. _____ Only 200 people have reached the summit of Mount Everest.

2. _____ The number of climbers has gone down over the years.

3. _____ Most people today use guides to climb Everest.

THINK ABOUT IT Discuss the questions with a partner or in a small group.

1. These days, climbing Mount Everest is not as hard as it was in the past. Is that good or bad? Explain.

2. If you could join an expedition to climb Mount Everest, would you go? Why or why not?

2.5 The Present Perfect with Indefinite Past Time —Overview

We use the present perfect for an action that occurred at an indefinite time in the past. This action still has importance to a present situation or discussion.

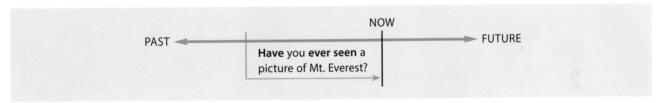

EXAMPLES	EXPLANATION
A: **Have** you *ever* **taken** a big risk? B: No, I *never* **have**.	We can use *ever* and *never* to show any time in the past. The time is indefinite.
I've *always* **wanted** to climb a mountain. I've *never* **heard** of Edmund Hillary.	We use *always* and *never* to connect the past to the present.
Has technology **come** to Everest *yet*? Technology **has** *already* **come** to Mount Everest.	We use *yet* to ask about an expected action. We use *already* with affirmative statements to show that an expected action happened.
Scientists **have** *recently* **begun** to study risk. *Lately*, Mount Everest **has become** dirty. The expedition **has** *just* **reached** the top.	We use *recently, lately,* and *just* with recent past actions.
Everest **has attracted** climbers from all over the world. Over 4,000 people **have** successfully **climbed** Everest.	Some present perfect sentences have no mention of time. The use of the present perfect indicates that the time is in the indefinite past.

EXERCISE 6 Listen to the conversation about mountain climbing. Write T for *true* or F for *false*. 🎧 2.4

1. _____ The speakers would both like to try mountain climbing.

2. _____ The book *Into Thin Air* was published in the twentieth century.

3. _____ The speakers have read the book.

EXERCISE 7 Fill in the blanks with the words that you hear. 🎧 2.4

A: I _ve thought_____ about mountain climbing. I'd love to climb Mt. Everest. It sounds so exciting.
　　　　　1.

B: I _____ that it's very dangerous. Many people _____ while
　　　　　2.　　　　　　　　　　　　　　　　　　　　　　　　　　　3.

　　 trying to reach the top. _____ any experience in mountain climbing?
　　　　　　　　　　　　　　　　　　4.

A: No. I _____ a course in rock climbing at my gym.
　　　　　　5.

B: I _____ interested in risky activities. But I'm happy reading adventure books and
　　　　　6.

　　 seeing exciting movies. In fact, I _____ a book about an expedition
　　　　　　　　　　　　　　　　　　　　　7.

　　 on Mt. Everest. It's called *Into Thin Air*. _____ of it?
　　　　　　　　　　　　　　　　　　　　　　8.

A: No, I _____ . Is it new?
　　　　　9.

B: No. It came out in the 1990s. But it's very exciting. I think you'd like it.

A: Does it have a good ending?

Athlete examining a rock wall in a gym

B: I _____ it yet. Do you want to borrow it when I'm finished?
10.

A: Lately, I _____ much time to read because of school. But thanks for the offer.
11.

EXERCISE 8 Use the words given to fill in the blanks.

A: I <u>'ve just seen</u> an amazing video of Nik Wallenda. _____ him?
1. just/see   **2.** you/ever/hear of

B: No, I _____ . Who is he?
3. never

A: He's a tightrope walker. He's from a famous family of circus performers. Take a look at this video online.

You can see what he does.

B: Wow! That looks terrific. I'd love to see a circus.

A: There's a circus in town. Do you want to go? I _____ two tickets
4. already/buy

for my girlfriend and me. But I think I can get another one.

B: I'd love to go. I _____ to the circus before. Have you?
5. never/be

A: Yes. But not since I was a child. I _____ one recently.
6. not/see

B: What kind of circus is it? Is one of the Wallendas going to be there?

A: No. It's a circus from China.

2.6 The Present Perfect with *Ever* and *Never*

EXAMPLES	EXPLANATION
A: Has a climber *ever* **died** on Mt. Everest? **B:** Yes. Many climbers **have died** on Mt. Everest.	We use *ever* to ask a question about any time in the past.
A: Have you *ever* **seen** a movie about Mt. Everest? **B:** No, I *never* **have**.	We use *never* in a negative answer.
A: Has Nick Wallenda *ever* **gone** across Niagara Falls on a tightrope? **B:** Yes, he **has**.	We can answer an *ever* question with the present perfect. The present perfect shows no reference to time. The time is indefinite.
A: Has anyone from the Wallenda family *ever* **had** an accident? **B:** Yes. Nik Wallenda's great-grandfather **fell** in 1978 at the age of 73.	We can answer an *ever* question with the simple past. The simple past shows a definite past time (*in 1978, last week, last summer, last Friday, two weeks ago,* etc.).

EXERCISE 9 Fill in the first blank with *Have you ever* and the correct form of the verb given. Then complete the rest of the conversation with the correct form of the verb given and any other words you see.

1. **A:** _Have you ever done_ anything dangerous?
   a. do

   B: Yes, I _____ have _____.
   b.

   A: What was it?

   B: Last year I _____ went _____ bungee jumping over a canyon.
   c. go

   A: Wow! I _'ve never done_ anything like that in my life.
   d. never/do

   And I never will!

2. **A:** _____ in a helicopter?
   a. fly

   B: No, I _____ . Have you?
   b. never

   A: No, I _____ . But I'd like to.
   c.

3. **A:** _____ a dangerous sport?
   a. play

   B: Yes, I _____ .
   b.

   A: Oh, really? What sport is that?

   B: When I lived in Spain, I _____ with the
   c. run

   bulls. It's very popular in Spain.

   A: Oh, yes. I think I _____ of that.
   d. hear

4. **A:** _____ money to a friend?
   a. lend

   B: No, I haven't. _____ you?
   b.

   A: Yes. One time I _____ $100 to my best
   c. lend

   friend.

   B: Did he pay you back?

   A: Yes. He _____ me back two months later.
   d. pay

5. **A:** _____ a mountain?
   a. climb

   B: No, I _____ . _____
   b. never   **c.**

   you?

   A: No. But my sister _____ Denali last year.
   d. climb

New York City
marathoners
running on
the Verrazano
Bridge, which
connects
Staten Island
to Brooklyn

B: I _____ Denali. Where is
   e. never/hear of
it?

A: It's in Alaska. It's the highest mountain in North America.

6. **A:** _____ a big mistake in
   a. make
your life?

   B: Of course, I _____ . I _____
   b.   **c.** make
many mistakes in my life.

7. **A:** _____ money in business?
   a. risk

   B: Yes, I _____ . Ten years ago, I
   b.

_____ a business.
   c. start

   A: How did that work out for you?

   B: Unfortunately, I _____ a lot of money.
   d. lose

8. **A:** _____ someone from a
   a. save
dangerous situation?

   B: No, I _____ . But my brother
   b.

_____ .
   c.

   A: Really? What did he do?

   B: A few years ago, he was passing a burning building. He

_____ in to save a child.
   d. run

9. **A:** _____ a serious accident?
   a. have

   B: Yes, unfortunately. Three years ago, I

_____ skiing. I _____
   b. go   **c.** fall
and _____ my leg.
   d. break

10. **A:** _____ in a marathon?
   a. run

   B: Yes. I _____ in the New York marathon five
   b. run
years ago. It was amazing!

ABOUT YOU Find a partner. Ask each other questions starting with *Have you ever . . . ?* and the past participle of the verb. If your partner answers *Yes, I have,* ask for more specific information.

> A: *Have you ever swum across a lake?*
> B: *Yes, I have.*
> A: *When did you do it?*
> B: *I swam across a lake when I was in high school.*

1. *swim* across a lake
2. *go* bungee jumping
3. *win* a contest or a prize
4. *be* in a car accident
5. *fly* in a helicopter
6. *break* a bone

7. *make* a big change in your life
8. *climb* a mountain
9. *lose* money in an investment
10. *risk* your safety to help someone
11. *run* a long distance
12. *play* a dangerous sport

2.7 The Present Perfect with *Yet* and *Already*

EXAMPLES	EXPLANATION
We **have read** about several risk takers *already*. Over 4,000 people **have** *already* **climbed** Mt. Everest.	We use *already* in affirmative statements for an indefinite time in the past. We can put *already* at the end of the verb phrase or between the auxiliary verb and the main verb.
A: I'm planning to climb a mountain next year. **B: Have** you **begun** to train for it *yet*? **A:** Yes, I **have**. But I **haven't trained** at a high altitude *yet*.	We use *yet* or *already* to ask about an expected action.
B: Have you **bought** your equipment *already*? **A:** No, not *yet*.	We use *yet* with a negative verb. We use *not yet* for a short answer.
A: Have you **written** your essay *yet*? **B:** Yes. I **wrote** it last week.	If we answer a present perfect question with a definite time, we use the simple past.

Note:

Using *already* in a question shows a greater expectation that something has happened. Using *yet* indicates you are not as sure.

> You expect it has happened: *Have you **already** planned your vacation?*
> You aren't sure it has happened: *Have you planned your vacation **yet**?*

GRAMMAR IN USE

In the U.S., the simple past may also be used with these adverbs, especially in speech:

> A: **Did** you **finish** the experiment *yet*?   B: Yes, I finished it **already**.

In the U.K., and other countries influenced by British English (e.g., Australia, South Africa), the present perfect is generally preferred.

> A: **Have** you **finished** the experiment *yet*?   B: Yes, I've **already** finished it.

EXERCISE 10 Fill in the blanks to complete each conversation using the correct verb form and *yet* or *already*.

1. **A:** _____Has_____ your brother come back from his skiing trip _____yet_____?
       a.   b.

   B: Yes. He _____came_____ back last week.
                        c.

   A: Did he have a good time?

   B: He _____hasn't had_____ time to call me _____yet_____.
                        d.   e.

2. **A:** Is that a good book?

   B: Yes, it is. It's about an expedition in South America. I haven't _____
                                                                                                              a.

       it _____. But when I finish it, you can have it.
                        b.

   A: Wait a minute. I think I've read it _____.
                                                                                    c.

3. **A:** I want to see the movie *Trapped on Mt. Everest* this weekend. Have you _____
                                                                                                                                a.

       it _____?
                        b.

   B: No, not _____.
                               c.

   A: Then let's go. I'm planning to go Friday night.

   B: Sorry. I've _____ _____ plans for Friday. Maybe we can
                                  d.   e.

       make plans for next week.

4. **A:** What are you going to do during summer vacation?

   B: I haven't _____ about it _____. It's only February. I'll think about it
                               a.   b.

       in April or May. What about you?

   A: I've _____ decided to go to Alaska.
                        c.

   B: You're going to love it. We _____ there a few years ago.
                                                                    d.

5. **A:** Let's have an adventure this summer.

   B: I _____ told you _____ that I'm not interested in an adventure.
                    a.   b.

   A: How do you know? You've never had one.

EXERCISE 11 Circle the correct words to complete this conversation between a grandmother (A) and granddaughter (B). In some cases, both answers are possible. If both answers are correct, circle both.

A: I'm planning to take a vacation next summer.

B: I see you have some information on the kitchen table. Have you (*look*/*looked*) at these brochures yet?
1.

A: No, not (*already*/*yet*). I've been so busy. I (*haven't*/*didn't*) had time (*already*/*yet*). But I've (*already*/*yet*)
2.   3.   4.   5.

decided that I want to have some kind of adventure.

B: Wow, Grandma. These look like exciting trips. How about this one? A kayak trip on the Mississippi River?

A: Oh. (*I've done that one already.*/*I've already done that one.*)
6.

B: I don't remember.

A: (*I've done*/*I did*) it two years ago with my friend Betty.
7.

B: How about skydiving? Have you tried that (*yet*/*already*)?
8.

A: No. I (*never have*/*never had*). But it's not for me. It's a bit too risky.
9.

B: How about this one: white-water rafting. It's so much fun. (*Have ever you tried*/*Have you ever tried*) it?
10.

A: No. I (*haven't*/*didn't*). (*Have*/*Did*) you?
11.   12.

B: Yes, I (*did*/*have*). Many times, in fact.
13.

A: It looks dangerous.

B: It really isn't. You wear a life jacket. And the rafting trips are rated according to difficulty. Look.

Here's an easy trip on the Colorado River. (*Have you*/*Did you*) seen this one yet?
14.

A: No, I (*haven't*/*didn't*). It looks interesting.
15.

B: Should we fill out the application?

A: Wait a minute. I haven't made up my mind (*already*/*yet*).
16.

White-water rafting on the
Karnali river in Nepal

2.8 The Present Perfect with *Lately, Recently,* and *Just*

EXAMPLES	EXPLANATION
Lately, Mt. Everest **has become** crowded. The number of climbers on Everest **has increased** *recently*. Companies **have** *recently* **begun** to collect garbage on Everest.	*Lately* and *recently* with the present perfect refer to an indefinite time in the near past. We often use these words at the beginning or end of the sentence. *Recently* can also come between *have* and the past participle.
A: Have you **taken** any risks *lately*? **B:** No, I **haven't**. **A: Has** your brother **done** anything adventurous *lately*? **B:** Yes. He **took** skydiving lessons last month.	Questions with *lately* and *recently* ask about an indefinite time in the near past. When the answer is *no*, we usually use the present perfect. When the answer is *yes*, we often give a definite time and use the simple past.
I've *just* **come** back from a rafting trip. I *just* **came** back from a rafting trip.	We use *just* for an action that happened close to the present. We can use either the simple past or the present perfect. The present perfect is more formal.

Notes:

1. In affirmative statements, *recently* or *lately* with the present perfect refers to something that happened over time (in recent weeks, in recent months, in recent years). With the simple past, *recently* usually refers to a single event.

   *Mt. Everest **has had** problems with garbage **recently**. (over a period of time; in recent years)*

   *My cousin **climbed** Mt. Everest **recently**. (one time)*

2. *Lately* refers to a repeated or continuous event.

   *We **have read** a lot of stories about risk **lately**.*

3. Another way to show recent activity is by using *these days*.

   *Everest **has become** crowded and dirty **these days**.*

EXERCISE 12 Fill in the blanks with the present perfect or the simple past of the verb given.

1. **A:** <u>Have you read</u> any good books lately?
   a. you/read

   B: I _____ much time lately. I've been busy with schoolwork. What about you?
   b. not/have

   A: I _____ an exciting book called *The Lost City of Z*.
   c. just/finish

   Lately, a lot of people _____ interested in finding this place in South America.
   d. become

2. **A:** I know you love adventure. _____ any exciting trips lately?
   a. you/take

   B: No, I _____. Lately, I _____ busy with my job. What about
   b. **c.** be

   you? _____ anything adventurous these days?
   d. you/do

   A: No, I _____. But my sister _____. Last month she
   e. **f.**

   _____ rock climbing.
   g. go

continued

3. **A:** Mt. Everest _____ problems with pollution. Many climbers

   a. have

   _____ behind garbage.

   b. leave

   B: _____ recently?

   c. conditions/improve

   A: Yes, they _____ . Recently a company _____ to pick up

   d.   e. start

   the garbage left behind by climbers.

4. **A:** I _____ an article about unusual climbers on Mt. Everest.

   a. just/read

   B: What do you mean?

   A: It's about the first woman, the youngest person, the oldest person, etc.

   B: How old was the oldest person to climb Mt. Everest?

   A: The oldest was 64; the youngest was 16.

5. **A:** In recent years there _____ a lot of deaths and accidents on Mt. Everest.

   a. be

   B: I wonder why.

   A: Lately, a lot of inexperienced climbers _____ to climb the mountain.

   b. try

ABOUT YOU Write *yes/no* questions using the present perfect. Then work with a partner. Ask and answer the questions. If the answer is *yes,* ask for more specific information.

   A: Have you gone swimming recently?
   B: Yes, I have.
   A: When did you last go swimming?
   B: I went swimming yesterday afternoon.

1. go swimming recently

   _____

2. see any exciting movies lately

   _____

3. take a vacation recently

   _____

4. read any good books recently

   _____

5. hear anything interesting lately

   _____

6. eaten any new foods lately

   _____

EXERCISE 13 Fill in the blanks with the correct form of the verbs given. Include other words you see.

A: There's a video online about space tourism. <u>Have you seen it yet</u>?
                                               1. you/see/it/yet

B: Yes, I have. I _____ it a few weeks ago. It was very exciting.
                          2. see

_____ about going into space?
               3. you/ever/dream

A: Yes. I _____ a lot about it lately.
            4. think

B: _____ how much it costs?
            5. you/see

A: No, not _____ .
               6.

B: A ticket costs $250,000.

A: I _____ my mind!
             7. just/change

2.9 The Present Perfect with No Time Mentioned

EXAMPLES	EXPLANATION
I've **made** a decision. I'm going to take skydiving lessons. He's **worked** very hard, so he should take a vacation.	We can use the present perfect to talk about the past without any reference to time. The time is not important. Using the present perfect, rather than the simple past, shows that the past is relevant to a present situation or discussion.

EXERCISE 14 Fill in the blanks with the present perfect using one of the words from the box.

attract	discover	give	save	walk
be	entertain	photograph✓	take	win

1. Paul Nicklen <u>has photographed</u> marine animals. He _____ awards
                          a.   **b.**

   for his photographs. He _____ afraid to take risks. He
                                     c. not

_____ us an amazing look at underwater life.
               d.

2. Scientists _____ certain chemicals in the brain that affect risk.
                        a.

3. Nik Wallenda _____ across Niagara Falls on a tightrope. He
                         a.

_____ people with his performances.
               b.

4. Mt. Everest _____ inexperienced climbers. One guide, Danuru Sherpa,
                        a.

_____ the lives of at least five people. Many feel that visitors
               b.

_____ care of the mountain.
            c. not

Exploring THE OCEAN

Read the following article. Pay special attention to the words in bold. 🎧 2.5

When she first explored the ocean, Sylvia Earle thought the sea was too large to suffer harm from people, but not today. In just a few decades, many marine animal species **have disappeared** or **become** scarce[1].

Sylvia Earle is an oceanographer, explorer, author, and lecturer. She **has taken** many risks to explore the ocean. If you added the hours she **has spent** underwater, it equals more than 7,000 hours, or about 292 days. So far, she **has led** over 100 expeditions. In the 1960s, she had to fight to join expeditions. Women weren't welcome. Today she fights to protect marine life.

What **has happened** to the ocean in recent years? Unfortunately, many harmful things **have happened**. For millions of years, sharks, tuna, turtles, whales, and many other large sea animals lived in the Gulf of Mexico without a problem. But by the end of the 20th century, many of these animals were starting to disappear because of overfishing[2]. Drilling[3] for oil and gas on the ocean floor **has** also **harmed** many sea animals.

Earle **has won** many awards for her work. She **has received** 26 honorary degrees from universities and **has been** on hundreds of radio and television shows. In her effort to protect the ocean, she **has lectured** in more than 90 countries and **has written** more than 200 publications. She **has** even **written** several children's books. In 1998, *Time* magazine named Earle its first Hero for the Planet.

Earle said, "As a child, I did not know that people could protect something as big as the ocean or that they could cause harm. But now we know: The ocean is in trouble, and therefore so are we."

She added, "We still have a really good chance to make things better than they are. They won't get better unless we take action and inspire others to do the same thing. No one is without power. Everybody has the capacity to do something."

---

1 scarce: not plentiful
2 overfishing: when people are fishing so much that the amount of fish available is reduced to very low levels
3 to drill: to open a hole in the earth

Dr. Sylvia Earle

COMPREHENSION Based on the reading, write T for *true* or F for *false*.

1. _____ Sylvia Earle is an ocean photographer.

2. _____ Drilling for oil on the ocean floor has harmed animal life.

3. _____ Earle's ideas about the ocean have changed over the years.

THINK ABOUT IT Discuss the questions with a partner or in a small group.

1. Do you think we should put limits on fishing and drilling in the ocean?

2. What are reasons for and against protecting the ocean? What's your opinion?

2.10 The Present Perfect with Repetition from Past to Present

We use the present perfect to talk about repetition in a time period up to the present.

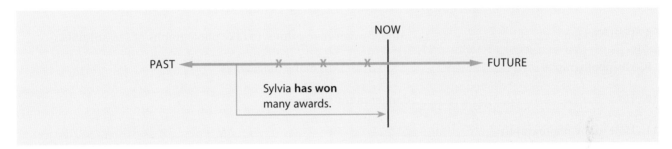

EXAMPLES	EXPLANATION
We **have read** several articles about risk **this week**. Earle **has taken** several risks **this year**.	We use *this week, this month, this year,* or *today* with the present perfect. It shows that the time period is open, and that it is possible for the action to occur again.
Earle **has written** more than 200 publications. (It's possible that Earle will write more books.)	If there is a possibility for a number to increase, we use the present perfect.
Sylvia Earle **has won many** awards. She **has lectured** in more than **90** countries.	We can use *a lot of, many, several,* or a number to show repetition from past to present.
So far over 4,000 people **have climbed** Mt. Everest. *Up to now*, more than 200 climbers **have died**.	*So far* and *up to now* show repetition from past to present.
How many women **have climbed** Mt. Everest? *How much* time **has** Earle **spent** under water?	To ask a question about repetition, use *how much* or *how many*.
Sylvia Earle **was** the chief scientist of a government organization from 1990 to 1992. Between 1953 and 1963, six people **reached** the top of Mt. Everest.	We use the simple past in a closed time period because the number of repetitions in this time period is final.
Karl Wallenda **performed** on a tightrope many times in his life. He died in 1978. Nik Wallenda **has performed** on a tightrope many times in his life.	If we refer to the experiences of a deceased person, we must use the simple past because nothing more can be added to that person's experience. A living person can repeat an action or experience.

EXERCISE 15 Fill in the blanks with the present perfect using one of the verbs from the box.

| appear   die   disappear   do   experience   go   lead   reach   spend   take   write✓ |

1. Sylvia Earle _____*has written*_____ several children's books.

2. Sylvia Earle _____ many interesting things in her life.

3. She _____ many expeditions.

4. She _____ more than 7,000 hours under water.

5. Many ocean animals _____. They will never come back.

6. Over two hundred Everest climbers _____.

7. More than 4,000 people _____ the top of Mt. Everest.

8. Paul Nicklen _____ under water many times to take photographs of sea animals.

9. His photographs _____ in many magazines.

10. He _____ danger many times.

11. How many photographs _____ he _____?

EXERCISE 16 Fill in the blanks with the present perfect or the simple past of the verb given.

1. In 1998, Sylvia Earle _____*won*_____ recognition from *Time* magazine.
    _{win}

2. She _____*has won*_____ many awards in her lifetime.
    _{win}

3. In 2012, she _____ an expedition near Florida.
    _{lead}

4. She's worried that we _____ a lot of sea life.
    _{lose}

5. She _____ many publications.
    _{write}

6. Sir Edmund Hillary _____ the top of Mt. Everest in 1953.
    _{reach}

7. Over 4,000 people _____ the top of Mt. Everest so far.
    _{reach}

8. One man, Apa Sherpa, _____ Mt. Everest many times.
    _{climb}

9. Between 1990 and 2012, he _____ Mt. Everest 21 times.
    _{climb}

10. Mt. Everest is getting crowded. On one day alone in 2012, 234 climbers _____ the summit.
    _{reach}

11. Karl Wallenda _____ a circus performer. He died in 1978.
    _{be}

12. His great-grandson, Nik Wallenda, _____ many times as a tightrope walker.
    _{perform}

13. In 2012, Nik Wallenda _____ Niagara Falls on a tightrope.
    _{cross}

EXERCISE 17 Fill in the blanks with the present perfect or the simple past of the verb given.

<u>Have you ever heard</u> of James Cameron? You may know him best as a famous movie director.
     1. you/ever/hear

He _____ many movies in his life. Some of his most popular movies are *The*
     2. direct

Terminator, Titanic, and *Avatar.*

    But he hasn't always been a filmmaker. When he was a young man, he _____ at several
                              3. work

different jobs. At one time, he _____ a truck driver. But he quit that job and moved to
     4. be/even

California to follow his dream—filmmaking.

    He _____ many award-winning films. In filming *Titanic* from 1995 to 1997 he
     5. make

_____ make 12 dives down to the ship. At that time, he _____ very
     6. have to   **7.** become

interested in ocean exploration. He _____ a company, Earthship Productions, in 1998 to
                                8. form

explore the ocean. Since his first expedition, he _____ at least eight more expeditions.
                                9. lead

So far, he _____ the *Titanic* site two more times.
           10. visit

    Cameron is not only interested in the ocean. He's also interested in space exploration.

He _____ with space scientists and engineers many times. One thing is for sure,
     11. work

Cameron's life _____ very interesting.
          12. be

Interior of a first-class cabin in the
shipwrecked *Titanic*

2.11 The Present Perfect with Continuation from Past to Present

EXAMPLES	EXPLANATION
Nik Wallenda **has been** a performer *for* many years.	We use *for* + an amount of time to show the duration of time.
Paul Nicklen **has been** interested in sea animals *all his life.*	We can use an expression with *all* (*all his life, all day, all week*) to show duration. We don't use *for* before *all*.
I climbed mountains many years ago, but I **haven't done** it *in* a long time.	In a negative statement, we often use *in* rather than *for*.
Nik **has been** a tightrope performer *since* 1992.	We use *since* + a past time or time period to show the starting time.
James Cameron **has been** interested in the ocean *(ever) since* he started work on the movie *Titanic*.	We use *since* or *ever since* to begin a clause that shows the start of a continuous action or state. The verb in the *since* clause is in the simple past.
I **have** *always* **been** interested in adventure.	*Always* with the present perfect shows the continuation of an action or state from the past to the present.
How long has Sylvia Earle **been** interested in the ocean?	We use *how long* to ask a question about duration.
Paul Nicklen **takes** photographs during his expeditions. He **has taken** many photographs during his expeditions.	Don't confuse the present perfect with the simple present. The simple present refers to habitual actions. The present perfect connects the past to the present.

Notes:

1. We can use the simple past with *for* when the event started and ended in the past.
   *Sylvia Earle **did** research at the University of California from 1969 to 1981. She worked there **for** 12 years.*

2. We can use the simple past with *how long* when the event started and ended in the past. Compare:
   ***How long have** you **lived** in the U.S.?* (still in the U.S.)
   ***How long did** you **live** in your country?* (all in the past)

3. We can put *ever since* at the end of the sentence to mean "from the past time mentioned to the present."
   *She became interested in the ocean as a child, and **has been** interested in it **ever since**.*

GRAMMAR IN USE

When we write a letter to apply for a job or for admission to a school, we often use the present perfect to introduce information about our experience. Then we switch to the simple past for specific details.

*I **have worked** as a volunteer on several occasions. In the summer of 2019, I **worked** with an organization to clean the beaches in my town. I **picked up** trash and **monitored** sea-turtle nests.*

EXERCISE 18 Fill in the blanks with the present perfect and any missing words.

1. Paul Nicklen ____has worked____ as a photojournalist ____since____ 1985.

a. work   b.

2. The Wallendas _____ circus performers _____

a. be   b.

   seven generations.

3. Sylvia Earle _____ a good team.
   a. always/have

4. _____ Earle first started to explore the ocean, it _____ a lot.
   a.   **b.** change

5. In 1953, Edmund Hillary was the first person to reach the top of Mt. Everest. Many people

_____ to reach the top ever _____ .
   a. try   **b.**

6. _____ 1990, Apa Sherpa _____ Mt. Everest over 20 times.
   a.   **b.** climb

7. Ever _____ James Cameron made his first deep-sea dive in 1985, he
   a.

_____ many deep-sea expeditions.
   b. lead

8. How _____ _____ a movie director?
   a.   **b.** Cameron/be

EXERCISE 19 Fill in the blanks using the correct form of the words given and any missing words. In some cases, no answer is needed in the blank. If that is the case, write Ø.

A: How do you feel about risk?

B: I __'ve been__ interested in risk taking _____Ø_____ all my life.
          1. be   **2.**

A: So you _____ a lot of articles and books about risk takers.
             3. probably/read

B: Well, yes, I have. But I _____ a lot of risks, too. I _____
                              4. take   **5.** have

three lessons in parachuting so far.

A: How long _____ interested in parachuting?
                   6.

B: Ever _____ I graduated from high school.
          7.

A: _____ you ever had an accident?
      8.

B: No, I never _____ . A few months ago, I read an article about bungee jumping,
                   9.

and I _____ to do it ever _____ .
       10. want   **11.**

A: I _____ interested in that. I can't even understand why people
      12. never/be

would want to put their lives in danger. In fact, I _____ to do safe things
                                                      13. try

_____ all my life.
   14.

B: Really? So you're not interested in taking risks?

A: I didn't say that. Since we _____ to talk about risk in this lesson, I
                                   15. start

_____ more interested. But my interest is in reading about it, not doing it!
   16. become

ABOUT YOU Fill in the blanks with the correct present perfect forms and other words to complete the questions. Ask and answer these questions with a partner.

A: **Has** your life **changed** since you left your country?

B: Yes! It**'s changed** a lot. I**'ve been studying** every day, and I **haven't been watching** as many TV shows.

1. _____Has_____ your life ___changed___ a lot since last year?
                                        change

2. _____ you _____ a new career in the last few years?
                            start

3. Since last year, _____ you _____ to do things you _____ before?
                                              learn   never/do

4. Have you _____ something dangerous?
                 ever/do

5. Have you _____ to do something no one else _____ before?
                 always/want   ever/do

6. Have you _____ to make a difficult decision?
                 ever/have

ABOUT YOU Write sentences using the present perfect. Then work with another pair and share your information. Ask follow-up questions.

A: I**'ve always wanted** to go on a safari in Africa.

B: **Have you ever visited** Africa?

A: No, I **haven't even been** there yet. I hope to go one day!

1. (something you've wanted to do ever since you were a child)

   _____

2. (something you've always thought about)

   _____

3. (an activity you've never tried but would like to)

   _____

4. (something you've been good at all your life)

   _____

5. (something you haven't done in a long time)

   _____

FUN WITH GRAMMAR

Make up a story. Work in a small group. Create a fictional adventurer or explorer. Write a story about the person's life and recent adventures. Include at least three verbs and three adverbs from the lists. Share your stories with the class and vote on the best one.

VERBS	ADVERBS
climb	always
eat	for
see	lately
discover	recently
jump	since
find	this year

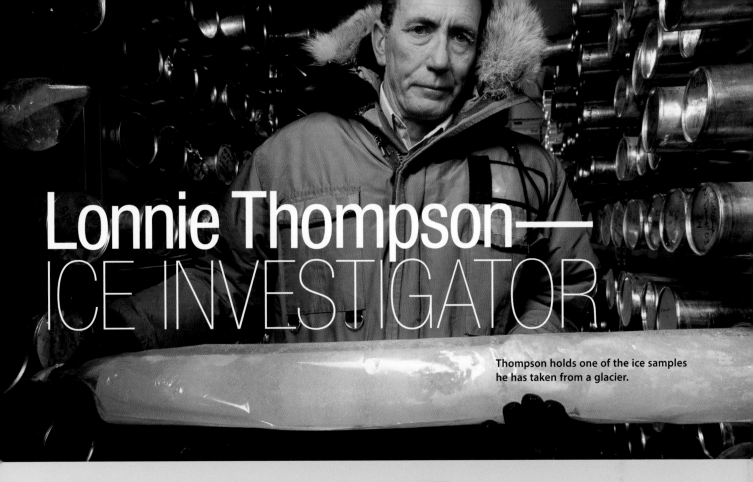

Lonnie Thompson—
ICE INVESTIGATOR

Thompson holds one of the ice samples he has taken from a glacier.

Read the following article. Pay special attention to the words in bold. 🎧 2.6

Lonnie Thompson **has been climbing** to the top of glaciers[1] for over 40 years. He **has been looking** for information that is hidden inside the ice. Some of these glaciers contain information that is thousands of years old. This information shows that the planet **has been warming** and that these glaciers **have been melting**. He wants to find out more about these glaciers before it's too late.

Thompson has probably spent more time above 18,000 feet than anyone else. Altogether he has spent over 1,100 days at this altitude. Many people have climbed to above 18,000 feet, but no one has stayed there as long as Thompson. Sometimes he has stayed at this altitude for up to six weeks.

He has faced many dangers and challenges. Getting six tons of camping and drilling equipment up to 23,500 feet is one. Lightning is another. "I've had lightning come down 10 feet in front of me," he reported. Other dangers are avalanches,[2] storms, and wind. What's amazing is that Thompson is in his 60s. At the age of 63, he had a heart transplant. His father died at 41 of a heart attack. "Maybe I'm living longer because I climb mountains," he said.

Thompson has gone to a glacier in Peru 26 times. His research **has been helping** us learn about the past. But the opportunities for gaining this knowledge **have been diminishing**[3]. "My work has become a way to capture[4] history before it disappears forever."

---

[1] glacier: a large mass of ice that moves slowly, usually down a mountain
[2] avalanche: a sudden break of snow down a mountain
[3] to diminish: to decrease in number, to lessen
[4] to capture: to catch

COMPREHENSION Based on the reading, write T for *true* or F for *false*.

1. _____ Lonnie Thompson has been finding important information in glaciers.

2. _____ He has been climbing glaciers for 26 years.

3. _____ Some of the glaciers have been melting.

THINK ABOUT IT Discuss the questions with a partner or in a small group.

1. In what ways might his research about the past be useful to humans today?

2. Lonnie Thompson takes personal risks to gather important information. Would you take risks like this? Explain. Give your reasons.

2.12 The Present Perfect Continuous

We use the present perfect continuous to talk about an action that started in the past and continues to the present.

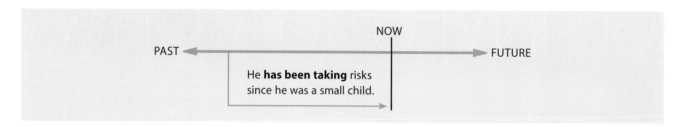

EXAMPLES	EXPLANATION
Lonnie Thompson **has been climbing** glaciers *for* many years. Paul Nicklen **has been taking** risks *since* he was a small child.	We use *for* and (*ever*) *since* to show the time spent at an activity.
Lately, people **have been thinking** about space tourism.	We use indefinite time words, like *lately*, with the present perfect continuous.
We **have been reading** stories about risk takers.	Sometimes there is no mention of time.
He **has worked** with glaciers for a long time. He **has been working** with glaciers for a long time.	With some verbs, we can use either the present perfect or the present perfect continuous with no difference in meaning. This is especially true with the following verbs: *live, work, teach, study, use, wear.*
How long **has** James Cameron **been making** movies? *How long* **has** Lonnie Thompson **been studying** glaciers?	To ask a question about the duration of an action, we use *how long*.
Thompson **studies** glaciers. He **has been studying** glaciers for over 40 years. Many glaciers **are melting**. They **have been melting** for many years.	Don't confuse the simple present or the present continuous with the present perfect continuous. The present perfect continuous connects the past to the present.

Notice these seven patterns with the present perfect continuous:

AFFIRMATIVE STATEMENT:	Thompson **has been studying** glaciers.
NEGATIVE STATEMENT:	He **hasn't been studying** the ocean.
YES/NO QUESTION:	**Has** he **been studying** glaciers in Peru?
SHORT ANSWER:	Yes, he **has**.
WH- QUESTION:	Which glaciers **has** Thompson **been studying**?
NEGATIVE WH- QUESTION:	Why **hasn't** he **been studying** the ocean?
SUBJECT QUESTION:	Who **has been studying** the ocean?

EXERCISE 20 Fill in the blanks with the present perfect continuous form of the verb given. Add *for* or *since* where necessary.

1. James Cameron <u>has been making</u> movies <u>   since   </u> 1984.
                                  make

2. He _____ the ocean _____ many years.
                      explore

3. Lately, he _____ with space scientists.
                        work

4. Lonnie Thompson _____ glaciers _____ over 40 years.
                             study

5. He _____ a lot about the past.
                      learn

6. _____ many years, the glaciers _____.
                                  melt

7. The Wallenda family _____ risky activities _____ seven
                            perform

   generations.

8. Scientists _____ more and more about how brain chemicals affect risk.
                      learn

9. Sylvia Earle _____ the ocean _____ many years.
                      study

10. People _____ Mt. Everest _____ 1953.
                      climb

EXERCISE 21 Fill in the blanks in the following conversations. Use the present perfect continuous. Fill in any other missing words.

1. **A:** I'm learning about glaciers.

   B: How long <u>have you been learning</u> about glaciers?
                           a.

   A: <u>   For   </u> about six months.
          b.

continued

Frozen core sections are carried down off
the ice field to refrigerated storage trucks.

2. **A:** My father works as a photographer.

   B: How long _____ as a photographer?

                                      a.

   A: _____ about 10 years.

       b.

3. **A:** Are you thinking about getting your pilot's license?

   B: Yes, I am.

   A: How long _____ about getting it?

                                      a.

   B: _____ I was in high school.

       b.

4. **A:** Someone told me that your mother is a mountain climber.

   B: That's right. She is.

   A: How _____ mountains?

                               a.

   B: _____ about 20 years.

       b.

5. **A:** James Cameron makes great movies.

   B: I agree. How _____ movies?

                               a.

   A: He's _____ making movies _____ over 35 years. And he's been _____

                b.   **c.**   **d.**

   risks to make some of these movies.

   B: Do you mean that he's put his life in danger?

   A: Sometimes. But he _____ taking financial risks, too.

                            e.

6. **A:** You've _____ reading that book for a long time.

             a.

   B: Yes, I _____. It's so interesting. It's called *Into Thin Air*.

               b.

   A: I've never heard of it.

   B: Yes, you have. I _____ you about it _____ a few weeks.

                             c.   **d.**

   A: Tell me again.

   B: It's about a tragedy on Mt. Everest.

7. **A:** I _____ an interesting book by Sylvia Earle.

                             a.

   B: I can't read books about science. They're too difficult for me.

   A: It's a children's book. So it's easy to understand.

Complete the sentences with information about yourself. Use the present perfect continuous. Then work with a partner and discuss your answers.

> A: **I've been thinking** about my future for a while.
>
> B: Oh really? Why?
>
> A: Because I'm ready for a new challenge. I **haven't been doing** anything new for a while.

1. I've been thinking about _____ for _____.

2. I've been _____ since I was _____ years old.

3. I've been _____ lately.

2.13 The Present Perfect, the Present Perfect Continuous, and the Simple Past

EXAMPLES	EXPLANATION
Lonnie Thompson **has been trying** to find information in glaciers. How long **has** Paul Nicklen **been working** as a photojournalist?	We use the present perfect continuous for actions that started in the past and are still happening now. These actions are ongoing and are not finished. For questions about duration, we use *how long*.
Thompson **has climbed** many glaciers. **Have** you **ever** climbed a mountain? I **have** always **wanted** to climb a mountain, but I **have** never **done** it. Lonnie Thompson **has been** interested in glaciers for many years. How many times **has** Thompson **gone** to Peru? How much time **has** he **spent** on glaciers?	We use the present perfect, not the present perfect continuous, in the following cases: • with repetition from past to present • with an indefinite time in the past • with *always* and *never* • for duration with nonaction verbs (See Appendix B for a list of nonaction verbs.) • with questions about repetition, using *how much* or *how many*
I**'ve read** some interesting articles lately. I **have been reading** a book about glaciers. I **have climbed** several mountains. My friend **has been climbing** a mountain in Alaska this week.	The present perfect sentences indicate indefinite past times. The present perfect continuous sentences indicate that the action is still in progress.
He **has worked** as a photographer for many years. He **has been working** as a photographer for many years.	In some cases, there is no difference in meaning between the present perfect and the present perfect continuous.
When he was in college, Lonnie Thompson **studied** geology. He **made** his first glacier exploration in the 1970s.	We use the simple past for an action that was completely in the past. Often a definite past time or time period is given.

EXERCISE 22 Listen to the story of Jill Seaman. Fill in the blanks with the missing words. 🎧 2.7

Jill Seaman _____is_____ an American doctor. She _____ as a
           1.   **2.**

doc tor _____ 1979. She _____ ways to bring modern
              3.   **4.**

medicine to South Sudan _____ many years. When she _____ in Sudan
                                 5.   **6.**

in 1989, many people in this region were very sick. At the same time, a war was going on. She

_____ to South Sudan with an organization called Doctors Without Borders. Doctors from this
    7.

organization _____ to countries all over the world to help where there is a
                           8.

need for medical care. When Seaman first _____ to South Sudan, there _____
                               9.   **10.**

no doctors treating patients in small villages. Over the past 20 years, the health of the people in South

Sudan _____. In one year alone, Doctors Without Borders
              11.

_____ 2,500 people.
    12.

Because of the war, Seaman _____ many terrible things. But she says she's not a
                           13.

risk taker. She says, "Everybody _____ risks. Life _____ a risk." But
                       14.   **15.**

_____ many years, she _____ thousands of people.
    16.   **17.**

"How could I be more lucky?" she says.

EXERCISE 23 Fill in the blanks with the present perfect, the present perfect continuous, or the simple
past of the verb given.

Alex Honnold is a mountain climber. He _has been climbing_ since he was a child. What's amazing
                                      1. climb

is that he _____ this many times without a rope or any protection. This kind of
               2. do

climbing is called "free soloing." He _____ more than a thousand free-solo climbs.
                           3. make

When he was a small child, he _____ by practicing at a gym in Sacramento,
                           4. begin

California, where he lived. He _____ there six days a week. Throughout his life,
                        5. go

he _____ his risk. In 2008, to prepare for a climb in Yosemite
             6. increase

National Park, he _____ ropes. He wanted to analyze the mountain. He was
             7. use

looking for the best places for his hands and feet. The next day, he _____ it to
                                        8. make

the top without ropes. And he _____ it in less than three hours.
                          9. do

He _____ on many TV shows and in many magazines. In 2011, he
             10. appear

_____ on the cover of *National Geographic* magazine.
    11. be

EXERCISE 24 Fill in the blanks with the present perfect or the present perfect continuous and any other words. Use context clues to help you. In some cases, more than one answer is possible.

1. Alex is climbing a mountain now. He _has been climbing_ that mountain _____ eight hours.

   He _____ that mountain five times.

2. Alex is preparing for his next climb. He _____ for several months.

3. **A:** I _____ the documentary "Free Solo," yet, _____ you?

   B: No, _____. I want to see it, though!

4. I _____ a few risks _____ my life. For example, I _____

   a risk when I left my country and went to live in another country.

5. The organization _____ people in poor countries. Because of its help, conditions

   _____ improving for these people.

6. Sylvia Earle _____ as a National Geographic explorer _____ 1998.

7. Let's move on to a new subject. We _____ about it _____

   too long!

Alex Honnold climbing Half Dome in Yosemite National Park, California, U.S.

SUMMARY OF UNIT 2

The Simple Present and the Present Perfect

SIMPLE PRESENT	PRESENT PERFECT
Paul Nicklen **is** a photojournalist.	He **has been** a photojournalist since 1985.

The Present Continuous and the Present Perfect Continuous

PRESENT CONTINUOUS	PRESENT PERFECT CONTINUOUS
Jill Seaman **is helping** people in Africa.	She **has been helping** people in Africa for many years.

The Simple Past and the Present Perfect

SIMPLE PAST	PRESENT PERFECT
James Cameron **made** 12 deep-sea dives between 1995 and 1997.	James Cameron **has made** many dives since 1995.
When **did** Sylvia Earle **write** her first book?	How many children's books **has** she **written**?
Did Thompson **find** something important last year?	**Has** Thompson ever **gone** to the South Pole?
Nik Wallenda's grandfather **had** an accident and **died**.	Nik Wallenda takes risks, but he **has** always **been** very careful.

The Present Perfect and the Present Perfect Continuous—No Change in Meaning

PRESENT PERFECT	PRESENT PERFECT CONTINUOUS
Thompson **has studied** glaciers for many years.	Thompson **has been studying** glaciers for many years.

The Present Perfect and the Present Perfect Continuous—Difference in Meaning

PRESENT PERFECT	PRESENT PERFECT CONTINUOUS
I need a new hobby. I **have thought** about mountain climbing.	Lately, I **have been thinking** a lot about my future.
He **has climbed** the mountain three times.	He **has been climbing** the mountain for three hours.

REVIEW

Fill in the blanks with the simple past, the present perfect, or the present perfect continuous of the verb given. Fill in any other missing words. In some cases, more than one answer is possible.

A: I _____haven't seen_____ you _____ a long time. Where _____ for
           1. not/see   **2.**   **3.** be

the past few months?

B: Lately, I _____ a lot of work. And I have a new hobby. So I _____
             4. have   **5.** not/have

a lot of time for social activities.

A: What's your new hobby?

B: I _____ skydiving lessons lately.
      6. take

A: Really? That sounds so interesting—and scary! How long _____ that?
                                  7. you/do

B: I _____ to take lessons about six months ago. So far, I _____ out
      8. start   **9.** jump

of an airplane about 10 or 12 times.

A: You're so brave. I can't imagine doing that. In fact, I _____
                                             10. never/even/think

about it.

B: I _____ to do it, ever _____ I was a little girl. Before I
            11. always/want   **12.**

started, I _____ to some experienced jumpers. I _____ a lot.
         13. talk   **14.** learn

A: _____ a scary jump?
      15. you/ever/have

B: No. I'm very careful.

A: I'm glad to hear that. Is it an expensive hobby?

B: Yes. It's very expensive. I _____ to buy a lot of equipment over the past
                        16. have

six months. And each jump costs me $150.

A: Wow! That's a lot of money.

B: That's why I _____ overtime a lot lately. _____
             17. work   **18.**

the past few months, I _____ to convince my husband to do it with me, but he's
                        19. try

not interested at all. What about you? What kind of hobbies do you have?

A: I'm not as brave as you are. My hobby is a very safe one. I knit. My grandmother _____
                                          20. teach

me how to knit when I _____ 10 years old, and I _____
               21. be   **22.** knit

ever _____ . I _____ hundreds of scarves and sweaters over the years.
      23.   **24.** make

B: Would you like to try skydiving with me sometime?

A: No, thanks! Would you like to learn to knit?

B: No, thanks.

FROM GRAMMAR TO WRITING

PART 1 Editing Advice

1. Don't confuse the present participle (verb–*ing*) and the past participle. In some cases, they sound similar.

   Paul Nicklen has ~~taking~~ *taken* many pictures.

   Has he ever ~~being~~ *been* to the South Pole?

2. Don't confuse *for* and *since*.

   Sylvia Earle has been studying the ocean ~~since~~ *for* many years.

3. Use the correct word order.

   I have ~~been never~~ *never been* to Niagara Falls.

   Has Wallenda ~~had ever~~ *ever had* an accident?

4. Use *yet* in negative statements. Use *already* in affirmative statements.

   He hasn't reached the top of the mountain ~~already~~ *yet*.

5. Don't forget the *-d* or *-ed* ending on past participles of regular verbs.

   We have learn*ed* many things about risk takers.

   I've decide*d* to take skydiving lessons.

6. Use correct subject-verb agreement.

   Some people ~~has~~ *have* had very interesting experiences.

PART 2 Editing Practice

Some of the shaded words and phrases have mistakes. Find the mistakes and correct them. If the shaded words are correct, write C.

My uncle Meyer is not a famous person. But he has ~~doing~~ *done* many great things in his life. He is a teacher.
1.

He has been teaching Hebrew and Jewish history since the past 45 years. He has inspire many young
2. *C*   **3.**   **4.**

people to love language and history. In some cases, he have taught three generations of the same family.
5.

He often receives letters and e-mails from students who have studied with him many years ago. Many of
6.   **7.**

them has finished college and started their own careers and families. They often tell him how much they
8.

learned from him and how much he has inspired them.
9.

Another great thing about my uncle is that he has always being a great teacher outside the classroom.
10.

When we have been children, he often took us to the library on Saturdays and to a museum on Sundays.
11.   **12.**

He has been always a member of several museums and has donated money to support them. Many times
13.   **14.**

we **have wondered** why it's important to support the museums. He once **has told** us, "The classroom is only
    15.   16.

one place to learn. But life is bigger than the classroom. There are many other ways to learn."

    A third great thing about Uncle Meyer is that he never stops learning. He's 68 years old now, and he

has recently decided to learn Chinese. He **has already learn** Russian and German pretty well, and now he
    17.   18.   19.

wants a new challenge. He **is studying** Chinese **for** the past two months. He speaks it a little now, but he
 20.   21.   22.

hasn't learned to read or write it **yet**. But he never gives up. He **has always wanted** to travel to China, and
    23.   24.   25.

now he's hoping to go there next year with the ability to speak some Chinese.

    Some people think he's old and he should retire. But he **has never been thinking** about retiring. He
                                                              26.

loves to teach and learn. He **has taught** me that it's important to learn and inspire other people to learn.
                                    27.

WRITING TIP
When writing about an experience, you can set the scene with the present perfect, and then switch to the simple past when you are ready to give more precise details such as dates, times, and so on.

*Paul Nicklen **has shown** us incredible images of the arctic. Last year, he **went** on an expedition...*

*I**'ve been** to France many times and I**'ve** always **had** a wonderful time, but I**'ve** never **forgotten** a single thing about my first trip. That **was** in 2003, when I **visited** the Côte d'Azur and **stayed** in a small village with some friends.*

PART 3 Write
Read the prompts. Choose one and write one or more paragraphs about it.

1. Choose a living person you know or have read about who has done great things. This person doesn't have to be famous or well known. Write a paragraph (or multiple paragraphs) describing what risks this person has taken and why you think he or she is great.
2. Sometimes we take a big risk or make a decision to do something new without thinking about the results. Write a paragraph (or multiple paragraphs) telling about a decision you made or a risk you took without thinking about it too much. What was the decision? How has this decision affected your life or the lives of those around you? What have you learned from this experience?

PART 4 Edit
Reread the Summary of Lesson 2 and the Editing Advice. Edit your writing from Part 3.

Passive and Active Voice

An outdoor movie playing
in Brooklyn Bridge Park,
New York City

THE MOVIES

When a movie character is really working, we become that character. That's what the movies offer: Escaping into lives other than our own.

ROGER EBERT

BASED ON A
TRUE STORY

Read the following article. Pay special attention to the words in bold. 🎧 **3.1**

Movie studios are always searching for stories that can become "blockbusters"—movies with massive audiences and high profits. While a lot of money **has been made** over the years with fictional stories, movies that **are based** on real-life events or people **are often seen** as another way to attract large audiences. Such movies **are frequently centered** on stories from the news or on historical events. Often these movies are about heartwarming[1], feel-good news stories or about dangerous, thrilling, and exciting events. Here are some examples.

- *Hachi: A Dog's Tale* (2009)

Sometimes, a story is not well known until a movie **has been produced** and **seen** by audiences around the world. Often such a story **is chosen** for its general interest or human appeal. *Hachi* **was based** on a Japanese story about a dog that waited at the train station every evening for its owner to come home. After the owner's death, the dog continued to wait at the station for him for over nine years. The movie shows the depth of emotion between this dog and its owner. When *Hachi* **was released**, it **was criticized** by some reviewers for sentimentality[2],

but it **was generally well received** by critics and the public alike.

- *Sully: Miracle on the Hudson* (2016)

On the afternoon of January 15, 2009, audiences of U.S. news channels **were fascinated** by the amazing story of a passenger airplane that **was forced** to land on the Hudson River in New York City. The plane **had been hit** by birds soon after takeoff, and the engines had failed. All 155 people on board **were rescued** by boats. There were few injuries, and the pilot, Chesley Sullenberger, or "Sully" as he **was nicknamed**, became a national hero.

Of course, audiences for all movies want drama, thrills, and conflict, and those qualities **are sometimes provided** by filmmakers whether they actually happened or not! The truth **may be stretched**[3] and some characters or events even **changed** completely to make a "better" story. So please do not believe *everything* you see in movies that are "based on a true story."

---

1. heartwarming: describes something that makes people feel good or happy
2. sentimentality: quality of being overly sad or too emotional to
3. stretch the truth: to exaggerate a story

Movie poster showing passengers as they wait to be rescued on the wings of an airplane that safely landed in the Hudson River after a flock of birds knocked out both its engines (New York City, January 2009)

COMPREHENSION Based on the reading, write T for *true* or F for *false*.

1. _____ Movies that are based on real life are not as popular as movies with fictional stories.

2. _____ The emotional story in *Hachi* was appreciated by everyone.

3. _____ The movie *Sully* was named after the pilot of the plane in the story.

THINK ABOUT IT Discuss the questions with a partner or in a small group.

1. Do you prefer movies based on real life or movies with fictional stories? Explain your reasons.

2. Which movie would you rather see, *Hachi* or *Sully*? Explain your reasons.

3.1 Active and Passive Voice—Introduction

EXAMPLES	EXPLANATION
subject verb object **Active:** Many people **saw** the movie. subject verb agent **Passive:** The movie **was seen** *by* many people.	Some sentences are in the active voice. The subject performs the action of the verb. Some sentences are in the passive voice. The subject receives the action of the verb. The passive voice is formed with *be* + the past participle. See Appendix C for a list of irregular past participles.
The plane was hit **by birds**. The movie has been seen **by the survivors**. The movie **is based** on a true story. The students **were given** free tickets.	Sometimes a passive sentence includes the agent, or the performer of the action. If so, *by* + agent is often added to the sentence. More often, the agent is omitted.
Active: He photographed her. **Passive:** She was photographed by him.	Notice the difference in pronouns in an active sentence and a passive sentence. After *by*, the object pronoun is used.
In 1929, tickets *were sold* for $10. (simple past) Today tickets *are* not *sold*. (simple present)	The tense of a passive sentence is shown in the form of the verb *be*.

Notes:

1. If two verbs in the passive voice are connected with *and*, we do not repeat the verb *be*.

   *Some popular older movies **have been watched and loved** for decades.*

2. An adverb can be placed between *be* and the main verb.

   *The movie was **widely** criticized for its historical inaccuracy.*

   *Successful movies are **often** adapted from novels.*

Notice these patterns with the passive voice in the past.

AFFIRMATIVE STATEMENT:	The movie **was filmed** in the United States.
NEGATIVE STATEMENT:	It **wasn't filmed** in Canada.
YES/NO QUESTION:	**Was** it **filmed** in Hollywood?
SHORT ANSWER:	No, it **wasn't**.
WH- QUESTION:	When **was** it **filmed**?
NEGATIVE WH- QUESTION:	Why **wasn't** it **filmed** in Hollywood?
SUBJECT QUESTION:	Which movie **was filmed** in Canada?

3.2 Comparison of Active and Passive Voice

	ACTIVE	PASSIVE
Simple Present	Critics **review** movies.	New movies **are reviewed** after special early screenings.
Present Continuous	They **are filming** the movie in 3D.	The movie **is being filmed** in Hollywood.
Future	The writer **will base** the story on an event from the news. The writer **is going to base** the story on an event from the news.	The story **will be based** on an event from the news. The story **is going to be based** on an event from the news.
Simple Past	The director **made** a new movie.	The movie **was made** in Paris.
Past Continuous	Reporters **were interviewing** the stars.	The stars **were being interviewed** on the red carpet.
Present Perfect	Woody Allen **has made** many movies.	Most of his movies **have been made** in New York.
Modal	You **should see** the movie in the theater.	The movie **should be seen** on a large screen.

GRAMMAR IN USE

Using an agent with *by* is only one of the ways a passive sentence can be completed. Here are other common ways.

*The movie was made **in 2017**.* (When?)
*The forest scenes were shot **in New Zealand**.* (Where?)
*The scene was filmed **using a new 3D camera**.* (How?)
*The script was designed **to surprise the audience**.* (Why?)

EXERCISE 1 Listen to the sentences and fill in the blanks with the words you hear. Then decide if the verb is active (*A*) or passive (*P*). 🎧 **3.2**

1. The director _____*wrote*_____ the screenplay. A

2. The screenplay ___*was written*___ by the director. P

3. The car company _____ a new model for the movie.

4. A new car _____ for the movie.

5. Starring roles _____ to unknown actors.

6. Who _____ the music for the movie?

7. Many American actors _____ in California.

8. _____ all American movies _____ in Hollywood?

9. The movie _____ in 3D.

10. Her next movie _____ on a true story.

11. The actress usually _____ in comedies.

12. Many well-known movies _____ in New York.

13. _____ you ever _____ *Gone With the Wind*?

14. When _____ this film _____?

15. Some movies _____ on TV.

16. I _____ to the movies lately.

17. The actor _____ for his performance.

18. Which movie _____ in Paris?

EXERCISE 2 Fill in the blanks with the passive voice of the verb given and any other words you see. Use the simple past form of *be*.

A: People associate American movies with Hollywood. But in the beginning, the American film industry

___wasn't based___ in Hollywood. It _____ in New York.
      1. not/base   2. base

B: When _____ in Hollywood?
          3. the first film/make

A: The first Hollywood film _____ in 1911. Did you know that early movie theaters
                        4. produce

_____ "nickelodeons?"
      5. call

B: Really? Why _____ that?
          6. they/call

A: Because they cost five cents, or one nickel.

B: I wonder how else nickelodeons were different from theaters today. _____
                                            7. snacks/sell

in nickelodeons?

A: At first, food _____ by the theaters. Then outside vendors _____
          8. not/sell   9. permit

to come in and sell snacks. But when theater owners realized that they could make money for themselves

by selling snacks, vendors _____ to come in anymore.
                              10. not/allow

B: What _____? Popcorn? I love eating popcorn at the movies.
          11. sell

A: Me, too. But popcorn came later.

continued

B: Early films had no sound, right? How did the audience know what was happening?

A: Some of the dialogue _____ on signs. And special music
12. show

_____ for a movie. A pianist or organist would play live music in the theater to
13. write

create a mood. For example, dramatic music _____ for stormy
14. usually/play

weather or scary scenes, and romantic music _____ for love scenes.
15. use

B: When _____ to films?
16. sound/add

A: In 1927.

B: And when _____ ?
17. the first color movie/make

A: The first color movies _____ in the early 1900s, but many of these
18. actually/make

films _____ .
19. lose

B: Wow! You know a lot about movies. How do you know so much?

A: I'm majoring in film. We _____ an assignment to write a paper about the early days of
20. give

the movies.

EXERCISE 3 Fill in the blanks with the passive voice of the verb given. Use the simple present or present continuous, as indicated.

Imagine: You have checked movie listings online. The theater website says the movie you

want to see will begin at 7:30 p.m. You arrive at 7:00. You relax into your seat, and now you're

ready to see your movie, right? Not so fast! First, you ___are shown___ a number of ads for
1. simple present: show

cars, soft drinks, TV shows, and more. Then you _____ to turn off your cell
2. simple present: tell

phone. Now the lights _____ and the theater is becoming dark.
3. present continuous: dim

The movie's ready to begin, right? Wrong! Next come the movie trailers. Trailers

_____ to advertise new movies that are coming soon or that
4. simple present: make

_____ in other parts of the same theater. A trailer _____ to
5. present continuous: show   6. simple present: limit

two and a half minutes, so the movie will begin soon. Right? Wrong again. Sometimes as many

as five or six trailers _____ . Again you _____ to turn
7. simple present: play   8. simple present: ask

off your cell phone. And no doubt, someone's phone will still ring. Finally, your movie begins and

you _____ to another world.
9. simple present: transport

3.3 Active and Passive Voice — Use

Active: George Lucas **directed** *Star Wars*. **Passive:** *Star Wars* **was directed** by George Lucas. **Active:** Jennifer Lawrence **will play** the starring role in the movie. **Passive:** The starring role in the movie **will be played** by Jennifer Lawrence.	When the sentence has a *strong* agent (a specific person), we can use either the active or passive voice. The passive with a strong agent is often used with the following verbs: *make, discover, invent, design, build, present, direct, write, paint, compose*. The active sentence calls attention to the subject. The passive sentence calls attention to the action or the receiver of the action.
A lot of food **was left** in the theater after the movie. *Sully* **was made** in 2016.	When the sentence has a *weak* agent (identity of the agent is not important, not known, or is obvious), the passive voice is used without a *by* phrase.
Active: The screenwriter is going to adapt his next **script** from a recent news story. **Passive:** The screenwriter's next **script** is going to be adapted from a recent news story. **Active:** The director bases most of her **movies** on real life. **Passive:** Most of the director's **movies** are based on real life.	The passive voice can be used to shift the emphasis to the object of the preceding sentence.
I **was told** that you didn't like the movie.	The passive voice can be used to hide the identity of the agent.
Informal: *Nobody* **knows** who the star of the movie is going to be. **Formal:** The star of the movie is not **known** yet. **Informal:** *They* **filmed** the movie in just three weeks. **Formal:** The movie **was filmed** in just three weeks.	In conversation, the active voice is often used with the impersonal subjects: *people, you, we,* or *they*. These are *weak* subjects. In more formal speech and writing, the passive is used with no agent.

GRAMMAR IN USE

Using active or passive voice is often based on the formality required by the situation. Passive often sounds more formal. For example:

Talking to friends: *They're **going to increase** the price of a movie ticket.*

In the news: *In the next year, ticket prices **are going to be increased**.*

EXERCISE 4 Some of the following sentences have a strong agent and can be changed to passive voice using the agent. Some have a weak agent and should be changed to passive voice without the agent. Change all sentences to passive voice.

1. Someone designs appropriate costumes to suit the period of the movie.

   Appropriate costumes are designed to suit the period of the movie.

2. James Cameron and Vince Pace designed the 3D camera for *Avatar*.

   The 3D camera for Avatar was designed by James Cameron and Vince Pace.

continued

3. They compose music to give the movie a mood.

_____

4. John Williams composed the music for _Star Wars_.

_____

5. They show credits at the end of the movie.

_____

6. They made the first Hollywood movie in 1911.

_____

7. Someone builds expensive sets for blockbuster movies.

_____

8. An Akita dog played the part of Hachi.

_____

9. You can buy movie tickets online.

_____

10. In _Sully_, Chesley Sullenberger saved all the passengers on the plane.

_____

11. They sell snacks in movie theaters.

_____

12. Someone gave me free tickets for the movie.

_____

EXERCISE 5 Fill in the blanks with the active or passive voice of the verb given. Use the simple present or the modal indicated.

_____Do you like_____ to watch movies in movie theaters? Well, I don't. First, movies are
     1. you/like

expensive. On Friday and Saturday nights, the movie theater is always crowded. I walk into the lobby,

and it _____ wonderful. I am tempted to buy some food, but it's so overpriced.
     2. smell

    In the movie theater close to my house, there's a free parking lot. When I enter, a small ticket

comes out. To get the free parking, the ticket _____ in the
     3. must/stamp

theater. I _____ to get it stamped, so I have to pay for parking.
     4. often/forget

If I _____ for the 7 p.m. show, the tickets _____,
　　　　5. arrive　　　　　　　　　　　　　　　　　　　　　　　　6. often/sell out

or the only seats left are in the first few rows. Tickets _____ earlier online, but
　　　　　　　　　　　　　　　　　　　　　　　　　　　　　　　7. can/buy

they're more expensive that way.

　　In a theater, I have to watch movie trailers. The trailer scenes _____ from the
　　　　　　　　　　　　　　　　　　　　　　　　　　　　　　　8. take

most exciting parts of the film, and they're often too loud. I heard that some of these scenes

_____ specifically for the trailer and don't even appear in the film!
　　9. create

　　I _____ to watch movies at home on my new large-screen TV. With my cable
　　　10. prefer

service, I _____ to watch newer movies for a reasonable price. Older movies
　　　　　11. can/pay

_____ from my local library for free. Even though DVDs _____
　　12. can/borrow　　　　　　　　　　　　　　　　　　　　　　　　　　　　　13. have

trailers too, they _____ .
　　　　　　　　14. can/skip

　　When I watch a movie at home, I _____ my phone so that I
　　　　　　　　　　　　　　　　　　　　15. turn off

_____ . Sometimes I _____ my friends and we
　　16. not/interrupt　　　　　　　　　17. invite

_____ popcorn in the microwave. We _____ money and don't have
　　18. make　　　　　　　　　　　　　　　　　19. save

any of the frustrations of going to the theater.

ABOUT YOU Underline the verbs in the following sentences. Write *P* if the verb is passive. Write *A* if the
verb is active. Work with a partner and discuss whether the statement is true in your native country.

1. Snacks <u>are sold</u> in movie theaters. P

2. Movie tickets can be bought online.

3. Several movies are played in the same theater at the same time.

4. Movie tickets are expensive.

5. A lot of American movies are shown in my country.

6. Actors earn a lot of money.

7. The best actors are given awards.

8. Senior citizens get a discount at a movie.

3.4 Verbs with Two Objects

EXAMPLES	EXPLANATION
Active: They gave the director an award. 　　　　　　　　　I.O.　　　　　　　D.O. **Passive 1:** The director was given an award. **Passive 2:** An award was given to the director.	Some verbs have two objects: a direct object (D.O.) and an indirect object (I.O.). When this is the case, the passive sentence can begin with either object. If the direct object (*an award*) becomes the subject of the passive sentence, *to* is used before the indirect object.

Note: Some verbs that use two objects are:

bring	hand	offer	pay	send	show	teach	write
give	lend	owe	sell	serve	take	tell	

EXERCISE 6 Change the following sentences to passive voice in two ways. Omit the agent.

1. They gave the actress a starring role.

   <u>The actress was given a starring role.</u>

   <u>A starring role was given to the actress.</u>

2. They will offer the actor the role.

   _____

   _____

3. Someone has given Alex two free tickets.

   _____

   _____

4. They showed us the new movie.

   _____

   _____

5. They serve you food at your seat.

   _____

   _____

FUN WITH GRAMMAR

Play a guessing game. In a group of three, write 4-5 sentences about a movie that was adapted from real life or from a book. Use the passive voice with these verbs or other verbs (compose, design, direct, film, play, release, write, watch). Read your sentences to your classmates, and they will guess the movie.

A: *The movie **was released** in 2009. The main character **was played** by Richard Gere. The dog **was played** by an Akita, a Japanese dog. The screenplay **was based** on a Japanese story…*

B: Is it *Hachi: A Dog's Tale?*

A: *Yes, it is!*

The HISTORY of ANIMATION

Read the following article. Pay special attention to the words in bold. 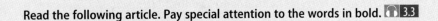 🎧 3.3

You have probably seen some great computer-animated movies, like *Toy Story, Finding Nemo,* or *Frozen.* Computer animation **has become** the norm[1] in today's world. But animation has been around for over one hundred years. It **has changed** a lot over time. How **was** it **done** before computers **were invented**?

Early animations **were created** by hand. At the beginning of the 1900s, Winsor McCay, who **is considered** the father of animation, **worked** alone and animated his films by himself. He drew every picture separately and had them photographed, one at a time. Hundreds of photographs **were needed** to make a one-minute film. It took him more than a year and 10,000 drawings to create a five-minute animation called *Gertie the Dinosaur.* It **was shown** to audiences in theaters in 1914.

After celluloid (a transparent material) **was developed,** animation became easier. Instead of drawing each picture separately, the animator could make a drawing of the background, which **remained** motionless, while only the characters **moved**.

Walt Disney, the creator of Mickey Mouse, took animation to a new level. He added sound and music to his movies and **produced** the first full-length animated film, *Snow White and the Seven Dwarfs.* Many people think he was a great animator, but he wasn't. Instead, he **worked** mainly as a story editor. He was also a clever businessman who had other artists do most of the drawings.

Toy Story, which **came** out in 1995, was the first computer-animated film. Computer animation **was** also **used** for special effects in movies such as *Star Wars* and *Avatar.* If you've seen *Life of Pi,* you may be surprised to learn that the tiger **was done** by animation. To create the illusion[2] of movement in these films, an image[3] **was put** on the computer and then quickly **replaced** by a similar image with a small change. While this technique is similar to hand-drawn animation, the work **can be done** much faster on the computer. In fact, anyone with a home computer and special software can create a simple animation.

continued

---

1 norm: a common expectation
2 illusion: a false idea of reality
3 image: a picture or drawing

One of the first animated films, *Gertie the Dinosaur* (1909)

Important Dates in Animation

1914	Winsor McCay **created** the first animation on film, *Gertie the Dinosaur*.
1918	Walt Disney **opened** a cartoon studio in Kansas City, Missouri.
1923	Disney **moved** his studio to Hollywood.
1928	The first Mickey Mouse cartoon **was introduced**. It was the first talking cartoon.
1937	Disney **produced** *Snow White and the Seven Dwarfs*, the first full-length animated cartoon.
1995	*Toy Story* **became** the first full-length film animated entirely on computers.
2014	*Frozen* **won** the Academy Award for best animated film.

COMPREHENSION Based on the reading, write T for *true* or F for *false*.

1. _____ Animation was seen in movie theaters over 100 years ago.

2. _____ *Gertie the Dinosaur* was created by Walt Disney.

3. _____ It's possible to create a realistic looking animal using computer animation.

THINK ABOUT IT Discuss the questions with a partner or in a small group.

1. Do you prefer watching movie-length animations or movies with actors? Explain.

2. What are some ways an animation might be better for telling a story than using real actors? What are some ways using real actors might be better?

3.5 Transitive and Intransitive Verbs

EXAMPLES	EXPLANATION
verb object **Active:** McCay **created** the first animated film. **Passive:** The first animated film **was created** in 1914. verb object **Active:** Walt Disney **didn't draw** his cartoons. **Passive:** His cartoons **were drawn** by studio artists.	Most active verbs are followed by an object and can be used in the active or passive voice. These verbs are called *transitive* verbs.
Disney **lived** in Hollywood most of his life. He **became** famous when he created Mickey Mouse. He **worked** with many artists. What **happened** to the first Mickey Mouse cartoon?	Some verbs have no object. These are called *intransitive verbs*. We don't use the passive voice with intransitive verbs. The following are examples: arrive go remain be happen sleep become live stay come occur wait die rain fall recover (from illness)
Some animations **look** so real. The popcorn **smells** fresh.	The sense perception verbs are intransitive: *look, appear, feel, sound, taste, smell, seem.*

EXAMPLES	EXPLANATION
(T) Someone **left** the DVD in the DVD player. It **was left** there last night. (I) Disney **left** Kansas City in 1923. (T) We **walked** the dog when we got home. The dog **was walked** in the morning, too. (I) We **walked** to the theater near our house.	Some verbs can be transitive (T) or intransitive (I), depending on their meaning and use. A transitive verb can be active or passive. An intransitive verb can only be active.
(I) Animation **has changed** a lot since the early days. (T) The janitor **changed** the light bulb. The light bulb **was changed** last night.	*Change* can be intransitive (I) or transitive (T). When a change happens through a natural process, it is intransitive. When someone causes the change, it is transitive.
(I) In an animated movie, it looks as if the characters **are moving**, but they are not. (T) The janitor **moved** the chairs. They **were moved** to another room.	*Move* can be intransitive (I) or transitive (T). When someone causes the move, it is transitive.
Walt Disney **was born** in 1901. He **died** in 1966.	We use *be* with *born*. We don't use *be* with *die*.

EXERCISE 7 Read the following sentences. Find and underline the main verb in each one. Then identify which sentences can be changed to the passive voice, and change those sentences. If no change is possible, write *no change* or *NC*.

1. Winsor McCay <u>made</u> the first animated film.

   <u>The first animated film was made by Winsor McCay.</u>

2. Winsor McCay <u>became</u> famous for *Gertie the Dinosaur*.

   <u>no change</u>

3. McCay worked in Cincinnati.

   _____

4. Someone offered him a job as a newspaper artist.

   _____

5. He left Cincinnati.

   _____

6. He moved to New York in order to work for the *New York Herald Tribune*.

   _____

7. People considered the *Herald Tribune* to have the highest-quality color.

   _____

continued

8. What happened to the animation *Gertie the Dinosaur*?

_____

9. Can we see it today?

_____

10. Did they preserve it?

_____

11. You can find it online.

_____

12. *Gertie the Dinosaur* seems very simple compared to today's animations.

_____

13. Animation has changed a lot over the years.

_____

14. Today they create most animation on computers.

_____

15. Someone left the movie tickets at home.

_____

EXERCISE 8 Listen to the text about Walt Disney. Write T for *true* or F for *false*. 3.4

1. _____ After high school, Walt Disney worked for a newspaper.

2. _____ Disney's character Donald Duck first appeared in *"Steamboat Willie."*

3. _____ Disneyland was built in 1955.

EXERCISE 9 Circle the correct words to complete this article about Walt Disney. Then listen and check your answers. 3.4

Walt Disney (was born/born) in Chicago in 1901. He (began/was begun) drawing and painting
        1.   2.
when he was a small child. When he was in high school, he (gave/was given) the job of drawing cartoons
                                                                        3.
for the school newspaper. After high school, Disney (worked/was worked) for a company making
                                                                4.
commercials. At that job, he (became/was become) interested in how to make animations. In 1923,
                                5.
Disney (moved/was moved) to California. There, he (started/was started) to work on his most famous
        6.   7.
character, Mickey Mouse. We can all (recognize/be recognized) this lovable little mouse. But when
                                            8.

Mickey and Minnie Mouse from Walt Disney's *Steamboat Willie* (1928)

Mickey (*first created/was first created*), he (*looked/was looked*) different. The original cartoon mouse
        9.   **10.**

(*named/was named*) "Mortimer," not "Mickey." Walt's partner (*changed/was changed*) Mickey's look
    11.   **12.**

to the character we know today.

At first, Mickey Mouse animations had no sound. But in 1929, after sound

(*introduced/was introduced*) into movies, Walt Disney (*created/was created*) "Steamboat Willie",
    13.   **14.**

with a talking mouse and music. The cartoon was an instant success. Later new characters

(*added/were added*): Minnie Mouse, Donald Duck, Goofy, and Pluto. In 1932, Disney's short animation
    15.

"*Flowers and Trees*" was the first animated movie that (*produced/was produced*) in color—and Disney
                                                       16.

(*won/was won*) his first Oscar.
    17.

In 1937, Disney's *Snow White and the Seven Dwarfs* was the first full-length animated film. Disney

(*earned/was earned*) $1.5 million and (*won/was won*) an honorary Academy Award for that film.
    18.   **19.**

In 1955, Disney (*built/was built*) Disneyland in California, which became a favorite vacation
                          20.

destination for families with small children. A new Disney park, called Disney World,

(*was building/was being built*) in Florida when Disney (*died/was died*) in 1966. As of today, five Disney
    21.   **22.**

theme parks (*have built/have been built*) in four different countries.
    23.

EXERCISE 10 Fill in the blanks with the active or passive form of the verb given. Use the past.

Ronald Reagan __was elected__ president of the United States in 1980. Before he _____
                 1. elect   **2. become**

president, he was governor of California. Even before that, he _____ as a Hollywood actor.
                                                               3. work

He _____ in 53 Hollywood movies between 1937 and 1964. He
   4. appear

_____ a great actor, and he never _____ an Oscar.
  5. not/consider   **6. win**

On March 20, 1981, the day the Oscar ceremony _____ to take place, something
                                                  7. schedule

terrible _____. Reagan _____ in an assassination attempt. Fortunately, he
     8. happen   **9. shoot**

_____ from his wounds. One of his aides, who was with him at the time,
   10. not/die

_____. Out of respect for the president, the Academy Awards ceremony
  11. also/wound

_____ for one day.
   12. postpone

Reagan _____ and continued to serve as president until he _____ his
         13. recover   **14. finish**

second term in 1989. He _____ in 2004 at the age of 93.
              15. die

Ronald Reagan in an old Western movie long before he became president of the U.S.

3.6 The Passive Voice with *Get*

EXAMPLES	EXPLANATION
A Hollywood actor **gets paid** a lot of money. I saw a violent movie, but I didn't like it. A lot of people **got shot**.	In conversation, we sometimes use *get* instead of *be* with the passive. get paid = be paid get shot = be shot *Get* is frequently used with: *shot, killed, injured, invited, wounded, paid, hired, hurt, fired, laid off, picked, caught, done, sent, stolen.*
He **was shot** by a cowboy.	If there is an agent, we use *be*, not *get*.
He **got shot** three times.	We usually omit the agent after *get*.
How much **do** actors **get paid** for a movie? Winsor McCay **didn't get paid** a lot of money.	When *get* is used in the simple present and the simple past, questions and negatives are formed with *do, does, did*.

EXERCISE 11 Change the following sentences to use *get* instead of *be*. If you see a *by* phrase, omit it.

1. Ronald Reagan was shot on the day of the Oscars.

   Ronald Reagan got shot on the day of the Oscars.

2. One of his aides was shot by the same man, too.

   One of his aides got shot, too.

3. Reagan wasn't killed by the shooter.

   _____

4. Was the aide killed by him?

   _____

5. Was the shooter caught by the police?

   _____

6. Movie stars are paid a lot of money.

   _____

7. Who will be picked for the starring role of the movie?

   _____

8. I wasn't invited to the Academy Awards.

   _____

Charlie Chaplin playing a burglar in a 1916 silent film

CHARLIE CHAPLIN

Read the following article. Pay special attention to the words in bold. 3.5

You have seen many movies and animations with the most **advanced** technology. And you can probably recognize many of today's popular actresses and actors. But have you ever heard of Charlie Chaplin? Charlie Chaplin was one of the greatest actors in the world. During the time of silent movies, Chaplin was the highest-**paid** person in the world—not just the highest-**paid** actor. His **amusing** character, the Little Tramp, with his **worn**-out shoes, round hat, and cane, is still well **known** to people throughout the world.

Chaplin had an **amazing** life. His idea for a poor tramp probably came from his childhood experiences. Born in poverty[1] in London in 1889, Chaplin was abandoned by his father and left in an orphanage[2] by his sick mother. He became **interested** in acting at the age of five. At 10, he left school to travel with a British acting company. In 1910, he made his first trip to the United States. He was talented, athletic, and **hardworking**. On his second trip to the United States, in 1912, his talent was recognized and he was offered a movie contract. In 1917, when his contract expired, he built his own

studio, where he produced, directed, and wrote the movies he starred in. He even composed the music that was played with his movies. Five years after arriving in the United States, he was earning $10,000 a week, which today is worth over $100,000.

Even though sound was introduced in movies in 1927, Chaplin continued to make silent movies. He didn't make a movie with sound until 1940, when he played a comic version of the **terrifying** dictator, Adolf Hitler.

As Chaplin got older, he faced **declining** popularity as a result of his politics and personal relationships. After he left the United States in 1952, Chaplin was not allowed to re-enter because of his political views. He didn't return to the United States until 1972, when he was given a special award for his lifetime achievements. Chaplin died in 1977 at the age of 88.

---

[1] poverty: lack of money and material possessions
[2] orphanage: a place where children without parents live and are cared for

COMPREHENSION Based on the reading, write T for *true* or F for *false*.

1. _____ When Chaplin was 10 years old, he moved to America.

2. _____ He composed the music for his movies.

3. _____ He started life poor but became very rich.

THINK ABOUT IT Discuss the questions with a partner or in a small group.

1. In what ways was Chaplin's career in movies similar to and different from the careers of modern film stars? Give examples.

2. Do you enjoy watching old movies? Why or why not?

3.7 Participles Used as Adjectives

EXAMPLES	EXPLANATION
Today's movies use **advanced** technology. Chaplin was not an **educated** man.	Some past participles are used as adjectives.
Chaplin had an **amazing** life. In later life, he faced **declining** popularity.	Some present participles are used as adjectives.
Chaplin was **extremely hardworking**. He was a **highly paid** actor.	An adverb sometimes precedes the participle.
Chaplin's life **interests** me. (*interest* = verb) (a) Chaplin's life is **interesting**. He made many **interesting** movies. (b) I am **interested** in learning more about Chaplin. Chaplin **amuses** us. (*amuse* = verb) (a) The Little Tramp was an **amusing** character. He did many **amusing** things. (b) We saw his movie and we were **amused**.	In some cases, both the present participle (a) and the past participle (b) of the same verb can be used as adjectives. The present participle (a) has an active meaning. Someone or something *actively* causes a feeling in others. The past participle (b) gives a passive meaning. It describes the person who *passively* experiences a feeling.
Chaplin was an **interesting** person. Chaplin was **interested** in acting from a young age. I saw a scary movie, and I was **terrified**.	A person can cause a feeling in others (be terrifying) or he can experience a feeling (be terrified).
The story about Chaplin is **interesting**. Chaplin's movies are **entertaining**.	An object (like a story or a movie) doesn't have feelings, so a past participle, such as *interested* or *entertained*, cannot be used to describe an object.

Note:
Some common paired participles are:

amazing	amazed	exhausting	exhausted
amusing	amused	frightening	frightened
annoying	annoyed	frustrating	frustrated
boring	bored	interesting	interested
confusing	confused	puzzling	puzzled
convincing	convinced	satisfying	satisfied
disappointing	disappointed	surprising	surprised
embarrassing	embarrassed	terrifying	terrified
exciting	excited	tiring	tired

EXERCISE 12 Use the verb in each sentence to make two new sentences. In one sentence, use the present participle. In the other, use the past participle.

1. The movie entertained us.

   The movie was entertaining.

   We were entertained.

2. Violent movies frighten children.

   _____

   _____

3. Chaplin amused the audience.

   _____

   _____

4. The adventure movie excited the audience.

   _____

   _____

5. The TV show bored me.

   _____

   _____

6. The end of the movie surprised us.

   _____

   _____

7. The movie confused her.

   _____

   _____

8. The movie terrified them.

   _____

   _____

EXERCISE 13 The following conversation is about a movie. Choose the correct participle to complete the conversation.

A: At the Oscars in 2012, a very (*interesting*/interested) movie called *The Artist* won five awards, including
   1.
best picture, best director, and best actor.

B: Why was this so (*surprising/surprised*)? A lot of popular movies win several awards.
                              2.

A: Well, the movie was filmed in black and white. It takes place in 1927. It's almost completely silent.

B: You're kidding! I'm really (*surprising/surprised*). Wasn't the audience (*confusing/confused*) about what
                              3.   4.
was happening?

A: Like the silent movies made many years ago, signs were used to show what the actors were saying.

B: What's the movie about?

A: It's about an older man, George, who's a silent film star. He discovers a pretty, young actress, Peppy.

George wants his boss to give her a small part in his film. George's boss isn't (*convincing/convinced*) that
                                                                                    5.
this is a good idea, but George insists. Peppy is very (*exciting/excited*) to get the part. When most movie
                                                          6.
studios stop making silent movies in 1929, Peppy goes on to become a popular star in sound movies, but

George faces (*declining/declined*) popularity. He becomes (*depressing/depressed*). I don't want to tell
              7.   8.
you the end of the movie. If I do, you won't be (*surprising/surprised*) by the ending.
                                                 9.

B: Don't worry. I'm not (*interesting/interested*) in seeing a silent movie. It sounds pretty (*boring/bored*)
                            10.   11.
to me.

EXERCISE 14 Fill in the blanks with the correct present (*-ing*) or past (*-ed*) participle, of the verb given.

Last night my friend and I went to see a new movie. We thought it was ____boring____. It had a
                                                                          1. bore

lot of car chases, which were not _____ at all. And I didn't like the characters. They
                                        2. excite

weren't very _____. We were pretty _____ because the reviewers
                  3. convince   4. disappoint

said it was a good movie. They said it had _____ visual effects. But for me, it wasn't
                                                5. amaze

_____. I was _____ that I wasted $10 and a whole evening just to
      6. interest   7. annoy

be _____. The only thing that was _____ was the popcorn.
      8. bore   9. satisfy

3.8 Other Past Participles Used as Adjectives

EXAMPLES	EXPLANATION
No one knows the winners' names because the envelope is **sealed**. The **sealed** envelope will be opened on Oscar night. The new movie is **finished** now. Would you like to see the **finished** product? The theater looks **crowded**. I don't like to be in a **crowded** theater.	Certain past participles can be used as adjectives after *be* or other linking verbs. They can also be used before a noun. The following are examples: air-conditioned injured pleased broken insured prepared closed involved related concerned known sealed crowded locked used educated lost worried finished married wounded
We**'re done** with the DVD. Do you want to borrow it? The actress's dress **is made** of silk. Children **are not allowed** to see some movies. **Is** this seat **taken**?	Other past participles come after *be*, but not usually before a noun. The following are examples: *accustomed, allowed, born, done, gone, located, made, permitted, taken* (meaning *occupied*).
That was a *well*-**made** movie. The theater is *extremely* **crowded** on Saturday night.	Adverbs can often precede past participles.

EXERCISE 15 Fill in the blanks with the past participle of one of the words from the box.

bear✓	educate	interest	locate	pay	worry
close	finish	know	marry	take	

1. Charlie Chaplin was _____ *born* _____ in England in 1889.

2. Chaplin was a highly _____ actor.

3. Was he an _____ man? Did he go to college?

4. Charlie Chaplin was _____ in making funny movies about serious topics.

5. His film studio was _____ in Hollywood.

6. He was _____ several times.

7. American actors are usually well _____ by fans throughout the world.

8. Movie theaters are usually _____ early in the morning. They usually open around

    11 a.m. or noon on weekends.

9. If you're _____ about getting a seat, you can buy your tickets beforehand online.

10. Excuse me. Is this seat _____ ?

11. When you're _____ with your popcorn, you should throw away the bag.

3.9 *Get* vs. *Be* with Past Participles and Other Adjectives

EXAMPLES	EXPLANATION
Is the actor **married**? You're yawning. I see you *are* **bored**.	*Be* + past participle describes the status of a person over a period of time.
When did she *get* **married**? Some people *got* **bored** with the movie and walked out.	*Get* + past participle means *become*. There is no reference to the continuation of this status.
Most movie stars *are* **rich**. Chaplin *was* **old** when he received an Oscar.	*Be* + adjective describes the status of a person over a period of time.
A lot of people would like to *get* **rich** quickly. Most stars don't want to *get* **old**. They want to look young forever.	*Get* + adjective means *become*.

Past Participles with *get*			Adjectives with *get*	
get accustomed to	get dressed	get scared	get angry	get old
get acquainted	get worried	get tired	get dark	get rich
get bored	get hurt	get used to	get fat	get sleepy
get confused	get lost		get hungry	get upset
get divorced	get married			

Note: Notice the difference between *to be married, to marry,* and *to get married.*

> The actor **is married**. (**Be married** describes one's status.)
>
> She **married** her costar secretly last summer. (*The verb* **marry** *is followed by an object.*)
>
> They **got married** in Scotland. (**Get married** *is not followed by an object.*)

EXERCISE 16 Circle the correct words to complete this conversation.

A: Angelina Jolie is my favorite actress. When she (*was*/*got*) divorced from Brad Pitt, I (*was*/*got*)
    1.   2.
 surprised, but happy.

B: Happy? Do you think Angelina (*is*/*gets*) interested in you? She doesn't even know you! She (*is*/*gets*) too
    3.   4.
 rich and famous to pay attention to you.

A: Well, I'm an actor too, you know. When I'm famous, Angelina will notice me if she (*gets*/*is*) still single.
    5.

B: Well, it's possible that she'll (*get*/*be*) single. But you'll be an old man when, and if, you are famous. You
    6.
 won't (*be*/*get*) interested in her anymore.
    7.

A: I'll always (*get*/*be*) interested in her.
    8.

B: Oh, really? What does your girlfriend have to say about that?

A: I never talk to her about it. Once I told her how much I like Angelina, and she (*was*/*got*) angry.
    9.

B: I don't think your girlfriend has anything to worry about.

SUMMARY OF UNIT 3

Passive Voice

PASSIVE VOICE = *BE* + PAST PARTICIPLE	
Mickey Mouse **was created** by Walt Disney. *Star Wars* **was directed** by George Lucas.	The passive voice can be used with a strong agent if we want to emphasize the action or the receiver of the action.
Hollywood **was built** at the beginning of the 20th century. Children **are** not **allowed** to see some movies. I **was told** that you didn't like the movie. The Oscar ceremony **is seen** all over the world.	The passive voice is usually used without an agent when: • the agent is not known, or it is not important to mention who performed the action • the agent is obvious • we want to hide the identity of the agent • the agent is not a specific person but people in general
Reagan **got shot** in 1981. No one **got killed**.	*Get* can be used instead of *be* in certain conversational expressions. *Get* is not used when the agent is mentioned.

Participles and other Adjectives

EXAMPLES	EXPLANATION
Silent movies are very **interesting**. Charlie Chaplin was an **entertaining** actor.	The present participle is used as an adjective to show that someone or something produced the feeling.
He **is interested** in the life of Charlie Chaplin. I saw a great movie and was very **entertained**.	The past participle is used to show that the subject experienced the feeling caused by someone or something else.
The movie theater is **closed**. The doors are **locked**. I don't like to see a movie in a **crowded** theater.	Other past participles are used as adjectives.
Some movie stars **get rich** quickly. Some movie stars **get married** many times.	*Get* is used with past participles and other adjectives to mean *become*.

REVIEW

Choose the correct form to complete the conversation.

A: I'm going to watch *Life of Pi* tonight. Do you want to watch it with me?

B: Is it a new movie?

A: No. It (*made/was made*) in 2012. I (*saw/was seen*) it once, but I want to (*see/be seen*) it again.
1.   2.   3.

B: I (*don't remember/wasn't remembered*) the name. What is it about?
4.

A: It's about a teenage boy from India. His father (*decides/is decided*) to travel with zoo animals on a ship.
5.

A storm (*is come/comes*), and the ship (*sinks/is sunk*). The boy (*survives/is survived*), but his parents
6.   7.   8.

(*die/are died*). The boy is on a lifeboat with one of the animals, a tiger.
9.

B: Oh, yes. Now I remember. It was a very (*interested/interesting*) movie. In some theaters it
10.

(*showed/was shown*) in 3D. How does it end? I can't (*be remembered/remember*).
11.   12.

A: They finally (*are arrived/arrive*) in Mexico and the tiger (*is disappeared/disappears*) and the boy
13.   14.

(*rescues/is rescued*).
15.

B: For me that was a very (*disappointed/disappointing*) ending.
16.

A: I don't agree. The boy (*saved/got saved*) and (*lived/was lived*) to tell the story.
17.   18.

B: Some of the scenes with the tiger were very (*frightened/frightening*).
19.

A: The tiger wasn't real, you know. The scenes with the tiger (*did/were done*) with computer technology.
20.

B: Really? I'm (*amazing/amazed*). Technology is so (*advanced/advancing*). Most of the story
21.   22.

(*happens/is happened*) when the boy is in a boat. (*Did/Was*) this movie (*make/made*) at sea?
23.   24.   25.

A: I don't know. Probably not. So much can (*do/be done*) by computer now. I (*read/was read*) the
26.   27.

book before I saw the movie. So I already (*knew/was known*) the story. But the movie
28.

(*amazed/was amazed*) me even more. It (*was directed/directed*) by a famous director, Ang Lee.
29.   30.

B: (*Was/Did*) the movie (*nominate/nominated*) for any awards?
31.   32.

A: Yes. It (*was/has*) nominated for many Academy Awards. So, do you want to watch it with me?
33.

B: I don't think so. When I know how the movie (*is ended/ends*), it no longer (*interests/interesting*) me.
34.   35.

FROM GRAMMAR TO WRITING

PART 1 Editing Advice

1. Use *be*, not *do,* to make negatives and questions with the passive voice.

   wasn't
   The movie ~~didn't~~ made in Hollywood.

2. Don't use the passive voice with intransitive verbs.

   The main character ~~was~~ died at the end of the movie.

3. Don't confuse the present participle with the past participle.

   eaten
   Popcorn is often ~~eating~~ during a movie.

4. Don't forget the *–d/–ed* ending for a regular past participle.

   ed   *d*
   Music was play∧during silent movies.   I got bore∧during the movie and fell asleep.

5. Don't forget to use a form of *be* in a passive sentence.

   was
   The movie ∧seen by everyone in my family.

6. Use *by* to show the agent of the action. Use an object pronoun after *by.*

   by   *him*
   Life of Pi was directed ~~for~~ Ang Lee.   *Hulk* was also directed by ~~he~~.

7. In present and past questions and negatives, use *do* when you use *get* with the passive voice.

   didn't
   My favorite movie ~~wasn't~~ get nominated.

8. Don't forget to include a verb (usually *be*) before a participle used as an adjective.

   is
   The movie theater ∧located on the corner of Main and Elm Streets.

9. Use *be*, not *do,* with past participles used as adjectives.

   Are
   ~~Do~~ you interested in French movies?

10. Make sure you use the correct past participle in the passive voice.

    built
    A new movie theater is being ~~build~~ near my house.

11. Don't confuse participles like *interested/interesting; bored/boring,* etc.

    boring   *bored*
    I fell asleep during the ~~bored~~ movie. I was ~~boring~~.

PART 2 Editing Practice

Some of the shaded words and phrases have mistakes. Find the mistakes and correct them. If the shaded words are correct, write *C.*

One of my favorite movies is *12 Years a Slave*. This is an amazing movie. Everyone ~~should be seen~~
     C   *should see*
                           1.   2.

it. The first time I saw it, I wasn't very interested in it. The movie shown on my flight from my country to
          3.   4.   5.

the United States. The screen was small and I was exhaust. I was fell asleep before the movie was ended.
                                                   6.   7.   8.

A few months ago, a friend of mine invited me to his house to watch a movie. I surprised when
                          9.   10.
he told me that the movie was *12 Years a Slave*. I told him that I saw part of the movie, but I never

saw the ending. I asked my friend, "Was the main character died? Or was he get rescue? Just tell me
                                   11.   12.   13.   14.
what was happened. That's all I need to know."
        15.

   "Let's watch it," my friend said. "I know you'll like it." I was agreed to watch it with him. It's
                                                              16.
based on a true story of a black man, Solomon Northup. He lived in the North and he was free, but
  17.   18.
he was kidnap. He was sold into slavery in the South. He was remained a slave for 12 years. I didn't
     19.   20.   21.
know much about slavery in the U.S., and I was shocked at how horrible life was for the slaves.
                                                   22.

   When I came home, I looked for more information about the movie. I looked for information on

the Internet. A lot of information can found on the film and the real person. The movie directed by
                                       23.   24.
Steve McQueen. I wanted to find other movies directed by he too, so I googled his name. I found
                                                   25.   26.
that he directed *Shame* and *Hunger*. He also wrote the script for these movies. However, *12 Years a*
        27.   28.
Slave was writing by someone else.
       29.

   12 Years a Slave was nominate for several Oscars. It won for Best Picture of 2013. The star did a
                          30.   31.
great job as Solomon, but he didn't chosen as Best Actor that year. I was disappointing.
                                   32.   33.

WRITING TIP

Many reference books tell you to avoid using passive sentences. This does not mean you should never use one. It is important to understand that the passive voice is useful in certain situations. For example, the passive voice is important when you want:

1. to maintain focus on the topic
   *There is a new **movie** that everyone is talking about. **The movie is considered** one of the best of the year.*
   *NOT: There is a new **movie** that everyone is talking about. Everyone considers it the best **movie** of the year.*

2. to avoid criticizing someone
   *The actor **was told** to cry a lot, which ruined the movie.*
   *NOT: The **director told** the actor to cry a lot, which ruined the movie.*

PART 3 Write

Read the prompts. Choose one and write one or more paragraphs about it.

1. How are American films different from films made in your country or another country you know about? Give several examples.
2. Talk about a movie that you enjoyed or that had an impact on you. Summarize the movie, and then explain how it made you feel or how it impacted you.

PART 4 Edit

Reread the Summary of Unit 3 and the Editing Advice. Edit your writing from Part 3.

4

The Past Continuous
The Past Perfect
The Past Perfect Continuous

Car enthusiasts from around the world come to the
Bonneville Salt Flats in Utah, USA, for Speed Week.

Travel by
LAND, SEA, AIR
and

Travel makes one modest. You see what a
tiny place you occupy in the world.

GUSTAV FLAUBERT

TRAVEL BY LAND: The LEWIS and CLARK EXPEDITION

Read the following article. Pay special attention to the words in bold. 🎧 4.1

Imagine a time when most people in the eastern part of the United States had no idea what was on the other side of the Mississippi River. That was the case at the beginning of the 19th century, when Thomas Jefferson was the third president of the United States. The nation was only 18 years old then and had about five million people. They **were living** between the Atlantic Ocean and the Mississippi River.

President Jefferson wanted control over the American Indian tribes, who were living throughout the continent. In addition, he wanted to find a land passage to the Pacific Ocean. He **was hoping** to create a country that went from sea to sea.

Meriwether Lewis **was working** as an aide to the president at the time. Jefferson appointed[1] Lewis and his friend William Clark to lead a dangerous, 33-man expedition[2] to the Northwest, through rivers and over the Rocky Mountains.

The expedition left St. Louis in May 1804. As the men **were going** down the Missouri River, Clark stayed on the boat and drew maps and planned the course. Lewis often stayed on land to study animals and plants. While they **were crossing** the continent, they met some Indian tribes who were helpful. But they also met some who were hostile[3].

By the time the expedition reached North Dakota, winter **was** fast **approaching**. They needed to wait until spring to cross the Rocky Mountains. As they **were waiting** out the winter, they met a Shoshone[4] woman, Sacagawea, and her Canadian husband. With their help, the expedition started the most dangerous part of the journey: crossing the Rocky Mountains. They were going to need horses. Sacagawea helped them get horses from her tribe.

While they **were traveling**, they faced many hardships: hunger, danger from grizzly bears, bad weather, and uncertainty about their future. Several times, while they **were sleeping**, their horses were stolen. They had no communication with anyone back east. No one even knew if they were still alive.

In November 1805, tired but successful, they finally made it to the Pacific. When they returned to St. Louis, almost two and a half years later, the people of St. Louis **were waiting** to greet them. They were heroes.

---

1   to appoint: to choose somebody to do something
2   expedition: a journey made by a group of people organized and equipped for a special purpose
3   hostile: hateful, angry
4   Shoshone: member of the Shoshone Indians, an American Indian tribe

Sculpture of Lewis, Clark, and Sacagawea at Fort Benton, Montana, USA

COMPREHENSION Based on the reading, write T for *true* or F for *false*.

1. _____ President Jefferson's main goal was to learn about American Indian life.

2. _____ Lewis and Clark couldn't cross the mountains in the winter.

3. _____ While traveling, they communicated with Jefferson about their location.

THINK ABOUT IT Discuss the questions with a partner or in a small group.

1. What was the biggest danger facing Lewis and Clark in your opinion? Explain.

2. If you had the chance to join an expedition into unknown territory/country like Lewis and Clark, would you go or not? Give your reasons.

4.1 The Past Continuous — Form

WAS/WERE + PRESENT PARTICIPLE (VERB + *ING*)

SUBJECT	WAS/WERE (+ NOT)	PRESENT PARTICIPLE	
I	was	reading	about Lewis and Clark.
Clark	was	making	maps.
You	were	looking	at the map of the U.S.
Lewis and Clark	were not	traveling	fast.

Note:

An adverb can be placed between *was/were* and the present participle.

> *Winter was **fast** approaching.*
>
> *They were **probably** getting worried.*
>
> *Clark wasn't **always** riding in the boat.*

STATEMENTS AND QUESTIONS

STATEMENTS	YES/NO QUESTIONS & SHORT ANSWERS	WH- QUESTIONS
They **were traveling** to the West.	**Were** they **traveling** far? Yes, they **were**.	How far **were** they **traveling**?
Lewis **wasn't making** maps.	**Was** Clark **making** maps? Yes, he **was**.	Why **wasn't** Lewis **making** maps?
Lewis **was working** for the president.	**Was** Lewis **working** in St. Louis? No, he **wasn't**.	Who else **was working** for the president?

Note:

The past continuous of the passive voice is *was/were* + *being* + past participle.

> *In 1803, preparations **were being made** for the expedition.*

EXERCISE 1 Listen to each conversation. Fill in the blanks with the words you hear. 🎧 4.2

1. **A:** Where <u>were most Americans living</u> at the beginning of the 1800s?

   B: They _____<u>were living</u>_____ east of the Mississippi River.

2. **A:** Lewis _____ for the president. _____ for President Jefferson

   at that time, too?

   B: No, he _____ .

3. **A:** While _____ the continent, did they meet a lot of American Indians?

   B: Yes, they did. They met a lot of American Indians while they _____ .

4. **A:** Why _____ during the winter?

   B: It was too cold. They had to wait until spring to cross the mountains.

5. **A:** Did they have any problems while _____ the mountains?

   B: Yes, they did. Sometimes at night while they _____ , their horses were stolen.

6. **A:** A Shoshone woman _____ them. How _____ them?

   B: The expedition needed horses. She got horses from her tribe.

7. **A:** How many people _____ to greet them when they returned to St. Louis?

   B: Almost all of the people of St. Louis were there. They _____ to see Lewis and Clark.

4.2 The Past Continuous — Use

EXAMPLES	EXPLANATION
In 1803, Lewis **was working** as an aide to the president. working as aide NOW PAST ←———●————↑————●———→ FUTURE 1803	The past continuous is used to show that an action was in progress at a specific past time. It didn't begin at that time.
When they **arrived** in St. Louis, many people **were waiting** for them. **While** they **were crossing** the continent, they **met** many Indians. crossing the continent NOW PAST ←——●—✗—✗—✗—●——→ FUTURE ⏐ ⏐ ⏐ met Indians	We often use the simple past in one clause and the past continuous in another clause to show the relationship of a longer past action to a shorter past action. The simple past is used to express the shorter action. The past continuous is used with the longer action. **When** is used with the shorter action. **While** or **as** is often used with the longer action.

Punctuation Note:

If the time clause (starting with **when, while,** or **as**) comes first, we separate the two clauses with a comma.

As they were traveling, Clark drew maps.

*Clark drew maps **as** they were traveling.*

GRAMMAR IN USE

When making requests, the past continuous is sometimes used to be more polite. It shows that the speaker is a little hesitant to ask.

Could you help me? (direct)

*I **was wondering** if you could help me.* (It's no problem if you can't help.)

EXERCISE 2 Read this article about a space mission that took place in 2003. Pay attention to the verb forms in **bold**. If the verb form describes a longer past action, write *L* over it; if it describes a shorter past action, write *S*. Then discuss your choice with a partner.

The United States National Aeronautics and Space Administration (NASA) sent the space shuttle

Columbia into space with seven crew members on January 16, 2003. While *Columbia* **was going** [L] around
                                               1.

the Earth, the crew **conducted** [S] science experiments. On February 1, 2003, it **was traveling** back to Earth
              2.   **3.**

after completing its mission. As *Columbia* **was flying** over east Texas, just 16 minutes from its landing in
                                 4.

Florida, it **broke** into pieces. While families **were waiting** for the return of their relatives, they **received**
      5.   **6.**   **7.**

the tragic news. People were shocked when they **heard** about the accident.
                                       8.

The causes of the disaster were studied, and this is what was found: As *Columbia* **was lifting** off, a
                                                 9.

piece of the fuel tank **broke** off and **hit** the wing.
             10.   **11.**

Columbia was the second major disaster in space. The first one was in January 1986, when the space shuttle

Challenger **exploded** while it **was lifting** off. All seven crew members were killed in that tragedy as well.
          12.   **13.**

ABOUT YOU Think of an important event that happened during your lifetime. Write what you were doing when you heard the news. Share your answers with a partner.

I was watching TV when I heard about the Challenger explosion.

_____

_____

_____

_____

4.3 The Past Continuous vs. the Simple Past

EXAMPLES	EXPLANATION
A: What **were** you **doing** *when* you **heard** the news about *Columbia*? **B:** I **was eating** breakfast. NOW was eating PAST ←————————→ FUTURE heard	*When* can mean "at that time" or "after that time," depending on whether the past continuous or the simple past is used. The past continuous shows what was in progress *at* the time a specific action occurred.
A: What **did** you **do** *when* you **heard** the news about *Columbia*? **B:** I **called** my friend. NOW heard PAST ←————————→ FUTURE called	The simple past shows what happened *after* a specific action occurred.
On February 1, 2003, relatives **were waiting** in Florida for the astronauts. They **were getting** ready to celebrate. Suddenly, just 16 minutes before landing, *Columbia* **broke** into pieces.	The past continuous shows the *events leading up to* the main event of the story. The simple past tense shows the *main event*.

EXERCISE 3 Fill in the blanks using the words given. Use the simple past or the past continuous.

1. **A:** I remember the *Columbia* accident well. I _____was living_____ in Texas at that time.

a. live

   B: What _____ the morning of the accident?

b. you/do

   A: I _____ ready for work. I _____ breakfast and _____

c. get   d. eat   e. listen

   to the radio. Then suddenly I _____ a loud noise.

f. hear

   B: What _____ when you heard the loud noise?

g. you/do

   A: I _____ outside. I saw pieces of metal on my property.

h. run

   B: What _____ when you found these pieces?

i. you/do

   A: I _____ the police.

j. call

2. **A:** Where _____ when the accident _____?

a. Columbia/go   b. happen

   B: It _____ to Florida.

c. travel

   A: What _____ when the accident happened?

d. you/do

B: I _____ ready for school. Then my sister called me. When she _____
    e. get   **f.** tell

me about the accident, I _____ on the TV. When they _____ the sad
                                              g. turn   **h.** show

faces of the relatives, I _____ to cry.
                                       i. start

3. A: As I _____ an article on my tablet about Lewis and Clark, I _____
                a. read   **b.** find

a word I didn't know: *tribe.*

B: What _____ to find out the meaning?
              c. you/do

A: I _____ my finger on the word, and the definition popped up.
          d. put

EXERCISE 4 Choose the correct tense (simple past or past continuous) to complete the following conversations.

1. A: While I (*researched/was researching*) online yesterday, I (*found/was finding*) a movie about
                                            a.   **b.**

Lewis and Clark.

B: What (*did you do/were you doing*) with it?
                                              c.

A: I (*watched/was watching*) it.
          d.

2. A: While Lewis and Clark (*crossed/were crossing*) the country with their team of 33 men, one of their men
                                                            a.

(*died/was dying*).
      b.

B: What (*did they do/were they doing*) when he died?
                                                c.

A: They (*buried/were burying*) him and continued their expedition.
                          d.

3. A: While the teacher (*explained/was explaining*) the lesson, I (*fell/was falling*) asleep.
                                                    a.   **b.**

B: What (*did the teacher talk about/was the teacher talking about*) when you fell asleep?
                                                                    c.

A: I think he (*talked/was talking*) about Lewis and Clark.
                                d.

B: I can't believe you fell asleep. The story was so exciting.

A: I thought so, too. But the night before, while I (*slept/was sleeping*), the phone rang and (*woke/was waking*)
                                                                                        e.   **f.**

me up. When I finished talking on the phone, I (*tried/was trying*) to go back to sleep but couldn't.
                                                                            g.

4. A: I haven't seen you for a while.

B: I (*visited/was visiting*) my cousin in Washington, DC, all week.
              a.

A: Did you have a good time?

B: Yes. We were planning to visit the Air and Space Museum, but it was closed for repair.

continued

A: So what (*did you do/were you doing*) instead?
b.

B: We (*went/were going*) to the National Museum of the American Indian instead.
c.

5. **A:** What (*did you do/were you doing*) at around eight o'clock last night? I called you and texted you, but you
a.

didn't reply.

B: I (*watched/was watching*) a documentary about American history.
b.

A: But I called you again around midnight. What (*did you do/were you doing*) around midnight?
c.

B: I'm sure I (*slept/was sleeping*). When I got in bed, I (*turned/was turning*) off the phone.
d.   e.

FUN WITH GRAMMAR

Play a memory game. Look at the old photo of brothers who survived the *Titanic* shipwreck. Write simple past or past continuous questions about the photo. Then close your books and take turns asking and answering your questions with a partner. Who answered the most questions correctly?

A: What **was** the younger boy **holding**?
B: He **was holding** a toy ship, I think.

A: What color hair **did** the older boy **have**?
B: I'm not sure. **Was** it brown?

Survivors of the *Titanic*: Michel and Edmond Navratil (aged 4 and 2), brothers whose father died in the sinking of the ship

TRAVEL BY SEA: The FIRST and LAST VOYAGE of the TITANIC

Read the following article. Pay special attention to the words in bold. 🎧 4.3

The year was 1912. The railroad across the United States **had** already **been built**. The Wright brothers **had** already **made** their first successful flight. Henry Ford **had produced** his first car. The *Titanic*—the ship of dreams—**had** just **been built** and was ready to make its first voyage from England to America, with over 2,000 people aboard[1].

The *Titanic* was the most magnificent[2] ship that **had** ever **been built**. It had luxuries that ships **had** never **had** before: electric light, elevators, a swimming pool, libraries, and more. It was built to give its first-class passengers all the comforts of the best hotels. Some of the wealthiest people in the world were on the *Titanic*. But not everyone on the *Titanic* was rich. Most of the passengers in third class were emigrants who **had left** behind their home country in hopes of finding a better life in America.

The *Titanic* began its voyage on April 10. The winter **had been** unusually mild, and by spring large blocks of ice **had broken** away from the Arctic region. On April 14, at 11:40 p.m., an iceberg was spotted right in the ship's path. The captain **had been receiving** warnings about ice, but he wasn't worried about it; he didn't realize how much danger the ship was in. The captain tried to reverse the direction of the ship, but it was too late. The ship was moving too fast. The *Titanic* hit

Painting of the sunken *Titanic*

the iceberg and started to sink. The ship was designed to hold 32 lifeboats, but 12 of those lifeboats **had been removed** before sailing to make the ship look more elegant[3]. There were enough lifeboats for only about half of the people aboard.

While the ship was sinking, some passengers were being put on lifeboats. First-class passengers boarded[4] the lifeboats before second- and third-class passengers. By the time the third-class passengers came up from their cabins, most of the lifeboats **had** already **left**. Within two hours and forty-five minutes, the ship **had sunk**.

Cold and afraid, people waited in the lifeboats all night, not knowing if they would be saved or if their loved ones **had survived**. In the early morning, the *Carpathia*, the ship that **had responded** to the *Titanic*'s call for help, arrived to rescue the survivors. Only one-third of the passengers survived this disaster.

---

1 aboard: on a ship
2 magnificent: very beautiful or impressive
3 elegant: stylish in appearance
4 to board: to enter a ship, airplane, train, etc.

A team exploring the bow (front) of the sunken *Titanic* wreck

COMPREHENSION Based on the reading, write T for *true* or F for *false*.

1. _____ By the time the *Titanic* was built, the airplane had already been invented.

2. _____ There were enough lifeboats for most of the passengers.

3. _____ The *Titanic* sank in under an hour.

THINK ABOUT IT Discuss the questions with a partner or in a small group.

1. Why were 12 of the 32 lifeboats removed before the voyage of the *Titanic*? Why do you think the safety of the passengers was not as much a concern?

2. What is another deep sea discovery that has been made? Would you like to dive to such sites? Explain your answer.

4.4 The Past Perfect — Form

HAD + PAST PARTICIPLE

SUBJECT	HAD (+ NOT)	PAST PARTICIPLE	
The previous winter	**had**	**been**	mild.
The captain	**had not**	**understood**	the danger.

Notes:

1. Pronouns (except *it*) can be contracted with *had*: *I'd, you'd, she'd, he'd, we'd, they'd.*

   The captain knew about the ice. **He'd** *had a chance to turn the ship around, but he didn't.*

2. The contraction for *had not* is *hadn't.*

   He **hadn't** *paid attention to the warnings.*

3. Apostrophe + d (*'d*) can be a contraction for both *had* or *would*. The verb form following the contraction indicates what the contraction means.

   They'd *left the ship.* = *They had left the ship.*

   They'd *leave the ship.* = *They would leave the ship.*

4. An adverb can be placed between *had* and the past participle.

   Some passengers **had never been** *on a ship before.*

5. The past perfect of the passive voice is *had been* + past participle.

   The Titanic **had been built** *as a luxury ship.*

STATEMENTS AND QUESTIONS

STATEMENTS	YES/NO QUESTIONS & SHORT ANSWERS	WH- QUESTIONS
The captain **had received** several warnings.	A: **Had** he **received** warnings early enough? B: Yes, he **had**.	How many warnings **had** he **received**?
He **hadn't realized** the danger he was in.	A: **Had** he **paid** attention to the warnings? B: No, he **hadn't**.	Why **hadn't** he **paid** attention to the warnings?
Some people **had gotten** on lifeboats immediately.	A: **Had** third-class passengers **gotten** on lifeboats immediately? B: No, they **hadn't**.	How many people **had gotten** on lifeboats?

EXERCISE 5 This is the story of a young passenger on the *Titanic*. Fill in the correct past perfect using one of the verbs from the box. If you see an adverb given, include that with the verb.

be	die	happen	jump	leave	meet	pass away	say ✓	survive

Jack Thayer was a 17-year-old passenger on the *Titanic*, traveling with his parents.

He ___had just said___ goodnight to his parents and was getting ready to go to bed when he felt a bump.
　　1. just

He and his father went out to see what _____. At first, the passengers remained
　　　　　　　　　　　　　　　　2.

calm. But one of the ship's designers, whom the Thayers _____ several times
　　　　　　　　　　　　　　　　　　　　　3.

during the short voyage, told them that the *Titanic* would not last an hour.

Passengers were trying to get on the lifeboats, but many lifeboats _____
　　　　　　　　　　　　　　　　　　　　　　　　　　4. already

half full. Thayer got separated from his parents. As the ship was sinking, he jumped into the icy

water and swam to an overturned boat. He heard splashes and the cries of passengers who

_____ into the icy waters. Thayer spent the night not knowing if his parents were
　　5.

dead or alive. In the morning, the passengers in the lifeboats were rescued by the *Carpathia*. It was then

that he learned that his mother _____ but, unfortunately, his father
　　　　　　　　　　　　　　　6.

_____ .
　　7.

Thirty years later, he wrote his story about that tragic night. But his account was never published. In

April 2012, on the 100th anniversary of the tragedy, his story was published.

Jack Thayer faced another tragedy in his life. His son, who _____ a fighter
　　　　　　　　　　　　　　　　　　　　　　　　8.

pilot, was killed in World War II. This was an especially sad time for him because his mother

_____ the same year.
　　9.

4.5 The Past Perfect — Use (Part 1)

When showing the time relationship between past events, the past perfect is used to show the event that took place first.

EXAMPLES	EXPLANATION
By 1950, Jack Thayer **had written** about his experience. NOW lost loved ones PAST ⟵ ✖ ✖ ⟶ FUTURE 1950	The past perfect can be used with *by* + a time reference. The past perfect shows that something occurred before that time.
time clause *main clause* **By the time** the rescue ship **arrived**, the *Titanic* **had sunk**. NOW rescue ship arrived PAST ⟵ ✖ ✖ ⟶ FUTURE ship sank *main clause* *time clause* I **had** never **heard** of Jack Thayer **until** I **read** about it today.	The past perfect can be used in a sentence with a time clause. The time clause shows the later past event and uses the simple past. The main clause shows the earlier past event and uses the past perfect.
When Jack's family got on the *Titanic*, they **had never been** on such a luxurious trip **before**. When Jack was rescued in the morning, he **hadn't learned** about his father's death **yet**.	*Never … before* or *not … yet* can be used in the main clause to emphasize the earlier time.
The ship **had been** at sea **for five days** when it hit an iceberg.	The past perfect can be used in the main clause with *for* + a time period to show the duration of the earlier past action.
Before he **jumped** into the water, he('d) **put** on a life jacket. Many years **before** he **died**, he **had written** his personal story and **given** copies to family and friends.	In sentences with a time clause that begins with *before* or *after*, the simple past is often used in both clauses. The past perfect is more common if the earlier event does not immediately precede the later one.
It **was** 1913. Most people **had heard** about the tragedy.	We can start with a simple past sentence and follow it with a past perfect sentence to go further back in time.

EXERCISE 6 Fill in the blanks with the simple past or the past perfect of the verb given.

1. By 1912, the airplane <u>had already been invented</u> .
   passive: already/invent

2. By the time the *Titanic* _____ England, some of the lifeboats _____ to
   leave   passive: remove
   make the ship look more elegant.

3. By the spring of 1912, pieces of ice _____ away from the Arctic region.
   break

4. The captain _____ several warnings by the time the ship _____ the iceberg.
   receive   hit

5. Jack _____ in his cabin for a short time when he _____ that there was
   _____be_____   _____realize_____

   a problem.

6. When Jack _____ a bump, many passengers _____ to bed.
   _____feel_____   ____already/go____

7. By the time Jack Thayer _____ into the water, he _____ separated from
   _____jump_____   _____get_____

   his parents.

8. He _____ the night in a lifeboat by the time he _____ .
   _____spend_____   ____passive: rescue____

9. When the rescue ship _____ , most of the passengers _____ .
   _____arrive_____   ____already/die____

10. When the *Titanic* _____ in 1985, it _____ on the ocean floor for 73 years.
    ____passive: find____   _____be_____

EXERCISE 7 Read the sentences below. Decide which underlined time or event took place first. Write *1* above the first action or event and *2* above the second.

1. When the Lewis and Clark expedition traveled to the West, no one had done it before.
                         2   1

2. They finally entered a territory that no white man had ever entered before.
         2   1

3. It was 1804. For almost 20 years, President Jefferson had thought about sending an expedition to the West.

4. The expedition had traveled more than 600 miles by the end of July.

5. Up to this time, most of the trip had been done by boat.

6. Lewis and Clark were the first white Americans to go west of the Rocky Mountains. But these lands had

   been occupied by native people for a long time.

7. Many American Indians had never seen a white man before they met Lewis and Clark.

8. Only one man had died by the end of the expedition.

9. He had died long before the expedition ended.

10. They returned to St. Louis almost two and a half years after they had left.

GRAMMAR IN USE

The past perfect is not used as often as the simple past. If the time is clear, we use the simple past. However, there are times when the past perfect is needed.

*Jack **left** for Brazil yesterday. (Yesterday makes the time clear.)*

*Before he **left**, he said "good-bye" to all his friends. (Before makes time clear.)*

*By the time he arrived in Brazil, he **had read** his travel guide. (By the time indicates a time period leading up to a past time, which requires the past perfect.)*

4.6 *When* with the Simple Past or the Past Perfect

Sometimes *when* means *after*. Sometimes *when* means *before*.

EXAMPLES	EXPLANATION
When Jack Thayer got on the *Carpathia*, he **found** his mother. **When** Jack Thayer was rescued, he **had been** in a lifeboat all night.	If the simple past is used in the main clause, *when* means *soon after*. If the past perfect is used in the main clause, *when* means *before*.

EXERCISE 8 Fill in the blanks with the correct form of the verb given. Use the simple past to show that *when* means *after*. Use the past perfect to show that *when* means *before*.

1. When the *Titanic* was first shown to the public, people ____had never seen____ such a magnificent
   never/see

   ship before.

2. When the ship left England, 12 lifeboats _____.
   passive: remove

3. The captain _____ several warnings when the ship hit the iceberg.
   receive

4. When Jack Thayer felt a bump, he _____ to investigate.
   go

5. When the passengers heard a loud noise, they _____ to get on the lifeboats.
   run

6. When the *Titanic* sent out a call for help, a rescue ship _____ to pick up the survivors.
   come

7. When he died, his story _____.
   passive: not/yet/ publish

8. When his story was published, people _____ more about what had happened that night.
   learn

9. When I saw the movie *Titanic*, I _____ my friends about it.
   tell

10. When I saw the movie *Titanic*, I _____ of this ship before.
    never/hear

ABOUT YOU Think about important past events in your life (good or bad). Then complete the sentences. When you are sure your sentences are correct, discuss them with a partner.

*When I **moved** to California, I **bought** a used car.*

*When I **moved** to California, I **had never spoken** to a native English speaker.*

1. When _____ (past event), I _____ (simple past).

2. When _____ (past event), I _____ (past perfect).

3. When _____ (past event), I _____ (simple past).

4. When _____ (past event), I _____ (past perfect).

5. When _____ (past event), I _____ (simple past).

6. When _____ (past event), I _____ (past perfect).

4.7 The Past Perfect — Use (Part 2)

EXAMPLES	EXPLANATION
Many people **died because** the lifeboats **had left** half empty. Jack **survived because** he **had jumped** into the water and **swum** to a lifeboat.	The past perfect is often used in a *because* clause to show that something happened before the verb in the main clause.
The captain **didn't realize** that his ship **had come** so close to an iceberg. Until he was rescued, Jack **didn't know** that his mother **had survived**.	The past perfect can be used in a noun clause when the main verb is past. (A noun clause begins with *know that, think that, realize that,* etc.)*
The *Titanic* **was the most** magnificent ship that **had ever been** built.	In a past sentence with the superlative form, the past perfect is used with *ever*.
One of the ship's designers, **whom** the Thayer family **had met, told** them that the ship would not last an hour.	The past perfect can be used in an adjective clause. (An adjective clause begins with *who, that, which, whom,* or *whose*.)**

*For more about noun clauses, see Unit 10.
**For more about adjective clauses, see Unit 7.

EXERCISE 9 Complete each sentence by circling the correct verb form. Use both the simple past and the past perfect in the same sentence.

1. Jack Thayer and his father (went/had gone) to investigate because they (felt/had felt) a bump.

2. Jack, who (got/had gotten) separated from his parents, (jumped/had jumped) into the water and was

   picked up by a lifeboat.

3. Some people in the lifeboats (reported/had reported) that they (heard/had heard) music as the ship

   was going down.

4. Jack was 17 years old. Losing his father (was/had been) the worst thing that

   (ever happened/had ever happened) to him.

5. Later, Jack (became/had become) depressed because his son and his mother (died/had died) in the

   same year.

6. People (didn't know/hadn't known) Jack Thayer's story because he (didn't publish/hadn't published) it.

7. Jack's family (knew/had known) about his story because he (gave/had given) them copies of it.

8. His story, which he (wrote/had written) in the 1940s, (wasn't/hadn't been) published until after his death.

A grizzly bear fishing for salmon in the McNeil River State Game Sanctuary, Alaska, USA

EXERCISE 10 Fill in the blanks with the simple past or the past perfect of the verbs given and any other words you see. Use both tenses in each item.

1. Lewis and Clark _____*entered*_____ a land that no white man _*had ever entered*_ .
                      enter   ever/enter

2. The expedition to the West _____ one of the most dangerous journeys that anyone
                                               be

   _____ .
            ever/do

3. During the winter, they _____ busy writing reports about what they _____ .
                                keep   see

4. During the winter, they _____ equipment that _____ damaged.
                                repair   become

5. They _____ grizzly bear territory. The American Indians _____
                    enter   warn

   them about these dangerous animals, but they thought it wouldn't be a problem because they had rifles.

   They were wrong. The grizzly bear _____ one of the most frightening animals they
                                            be

   _____ .
           ever/meet

6. On November 7, 1805, they saw a body of water. They _____ that they _____
                                                 think   reach

   the Pacific Ocean. They were disappointed to learn that what they saw was just a river.

ABOUT YOU Fill in the blanks and discuss your answers with a partner. Talk about travel or transportation.

1. Until I was _____ , I had never _____ before.

2. By the time I was _____ years old, I _____ already

   _____ .

4.8 The Past Perfect Continuous — Form

HAD BEEN + PRESENT PARTICIPLE

SUBJECT	HAD (+ NOT)	BEEN	PRESENT PARTICIPLE	
The *Titanic*	had	been	crossing	the Atlantic Ocean.
Jack Thayer	had	been	waiting	all night.
The captain	had not	been	paying	close attention.

Note:

An adverb can be placed between *had* and *been*.

Jack had **probably** been thinking of his parents all night.

STATEMENTS AND QUESTIONS

STATEMENTS	YES/NO QUESTIONS & SHORT ANSWERS	WH- QUESTIONS
The *Titanic* **had been crossing** the Atlantic.	**A: Had** the ship **been crossing** in the winter? **B:** No, it **hadn't.**	How long **had** it **been traveling**?
The captain **hadn't been listening** to the warnings.	**A: Had** he **been traveling** too fast? **B:** Yes, he **had.**	Why **hadn't** the captain **been listening** to the warnings?
Lewis and Clark **had been traveling** for several years.	**A: Had** American Indians **been traveling** with Lewis and Clark? **B:** Yes, they **had.**	Which American Indians **had been traveling** with them?

EXERCISE 11 Fill in the blanks with the verb forms you hear. 🎧 4.4

Millvina Dean was only a nine-month-old baby when her family took her on the *Titanic*. Mr. and Mrs.

Dean _____ in third class with Millvina and her two-year-old brother.
        1.

Millvina's father _____ a business in London for several years when an
        2.

American cousin invited him to help run his business in the U.S. But, unfortunately, that wasn't going to

happen. Millvina, her mother, and brother were rescued, but Mr. Dean _____. A week after
        3.

arriving in the United States, Millvina, her mother, and brother returned to England. For many years,

Millvina _____ about her experience because, of course, she couldn't remember
        4.

anything. What she knew she _____ from her mother. Millvina
        5.

_____ a quiet life for many years until 1985, when the *Titanic* was found. For
        6.

the next 20 years she was invited to *Titanic*-related events in the United States, England, and other

countries. When she died in 2009 at the age of 97, she had been the oldest and last survivor.

4.9 The Past Perfect Continuous—Use

EXAMPLES	EXPLANATION
The *Titanic* **had been traveling** for four days when it **hit** an iceberg. Millvina **had been living** a quiet life **for many years** when the *Titanic* was found.	The past perfect continuous is used with a continuous action that was completed before another past action. The duration of the continuous action is expressed with *for* + an amount of time.
Lewis **had known** Clark for almost 10 years by the time the expedition began. By the time the rescue ship arrived, most of the passengers of the *Titanic* **had** already **died**.	We use the past perfect, not the past perfect continuous, with: • nonaction verbs (See Appendix B for a list of nonaction verbs.) • actions of little or no duration

EXERCISE 12 Fill in the blanks with the simple past or the past perfect continuous of the verbs given. Use the passive where indicated.

1. When she _____*died*_____ , Millvina Dean ___*had been living*___ in a nursing home for several years.

　　　　　　die　　　　　　　　　　　　　　　　live

2. Lewis _____ for President Jefferson for two years when the president

　　　　　　　　　work

   _____ him for the expedition.

　　　　　choose

3. Lewis and Clark _____ for three months by the time they

　　　　　　　　　travel

   _____ American Indians.

　　　meet

4. When Lewis and Clark finally _____ the Pacific Ocean, they

　　　　　　　　　　　see

   _____ the continent for one and a half years.

　　　cross

5. By the time Jack Thayer _____ his story, he _____

　　　　　　　　　write　　　　　　　　　　　　　　　　　think

   about this tragedy for 30 years.

6. By the time Jack Thayer _____ , he _____

　　　　　　　　passive: rescue　　　　　　　　　　hold on

   to a lifeboat all night.

7. By the time the *Titanic* _____ , it _____

　　　　　　　　passive: find　　　　　　　　　　　rest

   on the ocean floor for over 70 years.

8. When the space shuttle *Columbia* _____ , it _____

　　　　　　　　　explode　　　　　　　　　　travel

   for 16 days.

EXERCISE 13 The following is a student's account of leaving her country and immigrating to the United States. Fill in the blanks with the simple past or the past perfect continuous of the verbs given.

1. When I _____came_____ to the U.S., I _had been studying_ English for three years.
   (come)   (study)

2. I _____ for two years when I _____ a chance to
   (wait)   (get)
   leave my country.

3. I _____ in the same house all my life when I _____
   (live)   (leave)
   my city.

4. I _____ very sad when I left my job because I _____
   (feel)   (work)
   with the same people for 10 years.

5. I _____ to be a nurse for six months when a war _____
   (study)   (break out)
   in my country.

6. When I _____ my country, the war _____ for three years.
   (leave)   (go on)

7. My family _____ in Germany for three months before we
   (wait)
   _____ permission to come to the U.S.
   (get)

8. By the time I _____ to the U.S., I _____ for four days.
   (get)   (travel)

ABOUT YOU Complete the following sentences. Give information about your life. Use the past perfect progressive.

   By the time I _finished high school_, I _had been studying English_ for _10 years_.

1. By the time I _____ (simple past), I _____
   _____ (past perfect continuous) for _____ years/months.

2. I _____ (past perfect continuous)
   for _____ years/months by the time I _____ (simple past).

3. My family _____ (past perfect continuous)
   for _____ years/months when I _____ (simple past).

4. When I _____ (simple past), my family _____
   _____ (past perfect continuous) for _____ years/months.

4.10 The Past Perfect (Continuous) vs. the Present Perfect (Continuous)

The past perfect (continuous) and the present perfect (continuous) cannot be used interchangeably.

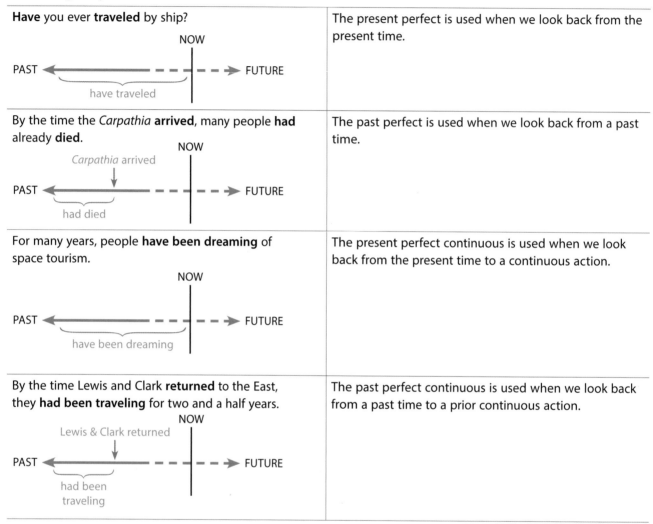

Have you ever **traveled** by ship?	The present perfect is used when we look back from the present time.
By the time the *Carpathia* **arrived**, many people **had** already **died**.	The past perfect is used when we look back from a past time.
For many years, people **have been dreaming** of space tourism.	The present perfect continuous is used when we look back from the present time to a continuous action.
By the time Lewis and Clark **returned** to the East, they **had been traveling** for two and a half years.	The past perfect continuous is used when we look back from a past time to a prior continuous action.

EXERCISE 14 Fill in the blanks with the present perfect, the present perfect continuous, the past perfect, or the past perfect continuous of the verb given. Include any other words you see.

A: I'm reading a great article about travel to Mars.

B: I didn't know that you liked to read about space exploration. How long ___*have you been*___
_____1. you/be_____
interested in it?

A: I _____ interested in it. When I was a child, we lived in Washington,
_____2. always/be_____

DC, so I _____ to the Air and Space Museum there many times. I
_____3. be_____

_____ going there. My fifth grade class _____
_____4. always/love_____   _____5. study_____

space exploration for three weeks when we went on a field trip there. That school trip really got me interested

in exploration. Lately, I _____ interested in other kinds of exploration, too, like the Lewis and
                                    6. become

Clark expedition. _____ the Ken Burns movie about it? I'm watching it now.
                              7. you/ever/see

B: I _____ of Ken Burns. Who is he?
          8. never/hear

A: He is a documentary filmmaker. He _____ a lot of interesting historical
                                                    9. make

documentaries. I _____ many of them.
                          10. see

B: I _____ to the movies lately.
          11. not/be

A: Oh, you can get his documentaries online. The Lewis and Clark documentary is a long one. I started

watching it last Sunday, and I _____ it all week. I'll let you know how it is.
                                            12. watch

B: Why do you think it's so interesting?

A: According to Ken Burns, the Lewis and Clark expedition was even more dangerous than a trip to the moon.

In fact, it was one of the most dangerous expeditions that _____ at that time.
                                                                  13. passive: ever/make

B: Sounds interesting.

A rocket display at the National Air and Space Museum in Washington, DC

TRAVEL BY AIR: The **DC-3**

DOUGLAS
DC 3

The DC-3, Smithsonian
National Air and Space
Museum, Washington, DC

Read the following article. Pay special attention to the words in bold. 🎧 4.5

An American Airlines airplane **left** the Newark Airport for Glendale, California. By the time the plane **arrived** in California, the passengers **had been traveling** for 18 hours and 40 minutes—and they **had made** several stops. This was an amazing flight.

Amazing? 18 hours? Several stops? Well, this **happened** in 1938. In the early days of aviation, airplanes **had been used** primarily in the military and to deliver mail. But airlines, hoping to make money, **were trying** to attract passengers away from train travel. The DC-3 airplane **changed** the airline industry and **started** to attract more and more passengers.

Before this time, a flight from New York to Los Angeles **had taken** 25 hours and **had required** 15 stops and several changes of plane. But the DC-3 **made** a number of improvements and **was** the first passenger plane to make money. However, air travel was not for everyone. A round trip, coast-to-coast flight **cost** $300, which is the equivalent of about $5,000 today.

But this **wasn't** the first passenger flight. Boeing **had built** another passenger airplane. United Airlines **bought** 60 of these early airplanes, which **carried** 10 passengers and **flew** at 155 miles (250 kilometers) per hour. But it **wasn't** a very attractive alternative to taking the train, even for those who could afford it.

Passengers **became** dizzy[1] on these planes, and some even **fainted**. Most people **considered** the airplanes to be unsafe. In fact, a famous football player **was killed** in a plane crash over Kansas in 1931.

If airlines **wanted** to attract passengers away from train travel, they **had** to become safer, faster, and more comfortable. The 1930s **was** one of the most innovative[2] periods in aviation history. Airplanes **became** lighter, which made them go faster. The noise level **was reduced**, and the air became easier to breathe.

Since the 1930s, airline travel **has been improving**. As more and more passengers **began** seeking air travel, even greater advances **were made**. More powerful jet engines **have made** it possible to carry hundreds of passengers thousands of miles quickly. And advanced radar systems **have allowed** air traffic controllers a way of safely separating the flow of traffic.

Airplanes soon **became** a regular mode of transportation. Today the original DC-3 hangs in the Smithsonian National Air and Space Museum in Washington, DC.

---

[1] dizzy: lightheaded, faint
[2] innovative: showing new ideas or improvements

COMPREHENSION Based on the reading, write T for *true* or F for *false*.

1. _____ The DC-3 was the first passenger plane.

2. _____ Early airplanes were used mostly for the military and mail.

3. _____ At first, passengers were afraid of airplane travel.

THINK ABOUT IT Discuss the questions with a partner or in a small group.

1. Do you prefer to travel by air when possible? Do you usually enjoy the experience? Explain.

2. Which is most important to you when making travel choices: speed, comfort, or low cost? Give your reasons.

4.11 Comparison of Tenses

EXAMPLES	EXPLANATION
The airplane **left** Newark on December 17, 1938. The trip **took** more than 18 hours. It **made** several stops.	The **simple past** is used for: • a short action • a long action • a repeated action
In the 1930s, airlines **were trying** to attract passengers. In 1931, Flight 599 **was flying** over Kansas when it **crashed**.	The **past continuous** shows that: • something was in progress at a specific time in the past • a longer past action (*was flying*) relates to a shorter past action (*crashed*)
By the time the airplane **landed** in California, it **had made** several stops.	The **past perfect** shows how an earlier action relates to a later past action (simple past). earlier = *had made*; later = *landed*
Passengers **had been traveling** *for* more than eighteen hours when they **landed** in California.	The **past perfect continuous** shows how an earlier continuous action relates to a later past action (simple past). *For* is used to show the duration of the continuous action. earlier = *had been traveling*; later = *landed*
Jet engines **have made** it possible to carry hundreds of passengers thousands of miles.	The **present perfect** looks back from the present time.
We're reading about transportation. We**'ve been reading** about it for two days.	The **present perfect continuous** looks back from the present time to a continuous action that is still happening.

Notes:

1. Sometimes the past continuous and the past perfect continuous can be used in the same case. The past perfect continuous is more common with a *for* phrase.

    *The airplane **was flying** over Kansas when it crashed.*

    *The airplane **had been flying** for one hour when it crashed.*

2. Sometimes the simple past or the past perfect can be used in the same case.

    *Before the plane arrived in California, it **made** several stops.*

    *Before the plane arrived in California, it **had made** several stops.*

3. Remember: We don't use the continuous form with nonaction verbs.

Assembly line workers inside the Ford Motor Company factory at Dearborn, Michigan, USA

EXERCISE 15 Listen to the conversation about Henry Ford. Write T for *true* or F for *false*. 🎧 4.6

1. _____ Henry Ford wanted to make the car available to a wider range of people.

2. _____ Ford's new production methods made cars more expensive.

3. _____ In the beginning, Ford's workers enjoyed their jobs on the assembly line.

EXERCISE 16 Complete the article about Henry Ford and his Model T car with the verb forms you hear. 🎧 4.6

When Henry Ford was born in 1863, most people _____*were living*_____ on farms and

_____ far from home. They _____ on foot, by bicycle, or on
　　　　2.　　　　　　　　　　　　　　　　　　3.

horseback. By the end of the 19th century, the railroad _____,
　　　　　　　　　　　　　　　　　　　　　　　　　　　　　　4.

so when it _____ necessary to go a longer distance, people _____
　　　　　5.　　　　　　　　　　　　　　　　　　　　　　　6.

trains. Henry Ford had other ideas. Some people think Henry Ford _____ the car.
　　　　　　　　　　　　　　　　　　　　　　　　　　　　　7.

But he didn't. By the time Henry Ford _____ producing cars, the car
　　　　　　　　　　　　　　　　　　8.

_____ invented. At first, the car was considered an expensive toy
　　　　9.

for the rich and _____ a "pleasure car." But Ford _____
　　　　　　　　10.　　　　　　　　　　　　　　　　　　　　　11.

to think about producing a car for middle-income people. He realized that other companies

_____ their products in large numbers and were able to sell them more cheaply.
　　　12.

By 1913, Ford _____ 13. the moving assembly line for automobiles. An assembly line is

when a different person adds each part or does each step in the process. With this method, he

_____ 14. able to produce cars faster and cheaper. When workers complained that

their job was very repetitive and boring, Ford _____ 15. their salaries. Ford was able to

keep his workers happy and mass-produce the Model T Ford. As a result of mass production, prices

_____ 16. and sales _____ 17. . During the 1920s, the term

"pleasure car" _____ 18. as it was being replaced by the term "passenger car."

EXERCISE 17 Read each conversation. Fill in the blanks with the correct tense of the verbs given. Use the passive voice and the adverbs where indicated. In some cases, more than one answer is possible.

1. **A:** <u>Have you ever heard</u> of Henry Ford?
        a. you/ever/hear

   B: Of course, I have. He _____ the car.
                                  b. invent

   A: No, he didn't. He _____ cars in large numbers and lowered the price.
                            c. produce

   B: Oh. I _____ that. I have a Ford SUV. I _____ Ford cars and
              d. not/know   e. drive

   trucks for many years. Ford _____ my favorite car maker.
                               f. always/be

   A: I _____ an American car. I _____ Japanese cars.
          g. never/have   h. always/prefer

2. **A:** My grandmother _____ me her car as a graduation present last month. She
                         a. give

   _____ for almost 50 years when she _____ to
   b. drive   c. decide

   stop. Her eyesight isn't so good anymore. Two months ago she _____ a bike and
                                                                 d. buy

   she _____ her bike around the neighborhood. Ever since she _____
         e. ride   f. start

   to ride her bike, her health _____ .
                                g. improve

   B: But how does she go long distances?

   A: Everyone in the family _____ her get around.
                                 h. help

3. **A:** _____ successful?
          a. space missions/always /be

   B: They _____ successful until 1986 when the first major accident
               b. be

   _____ .
   c. occur

   A: What about now? Are there still space missions?

   B: No. The last space mission _____ in 2011.
                                     d. be

continued

4. **A:** How did Ford learn so much about machines?

   B: He _____ about machines while he _____ for other
   　　　　　　　　a. learn　　　　　　　　　　　　　　　　　　　b. work

   　　people. He was happy while he _____ new things, but he
   　　　　　　　　　　　　　　　　　　c. learn

   　　_____ bored when there was nothing new to learn.
   　　　　d. become

5. **A:** The first cars were called "pleasure cars."

   B: Why _____ "pleasure cars"?
   　　　　　a. passive: they/call

   A: They were very expensive, and only rich people _____ them. They _____
   　　　　　　　　　　　　　　　　　　　　　　　　　b. have　　　　　　　　　　c. passive: use

   　　more for pleasure than for transportation.

6. **A:** While Ford _____ how other machines were produced, he suddenly
   　　　　　　　　　a. study

   　　_____ how to produce his cars more cheaply.
   　　　　b. realize

   B: What _____ when he _____ this?
   　　　　　　c. he/do　　　　　　　　　d. realize

   A: He _____ the assembly line for mass-producing cars.
   　　　　　e. develop

7. **A:** I _____ the story about Lewis and Clark last week. I really enjoyed it.
   　　　　a. read

   B: Me, too. I didn't realize that no one _____ the mountains before.
   　　　　　　　　　　　　　　　　　　　　　b. ever/cross

   A: By the time they returned from the West, only one man on the expedition _____.
   　　　　　　　　　　　　　　　　　　　　　　　　　　　　　　　　　c. die

   B: That's amazing, isn't it?

8. **A:** Lately, I _____ about buying a car. I'm tired of using public
   　　　　　　　a. think

   　　transportation. Do you have any suggestions for me?

   B: _____ a car before?
   　　　b. you/ever/buy

   A: No. This is my first time.

   B: _____ at a consumer magazine?
   　　　c. you/look

   A: What's a consumer magazine?

   B: It's a magazine that gives all kinds of information about buying a car.

   　　_____ about what kind of car you want?
   　　　d. you/think

   A: I want a small car less than five years old.

9. A: Do you know anything about the history of the *Titanic*?

   B: Yes. In 1912, it was the most magnificent ship that _____.

a. passive: ever/build

   A: So what went wrong?

   B: It _____ too fast when it _____ an iceberg and

b. travel   c. hit

   _____ to sink. Passengers wanted to get on lifeboats, but many of the lifeboats

d. start

   _____ .

e. already/leave

ABOUT YOU Write sentences about one or more trips you've taken by land, air, or sea. Use different past forms. When you are finished, share your sentences in small groups.

1. While I was traveling to Los Angeles, my car broke down. While a mechanic was fixing my car, I had to stay in a hotel for a few days. When they fixed my car, I continued my trip.

2. _____

3. _____

4. _____

5. _____

6. _____

SUMMARY OF UNIT 4

PRESENT PERFECT (RELATES THE PAST TO THE PRESENT)

So far, we **have read** three stories about transportation.
Have you **taken** any trips lately?
Ordinary citizens **haven't traveled** into space yet.
I have a driver's license now. I **have had** my license for three months.

PRESENT PERFECT CONTINUOUS (RELATES PAST TO PRESENT)

We **have been reading** about transportation for three days.
Ever since we started this unit, I **have been thinking** about taking a trip.
Is your son driving to California now? How long **has** he **been driving**?
We**'ve been learning** a lot about travel in the past few days.

SIMPLE PAST

Lewis and Clark **crossed** the Rocky Mountains on horseback.
They **returned** from the West two and a half years later.
They **were** very brave.
They **made** their expedition over 200 years ago.

PAST CONTINUOUS

While the *Titanic* **was crossing** the Atlantic, it hit an iceberg.
Jack Thayer **was getting** ready for bed when he felt a bump.
At 11:40 p.m. many passengers **were sleeping**.

PAST PERFECT

When Millvina Dean died in 2009, all the other *Titanic* survivors **had** already **died**.
In 1912, the *Titanic* was the most magnificent ship that **had** ever **been built**.
To make the *Titanic* look more elegant, lifeboats **had been removed**.
By the time the DC-3 airplane reached California, it **had made** several stops.

PAST PERFECT CONTINUOUS

By the time the DC-3 airplane reached California, passengers **had been traveling** for more than 18 hours.
The *Titanic* **had been traveling** for four days when it hit an iceberg.

REVIEW

Fill in the blanks with the correct form of the verbs given. Use the simple past, past continuous, present perfect, present perfect continuous, past perfect, or past perfect continuous. In some cases, more than one answer is possible.

A: I'm looking at a cool website, FlightAware.com. Do you want to see it?

B: I _'ve never heard_ of it. What's it for?
      1. never / hear

A: You can track a flight. My sister left for Poland last night. I can see when her plane _____,
                                                                                        2. depart

how long it _____ , and where it is right now.
              3. fly

B: _____ yet?
        4. she/arrive

A: Not yet. She _____ in Frankfurt this morning and _____
                     5. arrive   6. change

planes for Warsaw.

B: How many times _____ this website?
                        7. you/use

A: My family and I _____ it many times. While I _____ from Boston to
                        8. use   9. travel

Miami last month, my family _____ it. That was an awful trip.
                              10. use

B: Why? What _____ wrong?
                  11. go

A: I _____ a connection in Chicago, but my plane from Boston was two hours late. So I
         12. have

_____ my connection. The airline _____ me on another flight. By the time
13. miss   14. put

I _____ to Miami, I _____ for 14 hours. Then I
    15. get   16. travel

waited an hour for my luggage. All the other passengers _____ their luggage and
                                                          17. get

left, but mine didn't arrive.

B: What _____ ?
            18. you/do

A: I went to the luggage claim desk. They _____ me that they would do a search.
                                               19. tell

B: So _____ it?
         20. they/find

A: Yes. But by the time they _____ it, I _____ in Miami
                                  21. find   22. already/be

for a week. I _____ my brother, and, luckily, we are the same size, so he _____
               23. visit   24. give

me his clothes to wear. Wait a minute. I see that my sister's plane _____. Look. It
                                                                      25. just/arrive

_____ down five minutes ago.
26. touch

B: That's a cool website. I'm going to use it. I _____ the app.
                                                     27. already/download

I _____ it while you _____ it to me.
   28. do   29. show

FROM GRAMMAR TO WRITING

PART 1 Editing Advice

1. The simple past, in active voice, does not use an auxiliary.

   The plane ~~was~~ **arrived** at 6:44 a.m.

2. Don't forget *be* in a past continuous sentence. Don't forget the *-ing*.

   The *Titanic* ^*was* crossing the Atlantic when it hit an iceberg.

   While I was read^*ing* about the airplane, I came across some new words.

3. Don't forget *have* with perfect tenses.

   We ^*have* been learning about transportation for three days.

4. Use *when*, not *while*, for an action that has no continuation.

   Jack was getting ready for bed ~~while~~ *when* he felt a bump.

5. Choose the correct past tense.

   When I started this unit, I ~~have~~ *had* never heard of Lewis and Clark before.

   My trip to the U.S. from Japan last year was the longest trip I ~~had~~ *have* ever taken.

   The *Titanic* ~~was sinking~~ *sank* over 100 years ago.

   She has had her car ever since she ~~has come~~ *came* to the U.S.

6. Don't confuse the *-ing* form with the past participle.

   Jack had never ~~being~~ *been* on a ship before.

7. Don't use the simple present or the present continuous for an action that began in the past. Use the present perfect or present perfect continuous.

   The airplane ~~is~~ *has been* the most popular means of travel for many years.

   She ~~is~~ *has been* working as a pilot since 2012.

PART 2 Editing Practice

Some of the shaded words and phrases have mistakes. Find the mistakes and correct them. If the shaded words are correct, write *C*.

A few years ago, I ~~was~~ saw a TV program on the 100th anniversary of the *Titanic* tragedy. It was
$\quad\quad\quad\quad\quad$ **1.** $\quad\quad\quad\quad\quad\quad\quad\quad\quad\quad\quad\quad\quad\quad\quad\quad\quad\quad\quad\quad\quad\quad\quad\quad\quad\quad\quad\quad\quad$ *C*
$\quad\quad\quad\quad\quad\quad\quad\quad\quad\quad\quad\quad\quad\quad\quad\quad\quad\quad\quad\quad\quad\quad\quad\quad\quad\quad\quad\quad\quad\quad\quad\quad\quad\quad\quad\quad\quad\quad\quad\quad\quad\quad\quad\quad\quad\quad$ **2.**

a fascinating program about the survivors. I been interested in learning more about the survivors
$\quad\quad\quad\quad\quad\quad\quad\quad\quad\quad\quad\quad\quad\quad\quad\quad\quad\quad\quad\quad\quad\quad\quad\quad$ **3.**

ever since I have seen it. So I started to read more about it.
$\quad$ **4.** $\quad\quad\quad$ **5.**

One survivor was Eva Hart. She and her parents have originally planned to travel on another ship,
$\quad\quad\quad\quad\quad\quad\quad\quad\quad\quad\quad\quad\quad\quad\quad\quad\quad\quad\quad\quad\quad\quad\quad\quad\quad\quad\quad$ **6.**

but that trip was canceled. The Harts were transferred to the *Titanic*. While they were get on the ship,
$\quad\quad\quad\quad\quad\quad\quad\quad\quad\quad\quad\quad\quad\quad\quad\quad\quad\quad\quad\quad\quad\quad\quad\quad\quad\quad\quad\quad\quad\quad$ **7.** $\quad\quad\quad$ **8.**

Mrs. Hart was afraid, but seven-year-old Eva was excited about the trip. She had never even seeing a ship
$\quad\quad\quad\quad\quad\quad\quad\quad\quad\quad\quad\quad\quad\quad\quad\quad\quad\quad\quad\quad\quad\quad\quad\quad\quad\quad\quad\quad\quad\quad\quad\quad\quad\quad\quad\quad\quad$ **9.**

before, and now she was going to travel on the most luxurious ship that has ever been built.
$\quad\quad\quad\quad\quad\quad\quad\quad\quad\quad\quad\quad\quad\quad\quad\quad\quad\quad\quad\quad\quad\quad\quad\quad\quad\quad\quad\quad\quad$ **10.**

While Eva was sleeping, her parents were hearing a noise. Mr. Hart went up to see what had happened.
11.   12.   13.

He returned to their cabin and had taken Eva and her mother to the top deck. He was put them on a
                                                14.   15.

lifeboat and said to Eva, "Hold onto Mummy's hand and be good." That was the last time she has seen her
                                                                                                                                    16.   17.

father. While they were on the lifeboat, they heard people screaming. Then suddenly everything
                                                                                                    18.

had become quiet. The ship has gone down with her father and many others. Eva has died in 1996 at
19.   20.   21.

the age of 91.

  The last American survivor, Lillian Asplund, was just five years old when she traveling on the ship
                                                                                                                                                    22.

with her parents and brothers. They were returning to the U.S. from Sweden, where they had spent several
                                                                            23.   24.

years. While they went to the top deck, she and her mother got on a lifeboat with one of her brothers, but
              25   26

her father and three other brothers have waited for the next lifeboat. She never saw them again. Lillian
                                                                        27   28

has died in 2006, at the age of 99. She was the last person with a memory of the tragedy. Another person,
29

Millvina Dean, was the last survivor, but she was a baby at the time, so she hasn't remembered anything.
                                                                                                                                        30

WRITING TIP

When writing about the past, it is important to review your work to check for correct and consistent use of past verb forms. A basic reference:

- **past continuous** for background description

  It *was raining* hard and traffic *was moving* slowly.

- **simple past** for events at particular moments

  We arrived at the hotel after dark. The hotel *didn't have* any rooms.

- **past perfect** for related events that happened *before* those particular moments

  The hotel *had given* our room to someone else.

PART 3 Write

Read the two prompts. Choose one and write one or more paragraphs about it.

1. Find two articles about exploration or transportation. They can be articles about land, air, space, or sea. Or they can be about an explorer or inventor. Read the two articles and summarize them. Use your own words in the summary. Attach the articles to your summary.
2. Write about a trip you took where there were some difficulties to overcome.

PART 4 Edit

Reread the Summary of Unit 4 and the Editing Advice. Edit your writing from Part 3.

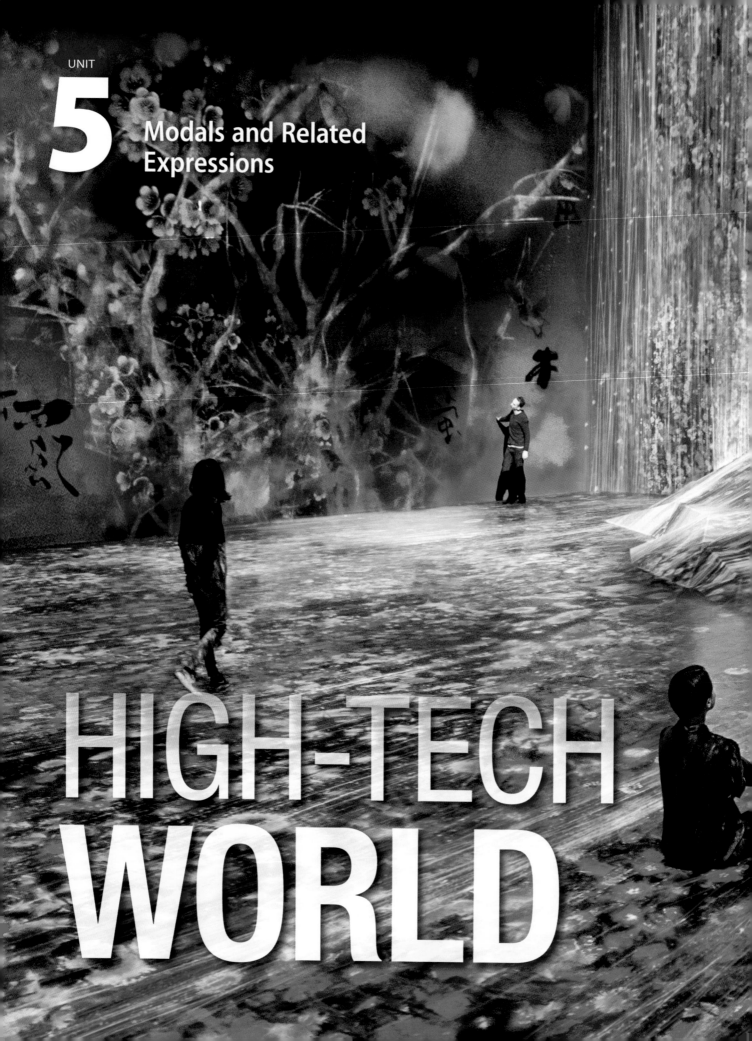

HIGH-TECH
WORLD

The exhibition teamLab Borderless, which covers 107,000 square feet and features 50 examples of moving artwork that is designed to respond to and stimulate each of the senses, The Mori Building Digital Art Museum in Tokyo, Japan

The real danger is not that computers will begin to think like men, but that men will begin to think like computers.

SYDNEY J. HARRIS

Updating Your Password?
UPDATE YOUR THINKING FIRST

Read the following article. Pay special attention to the words in bold. 🎧 5.1

Let's face it: Passwords are a pain! While you **might think** it's a good idea to use your pet's name or your birth year, research shows that passwords **must be** much stronger now than in the past. You may have noticed that you **have to create** longer and more complex passwords for your new accounts. Instructions **might say** something like: You **must include** uppercase letters, special symbols, numbers, and so on. They **may** also **tell** us that we **cannot use** dates, repeated numbers, or other patterns. This **is supposed to provide** better protection, but in reality, most people still follow a small number of predictable behaviors. Criminals, meanwhile, are happy that you are doing this.

So, what **can** you **do** to create a strong but easy-to-remember password? It **has to be** strong enough to protect your information from increasingly sophisticated cybercriminals, but it **should** still **be** easy to remember. Here are a few tips from the experts:

1. You **should not use** easy-to-guess information such as a birthday or other personal details.

2. Choose a short, memorable sentence. Then take the first letter of each word and use that as the base for your password. So, "Taylor Swift is my favorite singer." would become "TSimfs."

3. Whatever you choose as the base for your password, adding numbers and special symbols **can make** it stronger.

4. Do not keep your passwords in a notebook near your computer.

5. Yes, it's annoying, and yes, it takes time, but tell yourself that you **must create** a strong, safe password *every* time.

Of course, you **may be** tired of trying to remember different passwords for all your online activities, and this **could tempt** you to start using the same password for several different accounts. Bad idea! A recent study of 61 million passwords that hackers stole from websites found over 16 million passwords—more than 25 percent—that were reused or only slightly modified, making life very easy for hackers. This demonstrates that most of us do not take our online security seriously, but experts warn that we **had better start** to care, or one day, we **might regret** it.

COMPREHENSION Based on the reading, write T for *true* or F for *false*.

1. _____ It's a good idea to use personal information in your passwords.

2. _____ It's not advisable to use the same password for most of your accounts.

3. _____ According to a study, only around 25 percent of passwords are strong enough.

THINK ABOUT IT Discuss the questions with a partner or in a small group.

1. How concerned are you about cybercrime? Does it affect your enjoyment of the Internet? Explain.

2. Which of the password tips are the most important, in your opinion?

5.1 Modals—An Overview

The modal verbs are *can, could, should, would, may, might, must,* and *will.* Modals add meaning to the verbs that follow them.

EXAMPLES	EXPLANATION
You **should change** your password frequently. The password for my bank account **must include** at least one number.	A base form follows a modal. A modal never has an *-s* ending.
You **should not tell** anyone your password. I **cannot remember** so many passwords.	To form the negative, we put *not* after the modal. The negative of *can* is written as one word: *cannot.* The contraction for *cannot* is *can't.*
Passwords **should be changed** frequently. Passwords **must be entered** exactly.	To form the passive with a modal, we use the modal + *be* + past participle.
I **can't remember** so many passwords. = I **am not able to remember** so many passwords. You **must use** letters and numbers. = You **have to use** letters and numbers.	Expressions that are like modals in meaning are: *have to, have got to, be able to, be allowed to, be permitted to, be supposed to, had better.*

Observe these seven patterns with a modal:

AFFIRMATIVE STATEMENT:	You **should choose** a password.
NEGATIVE STATEMENT:	You **shouldn't choose** your name or birthday.
YES/NO QUESTION:	**Should** you **choose** a long password?
SHORT ANSWER:	Yes, you **should.**
WH- QUESTION:	Why **should** you **choose** a long password?
NEGATIVE WH- QUESTION:	Why **shouldn't** you **choose** your name?
SUBJECT QUESTION:	Who **should choose** a long password?

EXERCISE 1 Listen to the conversation. Write T for *true* or F for *false.* 🎧 5.2

1. _____ The woman has no trouble remembering her passwords.

2. _____ The man doesn't like having to create new passwords.

3. _____ The man and woman agree that technology has made life more complicated in some ways.

EXERCISE 2 Listen to the conversation. Fill in the blanks with the words you hear. 🎧 5.2

A: I'm trying to get into my credit card account, but I <u>can't remember</u> my password.

1.

B: It's so frustrating. I _____ my passwords, either. I

2.

_____ them down. Otherwise I _____ them. The problem is I

3.   4.

_____ where I put the paper.

5.

A: I was told that you _____ them down. What if someone _____ into

6.   7.

all your accounts?

B: Well, most sites have a "forgot your password" link.

A: The problem is, they often tell me I _____ a completely new password.

8.

They sometimes say, "You _____ a password that you haven't used in the past

9.

year." So then I _____ of something completely new—and remember it!

10.

B: Another frustration is this: If I'm doing online banking and I leave the computer for 10 minutes, I get

timed out. Then I _____ all over again.

11.

A: I thought technology _____ our lives easier.

12.

B: It _____ our lives in some ways, but in other ways, it has made our lives more

13.

complicated.

5.2 Possibility: *May, Might, Could*

EXAMPLES	EXPLANATION
The answer to my security question **might be** "King" or it **may be** "King High School" or it **could be** "King HS." I don't remember.	We use *may, might,* or *could* to show possibility about the present.
I **may open** a new account. I **might start** to do my banking online.	We use *may* or *might* to show possibility about the future.
You **may not remember** all your passwords. You **might not be** happy with technology.	For negative possibility, we use *may not* or *might not*. We don't make a contraction with *may not* or *might not*.
Maybe my password is my dog's name. My password **may be** my dog's name.	*Maybe,* written as one word, is an adverb. It usually comes before the subject. *May be,* written as two words, is a modal + verb. It comes after the subject.
I **may/might change** my password. **Maybe** I **will change** my password.	Compare using the modals *may* or *might* for the future with using *maybe* for the future.

Note:

We don't use *could not* for negative possibility. It means *was/were not able to.*

EXERCISE 3 This is a conversation between a granddaughter and a grandfather about technology. Change the *maybe* statement under each blank to a statement using the modal given.

A: _____*I might buy*_____ a new computer. If I do, Grandpa, do you want my old one? It's two years old.
  1. maybe I'll buy/might

B: _____ two years old is old, but for me it's practically new. The one I have now is
  2. maybe you think/may

good enough for me. I just do e-mail.

A: There's more than e-mail on a computer. _____ to try social media.
  3. maybe you'll want/may

B: I'm not interested in those things. _____ a lot of online friends, but I'd rather
  4. maybe you have/may

have two or three very good friends.

A: OK. But there are practical things you can do, too. Have you ever tried online banking?

_____ easier for you.
  5. maybe it will be/might

B: _____ right. But I like going into my bank and talking to real people.
  6. maybe you are/could

A: Why don't you just try it? Let me show you how.

B: No, thanks. I'll have to get a password. And _____ it.
  7. maybe I won't remember/may

A: If you think you'll forget it, you can keep a record of your passwords, using hints.

B: What do you mean?

A: For example, if my password is my dog's name, my hint is "DOG." Let me help you get a hint for

each password.

B: If I tell you my passwords, _____ all my money!
  8. maybe you will steal/might

A: Very funny, Grandpa.

5.3 Necessity/Obligation: *Must, Have to, Have Got to*

EXAMPLES	EXPLANATION
This password **must include** one uppercase letter. It **must be** at least eight characters long.	*Must* shows necessity or obligation based on a rule, a law, or an instruction. It has an official or formal tone.
Sometimes you **have to answer** security questions. Your password **has to have** at least one number.	*Have to* shows necessity or obligation. It has a less official tone than *must*.
For my bank account, I**'ve got to choose** a password. It**'s got to be** very strong.	*Have got to* is an informal way to show necessity or obligation. *Have* and *has* are usually contracted with the subject pronoun.
My old computer was too slow. I **had to buy** a new one last week.	For past necessity or obligation, we use *had to*.

continued

Note:

When using *have to*, don't make a contraction with the subject pronoun and *have*.

      *I **have to change** my password.*

  NOT *I've to change my password.*

Pronunciation Notes:

1. *Have to* is usually pronounced *hafta* or /hæftə/ and *has to* is usually pronounced *hasta* or /hæstə/.

2. With *have got to, got to* is often pronounced *gotta* or /gɑtə/.

GRAMMAR IN USE

When talking about a personal obligation, we tend to avoid *must* because it sounds very official or urgent and is too strong for personal situations. It is more natural to use *have to* or *have got to.*

    *I **have to** open an online account.*

    *I**'ve got to** choose a username and password.*

EXERCISE 4 Two friends are talking about online banking. Use the phrases from the box to fill in the blanks. Use contractions where possible.

have got to meet	must use	have to do	have to fill out	must have
have to remember	have to click	have got to leave ✓	have to log on	has got to match
have got to copy	have got to include	must be copied	had to learn	

A: Can you help me access my bank account online?

B: I <u>'ve got to leave</u> in about 15 minutes. But I think we have enough time. First you
        1.

    _____ . Have you ever signed in before?
          2.

A: I'm not sure. Maybe not.

B: Then you _____ "register here."
          3.

A: OK. Now I _____ this long form.
          4.

B: The information here _____ the information on your bank account. So if you
          5.

    used "David," you _____ "David" here, too. Don't use "Dave."
          6.

A: Of course, I knew that!

B: Now you need a password. It _____ at least one uppercase letter. And you
          7.

    _____ at least one number.
          8.

A: OK. But now I'm going to _____ one more password. Now what do I

9.

_____?

10.

B: See those funny letters and numbers? You _____ them.

11.

A: They're so hard to read. What's this for?

B: It's a safety feature. The letters and numbers _____ exactly.

12.

A: You're so good with computers.

B: I haven't always been so good. I _____, just like you. It's getting late, and I

13.

_____ a friend in half an hour.

14.

A: Thanks for your help! See you later.

ABOUT YOU Write a few obligations you have at your job, at your school, with your friends, or with your family. Use modals of necessity or obligation. Share your answers with a partner.

1. <u>My grandmother bought a new computer. I have to help her set it up on Saturday.</u>

2. _____

3. _____

4. _____

5. _____

5.4 Expectation: *Be Supposed To*

EXAMPLES	EXPLANATION
I'm **supposed to help** my parents with their smart phones. We **are supposed to change** our passwords every 30 days. Technology **is supposed to make** our lives simpler, but sometimes it doesn't.	Something may be expected because of: • a personal obligation • a law or a requirement • something we are told to expect
I know I'm **supposed to change** my password every month, but I don't do it. I know I'm **not supposed to write** down my passwords, but I do.	*Be supposed to* shows a rule that is frequently broken or an expectation that isn't met.
I **was supposed to help** you with your computer yesterday, but I forgot.	For the past, we use *was/were supposed to*. It shows an expectation or obligation that was not met.

Pronunciation Note:

The *d* and *t* in *supposed to* link together and form one sound. *Supposed to* sounds like *supposta* or /sʌpoʷztə/

EXERCISE 5 Fill in the blanks using a form of *be supposed to* and one of the words from the box. If you see *not,* use the negative. Use contractions where possible.

copy	make	memorize	pay	send	use
help	meet	open	read✓	text	

1. When you see "I accept," you <u>'re supposed to read</u> what it says, but most people don't.

2. Typing those funny letters and numbers _____ the website safer.

3. You _____ those numbers and letters exactly as you see them.

4. My friends and I share music online. I know we _____ for the music, but we often give it to each other for free.

5. I know I _____ all my passwords, but I can't. So I write them in a notebook.

6. Students (*not*) _____ in class, but I often see them texting under their desks.

7. My bank _____ me a statement each month, but I didn't get one this month. I'll look for it online.

8. I typed in my password, but I got an error message. Oh, now I know what I did wrong.

   I _____ uppercase for the first letter, but I used lowercase by mistake.

9. Children under 13 (*not*) _____ a social media account, but some kids lie about their age and open an account anyway.

10. My grandparents don't know much about computers. I _____ them this weekend.

11. You _____ me at 6:00 to help me with my computer. It's 7:30. Did you forget?

EXERCISE 6 Report some rules in the following places: in your home or dorm, in traffic, on the Internet, in a library, in class, on an airplane, or at an airport. Use *must* to give an official tone. Use *have to* or *be supposed to* to give an informal tone.

1. <u>In an airport, you must take off your shoes when you go through security.</u>

2. <u>In my dorm, we're not supposed to make noise after 11 p.m.</u>

3. _____

4. _____

5. _____

6. _____

7. _____

ABOUT YOU Write some rules, customs, or expectations that you don't (or didn't) follow. Discuss your answers with a partner.

1. <u>I'm supposed to turn off my cell phone in class, but I sometimes forget to do it.</u>

2. <u>I was supposed to write a paper for my history class, but I didn't have time.</u>

3. _____

4. _____

5. _____

5.5 Advice: *Should, Ought to, Had Better*

EXAMPLES	EXPLANATION
You **should change** your password every month. You **shouldn't use** your birthday.	*Should* shows advisability. It is used to say that something is a good idea. *Shouldn't* means that something is a bad idea.
Before I click "accept," I **ought to read** the terms, but I never do. You **ought to use** online banking. It's much quicker than going into a bank.	*Ought to* is another way of saying *should*. *Ought to* is not usually used for negatives and questions.
My password is too weak. I'**d better choose** a stronger one. Your password should be a secret. You'**d better not tell** it to anyone.	*Had better* is used in conversation and informal writing for advisability. It states or implies a negative consequence. We use *'d* to contract *had* with a pronoun.

Pronunciation Notes:

1. *Ought to* is sometimes pronounced like one word: *oughta*.

2. The *'d* in *had better* is often omitted or hard to hear and sounds like *you better*.

EXERCISE 7 Give advice for each situation. Practice *should, ought to,* and *had better*.

1. My computer is about seven years old. It's very slow.

   <u>In my opinion, you should throw it away and buy a new one. A seven-year-old computer</u>

   <u>is too old.</u>

2. I can't decide if I should buy a laptop or a desktop computer.

   _____

   _____

3. My little brother uses my laptop a lot. I think it has a virus now.

   _____

   _____

continued

4. My daughter is 10 years old and wants a social media account.

_____

_____

5. I have at least 25 passwords, and I can't remember them. So I wrote them all down and keep the

paper near my computer.

_____

_____

EXERCISE 8 Fill in the blanks with one of the phrases from the box.

you shouldn't make	I should give	he shouldn't play	should I buy ✓	I'd better do	you ought to protect	should I do
you'd better not use	you'd better be	you should choose	he ought to play	you ought to set up	'd better choose	

1. A: My old computer isn't fast enough. _____Should I buy_____ a new one or add more memory to
                                              a.

my old one? My computer's already nine years old.

B: That's a _very_ old computer.

A: Maybe _____ it to my grandson.
                                b.

B: He probably likes to play games, so he's probably not interested in a slow computer.

A: You're right. But I think _____ computer games.
                                          c.

_____ with friends, not just computers.
                      d.

2. A: Can I use your laptop for a few minutes? Can you fill in your password?

B: I don't have a password.

A: That's not good. _____ your laptop with a password.
                                a.

B: I don't think that's necessary. That's just one more password to remember.

A: What if someone steals your laptop? _____ it easy for the thief to access your
                                                                    b.

accounts. Mine was stolen in a coffee shop once.

B: Really? How did that happen?

A: I left it on the table and went to buy coffee. When I came back, it was gone! _____
                                                                                          c.

careful and password-protect your computer as soon as possible.

B: _____ it right now. I'll use my birthday.
　　　　　　　d.

A: _____ such an obvious password. Choose something that's more secure.
　　　　　　　e.

3. **A:** My younger brother uses my laptop when I'm at work. Sometimes he goes into my files.

　　What _____ ?
　　　　　　　a.

B: _____ a guest account. That way he can't get into your files.
　　　　　　　b.

A: How do I do that?

B: I can help you. Let me see your computer . . . OK. I set up a guest account for you. A guest doesn't need a

　　password, but your account does. _____ a password that your brother can't guess.
　　　　　　　　　　　　　　　　　　　c.

A: Even more important, I _____ a password that I can remember!
　　　　　　　　　　　　　d.

EXERCISE 9 Circle the correct modal or expression to complete the sentences. In some cases, both
answers are possible. In those cases, circle both choices.

1. You (_'d better not_/_must not_) write your passwords on a piece of paper. What if someone finds the paper?

2. For each new account, you (_'ve got to_/_should_) choose a password.

3. Some websites require an uppercase letter. For those sites, you (_'re supposed to_/_ought to_) include at least one

　uppercase letter.

4. I'm so tired of passwords. Why (_do I have to_/_should I_) remember so many passwords?

5. Sometimes when you forget your password, you (_have to_/_'d better_) answer some questions, such as

　"What's the name of your pet?"

6. You (_must_/_should_) choose a password that's hard for other people to guess. So it's not a good idea to use

　your birthday.

7. I know I (_ought to_/_should_) create a strong password, but I like using the same password for all my accounts.

8. I got timed out of my account when I answered the phone. When I came back, I (_had to_/_must_) log in again.

9. Your password is case-sensitive. That means you (_must_/_ought to_) type it exactly the way you typed it

　originally, with uppercase and lowercase letters.

10. They say you (_should_/_must_) change your password every month, but I never do.

11. My grandmother needs help with her online bank account. I promised to help her tomorrow. She

　(_is supposed to_/_must_) bring her laptop to my house. But it (_must_/_is supposed to_) snow tomorrow, so I don't

　know if she's still coming.

12. Those funny letters and numbers are so hard to read. You (_ought to_/_'ve got to_) copy them exactly.

ABOUT YOU Write sentences about computers, passwords, online shopping, online banking, or online music using the words given. Discuss your sentences with a partner.

1. have to <u>When I order something online, I sometimes have to pay for shipping.</u>

2. should _____

3. have got to _____

4. must _____

5. ought to _____

6. had better _____

7. be supposed to _____

5.6 Suggestion: *Can/Could*

EXAMPLES	EXPLANATION
To remember passwords, you **can create** a hint for each password. You **could keep** the hint in a notebook.	We use *can* and *could* to give suggestions.
You **can open** a bank account online, or you **could go** into the bank and do it in person. You **should change** your password frequently.	We use *can* or *could* when several options are possible. We use *should* when you feel that there is only one right way.

EXERCISE 10 Offer two suggestions to answer each of the following questions. You may work with a partner. Use *can* or *could*.

1. How can I make my password more secure?

   <u>You can mix uppercase and lowercase letters. You could include a number or symbol.</u>

2. How can I open a new bank account?

   _____

3. How can I remember all my passwords?

   _____

4. How can I pay for something online?

   _____

5. How can I compare prices on a new TV?

   _____

Taking a Break from Technology

Read the following article. Pay special attention to the words in bold. 🎧 5.3

Levi Felix has started a new kind of summer camp in California called Camp Grounded. Even though it's only three days long, campers can get away from their daily routine and swim, hike, take yoga classes, and enjoy nature. Most of all, campers can interact with each other. So what's so special about this camp? It's only for adults. And there's one important rule: Campers **must not be** connected to technology while there.

Many adults report that when they are on vacation, they **aren't able to stay away** from their devices and often check their work-related e-mails. Even when out in nature, they **may not take** the time to admire a spectacular mountain before pulling out their smartphone to take a picture.

Levi Felix wants people to interact with each other, not with their tech devices. At Camp Grounded, campers **are not allowed to talk** about their jobs. They **are not** even **permitted to use** their real names. They have to pick a nickname. They are supposed to get to know each other as people, not through their professional lives. Felix hopes that campers can get to know themselves better as well.

Why do people have to go to camp to do this? Why not just unplug for the weekend? Many people say that they **can't control** themselves when they have a device nearby. They know they **don't have to respond** every time they hear a beep from their phone, but they do.

Felix is not against technology, but he thinks technology **shouldn't control** us. We **don't have to give up** our devices, but we need more balance in our lives.

A young woman paddles a kayak in the morning near Vancouver, B.C., Canada.

COMPREHENSION Based on the reading, write T for *true* or F for *false*.

1. _____ Levi Felix has created a technology camp for adults.

2. _____ At Felix's camp, people talk about their professions.

3. _____ Felix wants adults to interact with each other at his camp.

THINK ABOUT IT Discuss the questions with a partner or in a small group.

1. Would you like to visit a place like Camp Grounded? What would you find enjoyable? What would you find difficult? Give your reasons.

2. Describe the role technology plays in your life. Do you feel you are too dependent on your computer, phone, and so on? Explain.

5.7 Negative Modals

EXAMPLES	EXPLANATION
Campers **must not be connected** to technology while there.	*Must not* shows that something is prohibited. It has an official tone.
Campers **cannot use** technology at this camp. They **may not talk** about work. They **are not allowed to use** a cell phone. They **are not permitted to use** their real names.	*Cannot* and *may not* show that something is not permitted. The meaning is similar to *must not* but is less formal. Other expressions that show prohibition are *be not allowed to* and *be not permitted to*.
Campers **are not supposed to talk** about their jobs. I **wasn't supposed to use** my cell phone at camp, but I did.	*Be not supposed to* is also used to show that something is not permitted. It is often used when a rule has already been broken.
Technology **shouldn't control** you. You should control technology.	*Should not* shows that something is not advisable.
If your phone beeps, you **don't have to respond** to it immediately. You can wait.	*Not have to* shows that something is not necessary or required.

Notes:

1. In the affirmative, *have to* and *must* have the same meaning, although *must* sounds more official.

    You **must give up** your cell phone for three days. = You **have to give up** your cell phone for three days.

2. In the negative, the meanings are completely different. *Must not* shows prohibition. *Not have to* shows that something is not necessary or required.

    One camp rule is that you **must not use** a cell phone for three days.

    When my cell phone rings, I **don't have to answer** it. I can wait.

EXERCISE 11 Circle the correct words in each item about Camp Grounded. In some cases, both answers are possible. In those cases, circle both choices.

1. At Camp Grounded, you (*may not*/*don't have to*) use a cell phone.

2. When your phone rings, you (*cannot*/*don't have to*) answer it if it's not an emergency.

3. According to Levi Felix, technology (*shouldn't*/*can't*) control you.

4. At Camp Grounded, you (*don't have to*/*are not allowed to*) use technology.

5. Campers (*aren't supposed to/don't have to*) bring their devices to camp, but some of them do.

6. According to the camp rules, you (*must not/may not*) use a tech device for three days.

7. If you don't want to take a yoga class at camp, you (*must not/don't have to*). It's your choice.

8. I want a break from technology. I (*don't have to/shouldn't*) go to camp. I can just turn off my phone.

9. You (*may not/don't have to*) use a computer at Camp Grounded.

EXERCISE 12 Circle the correct words to complete the conversation. In some cases, both answers are possible. In those cases, circle both choices.

A: Every time I get a credit card or bank statement, I just throw it in the garbage.

B: You (*shouldn't*/*don't have to*) do that. Someone (*can/should*) steal your identity. I read that thieves go
                1.   2.

through the garbage looking for personal information.

A: But they (*don't have to/can't*) use my number without my credit card.
                3.

B: They can and they do. They make purchases by phone and charge it to your credit card. You

(*may not/might not*) realize your information has been stolen till you review your bill a month later.
    4.

You (*must not/shouldn't*) just throw away papers with personal information. You (*must/should*) shred
          5.   6.

them. You (*could/can*) buy a shredder at an office supply store or online. Look. On this shopping site,
          7.

if you spend over $25, you (*are not supposed to/don't have to*) pay for shipping.
                              8.

A: OK. I'll buy one.

B: I do all my bill payments online. This way I (*don't have to/must not*) write any checks.
                                    9.

A: I don't know how to set up an online account. Can you help me?

B: Sure. Let's find your bank's website. OK. Now choose a password. You (*shouldn't/don't have to*) use
                                              10.

your birthday. It's too easy for a thief to figure out.

A: OK. Let me try my mother's maiden name. Oh. It rejected this.

B: You used all letters. You (*couldn't/can't*) use just letters. You (*have to/can*) include at least one number.
                           11.   12.

Now try to memorize it.

A: I (*'m not supposed to/can't*) memorize so many passwords. It's impossible.
          13.

B: You (*have to/'ve got to*) find a way to keep track of your passwords.
          14.

ABOUT YOU Write about a rule, law, or custom from your country or culture that other people may find strange.

_____

_____

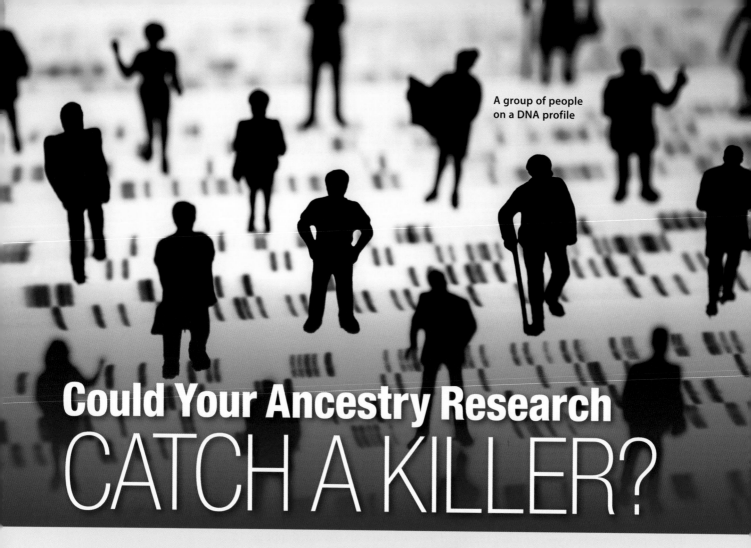

A group of people on a DNA profile

Could Your Ancestry Research
CATCH A KILLER?

Read the following article. Pay special attention to the words in bold. 🎧 5.4

We've all seen the ads for websites that provide you with information on your ancestry[1]. On some sites, you **can send** in a sample of your DNA[2] and in a short time find out more about where you came from and discover people around the world that you are related to. The availability of such sites has skyrocketed in recent years. The number of customers using ancestry sites was just a few hundred thousand in 2013 but jumped to over 15 million in 2018. Some people go to great lengths to trace their ancestry and **might spend** several hours a week on their search. Others **may** only **be** interested in a bit of fun. But how many of these millions of users realize that their hobby **might be helping** the police find a killer?

In 2018, police in Sacramento, California, **were able to track down** and **capture** a man known as the Golden State Killer. He had committed a series of horrible crimes in the 1970s and 80s, including 13 murders. With the use of ancestry sites, police **could compare** the DNA data that was collected from the crime scene with that of ancestry site users living in the area where the murders took place. Then, when a DNA match was found, the police **were able to locate** relatives that fit the killer's profile and who lived in the area. When they narrowed down their search to one suspect, they collected a new DNA sample from him. His sample matched the DNA of the killer. Without the use of ancestry sites, this individual **could** still **be walking** the streets as a free man.

So, on the face of it, this use of modern technology seems to be a good thing. But **should** we **be looking** at this issue with regard to personal privacy, too? Police **were able to get** genetic information of the murderer's relatives without permission. You put your information online for personal reasons and find out later that it was used without your knowledge. Is this acceptable?

---

[1] ancestry: people who were in your family in previous times
[2] DNA: a substance in human and animal cells that carries genetic information

COMPREHENSION Based on the reading, write T for *true* or F for *false*.

1. _____ Ancestry sites are more popular than they have ever been before.

2. _____ A relative told police the identity of the Golden Gate Killer.

3. _____ It is easy for the police to obtain information from ancestry sites.

THINK ABOUT IT Discuss the questions with a partner or in a small group.

1. Should the police get permission to use people's online DNA information?

2. What do you think about the man who was arrested in the California case? Explain.

5.8 Ability/Possibility: *Can, Be Able To*

EXAMPLES	EXPLANATION
You **can research** your family history on an ancestry site. You **can't stop** the police using your information.	*Can* shows ability or possibility.
Are you **able to find** distant relatives?	*Be able to* is another way to express ability/possibility.
Could you **do** the DNA test? = **Were** you **able to do** the DNA test? I **couldn't do** the DNA test. = I **wasn't able to do** the DNA test.	We use *could* or *was/were able to* for past questions and negative statements.
I **was able to find** several new cousins. I **could** only **find out** about close relatives before I joined an ancestry site.	In affirmative past statements, we use *was/were able to* for a single past action. We use *could* to express *used to be able to*.

Pronunciation Note:
Can is usually reduced in affirmative statements. The vowel almost disappears. In negative statements, *can't* is stressed, and the vowel is clear. We must pay attention to the stress to hear the difference between *can* and *can't*.

    I can go. I /k'n/ go.   *I can't go. I /kænt/ go.*

EXERCISE 13 Ancestry sites have advantages and disadvantages. Fill in the blanks with one of the phrases from the box to complete the statements about ancestry sites.

can catch	can't find	are you able to keep	are able to obtain can find out ✓
can find	wasn't able to get	can carry out	couldn't identify

1. On an ancestry site, you _____can find out_____ about relatives all around the world.

2. _____ your information private?

3. Currently, the police _____ information from ancestry sites without permission.

4. Do you think you _____ everyone in your family on an ancestry site?

continued

5. The police _____ criminals by locating one of their relatives and matching DNA with evidence from a crime scene.

6. The investigator _____ her DNA information until he got permission.

7. Starting your DNA research is easy: Anyone _____ the simple test.

8. You _____ all your relatives on an ancestry site because the databases are incomplete.

9. The police obtained DNA information from an ancestry site, but they _____ the criminal they were chasing.

5.9 Logical Conclusion: *Must*

EXAMPLES	EXPLANATION
When Ariana saw her DNA results, she thought, "This **must be** a mistake. I don't believe I am part Swedish." This site says you can find relatives you don't know exist. That **must be** exciting!	*Must* shows that something is probably true. It is used to make a conclusion based on information we have or observations we make.
A: How many living relatives do you have? **B:** I **must have** at least 50.	We can use *must* to make an estimate.
A: Are you going to the family reunion? **B:** Oh, you **must not know** that it's been postponed. **A:** No! Really? Why? **B:** Grandma and Grandpa **must not be** back from their trip yet.	For a negative conclusion, we use *must not*. We don't use a contraction.

EXERCISE 14 Fill in the blanks with an appropriate verb to make a logical conclusion. Use context clues to help you. Answers may vary.

1. **A:** I signed up for a no-tech camp. I plan on having a vacation from technology.

   B: You must ___feel___ nervous about being without your devices for a few days.

   A: I'm not nervous. I'm looking forward to a break from technology.

2. **A:** Kids love technology. They don't want to be without it for a minute.

   B: Teachers must _____ angry when cell phones ring during class.

   A: The kids are smart about it. They silence their phones in class.

3. **A:** I have a computer problem. I don't know how to fix it.

   B: Ask your teenage son. He's on his computer all day. He must _____ what to do. Kids know much more about computers than we do.

4. **A:** How many text messages do you send every day?

   B: A lot. I must _____ between 100 and 200 messages a day.

   A: You must not _____ using the telephone very much.

   B: For me, texting is more convenient than talking on the phone.

5. **A:** Do you use the same password for all your accounts?

   B: Of course not. Like most people, I must _____ more than 30 passwords.

   A: It must _____ hard to remember so many passwords.

   B: It is. It's very hard.

6. **A:** Katya always sends and receives text messages during class.

   B: Who's Katya?

   A: You must _____ who I'm talking about. She's the tall woman who sits between us

   in class.

   B: Oh, now I know. I always call her Kathy.

7. **A:** I hear your ringtone is a Beyoncé song.

   B: It is.

   A: You must _____ Beyoncé very much.

   B: I do. She's one of my favorite singers.

8. **A:** My sister has just joined an ancestry website. She's going to take a DNA test as soon as it arrives.

   B: Really? She must not _____ that the police can obtain your DNA information from

   those sites, then. You should tell her.

   A: Tell her what? I don't know anything about this.

   B: Oh, you must _____! We read an article about it in class last month!

9. **A:** Whenever I text my daughter, she usually writes "LOL." She probably means "Lots of love."

   B: You must not _____ much about texting abbreviations. "LOL" means "Laughing

   out loud."

5.10 Probability vs. Possibility: *Must* vs. *May, Might, Could*

EXAMPLES	EXPLANATION
A: You're getting the results of your DNA test this week, aren't you? You **must be** excited! **B:** Yes, I can't wait!	If something is probable because an observation leads to a logical conclusion, we use *must*.
A: You **might not realize** it, but ancestry websites can cause you a lot of problems. **B:** That's crazy. **A:** You **may not believe** it, but a man was arrested because of them. **B:** I suppose you **could be** right.	If something is possible but we don't have evidence to reach a conclusion, we use *may, might,* or *could*. These modals mean "maybe."

EXERCISE 15 Work with a partner to write a statement about the person who made each comment. Use *must, may, might,* or *could* to say who the person is, how the person feels, or any other information.

1. The police used my DNA information without my permission.

    The person must be angry.

2. I discovered I have cousins in Australia!

3. But I believed my DNA information was private!

4. I sent in my test weeks ago, but I haven't received my results yet.

5. The ancestry site lost my DNA sample.

6. A criminal relative was caught by police because I decided to research my family history through an ancestry site.

7. An innocent family member was arrested because police obtained my DNA sample.

8. Police came to my house and questioned me after reviewing my brother's DNA information on an ancestry site.

EXERCISE 16 Circle the correct words to complete each sentence.

1. **A:** I've decided not to do the DNA test for the ancestry site I joined.

   B: But you already paid, didn't you?

   A: Yes, I did. But I (*couldn't*/*can't*) go ahead after I realized the police can look at your information
   a.
   without your permission.

   B: How much (*should you*/*did you have to*) pay?
   b.

   A: $99, plus tax.

   B: You (*must*/*are supposed to*) be upset about that!
   c.

2. **A:** I just filled out this online application. I clicked "I accept."

   B: You (*were supposed to*/*had to*) read the agreement before accepting.
   a.

   A: Nobody reads that.

3. **A:** Did you read about Camp Grounded?

   B: Yeah. It's not for me. I (*don't have to*/*can't*) be without my cell phone for a whole weekend.
   a.

   A: You (*must*/*should*) be very dependent on it.
   b.

   B: I am.

continued

Many adults today go to special camps to "unplug" or take a break from technology.

4. **A:** What do you think about the case of the Golden State Killer? The police (*didn't have to/must not*)
a.
get permission to obtain DNA information from ancestry websites. I'm shocked!

B: Well, they (*couldn't/can't*) catch the murderer without that information. I think they (*had to/must*)
b.   c.
take the information to keep the local people safe.

A: I guess that's true. Still, I'm not sure what I'm going to write in my assignment.

B: Assignment?

A: Yes. For next week, we (*should/'ve got to*) write a composition. We (*'re supposed to/'re able to*) write
d.   e.
our opinions about the case.

5. **A:** Technology (*must/is supposed to*) make our lives easier. But I have so many passwords, and now I
a.
(*can't/don't have to*) remember all of them. I (*may/must*) have at least 25.
b.   c.

B: You (*should/must*) give yourself a hint for each one. For example, I have the hint "FRST SCHL."
d.

A: That's easy. It (*should/must*) mean "first school." What if someone (*is able to/is supposed to*)
e.   f.
understand your hint? Your friends (*might/are supposed to*) know it.
g.

B: I'm not worried about my friends. I'm worried about thieves!

6. **A:** I'm so happy. My vacation starts tomorrow. I (*must not/don't have to*) work for a week. I hope I won't
a.
be bored. Any ideas on what I can do?

B: You (*must/could*) read. Or you (*can/should*) just surf the Internet.
b.   c.

A: I (*must/could*) spend at least 20 hours a week on my computer at work. Now that I'm on vacation,
d.
I want a break from technology.

7. **A:** Can you help me with my computer problem this afternoon?

B: Sorry, I can't. I (*'m supposed to/could*) help my mom this afternoon. She's expecting me.
a.

8. **A:** I'm going to trace my ancestry online. Do you want to trace yours, too? We could do the DNA
test together.

B: No, I (*'d better not/might not*) —I can't stand the sight of blood!
a.

A: Oh, come on, it's just a drop. You (*may/should*) be braver!
b.

9. **A:** I heard your parents gave you $1,000 for your graduation. What are you going to do with the money?

B: I (*might/must*) buy a new computer. I (*don't have to/must not*) make up my mind right away.
a.   b.
I'm going to think about it first.

5.11 Continuous Modals

EXAMPLES	EXPLANATION
My son is at camp. I haven't heard from him all week. He **must be having** a good time.	We use the modal + *be* + present participle (verb -*ing*) for a present continuous meaning.
Sam is looking at his phone under his desk. He **might be texting**. Or he **could be using** the Internet. He **should be paying** attention.	

EXERCISE 17 Fill in the blanks with a verb phrase from the box.

could be charging	might be taking√	must be talking	shouldn't be texting
might be preventing	must be making	could be learning	shouldn't be using

1. **A:** My friend isn't answering his phone. I know he always has his cell phone with him.

   B: He __might be taking__ a shower now. I'm sure he doesn't take his phone into the shower!

   Or he _____ it now. Maybe his battery is dead.

2. **A:** I don't think the police should have access to public ancestry sites. They _____

   people's private information that way.

   B: But the police _____ further crimes, and that's a good thing.

3. **A:** You _____ in class.

   B: I know. But I have to send an important message to my mom right now.

4. **A:** My friends don't want to take a DNA test.

   B: That's odd. They _____ about their family.

5. **A:** It looks like that man is talking to himself.

   B: He _____ on a cell phone. Look carefully. He's wearing headphones.

6. **A:** More people than ever are signing up to online ancestry sites these days.

   B: I know. They _____ a huge amount of money!

FUN WITH GRAMMAR

Race your classmates! Work in a group of three. Read a situation. You must write as many sentences as possible in two minutes using modals of probability or possibility. Which group wrote the most sentences?

Example: You notice classmates cheating on a test.

*They **might misunderstand** the rules.*　　　*They **must be desperate** for a good grade.*
*They **must be** crazy!*　　　*They **shouldn't be cheating**.*

Situations:
1. You realize you lost your friends while hiking in the mountains.
2. Your doctor tells you that you need to exercise, but you feel fine.
3. You have been offered two jobs: one pays a lot of money, and the other pays very little, but is something you really want to do.

SUMMARY OF UNIT 5

EXAMPLES	MEANING
To use this ancestry site, you **must take** a DNA test. You **must not cheat** on the test.	Necessity or obligation because of a rule, law, or instruction (official tone) Negative: prohibition
I **have to choose** a password to bank online. She**'s got to send** a sample of her DNA. If your phone beeps, you **don't have to look** at it.	Necessity or obligation (unofficial tone) Negative: not necessary
I**'m supposed to read** the agreement before clicking "I accept." But I never do. Technology **is supposed to make** our lives easier. At a no-tech camp, campers **are not supposed to bring** their cell phones, but some people do.	Expectation because of a rule or requirement, or because we are told what to expect Negative: prohibition; rule often broken or instructions not followed
You **should change** your password frequently. You **ought to use** a combination of lowercase and uppercase letters. You **shouldn't use** your name or birthday in your password.	Advice
You**'d better think** carefully before providing your DNA to an online ancestry site. You**'d better not join** an ancestry site if you are concerned about privacy.	Warning: negative consequence is stated or implied
You **can/may discover** you have relatives you never knew existed. You **are allowed to/are permitted to join** as many ancestry sites as you wish. You **can't/may not prevent** the police from reviewing your online DNA information.	Permission Negative: prohibition; less formal than *must not*
I **can't understand** all the fuss about online ancestry sites. Before ancestry sites, you **could trace** your family history, but it took a lot of time and effort.	Ability/inability Past ability/inability
With your DNA information online, you **may/might/could get** some unpleasant surprises.	Possibility
How **can I get away** from technology? You **could turn off** all your devices for a few days. Or you **can go** to a no-tech camp.	Suggestions
It **must be** hard for some people to give up technology for a few days. I **must have** at least 50 passwords.	Logical conclusion about the present An estimate

REVIEW

Each item mentions an aspect of creating an online bank account. Circle the right words to complete the statement. In some cases, both answers are correct, so circle both options.

1. Sign up online or call this toll-free number: 800-555-1234

   I (*can*/*might*) enroll online, or I (*could/must*) call a toll-free number.

2. If you call us, please have your Social Security number ready.

   I (*don't have to/can't*) apply for online banking without a Social Security number.

3. Choose a password. Use at least one uppercase letter, one lowercase letter, one symbol, and one number.

   I (*can/'ve got to*) choose a complicated password. How (*am I supposed to/must I*) remember all of that?

4. Apply now. You can have an account in a few minutes.

   I (*must not/don't have to*) go into a bank. I (*can/should*) do my banking any time of day.

5. We need a driver's license or state ID.

   I don't have a driver's license. It says I (*am supposed to/can*) use a state ID.

6. What's the best phone number where we can reach you? What is your alternate number? (optional)

   I (*shouldn't/don't have to*) give an alternate phone number.

7. There are three types of accounts. Choose one.

   I'm not sure which is the best for me. I (*ought to/should*) call the bank for more information.

8. After you read the agreement, click "I accept."

   I (*'m supposed to/may*) read the whole agreement, but it's too hard to understand.

9. For information in Spanish, click here. (Para información en español, haga clic aquí.)

   Spanish speakers (*should/can*) get information in Spanish.

10. Do you want to sign up for automatic bill payment? (optional)

    I (*can/have to*) sign up for automatic bill payment if I want to.

11. There are so many questions on this application.

    There (*must/should*) be at least 30 questions. It (*could/was supposed to*) be an easy process, but it's not.

12. If you apply today, you will get a check for $50.

    That sounds like a good idea. I (*am supposed to/should*) apply today.

13. Only U.S. citizens can apply online. If you are not a U.S. citizen, please visit one of our banking locations.

    I (*must/have to*) be a U.S. citizen to apply online. I'm not a U.S. citizen, so I (*can't/must not*) apply online.

FROM GRAMMAR TO WRITING

PART 1 Editing Advice

1. Don't use *to* after a modal (exception: *ought to*).

   You should ~~to~~ drive more carefully.

2. Don't forget the *d* in *supposed to*.

   You are suppose_∧*d* to stop at a red light.

   You are suppose ⌃*d* to stop at a red light.

3. Don't forget the *d* to express *had* in *had better*.

   You ⌃*'d* better not provide your DNA if you are worried.

4. Use *have/has* before *got to*.

   You ⌃*'ve* got to have a password for each account.

5. Don't forget *be* or *to* in these expressions: *be supposed to, be able to, be permitted to, be allowed to.*

   You ⌃*are* supposed to be careful with your private information.

   I'm not able ⌃*to* remember so many passwords.

6. Use correct word order in a question with a modal.

   How ~~I can~~ *can I* trace my family history?

7. Don't put *can* after another modal. Change to *be able to*.

   You must ~~can~~ *be able to* pay in advance to receive your DNA test in the mail.

PART 2 Editing Practice

Some of the shaded words and phrases have mistakes. Find the mistakes and correct them. If the shaded words are correct, write C.

I don't think technology is good for small children. Kids should ~~to~~ play with other kids, not
1.

just devices. How can they develop social skills if they always play with devices? I have a five-
2. *C*

year-old nephew. He must to spend at least four hours a day on his tablet. He doesn't even like to
3.

watch TV anymore. He should spend more time outdoors with other kids. I often tell my brother,
4.

"You better put some limits on how much time Kyle can play with his tablet." My brother always
5.

tells me, "What we can do? We're too busy to take him to the park to play." I think my brother
6.

and his wife supposed to set a good example for their son. Instead, Kyle sees his parents always
7.

texting, tweeting, checking e-mail, etc. They think he should be able have good technology skills
8.

before he goes to school. I can't convince my brother and sister-in-law to change their habits.
9.

My sister is raising her daughter differently. Maya is four years old, and she not permitted
                                                                                          10.

use technology at all. My sister thinks that Maya got to learn social skills first. She's not allow to
                                                     11.   12.

watch more than one TV program a day. In nice weather, she's got to play outside and get some
                                                                        13.

exercise. Sometimes she sees her friends playing with a tablet. She asks my sister, "Why I can't
                                                                                            14.

have a tablet?" My sister has to explain to her that people are more important than electronic
                          15.

devices. It's not easy raising children today. But we got to set a good example for them.
                                                              16.

WRITING TIP

After you brainstorm ideas for a writing topic, it's always a good idea to organize those ideas. A T-chart is especially helpful when your topic can be divided into two sides, such as with advantages and disadvantages.

TECHNOLOGY IN DAILY LIVES

ADVANTAGES	DISADVANTAGES
convenience	distraction

PART 3 Write

Read the two prompts. Choose one and write one or more paragraphs about it.

1. Write about some advantages and disadvantages of technology in our daily lives.
2. Do you think it's important to take a break from technology from time to time? Why or why not?

PART 4 Edit

Reread the Summary of Unit 5 and the Editing Advice. Edit your writing from Part 3.

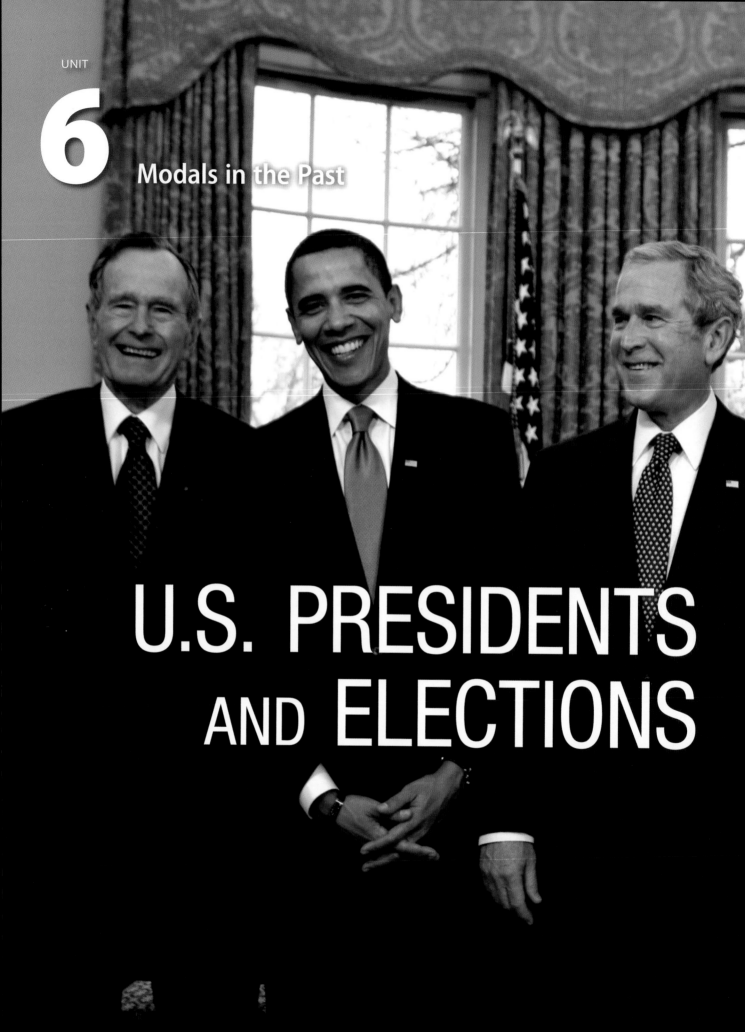

U.S. PRESIDENTS AND ELECTIONS

President-elect Barack Obama (second from left) is welcomed to the White House in Washington, DC, on Wednesday, Jan. 7, 2009, by President George W. Bush (third from left) and former presidents, from left, George H.W. Bush, Bill Clinton, and Jimmy Carter.

If your actions inspire others to dream more, learn more, do more and become more, you are a leader.

JOHN QUINCY ADAMS

LINCOLN and the GETTYSBURG ADDRESS

Read the following article. Pay special attention to the words in bold. 🎧 6.1

From the time of the first English colonies[1] in America, Africans were brought to America as slaves. Most of them worked on farms that produced sugar, cotton, and other crops[2]. Farmers in the South **couldn't have been** as prosperous without slaves. But many Northerners were against slavery. One of those was Abraham Lincoln, the president who finally brought an end to slavery in the United States.

Today, many people consider Abraham Lincoln to be one of the greatest presidents of the United States. But before he became president, many had doubts about his abilities. Lincoln's parents were poor and uneducated, and Lincoln had only 18 months of formal schooling. But he loved to read, and he educated himself.

Much to his opponents' surprise, Lincoln won the presidential election in 1860. At that time, southern slave owners wanted to continue slavery, but Lincoln wanted to stop the spread of slavery. What followed was the worst internal crisis in American history: the Civil War. Over half a million soldiers died in the conflict, the most of any war that the United States fought in.

On November 19, 1863, President Lincoln was invited to say a few words at Gettysburg, Pennsylvania, where a terrible battle had taken place. There were about 20,000 people there. Edward Everett, the main speaker, spoke first. His speech lasted two hours. Lincoln followed Everett with a two-minute speech. His speech was short, but those two minutes **might have had** more significance to U.S. history than any other two minutes. When he finished, everyone was silent. The audience **may have been surprised** that the speech was over. They **must have thought** that he hadn't yet finished. Seeing the reaction of the crowd, Lincoln turned to Everett and said he was afraid his speech had been a failure and that he **should have prepared** it more carefully. Everett disagreed. He said the speech was perfect. He said the president had said more in two minutes than he, Everett, had said in two hours. This speech, known as the Gettysburg Address, is one of the greatest speeches in American history. Lincoln said that the country was dedicated to freedom and that "government of the people, by the people, for the people" had to continue.

The Civil War continued until April 9, 1865, when the North finally won, and slavery was brought to an end.

---

[1] colony: a group of people who have moved to another area of land, but are still governed by their home country
[2] crop: plant grown as food, especially grains, vegetables, or fruit

Tourists visiting the Lincoln Memorial in Washington, DC

COMPREHENSION Based on the reading, write T for *true* or F for *false*.

1. _____ Lincoln didn't have much formal education.

2. _____ Lincoln's short speech surprised the audience.

3. _____ Lincoln was confident and believed his speech would go down in history.

THINK ABOUT IT Discuss the questions with a partner or in a small group.

1. What do you think it was like to be an American at the time of the Civil War? Give your reasons.

2. The Gettysburg Address was one of the greatest speeches in American history. What qualities does a great speaker need, in your opinion? Explain.

6.1 Modals in the Past—Form

EXAMPLES	EXPLANATION
"I **should have prepared** the speech more carefully," thought Lincoln. Southern farmers **could not have become** as rich without slaves.	To form the past of a modal, we use modal + (*not*) + *have* + the past participle.
Lincoln probably **could have been elected** again, but he was assassinated. Africans **should not have been brought** to the U.S. to work as slaves.	To form the passive of a modal, we use modal + (not) + *have been* + the past participle.

Pronunciation Note:

Informally, *have* in past modals is often contracted to *'ve* and sounds like the word "of." Sometimes it is reduced to just the schwa sound /ə/. These words are written in very informal writing as *shoulda* and *coulda*.

EXERCISE 1 Fill in the blanks with the words you hear to complete the conversations. 🎧 6.2

1. **A:** Did you read the story about Lincoln before class?

   B: No. I didn't have time.

   A: You _should have read_ it. Our lesson depends on it.

   B: I studied American history in high school.

   A: Then you _____ about Lincoln and the Civil War.

   B: Yes, I did.

2. **A:** Lincoln was a wonderful president.

   B: I agree. Without him, slavery _____ much longer.

   A: Farmers _____ slaves. That was terrible!

   B: I guess they just wanted to make money. They _____ rich without slaves.

   It's hard to believe that's how people were.

continued

3. **A:** Do you remember the story we read about Lewis and Clark?

   B: No. I _____ absent that day.

   A: You weren't absent. And we talked about it for almost a week.

   B: Oh. Then I _____ much attention.

   A: You _____ more attention in class. It was an interesting topic.

4. **A:** Lincoln's speech was very short.

   B: He _____ it very fast.

   A: I don't think he wrote it fast. I think he chose his words very carefully.

   B: Edward Everett's speech was two hours long. The audience _____ bored.

5. **A:** I rented the movie *Lincoln*, but it was very hard for me to understand.

   B: You _____ subtitles.

   A: I don't know how to do that.

   B: You _____ me. I do it all the time.

6.2 Past Regrets or Mistakes—*Should Have*

EXAMPLES	EXPLANATION
"I **should have given** a longer speech," thought Lincoln.	We use *should have* + the past participle to comment on mistakes or regrets or to rethink the advisability of a past decision.
I think Everett's speech was too long. He **shouldn't have talked** for such a long time.	We use *should not have* + the past participle to say that a past action was not advisable.

EXERCISE 2 Fill in the blanks to express past advisability. Use context clues to help you.

1. **A:** There was a great documentary on TV about Lincoln last night. You should ____*have seen*____ it.

   B: I didn't know about it. You should _____ me about it.

   A: I did tell you. You sometimes write things in your calendar. You should _____

   it down.

2. **A:** I rented the movie *Lincoln*, and I thought it was boring. I only watched about 20 minutes of it.

   B: You should _____ the whole thing. It was very good.

   A: I don't know much about American history. I never paid much attention to it in school.

   B: History's very important. You should _____ more attention.

3. A: Did you vote in the last election? I know you're a U.S. citizen now.

    B: I forgot about it. But I really don't like what some politicians are doing now.

    A: Then you should _____. You're giving me your opinion now. You should

    _____ your opinion on election day, too.

4. A: I gave a long speech in my English class, and everyone started to yawn. I should

    _____ it.

    B: You're right. It's best to shorten a speech as much as possible.

    A: You should _____ me. You're good at giving speeches.

    B: I didn't have time to help you. I had to prepare my own speech.

5. A: Slavery was a terrible thing. Farmers shouldn't _____ slaves to do their work.

    B: I agree. It's an awful thing to use people that way.

    A: They should _____ workers to do the work.

    B: They didn't want to pay workers. They wanted to make a lot of money for themselves.

ABOUT YOU Think of any regrets you have had about the following topics. Write your regret and what you now believe you should have done. Share your answers with your class.

Example: (a classmate)

    I told my classmate that her essay was terrible. **I should've told** *her something nice about it and* **given** *her advice to make it better.*

1. (a friend or family member) _____

_____

2. (a goal you had) _____

_____

3. (money) _____

_____

6.3 Past Possibility—*May / Might / Could + Have*

EXAMPLES	EXPLANATION
Why didn't the audience react after Lincoln's speech? They **could have been** surprised. They **may have expected** him to speak more. They **might have thought** that he wasn't finished.	We use *may/might/could + have* + the past participle to express a possibility about the past. It is not used to say something that was known to be true.
Everett's speech **may not have been** very interesting. Lincoln **might not have realized** how good his speech was.	To show negative possibility, we use *may not have* and *might not have*. We don't use *could not have* because it has a different meaning. (See Chart 6.7)

EXERCISE 3 Listen to the information about John Wilkes Booth. Write T for *true* or F for *false*. 🎧 6.3

1. John Booth was a better actor than his brother. _____

2. John Booth was familiar/known to people at the Ford Theater. _____

3. Edwin Booth saved the life of Lincoln's brother. _____

EXERCISE 4 Use past possibility to complete the text. Then listen again and check. 🎧 6.3

You may ___have learned___ about Abraham Lincoln in school, but here's something you might
   1. maybe you learned

_____. John Wilkes Booth, the man who assassinated Abraham Lincoln,
   2. maybe you didn't hear

was a famous actor. His brother, Edwin, was also an actor. John may _____
                                                                      3. maybe John was not

as good an actor as his brother, but he was very popular, especially with women. This could

_____ because he was very handsome. John Booth hated the president and was in
   4. maybe this was

favor of slavery. Edwin was on Lincoln's side. John and Edwin argued so much about Lincoln and slavery

that Edwin finally refused to have John in his house. John was planning to harm the president. At first, he

might _____ to kill the president, but later he decided to assassinate him.
        5. maybe he didn't plan

In a hotel in Pennsylvania, where John Booth often stayed, someone had written these words near a window:

"Abe Lincoln Departed This Life August 13th, 1864 By The Effects of Poison." After the death of Lincoln, people

thought that John Booth may _____ these words. But this is not certain. There were many
                             6. maybe John Booth wrote

people who hated Lincoln, and someone else could _____ that sentence.
                                                  7. maybe someone else wrote

In 1865, Lincoln was attending a play at the Ford Theater in Washington, DC. Booth was not an actor

in that play, but because he had acted there before, no one thought anything of his presence at the theater.

While Lincoln was sitting with his wife watching the play, Booth entered the president's box and shot him.

At first, it was thought that he may _____ Lincoln, but it was soon evident that
                                     8. maybe he stabbed Lincoln

Booth had shot him. The next morning, Lincoln died.

There's another interesting story about the Booth brothers. A few months before the assassination, Robert,

Lincoln's son, was standing on a train platform. Just as the train was arriving, Robert fell on the tracks. It could

_____ because of the crowds pushing. A stranger reached out and pulled Robert to
   9. maybe it was

safety just before the train arrived. This stranger was Edwin Booth, John Wilkes Booth's brother.

GRAMMAR IN USE

We use *should have* + the past participle when we give advice about the past. Parents often do this with their children, and friends often do this with each other.

> You **should've worn** a hat today. It's freezing!
> You **shouldn't have said** that her essay was bad.

6.4 Logical Conclusion about the Past—*Must Have*

EXAMPLES	EXPLANATION
Lincoln had very little schooling. He **must have been** very intelligent to learn so much on his own. I've seen pictures of Lincoln with other people. He looks so tall. He **must have been** over six feet tall.	We use *must have* + the past participle to make a logical conclusion, deduction, or estimate about the past. It means that something was probably true.
When Lincoln finished his speech after two minutes, some people thought that he **must not have been** finished. Lincoln thought, "They **must not have liked** my speech."	For the negative, we use *must not have* + the past participle. We don't use a contraction for *must not*.

EXERCISE 5 Fill in the blanks to express past probability or logical conclusion. Use the underlined verbs and context clues to help you. Answers may vary.

1. **A:** It sounds like Edwin Booth <u>was</u> a kind man.

   B: He risked his life to save Lincoln's son. He must <u>have been</u> a very kind man.

a.

   A: But Edwin's brother, John, was a terrible person.

   B: The brothers must not _____ each other.

b.

   A: It's obvious that they <u>didn't like</u> each other. Edwin didn't even want John in his house.

2. **A:** How did John Booth <u>enter</u> the theater to kill Lincoln?

   B: He must _____ like everyone else. He was a well-known actor, so people didn't

a.

   think anything of it.

   A: It's not easy to <u>plan</u> an assassination.

   B: He must _____ the assassination for a long time.

b.

   A: Today, presidents <u>have</u> a lot of security. They must not _____ so much security

c.

   in Lincoln's time.

3. **A:** Many people loved Lincoln. They must _____ very sad when he died. I <u>felt</u> very

a.

   sad when I read the story.

   B: But some people hated him. People who wanted to continue slavery must _____

b.

   happy when he died.

4. **A:** Slaves worked so hard. They must _____ a very hard life.

a.

   B: Yes. They <u>had</u> a very hard life.

   A: The slaves must _____ happy because Lincoln wanted to end slavery.

b.

   B: I'm sure they <u>were</u> very happy.

continued

5. **A:** Kennedy's death was such a tragedy.

   B: Who's Kennedy?

   A: You've never <u>heard</u> of Kennedy? He was so famous. You must _____ of him. There's a
   a.

   picture of him in this book on page 169.

   B: Wow. He <u>was</u> so handsome. He must _____ a movie star.
   b.

   A: No. He <u>was</u> an American president. He was assassinated in 1963 when he was only 46 years old.

   B: That's terrible. It must _____ a hard time for Americans.
   c.

   A: Yes, it <u>was</u>. I remember my grandparents telling me about it.

   B: How old were they at the time?

   A: They <u>were</u> in high school when it happened. They must _____ about 15 or 16 years old.
   d.

6. **A:** We read about Thomas Jefferson. Wasn't he the president who said "All men are created equal"? He must

   _____ against slavery.
   a.

   B: He <u>wasn't</u> against slavery. Even though he said that, he had a lot of slaves.

7. **A:** Have you ever seen the movie *Lincoln*?

   B: Is it a new movie? Did it just <u>come</u> out?

   A: It's not new. It must _____ out around 10 years ago.
   a.

   B: Was it good? Did you like it?

   A: I thought it was a little boring. I think I missed some of it because I must _____
   b.

   asleep in parts.

   B: I don't think I've ever <u>fallen</u> asleep during a movie.

FUN WITH GRAMMAR

Use your imagination. Read the situations and write as many sentences as you can about what the people could have done or what could have happened. Then give advice about what the people should have done. Share your answers as a class. Vote on the best ideas (and grammar) for each situation.

   *Pierre **could've told** his teacher he was sick. He **should have/shouldn't have** . . .*

1. Last week, Pierre was sick and couldn't do his homework. He copied a classmate's homework instead of telling his teacher he was sick.

2. Jill once went hiking by herself and got lost. She had left her cell phone in her car. She was rescued by a park ranger.

3. Bill and Tom often went surfing instead of going to English class. They both failed the class.

President Kennedy signs the order to block Soviet ships from delivering weapons to Cuba.

The CUBAN MISSILE CRISIS

Read the following article. Pay special attention to the words in bold. 🎧 6.4

It was October and people around the world were terrified. It seemed almost certain that World War III was about to begin, and the planet was in danger of complete destruction. The whole planet? Was this a science fiction story? Unfortunately, no. The danger of worldwide destruction was possible; some thought even probable. "October 27 is a day I'll never forget. The planet **could have been destroyed**," said a former CIA[1] agent. He was referring to October 27, 1962. "It **could have been** the end of the world, but here we are." Forty years later, many of the surviving leaders in this terrifying crisis met to reflect back on the time when their actions **could have resulted** in the end of the world.

From the 1940s, the United States and the Soviet Union[2] had not been friendly. Therefore, when the United States discovered that the Soviet Union was beginning to send nuclear missiles to Cuba, which is only about 90 miles from Florida, the American President, John F. Kennedy, saw this as a direct threat to national security.

These weapons **could have been** used to destroy major cities and military bases in the United States. Spy photos showed that missiles in Cuba **could have**

reached almost every part of the United States in a very short time.

On October 22, President Kennedy announced on TV that any attack from Cuba would be considered an attack from the Soviet Union, and he would respond with a full attack on the Soviets. He sent out the U.S. Navy to block Soviet ships from delivering weapons to Cuba. An attack on a U.S. ship **could have grown** into a full nuclear war. This crisis **could have changed** the world as we know it.

Fortunately, diplomacy[3] won over war. The Soviets agreed to send their missiles back and promised to stop building military bases in Cuba. In exchange, the United States promised to remove its missiles from Turkey. What **could have been** a tragic event is now only a chapter in history.

---

1 CIA: Central Intelligence Agency. A U.S. agency that gathers information about other countries
2 the Soviet Union: a country that included Russia, Ukraine, and 13 other republics. In 1991, the government collapsed and the Soviet Union broke up into 15 different countries, the largest of which is Russia.
3 diplomacy: skillful negotiation between countries to try to work out problems without fighting

COMPREHENSION Based on the reading, write T for *true* or F for *false*.

1. _____ Cuba was helping the Soviet Union in 1962.

2. _____ President Kennedy sent ships to attack the Soviet ships.

3. _____ In 2002, leaders met to discuss the decisions they had made in 1962.

THINK ABOUT IT Discuss the questions with a partner or in a small group.

1. Do people today see the world and other countries differently than they did when John F. Kennedy was president? Explain.

2. Are you worried about nuclear weapons in the modern day? Explain.

6.5 Past Direction Not Taken—*Could Have*

EXAMPLES	EXPLANATION
This crisis **could have changed** the world. The planet **could have been destroyed**.	We use *could have* + the past participle to show that it was possible for something to happen, but it didn't.
The U.S. **could have attacked** the Soviet ships. The U.S. **could have invaded** Cuba. But the president didn't do these things.	We use *could have* + the past participle to show that a past opportunity was not taken.
A: Before we got to class, I didn't know much about Lincoln. **B:** You **could have read** the article before class. Or you **could have googled** his name.	We use *could have* + the past participle to show suggestions that were not followed.

Note:

Remember, *could have* + the past participle can mean *may have/might have* (maybe). (See Chart 6.3)

GRAMMAR IN USE

We often use *I was so… I could have* + the past participle to exaggerate a result.

*I was so hungry, I **could've eaten** a horse!*

EXERCISE 6 Fill in the blanks with *have* + the past participle of one of the verbs from the box.

be killed	bomb	continue	end	make	send	start✓	speak

1. World War III could _____ *have started* _____ in 1962.

2. In 1962, the world as we know it could _____ .

3. Everyone could _____ .

4. The world leaders could _____ a wrong decision, but they made a sensible decision.

5. The Soviets could _____ to send ships to Cuba, but they stopped.

6. The Soviets could _____ missiles to all the major cities of the U.S. from Cuba.

7. The U.S. could _____ the missile sites in Cuba, but Kennedy decided against that.

8. Perhaps the leaders could _____ earlier and avoided the crisis completely.

EXERCISE 7 Fill in the blanks with *could have* + the past participle of one of the verbs from the box.

marry	kill	be	give	dress✓	break

1. Lincoln _____*could have dressed*_____ well, but he usually dressed poorly.

2. Lincoln _____ a farmer like his father, but he wanted to become a lawyer.

3. Mary Todd, Lincoln's wife, was from a wealthy family. Her parents thought she

   _____ a better man than Lincoln.

4. The South _____ away from the North, but Lincoln kept the nation together.

5. Lincoln _____ a long speech, but he decided to give a very short speech.

6. A train _____ Lincoln's son, but Edwin Booth saved him.

ABOUT YOU Write about a direction you could have taken in your life but didn't. Discuss your response with a partner.

   *I **could have gotten married** when I was 18, but I decided to finish college first.*

_____

_____

_____

EXERCISE 8 Write about something that almost happened in your country or another country you know about. Use *could have*. Discuss your response with a partner.

   *In Chile, 33 miners were trapped in a mine in 2010. They were there for over two months. They **could have died**, but luckily they were saved.*

_____

_____

_____

The Media and Presidential Elections

Read the following article. Pay special attention to the words in bold. 🎧 6.5

There's no doubt about it—the media influence elections. First newspapers, then radio, then television, and now social media—all of these have played an important part in getting out information and shaping public opinion.

One example of how the media **could influence** election results took place in the 1960 presidential race between John F. Kennedy and Richard Nixon. For the first time in history, two candidates debated[1] each other on TV. John Kennedy was the first candidate who understood the influence that television might have on the result of an election. Both candidates **had to answer** difficult questions. Many people who heard the Nixon-Kennedy debate on the radio thought that Nixon was the stronger candidate. But people who saw the debate on TV thought that the young, handsome Kennedy was the better candidate. Also, Nixon was sweating under the hot lights, and people thought that he **must have been** nervous and uncomfortable with the questions. It was a close election, but Kennedy won. Many people think Kennedy **couldn't have won** without TV.

If Kennedy was the first presidential candidate to understand the influence of TV, Barack Obama was the first candidate who understood the influence of social media. For the 2008 election, he reached out to the Internet generation; his opponent, John McCain, didn't use a computer. He depended on his wife to read and send e-mail. By the time of the 2012 election between Barack Obama and Mitt Romney, both parties understood the power of social media, but Obama's team **was able to collect** data online and use it more effectively.

When people started to use social media, they no longer **had to get** their information from TV or newspapers. With social media sites, people **could influence** each other. According to a media blog: "In the 2012 election, 30 percent of online users reported that they were urged to vote via social media by family, friends, or other social network connections, 20 percent actively encouraged others, and 22 percent posted their decision when they voted."

In the 2016 election between Donald Trump and Hilary Clinton, social media again played a role. Many now believe that "fake news" was spread purposefully on social media and that it **could have influenced** the election. One thing is for sure: media has throughout history impacted elections, and will no doubt continue to do so in the future.

---

[1] debate: to answer questions (before an audience) so that the public can judge who is the best candidate

John F. Kennedy (left) and Richard Nixon (far right) during their televised presidential debate

COMPREHENSION Based on the reading, write T for *true* or F for *false*.

1. _____ Some of the people who saw Kennedy on TV were influenced by his good looks.

2. _____ Candidates first started getting their political messages across with TV.

3. _____ Most people who use social media try to influence their friends and family in elections.

THINK ABOUT IT Discuss the questions with a partner or in a small group.

1. Why do you think radio listeners' reactions to the 1960 presidential candidates were different from those of TV viewers? Give your reasons.

2. Do you think the growing influence of social media is good or bad for politicians? Explain.

6.6 *Must Have* + Past Participle vs. *Had to* + Base Form

EXAMPLES	EXPLANATION
Kennedy and Nixon **had to answer** difficult questions. In the past, people **had to get** the news from newspapers or radio.	To show past necessity or obligation, we use *had to* + the base form. *Must*, for necessity or obligation, has no past form.
TV viewers thought that Nixon **must have been** nervous and uncomfortable during the debate. Social media sites **must have known** about fake news that was posted.	To show a logical conclusion or deduction in the past, we use *must have* + the past participle.

EXERCISE 9 Write *had to* + the base form for a past necessity. Write *must have* + the past participle for a past deduction or logical conclusion.

A: Remember the 2000 election between George W. Bush and Al Gore? It was very close, so they

_____had to count_____ the votes again to see who won. It took them five weeks to figure out who
        1. count

won the election.

B: Bush and Gore _____ nervous the whole time. They _____
                                    2. be   **3. wait**

a long time to find out the results.

A: This had never happened before. Everyone _____ surprised and confused at that
                                                                    4. be

time. There were so many problems counting the votes that the decision _____
                                                                                      5. *passive:* make

by the Supreme Court.

B: Did you vote in that election?

A: Of course. I always vote.

B: You usually vote for a Democrat, so you _____ for Gore.
                                                            6. vote

A: Yes, I did.

continued

B: You _____ very disappointed when they finally announced that Gore lost.
                    7. be

A: Yes, I was. What about you? Who did you vote for?

B: I _____ overtime that day, so I didn't vote. Anyway, one person's vote doesn't
                8. work

matter much.

A: It always matters!

6.7 Ability and Possibility in the Past

EXAMPLES	EXPLANATION
President Lincoln **could give** good speeches. He also had a good sense of humor and **was able to make** people laugh.	In affirmative statements, *could* + the base form means *used to be able to*. It shows ability or knowledge over a period of time. *Was/were able to* can also be used for ability over a period of time.
In October 1962, President Kennedy **was able to prevent** war. He **was able to convince** the Soviets to send back their missiles.	In affirmative statements, we use *was/were able to* for success in doing a single action. We don't use *could* for a single action.
I **couldn't understand** Lincoln's speech. **Were** you **able to understand** it?	In negative statements and questions, *could* and *was/were able to* are used interchangeably.
Our history test **could have been** much harder. I **could have given** a longer presentation, but I wanted to stay within the time limit.	We use *could have* + the past participle for an action that was possible but didn't happen.
Some people thought that Kennedy **couldn't have won** the election without TV. And maybe Barack Obama **couldn't have won** without social media.	We use *couldn't have* + the past participle to show that something was impossible in the past.
A: My grandparents liked to watch President Roosevelt on TV. **B:** They **couldn't have watched** him on TV. There was no TV back then.	*Couldn't have* + the past participle is used to show disbelief or to disprove a previous statement.

EXERCISE 10 Circle the correct words to complete each sentence. In some cases, both choices are possible, so circle both options.

1. I (*couldn't use*/*couldn't have used*) social media last night because I didn't have an Internet connection.

2. We listened to the Gettysburg Address online, but we (*couldn't understand*/*couldn't have understood*) it.

   The vocabulary was difficult for us.

3. Do you mean you listened to Lincoln's voice? You (*couldn't listen*/*couldn't have listened*) to Lincoln's voice.

   There was no recording of his voice. You must have listened to someone else reciting the Gettysburg Address.

4. (*Were you able to/Could you*) vote in the last election?

5. My mother has been a U.S. citizen for the last five years. She (*could vote/could have voted*) in the last election, but she's not interested in politics.

6. Around the time of the 2008 election in the United States, many people (*were able to use/could have used*) social media to get information.

7. You say President Kennedy was killed in a plane crash in 1999. That (*couldn't happen/ couldn't have happened*). He was assassinated in 1963. You're probably thinking of his son.

8. John McCain (*couldn't/wasn't able to*) use social media in 2008.

9. I (*couldn't/wasn't able to*) vote in the last election because I was out of the country.

10. My mother uses social media now. But she (*couldn't use/couldn't have used*) it five years ago. I had to show her how.

11. Lincoln (*could be/could have been*) a farmer like his father, but he was more interested in politics.

12. Lincoln's father (*couldn't read/couldn't have read*).

13. Lincoln (*was able to teach/could have taught*) himself law.

6.8 Modals in the Past: Continuous Forms

EXAMPLE	EXPLANATION
John Wilkes Booth **must have been planning** the assassination of Lincoln for a long time.	To give a continuous meaning to a past modal, we use modal + *have been* + the present participle.

EXERCISE 11 Fill in the blanks with one of the verbs from the box. Use the continuous form.

have	plan	protect	think	use✓	watch

1. Farmers shouldn't _____have been using_____ people as slaves.

2. What was Lincoln thinking after his speech? He might _____ about the audience reaction.

3. Lincoln must _____ doubts about his speech.

4. Booth must _____ the assassination for months.

5. Booth might _____ Lincoln for a long time.

6. Lincoln didn't have good protection. Someone should _____ him better.

SUMMARY OF UNIT 6

EXAMPLES	EXPLANATION
Lincoln **should have had** better protection. You **should have voted** in the last election. Every vote is important.	We use *should have* + the past participle to comment on mistakes or regrets or to rethink the advisability of a past decision.
In 1962, a nuclear attack was avoided. It **may have been** because of good diplomacy, or **might have been** because the Soviets feared a world war. When John Booth entered the theater, people **might have thought** he was an actor in the play that night.	*May/might/could have* + the past participle shows possibility about a past action or event.
People thought Nixon **must have been** nervous because he was sweating. The whole world **must have been** afraid in October 1962.	*Must have* + the past participle shows a logical conclusion or deduction about the past.
In 1962, a world war **could have started**, but it didn't. You **could have watched** the movie *Lincoln*, but you weren't interested.	*Could have* + the past participle shows a past direction not taken, a past possibility that didn't happen, or a past suggestion that wasn't followed.
A: I voted in the last presidential election. **B:** You **couldn't have voted**. You weren't even 18 at that time.	*Couldn't have* + the past participle can show disbelief or an attempt to disprove a previous statement.
When I was younger, I **could name** all the presidents in my country, but now I've forgotten. I **was able to read** Lincoln's speech without using a dictionary.	To express past ability, we use *could* + the base form or *was/were able to* + the base form. In affirmative statements, *could* means *used to be able to*. To show success in doing a single action, we use *was/were able to* for affirmative statements.
McCain didn't use a computer. He **had to depend** on his wife.	*Had to* + the base form shows an obligation or necessity in the past.
Booth **must have been planning** the assassination for some time.	For a continuous meaning of a past modal, we use modal + *have been* + the present participle.

REVIEW

Circle the correct words to complete each conversation. If both choices are possible, circle both.

1. **A:** Our grandparents (*had to rely*/*should have relied*) on TV or newspapers to get the news.

   B: I can't imagine a time without social media. Getting the news (*must*/*should*) have been so slow.

2. **A:** Did you read the article about Lincoln last night?

   B: I (*couldn't read*/*couldn't have read*) it. I didn't have time. What about you?

   A: I (*was able to*/*could*) read it, but I (*wasn't able to*/*couldn't*) understand every word.

3. **A:** Without Lincoln, slavery (*should*/*could*) have lasted much longer.

   B: Lincoln (*was able to end*/*could have ended*) slavery and keep the country together.

4. **A:** Lincoln's bodyguard (*couldn't*/*shouldn't*) have left the president alone. Where was he?

   B: I'm not sure. He (*might not*/*should not*) have been in the theater with Lincoln.

5. **A:** After Booth shot Lincoln, he jumped onto the stage.

   B: The audience (*had to think*/*must have thought*) this was part of the play.

6. **A:** Did they take Lincoln back to the White House?

   B: It was too far. They (*had to take*/*must have taken*) him to a house across the street. He died there the next morning.

7. **A:** When Lincoln died, the Secretary of War said something interesting, but people (*couldn't have agreed*/*weren't able to agree*) on what he said.

   B: Yes. He (*may*/*might*) have said, "Now he belongs to the ages" or he (*could*/*may*) have said, "Now he belongs to the angels."

8. **A:** When John Kennedy was president, a world war (*could happen*/*could have happened*), but it didn't. He had to make some difficult decisions.

   B: He (*could*/*must*) have made the right decision back then. He prevented a war.

9. **A:** Kennedy was another president who was assassinated. Who killed him?

   B: We don't know for sure, but the assassination (*must*/*could*) have been prevented. He was in an open car. He (*should*/*must*) have had better protection.

FROM GRAMMAR TO WRITING

PART 1 Editing Advice

1. After a modal, always use a base form.

   Lincoln should ~~has~~ *have* had more protection.

2. To express the past with some modals, use modal + *have* + the past participle.

   The bodyguard shouldn't ∧*have* left the theater.

3. Don't use *of* after a modal to express past. Use the auxiliary verb *have*.

   The Cuban Missile Crisis could ~~of~~ *have* caused a third world war.

4. Use the correct form for the past participle.

   Lincoln shouldn't have ~~went~~ *gone* to the theater that night.

5. *Can* is never used for the past.

   I ~~can't voted~~ *couldn't vote* in the last election.

6. Don't confuse *couldn't have* + the past participle with *couldn't* + the base form.

   When we read the article about Lincoln, I couldn't ~~have understood~~ *understand* a few words.

   If you didn't understand the article, you could ∧*have* use∧*d* a dictionary.

PART 2 Editing Practice

Some of the shaded words and phrases have mistakes. Find the mistakes and correct them. If the shaded words are correct, write *C*.

You probably know about the assassination of President Kennedy. But do you know about the tragic

death of his son in 1999?

John Junior was less than three years old when his father was killed. Because he was so young, he

~~can't remembered~~ *couldn't remember* much about him. But of course he must have heard *C* a lot about his father from his
1.   2.

family and from history. And he must remembered his uncle Robert, who was assassinated when John was
3.

eight years old.

John Junior could be a politician like his dad and uncles. He might have been discouraged from
4.   5.

going into politics, though, because both his father and his uncle were assassinated. Instead, he wanted

to become a lawyer. After awhile, though, he decided to publish a political magazine, so he must of been
6.

interested in politics.

Because he was so famous, he couldn't go out in public without being followed by photographers. When
7.

he flew on commercial airlines, other passengers asked him questions, took his picture, and wanted his

autograph. He can't got any privacy at all. So he decided to get his pilot's license and fly his own airplane.
8.

Only 15 months after getting his license, he planned to fly with his wife to his cousin's wedding in Massachusetts. They were supposed to be there after a short flight. Family members waited and waited. They couldn't have understood why John didn't arrive on time. After waiting all night with no word from John, they must knew that something terrible had happened.

The following morning, searchers found their suitcases on the shore. They concluded that the plane must has crashed. Family members couldn't go on with the wedding. Six days later, the bodies were found.

Experts tried to understand the reason for the crash. John didn't have a lot of experience as a pilot and flew over water, which is difficult for new pilots. Experts say he should have flew over land. Also, the weather wasn't good that evening. So he should have waited. He had broken his ankle a few months before. Some people think he may not been able to handle the foot pedals of the airplane.

This tragedy could be prevented. He could of used a commercial airline. Or he could have hired a professional pilot to take him there in his own airplane.

John Kennedy Jr. was only 38 years old. This was just one more tragedy for the Kennedy family.

WRITING TIP

When writing about past events, you can use the past modal forms to express your own opinions.

*President Kennedy **should not have been riding** in an open-topped car.*

*John Junior **should have waited** for better weather before flying.*

PART 3 Write

Read the two prompts. Choose one and write one or more paragraphs about it.

1. Write about an event that had a big impact on the U.S., your country, or the world. Or write about a tragedy that was avoided. Provide the sources you used to write your paragraphs. Give your opinion about the event.
2. Write about how the media influenced an election or a president you are familiar with. Provide the sources you used to write your paragraphs. Write your opinion about the situation.

PART 4 Edit

Reread the Summary of Unit 6 and the Editing Advice. Edit your writing from Part 3.

ONLINE INTERACTIONS

The Internet could be a very positive
step towards education, organization,
and participation in a meaningful society.

NOAM CHOMSKY

"Digital humanitarian" and National Geographic Explorer, Patrick Meier, analyzes crowd-sourced social media data and satellite imagery to help with disaster relief efforts around the world.

Pierre Omidyar AND eBAY

Read the following article. Pay special attention to the words in bold. 🎧 7.1

Did you ever want to sell a birthday present **that you didn't like?** Or an old guitar **that is taking up space in your closet?** In the old days, buyers and sellers were limited to newspapers, garage sales, and flea markets[1] in the area **where they lived.** But in the early 1990s, **when people started to use the Internet,** Pierre Omidyar had an idea. Omidyar, **who was working as a computer programmer,** realized that sellers no longer had to be limited to finding buyers **who lived in their local area.** He came up with the idea of eBay, **which he started as a hobby.** He didn't charge money at first because he wasn't sure eBay would work. Buying online requires you to trust sellers **whom you've never met.** But people liked eBay. Soon there was so much activity on eBay that his Internet service provider upgraded his site to a business account, **which was no longer free.** So Omidyar started to charge the sellers a small fee for each sale. Before long, this hobby grew into a big business.

By 1998, eBay had become so big that Omidyar needed a business expert. He brought in Meg Whitman, **whose knowledge of business helped make eBay a success.** She changed eBay from a company **that sold used things in several categories** to a large marketplace of 78 million items, both new and used, in 50,000 categories.

Many companies **that start out well on the Internet** later fail. When Whitman left the company, it started to decline. In 2008, John Donahoe was brought in as the new CEO[2]. He fired many people **who had been working there for years.** He understood that smartphones and tablets were changing the way **that people shopped;** people no longer had to shop from their home computers. He created an eBay app so that people could shop 24/7 and could pay with one click. eBay, **which was about to follow other Internet businesses into decline,** was brought back to life.

By the time Omidyar was 31, he was worth more than $7 billion. The money **that he has earned** is much more than he needs. He and his wife signed a promise, the Giving Pledge, to donate the majority of their wealth during their lifetime.

---

[1] flea market: a place where used items are sold
[2] CEO: Chief Executive Officer; the person in charge of a company

COMPREHENSION Based on the reading, write T for *true* or F for *false*.

1. _____ Omidyar did not start out with the intention of making money.

2. _____ Because of John Donahoe, eBay was starting to fail.

3. _____ Omidyar believes in sharing his wealth.

THINK ABOUT IT Discuss the questions with a partner or in a small group.

1. How much of your shopping do you do online? What are the advantages and disadvantages?

2. Why do you think John Donahoe fired a lot of people? Do you agree with his actions? Explain.

7.1 Adjective Clauses—Introduction

EXAMPLES	EXPLANATION
I received a birthday present **that I didn't like.** You have to trust sellers **whom you've never met.** Omidyar changed to a business account, **which was not free.**	An adjective clause is a group of words that contains a subject and verb. It describes or modifies a noun before it. In these examples, the adjective clauses describe the nouns: *birthday present*, *sellers*, and *business account*.

Notes:

1. The following words mark the beginning of an adjective clause: *who, whom, that, which, whose, where, when.*

2. Sometimes an adjective clause begins with no marker.

 *I received a birthday present **I didn't like**.*

3. Some adjective clauses are set apart from the rest of the sentence by commas.

 *John Donahoe saved eBay, **which was declining**.*

4. An adjective clause can follow any noun in a sentence. Often it follows immediately after the noun.

 *The company hired Meg Whitman, **who knew a lot about business**.*

 *Meg Whitman, **who left the company to go into politics**, helped make eBay a success.*

ABOUT YOU Notice the underlined adjective clause in each sentence. Then check the sentences that are true about you. Explain your answers to a partner.

1. _____ I have a lot of old things <u>that take up space in my house</u>.

2. _____ I sell things <u>that I don't use anymore</u>.

3. _____ I collect things <u>that someone might want to buy</u>.

4. _____ I have friends <u>who buy and sell things online</u>.

EXERCISE 1 Listen to the sentences about the online retailer Amazon. Write T for *true* or F for *false*. 🎧 7.2

1. _____ Amazon began as an online bookstore.

2. _____ Bezos's choice of house was influenced by ideas about online companies.

3. _____ Bezos's parents immediately understood his plan.

EXERCISE 2 Listen again and complete the adjective clause. 🎧 7.3

1. Amazon was founded in 1994 by Jeff Bezos, _____*who*_____ predicted that the Internet offered an opportunity to make money.

2. Amazon, _____ is now the largest online retailer, began by selling books.

3. First, Bezos made a list of about 20 products _____ could be sold online. He eventually decided on selling books.

4. Bezos wanted a name _____ began with "A." He decided on Amazon, because it is a place _____ is "exotic and different."

5. But a good company name is not enough. Bezos needed to hire people _____ talents would improve the company.

6. Since many big Internet companies started in a garage, Bezos decided to buy a house _____ had a garage.

7. Bezos needed money to start his company. He went to his parents, _____ first response was "What's the Internet?"

8. Some people thought his parents would lose all the money _____ they invested.

9. His parents, _____ invested $300,000 in his business, believed in their son's project.

10. Bezos created a place _____ customers could make recommendations to other users.

EXERCISE 3 Underline the adjective clause in each sentence.

1. Amazon was founded in 1994 by Jeff Bezos, <u>who predicted that the Internet offered an opportunity to make money.</u>

2. Amazon, which is now the largest online retailer, began by selling books.

3. First, he made a list of about 20 products that could be sold online.

4. Bezos decided on the name *Amazon* because it is a place that is "exotic and different."

5. But a good name is not enough. He needed to hire people whose talents would improve the company.

6. Since many big Internet companies started in a garage, he decided to buy a house that had a garage.

7. He needed money. He went to his parents, whose first response was "What's the Internet?"

8. Some people thought his parents would lose all the money that they invested.

9. The 1990s was a time when people were just beginning to use the Internet.

10. Bezos created a place where customers could make recommendations to other users.

7.2 Relative Pronoun as Subject

The relative pronouns *who, that,* and *which* can be the subject of the adjective clause.

THINGS

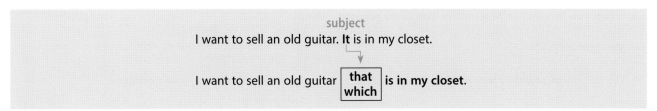

PEOPLE

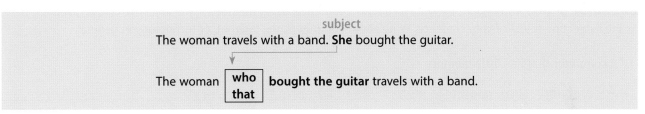

Notes:

1. Use the relative pronouns *that* and *which* for things and use *who* and *that* for people.

2. A verb in the adjective clause must agree in number with its subject.

    People *who* ***buy*** *things online like the convenience.*

    A person *who* ***buys*** *things online likes the convenience.*

GRAMMAR IN USE

Notice that *that* is used for both things and people. In other words, *that* is a safe choice when the relative pronoun is the subject of the adjective clause.

   I have a friend ***that*** *plays electric guitar.*

   She has a guitar ***that*** *is easy to find on eBay.*

EXERCISE 4 Fill in the blanks with *who* or *that* + the correct form of the verb, using the tense given to complete the adjective clauses.

1. I have a friend _____who/that buys_____ all her books online.

                   present: buy

2. People _____ books online can write reviews and give a book 1-5 stars.

                  present: buy

3. A person _____ the reviews can be influenced by the opinions of others.

                  present: read

4. There are many neighborhood bookstores _____ business and had to close

                                        past: lose

because of online competition.

continued

5. There are people _____ successful businesses on the Internet.

present perfect: create

6. Omidyar and Bezos are two people _____ the potential of the Internet.

past: understand

7. Jeff Bezos is lucky to have parents _____ in his idea.

past: believe

8. Friendster and MySpace were two Internet companies _____ successful and

past: become

   then failed.

9. When you buy something online, you often see this: "People _____ this product

past: buy

   also bought. . . "

10. You are encouraged to buy products _____ similar to your purchase.

present: be

11. Pierre Omidyar gives a lot of his money to organizations _____ people in need.

present: help

EXERCISE 5 Work with a partner. Write a complete sentence, using the noun + the adjective clause given as the subject or object of your sentence. Write about computers, the Internet, or technology in general.

1. a computer that has little memory

   <u>A computer that has little memory is not useful today. OR</u>

   <u>No one wants a computer that has little memory.</u>

2. students who don't have a computer

   _____

3. children who spend all their time playing computer games

   _____

4. e-mail that comes from an unknown sender

   _____

5. websites that offer music downloads

   _____

6. people who don't know anything about computers

   _____

7. kids who are born into today's world

   _____

8. a flash drive that has 10 MB of memory

   _____

7.3 Relative Pronoun as Object

The relative pronouns *who(m)*, *that*, and *which* can be the object of the adjective clause.

THINGS

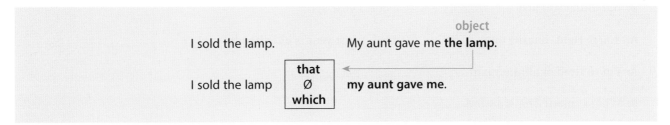

PEOPLE

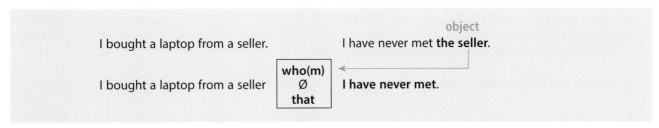

Notes:

1. The relative pronoun is usually omitted in conversation when it is the object of the adjective clause.

    *I sold the lamp ~~that~~ **my aunt gave me**.*

    *I bought a laptop from a seller ~~whom~~ **I've never met**.*

2. *Whom* is considered more formal than *who* when used as the object of the adjective clause. However, as seen in the note above, the relative pronoun is usually omitted in conversation.

    Pierre Omidyar is a man whom I greatly admire. (very formal)

    Pierre Omidyar is a man who OR *that I greatly admire. (common)*

    Pierre Omidyar is a man I greatly admire. (most common when speaking)

3. When there is no new subject after the relative pronoun, the relative pronoun is the subject of the adjective clause and cannot be omitted.

    *My neighborhood has a bookstore **that has a reading hour for children**.*

    NOT *My neighborhood has a bookstore ~~that~~ has a reading hour for children.*

4. When a new subject is introduced in the adjective clause, the relative pronoun is the object of the adjective clause and can be omitted.

    *My neighborhood has a bookstore **(that) the children love**. (the children → new subject)*

> **GRAMMAR IN USE**
>
> A common error is to repeat the object at the end of the adjective clause. Be sure to avoid this.
>
> *I bought it from a seller **that I've never met**.*
>
> NOT *I bought it from a seller **that I've never met ~~him~~**.*

EXERCISE 6 In the conversations below, use the underlined words and other context clues to help you fill in the blanks with adjective clauses. Answers may vary.

1. **A:** I just bought a new computer.

   B: But didn't you just _____*buy*_____ one a year ago?

a.

   A: You're right. But the one _*(that) I bought*_ last year is old already.

b.

2. **A:** I'm so tired of all the spam _____.

a.

   B: What's spam? That's a word _____.

b.

   A: You don't <u>know</u> the word "spam"? It's junk e-mail. Everyone <u>gets</u> it.

   B: I don't <u>get</u> much spam. I have an e-mail address _____ just for shopping online.

c.

   I don't <u>use</u> it for anything else. I often <u>buy</u> shoes online.

   A: How do you know if they're going to fit?

   B: The shoes _____ are always the same, so I don't have to worry about the size.

d.

   Besides, if I don't want the item, I can return it.

   A: Don't you have to pay to send things back?

   B: That depends on the company _____. If you <u>use</u> certain companies, they

e.

   offer free returns. You should try online shopping. You can save a lot of time.

   A: You <u>prefer</u> that method. But that's not for me. The method _____ is driving to

f.

   a mall, getting exercise by walking into the store, trying on the shoes, and walking back to my car.

   B: I don't <u>need</u> exercise walking into a store. I get all the exercise _____ with

g.

   my new running shoes.

3. **A:** Do you want to see a picture of my new girlfriend, Nina?

   B: I didn't know you <u>had</u> a new girlfriend. What happened to the last girlfriend

   _____? Carla, right?

a.

   A: Yeah, Carla. She thought I spent too much time taking pictures, texting, and using the Internet.

   So she broke up with me.

   B: I see you still <u>have</u> some pictures of Carla on your phone.

   A: Oh, right. I'd better delete the pictures _____ of Carla before Nina sees them.

b.

   B: Let me <u>give</u> you some advice. You'd better put down your phone and spend more time with Nina.

   A: I hope I can follow the advice _____ me. If not, I'll lose Nina.

c.

4. A: Can I see your new phone? Wow. Look at all the apps _____.

   _{a.}

B: I know I've got a lot of apps.

A: You must spend a lot of money on new apps.

B: Not really. Most of the apps _____ are free.

   _{b.}

A: I see you've got a new phone case. It's not as cool as the last one _____. Why did

   _{c.}

   you change?

B: This was a gift from my grandmother. It was the present _____ me for my

   _{d.}

   birthday. I don't want her to feel hurt. I just wish she'd <u>give</u> me a gift card and let me pick out my

   own present.

A: I'm sure she meant well.

5. A: I found a great site for planning a trip. Owners <u>rent</u> out their houses to vacationers. Look. I'll show it

   to you.

B: Wow! I <u>see</u> that's a beautiful house with a swimming pool. Does it really look like that?

A: The pictures _____ here are pretty accurate. This is the house

   _{a.}

   _____ last summer, and it was great. The house _____

   _{b.}   _{c.}

   next year is even more beautiful.

B: Why don't you just <u>get</u> a hotel room? What's the advantage of renting a home?

A: The hotel rooms _____ in the past were small. By renting a home, we have

   _{d.}

   a kitchen, so we can cook and save money that way.

B: How much does it cost?

A: This one costs $1,500 for the week, plus a security deposit.

B: Wow! $1,500 sounds like a lot of money.

A: We split the money between the number of people in our group. And the more friends

   _____ to go with us, the cheaper it'll be.

   _{e.}

B: If you can't <u>find</u> anyone else, I'll go with you!

7.4 Relative Pronoun as Object of Preposition

The relative pronoun can be the object of a preposition (*to, about, with, of,* etc.). Usually the preposition is at the end of the adjective clause.

PEOPLE

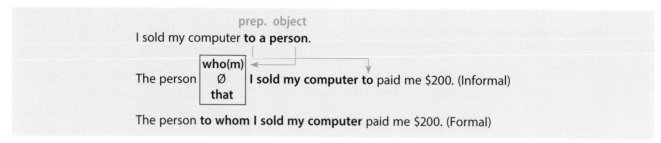

THINGS

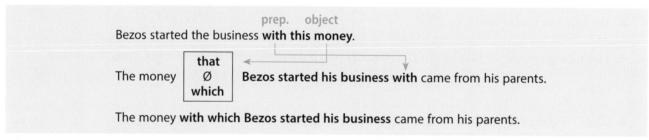

Notes:

1. We usually put the preposition at the end of the adjective clause and omit the relative pronoun.

    The person *I sold my computer to* paid me $200.

    Do you know the person *you bought your laptop from?*

2. In very formal English, we put the preposition before *whom* and *which*. *That* is not used directly after a preposition.

    The person **to whom I sold my computer** paid me $200. (NOT: to who or to that)

    The money **with which Bezos started his business** came from his parents. (NOT: to that)

EXERCISE 7 Make these sentences more informal by taking out the relative pronoun and putting the preposition at the end of the adjective clause.

1. There are several travel websites in which I am interested.

    There are several travel websites I'm interested in.

2. There is a new website about which everyone is talking.

    _____

3. The link on which you click will take you to that site.

    _____

4. The information for which you are looking can be found on that site.

    _____

5. Vacation Rentals is not a website with which I'm familiar.

_____

6. Finding a vacation home online is not a method to which I'm accustomed.

_____

7. The house on which we decided is in the mountains.

_____

8. The owner to whom I spoke was very helpful.

_____

9. There's one thing about which I'm sure: Renting a vacation home is a good deal.

_____

EXERCISE 8 Combine the two sentences to make one. Write each sentence in the formal and informal way, starting with the words given.

1. This site has vacation rentals. I'm interested in these vacation rentals.

This site _has vacation rentals (which/that) I'm interested in._

This site _has vacation rentals in which I'm interested._

2. I'm interested in a house. The house has three bedrooms.

The house _____

The house _____

3. I'm taking a vacation with some friends. These friends want to rent a house.

The friends _____

The friends _____

4. I got a lot of information from a person. I spoke to the person.

I got a lot of information from the person _____

I got a lot of information from the person _____

5. We are responsible for only one thing. We are responsible for cleaning the house.

The only thing _____

The only thing _____

The FREECYCLE NETWORK™

Read the following article. Pay special attention to the words in bold. 🎧 7.4

Do you have an old computer that you don't need anymore? Or are you trying to find an extra TV but don't want to spend money? Then The Freecycle Network™ is for you. The name combines the word "free" and the word "recycle." The Freecycle Network™ is an online community **whose members help each other get what they need—for free!** Unlike eBay, Freecycle is a geographical community. You join in the area **where you live**.

The Freecycle Network™ was created in 2003 by Deron Beal, **whose idea was to protect the environment by keeping usable goods out of landfills.** Americans generate almost five pounds of garbage per person per day. About 55 percent of this garbage is buried in what is called a "landfill." Buried garbage can cause environmental problems. This garbage often contains useful items that other people may need.

Beal also wanted to encourage neighbors to help each other. He started The Freecycle Network™ in Tucson, Arizona, **where he lives**. He sent an e-mail to about 30 or 40 friends to see if they wanted to join. His Freecycle community grew quickly. Today there are more than seven million members in over five thousand groups around the world. The Freecycle Network™ reports that its members are keeping 500 tons of goods out of landfills each day.

How do members deliver or receive the item? The person **whose offered item you want** will let you know the place **where you can pick it up**. Very often, the item will be left in front of the giver's house for the receiver. The giver will specify a time **when the receiver can pick up the item**. Sometimes the giver and receiver will meet.

Via The Freecycle Network, people not only interact online, but also in person. It is a great way to use the Internet to build a community **where people with common interests come together.**

Artist Mike Stilkey creates art pieces by painting books that are thrown away

COMPREHENSION Based on the reading, write T for *true* or F for *false*.

1. _____ Users of Freecycle sometimes have to send packages to other cities.

2. _____ Unwanted items are often buried in a landfill.

3. _____ Freecycle is similar to eBay.

THINK ABOUT IT Discuss the questions with a partner or in a small group.

1. Would you use Freecycle, or do you prefer to buy new products? Give your reasons.

2. Do you think you generate five pounds of garbage per day? How do you feel about your garbage, and what do you do about it?

7.5 Place and Time in Adjective Clauses

EXAMPLES	EXPLANATION
The city **where I live** has a recycling group. The city **in which I live** has a recycling group. The city **(that) I live in** has a recycling group.	We can express place in an adjective clause with: • *where* to mean "in that place" • a preposition + *which* (formal) • *that/which* or Ø + clause + preposition
Please specify times **(when) you 'll be home.**	We can express time in an adjective clause with *when* or Ø.
This is the place **where I used to live.** This is the restaurant **that I'm always talking about.** I can't remember a time **when there was no Internet.** I felt bad that time **that I lost a person's package.**	*Where* means *in that place* or *there.* *That* refers to the noun that precedes it. *When* means *at that time* or *then.* *That* refers to the noun that precedes it.

EXERCISE 9 Circle the correct words to complete the conversation. In some cases, both choices are correct, so circle both options.

A: Grandma, I can't imagine a time (*when*/*where*) there were no computers.
              1.

B: It wasn't such a long time ago. When I was in high school, we had never seen a computer. We used typewriters

   to write our papers. There was a special room in my school (*where*/*that*) you could go and use the typewriters.
                                                                                          2.

A: You mean like a computer lab?

B: Something like that. Later I read a book about computers, and I wanted to know more. At the

   time (*Ø*/*when*) I first became interested in computers, I didn't know anyone who had one.
          3.

A: Did you buy your computer online?

B: Oh, no. I'm talking about a time (*when*/*about which*) no one had even heard of the Internet. There were very
                                         4.

   few stores (*Ø*/*where*) you could buy computers. And they were so expensive.
        5.

A: More than $500?

B: More than $2,000!

continued

A: Wow! It must have had a lot of memory.

B: Absolutely not. I'm talking about a time (*when/that*) 100 kilobytes was considered a lot of memory. The
                                                                6.
computer tower was very big. I had to find a place under my desk (*that/where*) I could put the tower.
                                                                                    7.

A: Who taught you to use it?

B: I had to find a time (*which/when*) I could study on my own because I had no one to help me. Later I started
                            8.
taking a class at a community college near my house. Did you know that there was a time (*Ø/when*) most
                                                                                            9.
computer students were guys? I was the only woman in the class.

A: Grandma, I'm so proud of you. What happened to your first computer?

B: For many years, it was in my garage. Then I decided to put it on a website (*where/that*) people go in order to
                                                                                    10.
buy old computers.

A: Why would anyone want such an old computer?

B: There are collectors who consider my first computer a collector's item.

A: Cool. So, Grandma, you were ahead of your time.

B: I guess I was. But now, when I have a computer question, I have to ask my grandchildren. It's just hard to find
a time (*when/where*) you're not too busy with schoolwork and other activities.
        11.

A "grape" colored iMac
personal computer from
the late 1990's

ABOUT YOU Write the name of three websites you use frequently. Tell what a person can find on these websites. Share your answers with a partner.

1. Weather.com is a site where you can find out the weather in your area.

2. CCC.edu is a site that has a listing of college courses in Chicago.

3. _____

4. _____

5. _____

ABOUT YOU Write three years or time periods. Tell what happened in your life at that time. Share your answers with a partner.

1. 2012 was the year (when) I got married.

2. December 22 through January 5 were the weeks during which we had our winter break.

3. _____

4. _____

5. _____

7.6 *Whose* in Adjective Clauses

Whose is the possessive form of *who*. It stands for *his, her, its, their,* or the possessive form of the noun.

SUBJECT OF ADJECTIVE CLAUSE

subject

Freecycle is an online community. **Its members** help each other.

Freecycle is an online community **whose members help each other.**

subject

People can donate their kids' old clothes. **Their children** are growing.

People **whose children are growing** can offer their kids' old clothes.

continued

OBJECT OF ADJECTIVE CLAUSE

object
You should always thank the person. You received **her item**.

You should always thank the person **whose item you received**.

object
You want **a person's item**. The person will suggest a way for you to get it.

The person **whose item you want** will suggest a way for you to get it.

EXERCISE 10 Imagine you see these comments on a recycling website. Write one sentence using *whose* to tell what each person needs or offers to give away.

1. "My basement was flooded. I need new furniture."

   A person <u>whose basement was flooded needs new furniture.</u>

2. "My radio broke. I need a new one."

   A person _____

3. "My daughter needs a violin. She's in the school orchestra."

   A person _____

4. "My bicycle was stolen. I need one to get to work."

   A person _____

5. "My new apartment is small. I want to give away a lot of books."

   A person _____

6. "My laptop doesn't work anymore. I need a new one."

   A person _____

7. "My children are grown now. I want to give away their toys."

   A person _____

8. "My kids are starting school. I need two backpacks."

   A person _____

EXERCISE 11 Use the sentence given to form an adjective with *whose*.

1. The person _____whose tablet I bought_____ wanted to get the latest model.

I bought this person's tablet.

2. The person _____ was very helpful.

I found this person's vacation rental online.

3. The person _____ didn't charge me for shipping.

I bought this person's computer online.

4. I have a friend on a social media site _____ .

I don't like this person's profile picture.

5. The person _____ is an old friend of mine.

I received her picture by e-mail.

6. I need to re-enter the e-mail addresses of people _____ .

I accidentally deleted their names.

7. The person _____ is my best friend.

You see his picture on my page.

8. The teacher _____ has a course website.

We're taking this teacher's class.

7.7 Adjective Clauses after Indefinite Pronouns

EXAMPLES	EXPLANATION
Everyone **who sells on eBay** has to pay a fee. I know someone **who always shops online**.	The relative pronoun after an indefinite pronoun (*someone, something, everyone, everything, no one, nothing, anything*) can be the subject of the adjective clause. The relative pronoun cannot be omitted.
No one wanted anything **(that) I posted online**. Almost everyone **(that/who/whom) I know** has posted a photo online.	The relative pronoun after an indefinite pronoun can be the object of the adjective clause. In this case, it is usually omitted.

EXERCISE 12 Fill in the blanks with an adjective clause. Use the underlined verb to help you. Use the correct verb tense.

1. **A:** I know you've <u>gotten</u> a lot of things online. How has that worked out for you?

   B: I'm happy with everything ___(that) I have gotten___ online.

2. **A:** Do you <u>need</u> to buy anything for your new apartment?

   B: Not anymore. I found almost everything _____ for free on Freecycle.

3. **A:** I heard you've <u>bought</u> a lot of things online.

   B: So far, everything _____ has been great.

continued

4. A: My mother still <u>uses</u> a flip phone. Can you believe it?

    B: I don't know anyone _____ a flip phone anymore. Everyone

    _____ uses a smartphone.

    A: I <u>know</u> one person who doesn't use a cell phone at all—my grandpa.

5. A: I <u>sent</u> you an e-mail about vacation rentals. Did you get it?

    B: I didn't see anything _____ me about vacation rentals. Oh, wait.

    Now I see it.

6. A: Something _____ me about this shopping website was very important,

    but I forgot it.

    B: I <u>told</u> you that this site offers free shipping.

7. A: I <u>saw</u> the beautiful pictures of your vacation rental online. Were the pictures accurate?

    B: The house was exactly like everything _____ in the pictures. Maybe the house

    was even prettier.

8. A: I heard you can <u>rent</u> this vacation home online. Do you have to pay a security deposit?

    B: Yes. Everyone _____ this house has to pay a security deposit.

9. A: Do you <u>want</u> to spend money on a new bicycle or get a used one for free?

    B: I don't know anyone _____ to spend money when you can get something for free.

10. A: Grandma, you should <u>have</u> a social media account. You can communicate with all your friends that way.

    B: I don't know anyone my age _____ a social media account. People my age prefer to pick

    up the phone and talk.

Girls Who CODE

Read the following article. Pay special attention to the words in bold. 🎧 7.5

The first fully developed computer program, **which was published around 1843**, appeared around a hundred years before the beginning of the modern computer age. And it was created by Ada Lovelace, **the daughter of the famous English poet, Lord Byron**. Ada achieved this when the world of science and technology was dominated by men such as Charles Babbage, **with whom Ada collaborated**. Babbage, **whose Analytical Engine is regarded by many as the first real computer**, was mainly concerned with the calculating power of his machine, but Ada realized that computers would be able to create art, music, and much more.

Fast-forward to the modern day, and women still play only a small part in the world of computer technology. In the United States, **where tech jobs are in one of the fastest growing employment sectors**, fewer than one in five computer science graduates are women, and the gap between the genders, **which has always been large**, has widened in recent years. In 1995, for example, 37 percent of computer scientists were women, but by 2017, that figure had fallen to just 24 percent.

This situation is a source of great concern to Reshma Saujani, **who founded the nonprofit organization Girls Who Code in 2012**. Its sole mission is to reduce the gender gap in technology. In its first six years, the organization reached 90,000 girls from all backgrounds and across all 50 states. Using the Internet, summer camps, and a network of clubs across the country, Girls Who Code works to increase female representation in the tech industry. Despite the 2017 gender statistics, **which were an obvious disappointment**, Saujani believes that things are beginning to change and that the number of women in the field will be equal to that of men by 2027.

Ada Lovelace would certainly have approved.

COMPREHENSION Based on the reading, write T for *true* or F for *false*.

1. _____ Ada Lovelace designed the first real computer, the Analytical Engine.

2. _____ Less than 20 percent of computer science graduates in the U.S. are women.

3. _____ Reshma Saujani is not optimistic/hopeful about the future of women in computing.

THINK ABOUT IT Discuss the questions with a partner or in a small group.

1. Do you think it is possible for an organization like Girls Who Code to make a difference in a traditionally male-dominated employment area? Why or why not?

2. How important is it that there should be a balance between the genders in a given profession? Explain.

7.8 Nonessential Adjective Clauses

EXAMPLES	EXPLANATION
Technology was dominated by men such as Charles Babbage, **with whom Ada Lovelace collaborated.** Girls Who Code, **which operates in the U.S.,** has reached almost 90,000 girls so far. Most people have heard of Steve Jobs, **whose name is associated with Apple computers.**	Some adjective clauses are not essential to the meaning of the sentence. A nonessential adjective clause adds extra information. The sentence is complete without it. • A nonessential adjective clause is separated by commas from the main part of the sentence. • A nonessential adjective clause begins with *who, whom, which, where, when,* or *whose.* • *That* is not used in a nonessential adjective clause.

EXERCISE 13 Put commas in the following sentences to separate the nonessential adjective clause from the main clause.

1. The first modern computer, which was called ENIAC, took up a lot of space.

2. ENIAC was created in 1942 when the U.S. was involved in World War II.

3. Personal computers which were introduced in the 1970s were smaller and faster than previous computers.

4. Reshma Saujani whose name is not widely recognized is making a big difference in many women's lives.

5. Bill Gates went to Harvard University where he developed the programming language BASIC.

6. Bill Gates dropped out of Harvard to work with Paul Allen who was his old high school friend.

7. Bill Gates and his wife, Melinda, set up the Bill and Melinda Gates Foundation which helps people in need all over the world.

8. Jeff Bezos got money from his parents who lent him $300,000 to start Amazon.

9. Gina has started to take free classes with Girls Who Code which started a project at her school.

10. The iMac which was popular in the 1990s came in various colors such as grape and blueberry.

11. Apple computers have been popular due to their attractive design which is often sleek and colorful.

12. The new company is in California where many tech giants are based.

7.9 Essential vs. Nonessential Adjective Clauses

EXAMPLES	EXPLANATION
Reshma Saujani, **whose organization helps girls get into computer science**, believes the gender balance in the field will improve. Girls Who Code is based in the U.S., **where it has reached girls in all 50 states.**	In these examples, the adjective clause is nonessential because we can identify the noun in the main clause without the added information. Read the sentences without the adjective clause. The adjective clause adds extra information to an already complete sentence.
Smartphones changed the way **(that) people shop.** Jeff Bezos wanted a company name **that began with A.** People **who want quick information** can use the Web.	In these examples the adjective clause is essential, because, without it, we can't identify the noun. If we take the adjective clause out, the noun isn't properly identified, and the idea isn't complete.
(a) Saujani, **who founded Girls Who Code in 2012,** thinks there should be more women in computer science. b) The computer, **which was invented in the 1940s,** has become part of our everyday lives. (c) The computer **that I bought two years ago** is slow compared to today's computers.	In example (a), Saujani is unique and does not need to be identified. The clause is nonessential. Example (b) refers to the whole class of computers as an invention. The clause is nonessential. Example (c) refers to only one computer, which is identified by the adjective clause. The clause is essential.
The computer **(that) she just bought** has a lot of memory. The Web, **which Tim Berners-Lee created,** is a useful tool.	In an essential adjective clause, the relative pronoun *that* can be used or omitted. In a nonessential adjective clause, the relative pronoun *that* cannot be used. The relative pronoun cannot be omitted.

Notes:

Here are some questions to help you decide if the adjective clause needs commas. If the answer to any of these questions is *yes*, then the adjective clause is set off by commas.

✓ Can I put the adjective clause in parentheses?
> Google **(which was founded in 1998)** *is a popular search engine.*

✓ If the adjective clause is deleted, does the sentence still make sense?
> *Google is a popular search engine.*

✓ Is the noun a unique person, place, or thing?
> ***Reshma Saujani,** who is an advocate for more women in computer science, founded Girls Who Code.*

✓ If the noun is plural, am I including all members of a group?
> *Personal computers, **which became popular in the 1990s,** have changed the way we get information.*
> *(all personal computers)*

EXERCISE 14 Decide which of the following sentences contain a nonessential adjective clause. Put commas in those sentences. If the sentence doesn't need commas, write *OK*.

1. People who text use abbreviations. OK

2. My father, who texted me a few minutes ago, is sick.

3. Kids who spend a lot of time on the computer don't get much exercise.

4. The Freecycle Network™ which was created in 2003 helps keep things out of landfills.

continued

5. People usually have a lot of things they don't need.

6. Saujani whose organization has an impressive website has provided help to thousands of girls around the country.

7. At first, Amazon was a company that sold only books.

8. Meg Whitman who ran eBay for 10 years left the company in 2008.

9. Young women can go to the Girls Who Code website where there is a lot of useful information.

10. The Windows operating system which was developed by Microsoft came out in 1985.

11. Did you like the story that we read about Reshma Saujani?

12. The computer that I bought three years ago doesn't have enough memory.

13. The Web which is one of the most important inventions of the 20th century has changed the way people get information.

14. Bill Gates who created Microsoft with his friend became a billionaire.

15. Steve Jobs who died in 2011 helped create the Apple computer.

16. It's hard to remember a time when computers were not part of our everyday lives.

EXERCISE 15 Combine the two sentences into one. The sentence in parentheses ( ) is not essential to the main idea of the sentence. It adds extra information.

1. eBay is now a large corporation. (It was started in Pierre Omidyar's house.)

   eBay, which was started in Pierre Omidyar's house, is now a large corporation.

2. Reshma Saujani runs Girls Who Code. (She thinks there should be more women in computing.)

3. Pierre Omidyar started eBay as a hobby. (His wife became part of the company.)

4. eBay hired Meg Whitman in 1998. (More expert business knowledge was needed at that time to run the company.)

5. In 2008, eBay hired John Donahoe. (He fired a lot of people.)

6. E-mail did not become popular until the 1990s. (It was first created in 1972.)

_____

_____

7. Pierre Omidyar had to charge money for each sale. (His idea started to become popular.)

_____

_____

8. Saujani's focus is on the area of computer science. (Few women work there at the moment.)

_____

_____

7.10 Descriptive Phrases

Compare sentences (a) with an adjective clause to sentences (b) with a descriptive phrase.

EXAMPLES	EXPLANATION
(a) There are millions of items **that are listed on eBay**. (b) There are millions of items **listed on eBay**.	This descriptive phrase begins with a past participle.
(a) I sold some things **that were taking up space in my closet**. (b) I sold some things **taking up space in my closet**.	This descriptive phrase begins with a present participle (verb -ing).
(a) Pierre Omidyar, **who is the founder of eBay**, is one of the richest men in the world. (b) Pierre Omidyar, **the founder of eBay**, is one of the richest men in the world.	This descriptive phrase is a noun phrase. It gives a definition or more information about the preceding noun. This kind of descriptive phrase is called an _appositive_.
(a) Pierre Omidyar, **who is from France**, created eBay. (b) Pierre Omidyar, **from France**, created eBay.	This descriptive phrase begins with a preposition (_with, in, from, of_, etc.).

Notes:

1. We can only shorten an adjective clause to a descriptive phrase if the relative pronoun is followed by the verb _be_.

    I often use the computers ~~that are~~ in the library.

2. A descriptive phrase can be essential or nonessential. A nonessential phrase is set off by commas.

    I have two computers. The computer **in my bedroom** is newer. (Essential)

    The Amazon office, **in Seattle**, has over 100,000 employees. (Nonessential)

3. An appositive is always nonessential.

    Amazon, **an online retailer**, is a well-known company.

EXERCISE 16 Shorten the adjective clause to a descriptive phrase by crossing out the unnecessary words.

1. On eBay, people ~~who are~~ living in California can easily sell to people ~~who are~~ living in New York.

2. Google, which is a popular search engine, is used by millions of people.

3. Bill Gates, who is the founder of Microsoft, has set up a foundation to help others.

4. eBay takes a percentage of each sale that is made on its website.

5. Reshma Saujani, who is the head of Girls Who Code, works to improve the position of women in computing.

6. The Girls Who Code website, which is a good source of relevant statistics, is very clearly designed.

7. Saujani wants to change the situation in computer science, which is a subject she cares deeply about.

8. The number of girls that have been reached by Girls Who Code is very impressive.

9. People who are interested in reading newspapers from other cities can find them on the Web.

10. The World Wide Web, which is abbreviated WWW, was first introduced on the Internet in 1991.

11. The Internet, which was designed in the 1970s, didn't attract casual users until Berners-Lee created the Web.

12. Some wealthy people signed a Giving Pledge, which is a promise to give away most of their money in their lifetime.

13. Pierre Omidyar, who is a billionaire, signed the Giving Pledge.

14. Computers that are sold today have much more memory and speed than computers that were sold 10 years ago.

15. Deron Beal, who is from Arizona, created The Freecycle Network™.

EXERCISE 17 Combine the two sentences into one sentence. Use the second sentence as the adjective clause or descriptive phrase. (The second sentence adds nonessential information.)

1. Pierre Omidyar came to the U.S. when he was a child. His father was a professor.

   Pierre Omidyar, whose father was a professor, came to the U.S. when he was a child.

2. Pierre Omidyar wrote his first computer program at age 14. He is from France.

3. He lived in California. He started his business there.

4. Pierre Omidyar saw a good use for computer technology. He started eBay as a hobby in his home.

5. *BusinessWeek* named Meg Whitman among the 25 most powerful business managers. *BusinessWeek* is a popular business magazine.

6. Meg Whitman resigned from eBay in 2008. She decided to go into politics at that time.

_____

_____

7. John Donahoe got the company out of decline. Pierre Omidyar hired him in 2008.

_____

_____

8. Bill Gates started Microsoft at the age of 19. He dropped out of Harvard during his second year.

_____

_____

9. Amazon began by selling books. It is now the largest online retailer.

_____

_____

10. Jeff Bezos's parents invested money in Amazon. They had never heard of the Internet.

_____

_____

11. Reshma Saujani wants to see more women in computer science. Computer science is one of the fastest growing employment areas today.

_____

_____

FUN WITH GRAMMAR

Quiz you classmates! Work with a partner. Complete the questions about people and places you've learned about so far in this book. Use adjective clauses or descriptive phrases. Once you are finished, take turns quizzing another pair.

A: _What is the name of the woman **who started** Girls Who Code?_

B: I believe her last name was Saujani?

1. Who is the man _____

_____

2. What is the name of the place _____

_____

3. Who is the woman _____

_____

4. How did the president _____ die?

5. ___ _____

_____

SUMMARY OF UNIT 7

	ESSENTIAL ADJECTIVE CLAUSES	NONESSENTIAL ADJECTIVE CLAUSES
Pronoun as subject	People **who/that sell things on eBay** have to pay a fee. Amazon is a website **that/which sells a lot of different things.**	Berners-Lee, **who created the Web,** didn't make money from it. Pierre Omidyar created eBay, **which helps people buy and sell items online.**
Pronoun as object	The people **(who/whom) Omidyar hired** helped him build his company. The first computer **(that/which) I bought** didn't have much memory.	Pierre Omidyar, **who(m) I admire,** believes in donating money to help others. I'm very happy with my present computer, **which** I bought online.
Pronoun as object of preposition	INFORMAL: The person **(who/that) I sold my computer to** paid me $200. FORMAL: The person **to whom I sold my computer** paid me $200.	INFORMAL: Reshma Saujani, **who(m) we read about,** is very creative. FORMAL: Reshma Saujani, **about whom we read,** is very creative.
Where	I want to go to a college **where I can study computer science.**	Berners-Lee worked in Switzerland, **where he met other scientists.**
When	My grandparents grew up at a time **when there were no personal computers.**	The Web was created in 1991, **when most people did not have personal computers.**
Whose + noun as subject	Freecycle is a community **whose members help each other.**	Berners-Lee, **whose parents worked on computers,** learned a lot about technology when he was young.
Whose + noun as object	I sent a thank-you e-mail to the person **whose radio I received through Freecycle.**	Meg Whitman, **whose business expertise Omidyar needed,** started to work at eBay in 1998.
Adjective clause after indefinite pronoun	I don't know anyone **who doesn't have a cell phone.** Everything **(that/which) I've learned about the Internet** is fascinating.	
Descriptive phrase	Computers **made in the 1980s** had very little memory.	Bill Gates, **the founder of Microsoft,** never finished college.

REVIEW

PART 1

Circle the correct words to complete the sentences. Ø means no word is necessary. In some cases, more than one answer is possible. If so, circle all possible answers.

1. What is a computer virus? A virus is a computer code (*that*/who/whose/*which*) attaches itself to other programs and causes harm to programs, data, or hardware.

2. Who is Deron Beal? Deron Beal is the man (*who/whom/which/that*) created the Freecycle Network™.

3. Tim Berners-Lee was born at a time (*when/that/which/Ø*) personal computers were not even in people's imaginations.

4. Tim Berners-Lee is a name (*which/with which/that/Ø*) people are not familiar.

5. Omidyar needed to bring in someone (*who/whose/that/which*) knowledge of business was greater than his own.

6. The Web is a tool (*Ø/that/about which/which*) most of us use every day.

7. The Web, (*which/that/about which/about that*) we read on page 199, is not the same as the Internet.

8. What is eBay? eBay is a website (*that/where/whom/which*) you can buy and sell items.

9. The people (*Ø/which/whose/where*) I've met in online recycling sites have been very helpful.

10. Do you save all the e-mails (*that/where/whose/Ø*) your friends have sent to you?

11. The computer lab is never open at a time (*which/where/when/during which*) I need it.

12. I always delete the spam (*what/that/when/whose*) I receive.

13. You can create an address book (*when/that/where/in which*) you can keep the e-mail addresses of your contacts.

14. Do you know anyone (*Ø/who/whom/which*) doesn't own a computer?

15. The person (*who/that/whose/Ø*) computer I bought wanted a much more powerful computer.

16. Don't believe everything (*that/who/whom/Ø*) you read on the Internet.

PART 2

Some of the following sentences need commas. If they do, put them in. If the sentence doesn't need commas, write *OK*.

1. John Donahoe, who replaced Meg Whitman, saved eBay from decline.

2. In 2008 when John Donahoe came to work at eBay many top employees were fired.

3. Many online businesses that do well in the beginning later fail.

4. Amazon an online retailer was created by Jeff Bezos.

5. At first, Amazon was a place where you could buy only books.

6. Now Amazon is a retailer that sells almost anything.

7. I can't remember a time when there were no smartphones.

8. Berners-Lee is a name that most people don't recognize.

9. Everything that we read in this unit is related to the Internet.

10. Many people confuse the Web with the Internet which was created in the 1970s.

11. There are many websites where you can get travel information.

FROM GRAMMAR TO WRITING

PART 1 Editing Advice

1. Never use *what* as a relative pronoun.

   I bought a used computer from a person ~~what~~ [who] lives in another state.

   Everything ~~what~~ [that or Ø] we learned about the Internet is interesting.

2. You can't omit a relative pronoun that is the subject of the adjective clause.

   I have a cousin ^[who] doesn't have a computer.

3. If the relative pronoun is the object of the adjective clause, don't put an object after the verb.

   The software that I bought ~~it~~ online was very useful.

4. Make sure you use subject-verb agreement in the adjective clause.

   I have a friend who use^[s] e-mail a lot.

5. Put a noun before an adjective clause.

   ~~Who~~ [A person who] doesn't know how to use a computer in today's world is lost.

6. Don't confuse *whose* with *who's*.

   The person ~~who's~~ [whose] computer I bought didn't charge for shipping.

7. Put the subject before the verb in an adjective clause.

   The computer that ~~uses my grandfather~~ [my grandfather uses] is very old.

8. Use *whose*, not *his*, *her*, or *their* to show possession in an adjective clause.

   I have a friend ~~who his~~ [whose] knowledge of programming is very advanced.

PART 2 Editing Practice

Some of the shaded words and phrases have mistakes. Find the mistakes and correct them. If the shaded words are correct, write *C*.

Last semester I took a photo-editing class that [C] has helped me a lot. The teacher ~~what~~ [who] taught the class
1.   2.

is an expert in photo editing. This teacher, whose name is Mark Ryan, is patient, helpful, and fun. A lot of
3.

the photos I took were too dark. I learned how to lighten the parts needed lightening without lightening
4.   5.

the whole photo. I also learned to cut out parts I don't want them. For example, I have a family picture, but
6.

it has one person who's not in the family. It's a woman who live next door to us. She came right at the time
7.   8.

when was taking the picture my friend, and she wanted to be in it. It's a great photo, except for her. I tried
9.

scanning it and editing it at home, but I didn't do a good job. My teacher, who his scanner is much better

10.

than mine, scanned the photo and showed me how to cut the neighbor out. I learned many things in this

class. Everything what I learned is very helpful.

11.

    I started to take another photo class this semester. The teacher who's class I'm taking now is not

12.

as good as last semester's teacher. Who wants to learn a lot about photo editing should take Mark

13.

Ryan's class.

WRITING TIP

Check your work for short sentences or simple sentences with *and*. Combining short ideas with relative pronouns can improve the quality of your writing.

> *RottenTomatoes.com is an informative website. It has reviews of all the latest movies.*
>
> *RottenTomatoes.com is an informative website **that has reviews of all the latest movies**.*

PART 3 Write

Read the two prompts. Choose one and write one or more paragraphs about it.

1. Write about the ways computers and the Internet have made life simpler.
2. Write about two websites or apps that you like. Explain how they are helpful or enjoyable for you.

PART 4 Edit

Reread the Summary of Unit 7 and the Editing Advice. Edit your writing from Part 3.

Infinitives and Gerunds

HELPING
OTHERS

Many National Football League (NFL) players create foundations to help others. Player Torrey Smith started a foundation in Baltimore, Maryland, which helps children learn to read.

Remember that the happiest people are not those getting more, but those giving more.

H. JACKSON BROWN JR.

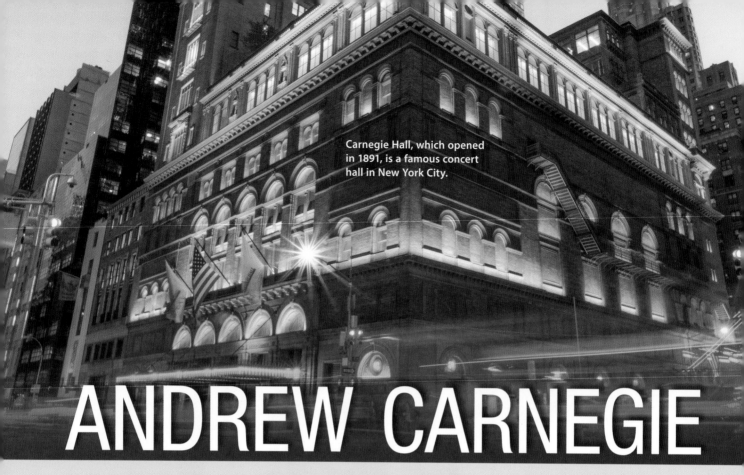

Carnegie Hall, which opened in 1891, is a famous concert hall in New York City.

ANDREW CARNEGIE

Read the following article. Pay special attention to the words in bold. 🎧 8.1

Andrew Carnegie was one of the world's richest men. He made a fortune[1] in the oil and steel industries. Did he enjoy his wealth? Of course he did. But there is something he enjoyed even more: giving away his money.

Carnegie was born in Scotland in 1835 to a very poor family. When his father lost his job, his mother started working **to support** the family. When Andrew was 13 years old, his mother persuaded his father **to leave** Scotland for the "possibilities of America." A year later, Andrew started **to work** in a factory in Pittsburgh, in the state of Pennsylvania. He met a man who let him and other working boys use his small library. Andrew was eager **to read** and **learn** as much as he could. He was intelligent and hardworking, and it didn't take him long **to become** rich.

As Carnegie's fortunes grew, he started **to give** his money **away**. One of his biggest desires was **to build** free public libraries so that everyone would have access to knowledge. He believed that education was the key to a successful life. In 1881, there were only a few public libraries. Carnegie started **to build** free libraries all over the U.S. and the world. Over the doors of the Carnegie Library of Pittsburgh, carved in stone, are the words, "Free to the People." By the time Carnegie died in 1919, there were more than 2,500 public libraries all over the world.

But building libraries was not his only contribution. In his book *The Gospel of Wealth,* he tried **to persuade** other wealthy people **to give away** their money. These are some of the ideas he wrote about in his book:

- **To give away** money is the best thing rich people can do.
- It is the moral obligation of the wealthy **to help** others.
- It is important for a rich person **to set** an example for others.
- It is not good **to have** money if your spirit is poor.
- It is a disgrace[2] **to die** rich.

By the time he died in 1919, Carnegie had given away more than $350 million[3].

---

[1] fortune: a very large quantity of money
[2] disgrace: something that brings shame or dishonor
[3] Today, this is equivalent to over 5 billion dollars.

COMPREHENSION Based on the reading, write T for *true* or F for *false*.

1. _____ The Carnegie family left Scotland because they saw more economic possibilities in the United States.

2. _____ When Carnegie was young, he had no help from anyone.

3. _____ Carnegie encouraged rich people to help others.

THINK ABOUT IT Discuss the questions with a partner or in a small group.

1. Carnegie believed that "education is the key to a successful life." Is this always true, in your view? Explain.

2. Do you agree that rich people have a "moral obligation" to help others? Give reasons for your opinion.

8.1 Infinitives—Overview

An infinitive is *to* + the base form of the verb (e.g., *to go*). An infinitive can be used in the following ways.

EXAMPLES	EXPLANATION
Carnegie wanted **to help** others.	after certain verbs
He wanted rich people **to give away** their money.	after the object of a verb
I'm happy **to help**.	after certain adjectives
It's important **to help** others.	after certain expressions that begin with *it*
To help others makes a person feel good.	as the subject of a sentence
Do you volunteer your time in order **to help** others?	to show purpose
He's old enough **to help**. She's too young **to help**.	after expressions with *too* and *enough*

Notes:

1. In a sentence with two infinitives connected by **and** or **or**, the second *to* is usually omitted.

   *I want **to make** money and **help** others.*

   *You can choose **to volunteer** time or **donate** money.*

2. Put *not* before an infinitive to make it negative.

   *Carnegie decided **not to die** rich.*

3. For a passive infinitive, we use *to be* + past participle.

   *Everyone wants **to be given** an opportunity to succeed.*

EXERCISE 1 Listen to the information about a teacher in Niger. Write T for *true* or F for *false*. 🎧 8.2

1. _____ Leslie Natzke first went to Niger on vacation.

2. _____ Girls in Niger often got married very young.

3. _____ Expanding Lives encouraged girls from Niger to start businesses in the United States.

EXERCISE 2 Fill in the blanks with the words you hear. 🎧 8.2

About 25 years ago, Leslie Natzke, an ESL teacher from Chicago, went to Niger _____*to work*_____

as a Peace Corps volunteer. She was surprised _____ that so few girls finished high
2.

school. According to an organization, Save the Children, Niger is the worst place in the world to be a

mother. Very poor parents often marry off their daughters at a very young age in order

_____ money from the husband's family. Natzke thought that these girls were too young
3.

_____ married and needed _____ their education first.
4.   5.

When Natzke returned to the United States, she continued _____ about the girls in
6.

Niger. She wanted _____ more for them. In 2008, she started a program called
7.

Expanding Lives. This program brings teenage girls from Niger to Chicago for the summer.

_____ experience with Americans, Natzke found volunteer families to give these girls a
8.

place to live during the summer. At first, Natzke just wanted them _____ their education
9.

and _____ high school. Then she decided _____
10.   11.

leadership training.

As the program grew, Natzke wanted the girls _____ about finance so that they
12.

could start a business back home. But most of all, she wanted them _____ health
13.

education. It is important for Natzke _____ these girls become leaders. She wants them
14.

_____ their new skills to other girls in Niger and help them expand their lives, too.
15.

8.2 Verbs Followed by an Infinitive

EXAMPLES	EXPLANATION
Carnegie *didn't want* **to die** rich. Everyone *deserves* **to have** an education.	Some verbs can be followed by an infinitive.

Notes:

1. The verbs below can be followed by an infinitive:

agree	decide	intend	offer	refuse
appear	deserve	learn	plan	seem
attempt	expect	like	prefer	start
begin	forget	love	prepare	try
choose	hate	manage	pretend	want
continue	hope	need	promise	wish

2. The following modal phrases are also followed by an infinitive: *can afford, can't stand, would like.*

EXERCISE 3 Fill in the blanks with the infinitive form of the verbs from the box. Try to use each verb only once, though some verbs may work in more than one place.

follow✓	give	help	provide
get	give away	persuade	use

Bill Gates and Warren Buffet, two of the richest people in the world, appear _____*to follow*_____ the
1.

example of Andrew Carnegie: they have also chosen _____ people less fortunate. They
2.

signed a document called the Giving Pledge, where they promise _____ more than
3.

half of their wealth during their lifetimes. They want _____ their money to make life better
4.

for others.

Gates and Buffet have managed _____ over 100 American billionaires to sign the Giving
5.

Pledge. Pierre Omidyar, of eBay, has promised _____ at least half of his wealth to charity.
6.

Now Gates and Buffet are attempting _____ billionaires in other countries to sign the Giving
7.

Pledge, too. Gates wants _____ all children with a good education and medical care.
8.

EXERCISE 4 Fill in the blanks with an infinitive. Use the verbs from the box.

build	educate	give	learn	start over
die	get	have	leave	work✓

1. Andrew Carnegie started _____*to work*_____ when he was very young.

2. His parents chose _____ Scotland.

3. They hoped _____ in the U.S.

4. Carnegie wanted _____ free public libraries.

5. He didn't want _____ a rich man.

6. Children in all countries deserve _____ a good education.

7. Everyone wants _____ *(passive)* a chance to succeed in life.

8. In some countries, poor children can't go to school. Children in all countries need
   _____ *(passive)*.

9. Girls in Niger want _____ a better life than their parents had.

10. They need _____ about computers, health, and finance.

ABOUT YOU Imagine that you are a billionaire. Complete the sentence with an infinitive phrase to tell how you would like to help others. Share your answers with a partner.

I would like _____

_____

8.3 Verb + Object + Infinitive

EXAMPLES	EXPLANATION
Carnegie **wanted** *poor people* **to have** the same opportunities as rich people.	The object can be a noun.
He **encouraged** *them* **to use** libraries.	The object can be a pronoun.

Note:

The verbs below can be followed by a noun or an object pronoun + an infinitive:

advise	beg	expect	need	remind	urge
allow	convince	force	permit	teach*	want
ask	encourage	invite	persuade	tell	would like

* After *teach, how* is sometimes used: *My parents taught me **how** to help others.*

EXERCISE 5 Fill in the blanks with an object pronoun and the infinitive of one of the verbs from the box.

become	do	go	save	suffer	teach	use✓
buy	finish	help	sign	take	think	volunteer

1. **A:** My brother likes to buy a lot of expensive tech gadgets.

   B: You should encourage ____him to use____ his money in better ways.

2. **A:** How do Bill and Melinda Gates persuade billionaires to give away their money?

   B: They talk to them. They encourage _____ about helping others. They

   ask _____ the Giving Pledge.

3. **A:** Andrew Carnegie's mother was worried about her children. She didn't want _____.

   She talked to her husband about the possibilities of a better life.

   B: What did she want _____?

   A: She wanted _____ the family to America.

4. **A:** My sister is a very generous person.

   B. Do you mean she gives her children a lot of things?

   A: No. She teaches _____ others.

   B: That's nice to hear. Those words encourage _____ my children to be generous, too.

5. **A:** My parents weren't rich, but they always helped other people.

   B: How did they do that?

   A: They donated their time. They taught _____ during my free time. So I tutor

   high school kids after school. I want _____ their education.

6. A: My parents always gave me money when I was a child.

   B: Did you buy a lot of toys?

   A: No. They didn't allow _____ a lot of things. They encouraged

   _____ my money.

   B: Save for what?

   A: I saved my money for a charity project.

7. A: Why does Leslie Natzke bring African girls to Chicago every summer?

   B: She wants _____ to college. She also wants _____

   leaders and teach other girls.

EXERCISE 6 Change the following imperative statements to statements with an object pronoun + an infinitive.

1. A woman says to her husband, "Teach the children good values."

   She wants <u>him to teach the children good values.</u> _____

2. My parents always said to me, "Help others."

   They expected _____

3. A mother says to her children, "Don't forget about other people."

   She wants _____

4. The father said to his children, "Give to charity."

   He advised _____

5. Parents say to their children, "Be kind to others."

   They want _____

6. I said to you, "Work hard."

   I would like _____

7. My parents said to us, "Give money to people in need."

   They encouraged _____

8. A father says to his daughter, "Be generous."

   He wants _____

9. My parents said to me, "Don't be selfish."

   They encouraged _____

10. Parents say to their children, "Be polite."

    They expect _____

ABOUT YOU What did your parents expect from you when you were growing up? Use each verb to write a sentence with an object + an infinitive. Share your answers with a partner.

1. expect

   My parents expected me to be polite.

2. advise

   _____

3. permit

   _____

4. tell

   _____

5. expect

   _____

6. encourage

   _____

8.4 Causative Verbs

Some verbs are called *causative* verbs because one person or thing causes, enables, or allows another person or thing to do something.

EXAMPLES	EXPLANATION
Gates **has gotten** billionaires **to sign** the Giving Pledge. Carnegie **persuaded** wealthy people **to give away** their money. You **convinced** me **to help** others.	*Get, persuade,* and *convince* are followed by an object + infinitive. *Get,* in this case, means persuade.
Carnegie **helped** people **(to) get** an education. Leslie **helps** girls **(to) improve** their lives.	After *help* + object, either the infinitive or the base form can be used. The base form is more common.
When Carnegie was a child, he met a rich man who had a small library. This man **let** children **use** his library. This man **permitted** children **to use** his library. This man **allowed** children **to use** his library.	*Let, permit,* and *allow* have the same meaning. *Let* is followed by an object + base form. *Permit* and *allow* are followed by an object + infinitive.
This reading **made** me **think** about wealth and happiness. No one can **make** you **give** to charity. Giving to charity **makes** me **feel** good.	*Make* is followed by an object + base form. *Make* can mean *force.* *Make* can mean *cause something to happen.*
Warren Buffet **had** his children **sign** the Giving Pledge. The teacher **had** us **write** an essay about charity.	*Have* means to give a job or task to someone. *Have,* in this case, is followed by an object + base form.

EXERCISE 7 Circle the correct verb form to complete each conversation.

1. **A:** Do you always give to charity?

   B: I know I should. But I don't always do it.

   A: Whenever I get a gift in the mail from a charity, I send a check. I think this is a good way to get

   people (*give*/(*to give*)).

   B: What kind of gifts do you receive in the mail?

   A: I often get address labels. Don't you?

   B: Yes, but that doesn't persuade me (*donate/to donate*) money. I just use the labels and throw away

   the donation envelope.

2. **A:** I volunteered for the public TV station last month.

   B: What did they have you (*do/to do*)?

   A: My job was to address envelopes. It was fun. I met other volunteers. And it made me (*feel/to feel*)

   good about watching the station.

3. **A:** I have a doctor's appointment on Friday, and my car doesn't work.

   B: Let me (*drive/to drive*) you.

   A: I don't want to bother you.

   B: It's not a bother. I love to volunteer my time.

4. **A:** When I was a child, my parents gave me money once a week.

   B: Did they let you (*buy/to buy*) whatever you wanted?

   A: They allowed me (*use/to use*) half of the money. They had me (*save/to save*) the other half.

   They convinced me (*give/to give*) part of my savings to charity.

EXERCISE 8 Fill in the blanks with the base form or the infinitive of the verb given.

There are many ways to help others. Some people donate money. I volunteer for my local

public radio station. The radio station needs money from listeners. Several times a year, the

station tries to persuade listeners _____*to give*_____ money to the station. Without their
                                         1. give

support, the radio station could not exist. The station managers have us _____
                                                                              2. answer

the phones when people call to contribute. We let callers _____ us about their
                                                              3. tell

favorite programs. To get people _____, the station offers some gifts. For
                                     4. contribute

example, for a $60 contribution, you can get a coffee mug. For a $100 contribution, you can get a

book. Everyone can listen to public radio for free. No one makes you _____ for it.
                                                                          5. pay

But listeners should pay for this service, if they can. I'd like to convince my friends

_____ or _____ in money.
   6. volunteer   **7.** send

8.5 Adjective + Infinitive

EXAMPLES	EXPLANATION
Some people are *happy* **to help** others. It makes me *sad* **to see** so many poor people. I am *proud* **to be** a volunteer. We are *pleased* **to help**.	Certain adjectives can be followed by an infinitive. Many of these adjectives describe a person's emotional or mental state.

Note:

The following adjectives can be followed by an infinitive:

afraid	eager	pleased	sad
ashamed	glad	prepared	sorry
delighted	happy	proud	surprised
disappointed	lucky	ready	willing

EXERCISE 9 A college student has volunteered her time with an agency that delivers food to families in need. She is discussing her duties with the volunteer coordinator. Fill in the blanks with an appropriate infinitive. Answers may vary.

A: Are you willing _____*to donate*_____ your time on the weekends?
                          1.

B: Yes. I'm eager _____ people who need my help. I'm ready _____
                        2.   **3.**

whatever you need me to do.

A: You're going to deliver meals to people in this neighborhood who don't have enough food.

B: I'm surprised _____ that some people don't have enough to eat. This seems like a
                       4.

middle-class neighborhood.

220 Unit 8

A: It is. But the economy is bad. Most people are lucky _____ a job. But some people have
                                             5.

  lost their jobs. Often people are ashamed _____ for help.
                                                        6.

B: I can understand that. But don't worry. I'm willing _____ anyone who needs my help.
                                                          7.

A: Don't be afraid _____ into a stranger's home. Someone will always go with you.
                                8.

B: I'm happy _____ food to people who need it.
                      9.

A: I'm glad that you're going to work with us. Your parents must be proud _____ such a
                                                                       10.

  generous daughter.

B: And I'm lucky _____ such generous parents. They taught me about giving when I was
                            11.

  very young.

ABOUT YOU Complete the sentences so they are true about you. Use an infinitive phrase. Then share
your sentences in a small group.

1. I'm afraid _____

2. My friend was pleased _____

3. I am not willing _____

4. I am eager _____

5. I was sad _____

EXERCISE 10 Fill in the blanks with an infinitive or a base form in this conversation between an uncle
and his nephew. Answers may vary.

A: What do you plan _____*to do*_____ this summer?
                          1.

B: I wanted _____ a summer job, but I couldn't find one. It's going to be boring. I'm ready
                   2.

  _____, but no one wants _____ me. And my parents expect me
        3.   **4.**

  _____ a job. My mom won't let me _____ home all day and watch TV or
        5.   **6.**

  hang out with my friends at the swimming pool.

A: Are you trying _____ money for your college education?
                   7.

B: Not really. I haven't even thought about saving for college yet. I want a job because I'm planning

  _____ a car.
        8.

A: You need _____ about college, too. You're going to graduate next year.
                 9.

continued

B: I'm planning _____ to a community college, so it won't be so expensive. And my parents
10.

are willing _____ for my college tuition.
11.

A: Have you thought about volunteering your time this summer?

B: Not really. I just want _____ money.
12.

A: Don't just think about money. Try _____ about how you can help other people. You can
13.

help little kids _____ to read. Or you can help _____ the parks by
14. 15.

picking up garbage.

B: I keep telling you. I just want _____ money. What will I get if I do those things? I won't
16.

get my car.

A: You'll get satisfaction. Helping others will make you _____ good. And you'll learn
17.

_____ responsible. After you finish community college and go to a four-year college, it
18.

will look good on your application if you say you volunteered. It will help you _____ into
19.

a good college.

B: Why are you trying so hard to get me _____ a volunteer?
20.

A: I volunteered when I was your age, and I found that it was more valuable than money.

B: OK. I'll volunteer if you're willing _____ me the money for the car.
21.

FUN WITH GRAMMAR

Play team Tic-Tac-Toe. Each team takes turns choosing a word and using it in an original sentence. If the
sentence is correct, place an X or O where the word is. The team who first gets three in a row across, down,
or diagonally, wins.

Example: *We choose "sorry." Our sentence is: We'll be sorry to see you lose this game.*

pretend	convince	sorry		forget	expect	persuade
lucky	get (someone)	encourage		proud	make (me)	hope
would like	refuse	prepared		want	surprised	remind

CRAFTY ways to CONTRIBUTE

Read the following article. Pay special attention to the words in bold. 🎧 8.3

Joyce Koenig was an artist who believed that it's important **to help** others. When she heard of a summer camp in Wisconsin for children with cancer, she came up with an idea. It costs money for these kids **to go** to camp, so Joyce decided **to see** what she could do to help. It was impossible for her **to donate** a lot of money, so she had to think of another way **to help**.

She wanted **to combine** her love of art and her desire **to help** others. So she started making and selling beautiful cards in order **to raise** money for these kids. Because these cards are all handmade, it was taking her a long time **to make** a lot of them. So Joyce had another idea. She started inviting friends to her house **to help** her make the cards. At first, her

friends were hesitant[1]. Many said that they were not artistic and didn't know how **to make** cards. But once they saw the beautiful materials that she had in her studio, her friends felt more comfortable designing, cutting, and pasting in order **to make** an original card.

But the materials were expensive. **To make** money without spending money, Joyce asked for and got donations of paper, glue, scissors, ribbon, and other supplies from nearby stores. She sold her cards for two dollars each at various art fairs during the year. Joyce raised more than $40,000 in her 20 years making cards—two dollars at a time.

_____
[1] hesitant: unsure

COMPREHENSION Based on the reading, write T for *true* or F for *false*.

1. _____ Joyce used her love of art to find a way to make money for kids with cancer.

2. _____ To produce a large number of cards, she needed the help of her friends.

3. _____ At first, her friends were eager to help her.

THINK ABOUT IT Discuss the questions with a partner or in a small group.

1. Can you think of other small ways to raise money for good causes? Have you ever done this? Share your ideas.

2. What good causes do you support or would you like to support? Give your reasons.

8.6 Infinitives as Subjects

EXAMPLES	EXPLANATION
To give money away is a nice thing to do. **To help** others gives a person satisfaction.	Sometimes we begin a sentence with an infinitive phrase. This tends to sound formal.
It's important **to help** other people. **It's** fun **to make** cards.	It's common to use *It* at the beginning of a sentence with the infinitive coming later to express the same idea as an infinitive in the subject position. In this case, the infinitive is a "delayed subject" and sounds less formal.
It was important **for Joyce to help** others. It wasn't possible **for her to make** a lot of cards alone.	*For* + an object gives the infinitive a specific subject.
It **costs** a lot of **money to send** the kids to camp. It takes **time** and effort **to raise** money.	An infinitive is often used after *cost* + money and *take* + time.
It **cost her** very little to make cards.	An object can follow *take* and *cost*.

EXERCISE 11 Fill in the blanks with any missing words. Use the simple past tense when necessary.

1. It was enjoyable _____to_____ make cards.

2. It didn't _____ a lot of time to make a card.

3. _____ fun to get together and make cards.

4. It wasn't hard _____ Joyce's friends to make cards.

5. _____ help sick children was Joyce's goal.

6. It _____ only two dollars _____ buy a card.

7. "_____ give away money is the best thing rich people can do," said Carnegie.

EXERCISE 12 Complete each statement with an infinitive phrase to talk about volunteering, donating money, etc. Share your answers with a partner.

1. It's important _to think about the needs of others._____

2. It isn't necessary _____

3. It's a good idea _____

4. It's everyone's responsibility _____

5. It costs a lot of money _____

6. It's important _____

7. It takes a lot of time _____

8. It doesn't take long _____

EXERCISE 13 Complete each statement. Begin with an *It* phrase. Share your answers with a partner.

1. _____It's impossible_____ to get every billionaire to sign the Giving Pledge.

2. _____It isn't hard_____ to get donations of materials.

3. _____ to help other people.

4. _____ to give away money.

5. _____ to die rich.

6. _____ to have a lot of money.

7. _____ not to have a good education.

8. _____ to live in the U.S.

EXERCISE 14 Change these statements to make them less formal by starting them with *It*.

1. To raise money for charity is a good thing.

   It's a good thing to raise money for charity.

2. To raise $1 million is not easy.

   _____

3. To fight disease takes a lot of money.

   _____

4. To help poor people is everyone's responsibility.

   _____

5. To produce high-quality education takes a lot of money.

   _____

6. To build libraries was Carnegie's dream.

   _____

7. To raise money for sick children was Joyce's goal.

   _____

8. To fight disease in poor countries will take time.

   _____

8.7 Infinitives to Show Purpose

EXAMPLES	EXPLANATION
Joyce sold cards **in order to raise** money.	*In order to* shows purpose. It answers the question *Why?* or *What for?*
Joyce sold cards **to raise** money.	*In order to* can be shortened to *to*.
In order to raise money, Joyce sold cards.	The purpose phrase can come before the main clause. If so, we use a comma after the purpose phrase.

EXERCISE 15 Fill in the blanks to complete the sentences. Answers may vary.

1. In order to _____*learn*_____ more about volunteering, you can use the Internet.
2. Carnegie donated his money to _____ libraries.
3. You can volunteer in order to _____ job experience.
4. To _____ a job, you need experience. To _____ experience, you need a job.
5. You can volunteer your time in order to _____ people. There are many people who need help.
6. Joyce started making and selling cards in order to _____ money to send kids to camp.
7. Leslie Natzke went to Africa in order _____ in the Peace Corps.
8. She brings girls from Niger to Chicago _____ them a better education.

8.8 Infinitives with *Too* and *Enough*

Too with an infinitive shows excess for a specific purpose (. . . *too big to fail*). *Enough* shows sufficiency for a specific purpose (*enough time to do* . . .). There are various patterns using *too* and *enough* with an infinitive.

EXAMPLES	EXPLANATION
You are never **too young to help** others. I worked **too slowly to finish** the card.	*too* + adjective/adverb + infinitive
I have **too much work to do**, so I have no time to volunteer.	*too much* + noncount noun + infinitive
There are **too many problems** in the world **to solve** in one day.	*too many* + plural count noun + infinitive
I'm not **talented enough to design** a card. Joyce sold cards **easily enough to raise** money.	adjective/adverb + *enough* + infinitive
I have **enough time to volunteer** this summer.	*enough* + noun + infinitive
Making cards is not too hard **for us to do**.	The infinitive phrase can be preceded by *for* + object.
I can't volunteer this summer because I'm **too busy** (to volunteer). Carnegie could build libraries because he had **enough money** (to build them).	Sometimes the infinitive phrase can be omitted. It is understood from the context.

EXERCISE 16 Fill in the blanks with the words given. Put the words in the correct order. Add *to* where necessary.

A: I heard about your card project, and I'd like to help you. But I don't have _____enough talent_____ .

1. talent/enough

I'm _____ something new.

2. old/too/learn

B: It's so _____ cards. Anyone can do it.

3. easy/make

A: I think it takes _____ a card. I don't have _____

4. long/too/make   5. time/enough

and I'm not _____ .

6. talented/enough

B: It only takes about 15 minutes _____ a card.

7. make

A: I'd really like to help, but I'm _____ you at this time.

8. busy/too/help

I have _____ at my job.

9. work/too much/do

B: That's not a problem. When people have _____ ,

10. time/enough/help

they help. If not, that's OK, too.

A: But I'd really like to help. Is there anything else I can do?

B: You can make a donation. You can buy just one card for two dollars.

A: Really? They're so inexpensive. I have _____ five cards now.

11. money/enough/buy

B: Great! Every dollar helps.

EXERCISE 17 Fill in the blanks with *too, too much, too many,* or *enough* to complete the conversation.

A: I heard about a volunteer project at the park. Some friends and I are going to pick up garbage.

B: Why would you want to do that? I don't have _____enough_____ time to pick up garbage. I have

1.

_____ things to do.

2.

A: You always say you want to volunteer. About 50 volunteers are coming. It won't take

_____ time to finish the job.

3.

B: But it's _____ hot to spend the whole day in the sun. It's almost 90 degrees today.

4.

A: We can go swimming afterward. The park has a big swimming pool. You swim, right?

B: Yes, but I don't swim well _____ to swim in deep water.

5.

A: Don't worry. There's a shallow end and a deep end. You can stay in the shallow end.

B: The shallow end has a lot of kids. And the kids make _____ noise.

6.

A: OK. It sounds like this project isn't a good match for you.

FORKLIFT
PHILANTRHOPIST

Matel "Mat" Dawson, Jr.

Read the following article. Pay special attention to the words in bold. 🎧 8.4

When we think of philanthropists[1], we usually think of the very rich and famous, such as Andrew Carnegie or Bill Gates. However, Matel Dawson, a forklift[2] driver in Michigan, was an ordinary man who did extraordinary things.

Dawson started **working** at Ford Motor Company in 1940 for $1.15 an hour. By **working** hard, **saving** carefully, and **investing** his money wisely, he became rich. But he didn't care about **owning** expensive cars or **taking** fancy vacations. Instead of **spending** his money on himself, he enjoyed **giving** it away. During his lifetime, he donated more than $1 million for college scholarships to help students get an education.

Why did Dawson insist on **giving** his money away to students? One reason was that he did not have the opportunity to finish school. He had to drop out of school after the seventh grade to help support his poor family. He knew that not **having** an education limits job possibilities. Also, he learned about **giving** from his parents. He watched them work hard, save their money, and help others less fortunate. His mother made Dawson promise to always give something back. He was grateful to his parents for **teaching** him the importance of **helping** others.

When he became rich, he didn't change his lifestyle. He continued **driving** his old car and **living** in a one-bedroom apartment. And he didn't stop **working** until shortly before he died at the age of 81. When asked why he worked long past the time when most people retire, he replied, "It keeps me **going**, **knowing** I'm helping somebody."

_____
[1] philanthropist: a person who gives away money to help other people
[2] forklift: a vehicle used to lift and carry boxes

COMPREHENSION Based on the reading, write T for *true* or F for *false*.

1. _____ Matel Dawson started out poor but became rich.

2. _____ When he was rich, he changed his lifestyle.

3. _____ His goal was to help students get an education.

THINK ABOUT IT Discuss the questions with a partner or in a small group.

1. What do you think of Matel Dawson's achievement? Do you know anyone else who has done something similar? Share your ideas.

2. Would you change your lifestyle if you became rich? Why or why not? Explain.

8.9 Gerunds—Overview

To form a gerund, we put an *-ing* ending on a verb. A gerund is used as a noun (subject or object).

EXAMPLES	EXPLANATION
Contributing money is one way to help. **Volunteering** your time is another way to help.	A gerund (phrase) can be used as the subject.
Dawson started **working** in 1940. He continued **driving** an old car even after he became rich.	A gerund (phrase) can be used after certain verbs.
Dawson insisted *on giving* away his money. He understood the importance *of helping* others.	A gerund (phrase) can be used as the object of a preposition.

Notes:

1. To make a gerund negative, we put *not* before the gerund.

    Not *finishing high school limits job possibilities.*

2. For a passive gerund, we use *being* + past participle.

    *We appreciate **being given** the opportunity to have an education.*

3. A gerund subject takes a singular verb.

    *Helping others **gives** a person pleasure.*

EXERCISE 18 Listen to the following article and fill in the blanks with the missing words. 🎧 8.5

Patty Stonesifer isn't worried about _____ making _____ money or _____ her career.
                                                    1.   **2.**

She quit _____ for money and has started _____ . She now works at
                      3.   **4.**

Martha's Table, a Washington, DC, organization that is dedicated to _____ food,
                                                                                           5.

clothing, and education to poor people. What did Patty do before this? She made a lot of money

_____ at Microsoft. In fact, she was the highest-ranking woman there. She helped start
          6.

the Bill and Melinda Gates Foundation, which works on _____ preventable
                                                                              7.

diseases in poor countries. But she didn't feel satisfied _____ so far away from the people
                                                                          8.

she helped. She became more interested in _____ close to people who are in need. When
                                                           9.

she started her new volunteer job at Martha's Table, she tried _____ for a week on a small
                                                                              10.

budget. She realized that _____ a healthy diet is impossible for low-income people. She's
                                      11.

concerned about_____ healthy meals for as many hungry people as possible
                              12.

in DC, but mostly she's interested in _____ child hunger. She doesn't mind
                                                    13.

_____ long hours at Martha's Table without pay. And she doesn't miss
          14.

_____ a fancy office. _____ something to help others gives her satisfaction.
          15.   **16.**

8.10 Gerunds as Subjects

EXAMPLES	EXPLANATION
Volunteering is enjoyable for Stonesifer.	A gerund or a gerund phrase can be the subject of the sentence.
Helping others *makes* Stonesifer feel good.	A gerund subject takes a singular verb (*is, was, gives*).

EXERCISE 19 Fill in the blanks with a gerund. Underline the main verb. Answers may vary.

1. _____*Giving*_____ away money made Dawson feel good.

2. _____ in a factory is not easy.

3. Not _____ an education always bothered Dawson.

4. _____ a college education is expensive in the U.S.

5. _____ money didn't give Dawson satisfaction.

6. _____ an old car was not a problem for Dawson.

7. _____ a vacation wasn't important for Dawson.

8. _____ that he was helping people was very important for Dawson.

9. _____ at Martha's Table gives Patty Stonesifer satisfaction.

10. _____ childhood hunger is Stonesifer's goal.

EXERCISE 20 Complete each statement with your own ideas. Share your answers with a partner.

1. Owning a lot of things *doesn't give people much satisfaction.*_____

2. Helping less fortunate people _____

3. Volunteering your time _____

4. Getting an education _____

5. Working hard _____

ABOUT YOU Use a gerund or gerund phrase as a subject to write sentences about you. Use the sentences in Exercises 19 and 20 as a guide.

Getting a college education is important to me.

1. _____

2. _____

3. _____

4. _____

8.11 Gerunds after Prepositions and Nouns

There are various patterns for using gerunds after prepositions.

EXAMPLES	EXPLANATION
Dawson **didn't care about owning** fancy things. He **believed in helping** others.	Verb + preposition + gerund
Carnegie was **famous for building** libraries. Stonesifer is **concerned about helping** people.	Adjective + preposition + gerund
Dawson **thanked his parents for teaching** him to save money.	Verb + object + preposition + gerund
Dawson **didn't spend money going** on vacations or **eating** in expensive restaurants. Stonesifer **has satisfaction helping** others.	A gerund is used after the noun in the following expressions: *have a difficult time, have experience, have fun, have a good time, have a hard time, have a problem, have trouble, have satisfaction, spend time, spend money.*

EXERCISE 21 In the article from Exercise 18, some gerunds are preceded by a preposition. Circle the prepositions that precede a gerund.

EXERCISE 22 Fill in each blank with the gerund form of a word from the box.

build	drive✓	have	make	quit	sign
create	give	help	provide	sell	volunteer

1. Dawson didn't have a problem _____*driving*_____ an old car.

2. Dawson was interested in _____ students get an education.

3. He insisted on _____ away his money.

4. Stonesifer cares about _____ .

5. She had a good reason for _____ her high-paying job.

6. She doesn't complain about not _____ a fancy office.

7. Carnegie was famous for _____ libraries.

8. Bill Gates is well known for _____ Microsoft.

9. He's also well known for _____ the Giving Pledge.

10. Joyce Koenig spent a lot of time _____ and _____ cards to help kids

    with cancer.

11. Leslie Natzke cares about _____ girls from Niger with a good education.

8.12 Prepositions after Verbs, Nouns, and Adjectives

VERB + PREPOSITION	COMMON PHRASES		EXAMPLES
verb + *about*	care about complain about dream about forget about	talk about think about worry about	You **care about helping** people.
verb + *to*	adjust to look forward to		I **look forward to getting** a volunteer job.
verb + *on*	depend on insist on plan on		Dawson **insisted on giving** away his money.
verb + *in*	believe in succeed in		Bill Gates **succeeded in becoming** a billionaire.

VERB + OBJECT + PREPOSITION	COMMON PHRASES		EXAMPLES
of	accuse . . . of suspect . . . of		You can't **accuse Gates of not caring** about other people.
for	apologize to . . . for blame . . . for	forgive . . . for thank . . . for	Stonesifer **thanks her parents for teaching** her about charity.
from	keep . . . from prevent . . . from	prohibit . . . from stop . . . from	No one could **stop Dawson from giving** away his money.
about	warn . . . about		Martha's Table **warns people about eating** too much junk food.

NOUN + PREPOSITION	COMMON PHRASES	EXAMPLES
of	in danger of in favor of	My friends are **in favor of volunteering** on Saturday.
for	need for reason for excuse for	What is Stonesifer's **reason for leaving** a high-paying job?

ADJECTIVE + PREPOSITION	COMMON PHRASES		EXAMPLES
of	afraid of capable of guilty of	proud of tired of	Dawson was **proud of helping** others get an education.
about	concerned about excited about	upset about worried about	Stonesifer was **excited about volunteering** with Martha's Table.
for	responsible for famous for		Carnegie is **famous for building** public libraries.
to + object + *for*	grateful to . . . for		He was **grateful to his parents for teaching** him about giving.
at	good at successful at		Joyce was very **good at making** cards.
to	accustomed to used to		Stonesifer is **accustomed to working** with young people.
in	interested in		Are you **interested in getting** a volunteer job?

Notes:

1. *Plan, afraid,* and *proud* can also be followed by an infinitive.

> I **plan on volunteering** on weekends. / I **plan to volunteer** on weekends.

> I'm **afraid of making** a mistake. / I'm **afraid to make** a mistake.

> He's **proud of being** a volunteer. / He's **proud to be** a volunteer.

2. Sometimes *to* is part of an infinitive.

> I need **to help** my family.

3. Sometimes *to* is a part of a verb phrase and is followed by a gerund.

> I **look forward to starting** my new volunteer job.

EXERCISE 23 Fill in the blanks with a preposition and the gerund of the verb given. In some cases, no preposition is necessary.

A: My father's going to retire next month. He's worried ___*about having*___ too much time on his hands.

1. have

B: I don't blame him _____ worried. For a lot of people, their self-worth depends

2. be

_____ , and when they retire, they feel empty.

3. work

A: My mother is afraid that he'll spend all his time _____ TV. Besides, she's not accustomed

4. watch

_____ him home all day.

5. have

B: Doesn't he have any interests?

A: Well, he's interested _____ , but my parents live in an apartment now, so they don't have

6. garden

a garden. When they had a house, my dad was always proud _____ the nicest garden on

7. have

the block.

B: Has he thought _____ at the Botanical Gardens?

8. volunteer

A: Do they use volunteers?

B: I think so. He would have a great time _____ there.

9. work

A: You're right. He would be good _____ tours because he knows so much about flowers.

10. give

Thank you _____ me this idea. I can't wait to tell him.

11. give

ABOUT YOU Write answers to the questions. Then discuss your answers with a partner.

1. Have you ever volunteered to help others? If so, how?

   _____

   _____

2. In your native country, do some people have a hard time feeding their families? Is there help from the government or other organizations?

   _____

   _____

3. In your native country, is there someone who is famous for helping people in need? What do (or did) they do?

   _____

   _____

4. What kind of volunteer work might interest you?

   _____

   _____

8.13 Verbs Followed by Gerunds

EXAMPLES	EXPLANATION
Dawson enjoyed **giving** money away. He couldn't imagine not **helping** others. Students appreciate **receiving** financial aid.	Many verbs are followed by a gerund or gerund phrase.
My friend **goes bowling** on Saturdays, but I prefer volunteering.	*Go* + gerund is used in many idiomatic expressions of sports and recreation.

Here are expressions with *go* + gerund.

go boating	go fishing	go sailing	go skiing
go bowling	go hiking	go shopping	go swimming
go camping	go hunting	go sightseeing	
go dancing	go jogging	go skating	

Notes:

1. The following verbs can be followed by a gerund:

admit	can't stand	dislike	keep (on)	postpone	resent
advise	consider	enjoy	like	practice	risk
appreciate	continue	finish	love	prefer	start
avoid	delay	follow	mind	put off	stop
begin	deny	hate	miss	quit	suggest
can't help	discuss	imagine	permit	recommend	try

2. Some two-part verbs have special meanings:
   - *Can't help* means to have no control: When I see hungry children, I *can't help* feeling bad.
   - *Can't stand* means can't tolerate: I *can't stand* seeing children go hungry.
   - I *mind* means that something bothers me. I *don't mind* means that something is OK with me; it doesn't bother me.
   - *Put off* means postpone: Don't *put off* applying for a volunteer position.

EXERCISE 24 Fill in the blanks with a gerund to complete these statements. Answers may vary.

1. Matel Dawson liked _____helping_____ students.

2. Students appreciated _____ help from Dawson.

3. He didn't mind _____ an old car.

4. He didn't mind _____ in a small apartment.

5. He kept on _____ until shortly before he died at the age of 81.

6. People appreciate _____ help from Stonesifer.

7. Stonesifer enjoys _____ people with food, clothing, and an education.

8. At the end of the day, when she finishes _____, she feels satisfied.

9. She doesn't mind not _____ money.

continued

10. Joyce Koenig appreciated _____ donated materials for her cards.

11. When she finished _____ cards, she tried to sell them at art fairs.

12. Leslie Natzke has many fun activities for the girls from Niger. It's hot in Chicago in the summer.

Sometimes they go _____ in Lake Michigan.

8.14 Verbs Followed by a Gerund or Infinitive

EXAMPLES	EXPLANATION
(a) Dawson liked **giving** money away. (b) He liked **to give** money away. (a) He started **working** in 1940. (b) He started **to work** in 1940.	Some verbs can be followed by either a gerund (a) or an infinitive (b) with no difference in meaning.

Note:

The verbs below can be followed by either a gerund or an infinitive with no difference in meaning:

begin	can't stand	continue	hate	like	love	prefer	start

EXERCISE 25 In the following sentences, change gerunds to infinitives and infinitives to gerunds.

1. Dawson's parents loved to help others.

<u>Dawson's parents loved helping others.</u>

2. They hated seeing people suffer.

<u>They hated to see people suffer.</u>

3. Dawson began working when he was 19 years old.

_____

4. He liked giving away money.

_____

5. He continued to work until his 80s.

_____

6. He preferred to live in a small apartment.

_____

7. He loved to help students get an education.

_____

EXERCISE 26 This is a conversation between a teenager and her older brother. Fill in the blanks with an appropriate gerund or infinitive. It doesn't matter which one you use. Answers may vary.

A: I want to work this summer, but I can't decide what to do.

B: How about volunteering in a museum?

A: I can't stand ___being OR to be___ indoors all day. I prefer _____ outdoors.
                           1.   **2.**

B: You're a great swimmer. Why don't you volunteer to teach kids how to swim?

A: I hate _____ with kids. It's hard work.
                    3.

B: Well, what do you like?

A: I love _____ at the beach.
                    4.

B: Maybe you should get a job as a lifeguard.

A: Great idea! I'll start _____ for a job tomorrow.
                       5.

B: That's what you said yesterday.

A: I guess I'm lazy. I just don't like _____ .
                             6.

8.15 Gerund or Infinitive as Subject

Either a gerund or an infinitive can be the subject of the sentence with no difference in meaning.

EXAMPLES	EXPLANATION
Helping others makes me feel good.	A gerund phrase can be used as the subject.
It makes me feel good **to help others.**	An infinitive phrase can be a delayed subject.
To help others makes me feel good.	An infinitive phrase can begin a sentence.

EXERCISE 27 Change these statements to begin with a gerund phrase.

1. It is wonderful to help others.

   Helping others is wonderful.

2. It costs a lot of money to go to college.

   _____

3. It is hard to work and study at the same time.

   _____

4. It is important to help students get an education.

   _____

continued

5. It is difficult to work in a factory.

_____

6. To die rich is a disgrace (according to Carnegie).

_____

7. It is satisfying to help others.

_____

8. It is a wonderful thing to sign the Giving Pledge.

_____

8.16 Gerund or Infinitive after a Verb: Differences in Meaning

EXAMPLES	EXPLANATION
Dawson loved to work. He didn't **stop working** until his 80s.	_Stop_ + gerund = quit or discontinue an activity
Dawson **stopped school to get** a job.	_Stop_ + (noun) + infinitive = quit one activity in order to start another activity
Do you **remember reading** about Carnegie?	_Remember_ + gerund = remember that something happened earlier
Dawson's mother said, "Always **remember to help** other people."	_Remember_ + infinitive = remember something and then do it
I **tried working** with kids but didn't like it. Then I **tried volunteering** at the park.	_Try_ + gerund = experiment with something new. You try one method, and if that doesn't work, you try a different method.
Joyce **tried to sell** her cards at art fairs. She **tried to make** money for sick kids.	_Try_ + infinitive = make an effort or an attempt

Note:
There is a big difference between _stop/remember_ + gerund and _stop/remember_ + infinitive. For _try_, the difference is mostly evident in the past tense.

EXERCISE 28 Read the following conversation between a son and his mother. Fill in the blanks with the gerund or infinitive of the word given.

A: Hi, Mom. I'm calling to say good-bye. I'm leaving for California tomorrow.

B: Really? You didn't tell me this.

A: Of course I did. I remember _____*telling*_____ you about it when I was at your house for dinner last
                                           1. tell

    week.

B: Oh, yes. Now I remember _____ you say something about it. Why are you going?
                                            2. hear

A: I have a friend there, and we've decided to do some volunteer work in a forest this summer.

B: Have I met your friend?

A: He was at my birthday party last year. You met him then.

B: I don't remember _____ him. Anyway, how are you getting to California?
  3. meet

A: I'm driving.

B: That's a long drive. If you get tired, you should stop _____ at a rest area. And you can
  4. rest

stop _____ a cup of coffee every few hours.
  5. get

A: I know. I will.

B: Don't stop _____ strangers. It could be dangerous.
  6. pick up

A: Of course I won't.

B: And remember _____ your cell phone on in case I want to call you. Last night I tried
  7. leave

_____ your cell phone, and I couldn't reach you.
  8. call

A: Did you leave a message?

B: I tried _____ a message, but your mailbox was full. So then I tried _____
  9. leave   10. text

you, but I'm not good at texting.

A: Don't worry. I'll leave my phone on.

B: You'll be outdoors all day for your job. Remember _____ sunscreen.
  11. use

A: Mom, stop _____ so much. And stop _____ me so much advice. I'm
  12. worry   13. give

24 years old!

B: Try _____. I'm your mother. Of course I worry.
  14. understand

ABOUT YOU Complete the sentences so they are true about you. Use a gerund or infinitive.

1. I often stop _____ when I am walking down the street.

2. I stopped _____ when I grew up.

3. I can't remember _____.

4. Whenever I go on vacation, I remember _____.

5. I tried _____, but I didn't like it.

6. I tried _____, and I loved it.

CYCLING
for a CAUSE

Cyclists during the Sac Valley World AIDS Day Bike Ride in Davis, California, USA

Read the following article. Pay special attention to the words in bold. 🎧 8.6

In 1994, a Californian named Dan Pallotta **saw** many people around him **die** of AIDS. He decided to see what he could do to raise money for AIDS research. He organized a bike ride from Los Angeles to San Francisco. Each rider asked friends and relatives to give donations to support the ride. His AIDS rides continued to grow. After nine years, 182,000 riders had participated, raising almost $600 million for charity research. Many more organizations started to have AIDS bike rides, raising millions of dollars.

Mimi Gordon, who has done several AIDS rides, wrote this in her journal:

I **used to think** that one person's contribution was not very important. But I was wrong. In 1998, I went on my first AIDS ride, from San Francisco to Los Angeles. Even though I bike to and from work every day (20 miles round trip), I **wasn't used to riding** long distances all at once. Also, I live in Chicago, where I **was used to riding** on flat land. I trained for about six months before the ride, riding at least 150 miles a week.

I **used to own** just a 10-speed road bike, but I realized that I would need a suitable bike for the long, hilly ride. I bought a new 24-speed mountain bike. I completed the ride and raised almost $5,000 for AIDS research. I felt so good about it that I started looking for more rides to do.

In 2001, I did the Alaska ride, which was especially difficult. It was mountainous, but that was not all: It was much colder than expected. Some of the riders couldn't **get used to** the cold and had to quit. But I'm proud to say that I finished it. I can't believe I **used to doubt** what one person can do.

COMPREHENSION Based on the reading, write T for *true* or F for *false*.

1. _____ In the first year of the AIDS ride, Dan Pallotta raised $600 million.

2. _____ The first AIDS ride was from Los Angeles to San Francisco.

3. _____ Mimi did a total of four AIDS rides.

THINK ABOUT IT Discuss the questions with a partner or in a small group.

1. What are some other sports people take part in to raise money? Give some examples.

2. Why are sports an especially good way to persuade people to make donations to good causes? Explain.

8.17 *Used To / Be Used To / Get Used To*

EXAMPLES	EXPLANATION
Mimi **used to own** a 10-speed bike. Now she owns a 24-speed bike. I **didn't use to exercise** much. Now I exercise almost every day.	*Used to* + the base form shows that an activity was repeated or habitual in the past. This activity has been discontinued. For the negative, we use *didn't use to*. We omit the *d* in the negative.
Mimi **is used to riding** her bike in Chicago, which is flat. She **isn't used to the cold wind** in Alaska.	*Be used to* + gerund or noun means to be accustomed to. This phrase describes a person's habits. It shows what is normal and comfortable. For the negative, we use *be* + *not* + *used to*. We don't omit the *d* in the negative.
Chicago is flat. Mimi had to **get used to** riding her bike in the mountains. Some of the riders **couldn't get used to** the cold wind and had to quit.	*Get used to* + gerund or noun means "become accustomed to." For the negative, we often use *can't* or *couldn't* before *get used to*. We don't omit the *d* in the negative.

Pronunciation Note:
The *d* in *used to* is not pronounced.

EXERCISE 29 Finish these statements. Answers may vary.

1. I used to _____*exercise once a week*_____, but now I exercise every day.

2. I used to _____ to work. Now I ride my bike. It's good exercise and I save money.

3. I used to _____ my bike only in the summer. But now I do it all year-round.

4. I used to _____ only money. Now I donate time and money to help others.

5. I used to _____ my extra money, but now I donate it to charity.

ABOUT YOU Complete the sentences so that they are true for you.

1. I used to _____.

2. I didn't use to _____, but now I _____.

3. I'm used to _____ in the morning.

4. I'm not used to _____ on weekends.

5. When I _____ I had to get used _____.

EXERCISE 30 Fill in the blanks with *be used to* and the correct form of the verb given.

1. **A:** I heard you volunteer with children now. Do you like it?

   B: I'm not sure yet. I've always worked with adults. I <u>'m not used to working</u> with children.

                                                         work

2. **A:** Do you want to train for the next California AIDS ride with me?

   B: California is mountainous. I _____ a bike in the mountains, so

                                           ride

   I think it's going to be hard for me.

3. **A:** Do you think it's hard for Bill Gates to give away money?

   B: I don't think so. He's been doing it for a long time. So I think he _____

                                                                              give

   away a lot of money.

4. **A:** Don't you think the story about Dawson is strange?

   B: Why?

   A: He had a lot of money, but he continued to drive his old car.

   B: Well, he _____ his old car. So it wasn't a problem for him.

                        drive

5. **A:** Patty Stonesifer had a high-paying job, but now she works with people in need. It must be hard.

   B: She loves it. She learned from her parents to help others. So she _____

                                                                              help

   other people.

6. **A:** I have a volunteer job on the weekends.

   B: Do you like it?

   A: I like the job, but I _____ on the weekend. I always used to relax

                              work

   and watch sports on TV on the weekend.

7. **A:** Joyce invited people to her house to make cards.

   B: I'm glad she never invited me. I _____ anything artistic.

                                            do

   A: Everyone told her the same thing. She _____ that. But she always explained

                                                 hear

   that no artistic talent was necessary.

8. **A:** I want to do an AIDS bike ride. I have a lot of experience riding a bike.

   B: Why don't you do it, then?

   A: There's just one problem. I'm from Thailand, where we always ride on the left side of the street.

   I _____ on the right side. I'm afraid I'll have an accident.

          ride

EXERCISE 31 Here is a story of a San Francisco man who did the Alaska AIDS ride. Circle the correct words to complete the story.

In 2001, I went on the AIDS bike ride in Alaska. My friends told me about it and asked me to join them. At first, I was afraid. My friends are good cyclists. They (used to ride/*are used to riding*) long distances because they
1.
do it all the time. They persuaded me to try it because it was for such a good cause. To get ready for the ride, I had to make some lifestyle changes. (*I'm/I*) used to be a little overweight,
2.
so I had to slim down and get in shape. First, I went on a diet. (*I/I was*) used to eating a lot of bread and rice, but now I eat
3.
mostly vegetables and lean meats. Also, I decided to get more exercise. I used to (*take/taking*) the bus to work every day,
4.
but I decided to start riding my bike to work. I work 10 miles from home, so it was hard for me at first. But little by little, I (*got used to/used to*) it. On the weekends, I started to take
5.
longer rides. Eventually I got used to (*ride/riding*) about
6.
45–50 miles a day. When the time came for the AIDS ride, I thought I was prepared. I live in San Francisco, which is hilly, so I was used to (*ride/riding*) up and down hills. But it's not
7.
cold in San Francisco. On some days the temperature in Alaska was only 25 degrees Fahrenheit, with strong winds. At first, I (*wasn't/couldn't*) get used to the cold. It was especially
8.
hard to (*used/get used*) to the strong winds. But eventually, I
9.
got (*use/used*) to it. I am proud to say I was one of the 1,600
10.
riders who finished the ride. I didn't (*use/used*) to think that
11.
one person could make a difference, but I raised close to $4,000. As a group we raised $4 million. And I've become a much healthier person because of this experience.

A group of people cycling in Skagway, Alaska, USA

8.18 Sense-Perception Verbs

The sense-perception verbs are: *hear, listen, feel, smell, see, watch, observe*. After these verbs, we can use either the *-ing* form or the base form with a slight difference in meaning.

EXAMPLES	EXPLANATION
I **heard** you **talk** about the Giving Pledge a few days ago. Dan Pallotta **saw** many people around him **die** of AIDS.	When the base form is used after a sense-perception verb (*saw, heard,* etc.), it indicates completion.
I **heard** you **talking** about a charity project. I **saw** some teenagers **volunteering** in the park last week.	Use the *-ing* form to show that something is sensed while it is in progress.

EXERCISE 32 Fill in the blanks with the base form or *-ing* form of the verb given. In some cases, both forms are possible.

By their example, my parents always taught me to help others. One time when I was a child, on

the way to a birthday party with my father, we saw a small boy _____walking_____ alone on the
                                                                    1. walk

street. As we approached him, we heard him _____. My father went up to him and
                                                    2. cry

asked him what was wrong. The boy said that he was lost. I saw my father _____ his
                                                                                3. take

hand and heard him _____ the boy that he would help him find his parents. My father
                         4. tell

called the police. Even though we were in a hurry to go to the party, my father insisted on staying with

the boy until the police arrived. I really wanted to go to the party and started to cry. I felt my father

_____ my hand and talk to me softly. He said, "We can't enjoy the party while this
    5. take

little boy is alone and afraid." Before the police arrived, I saw a woman _____ in our
                                                                                6. run

direction. It was the boy's mother. She was so grateful to my father for helping her son that she offered

to give him money. I heard my father _____ her, "I can't take money from you. I'm
                                            7. tell

happy to be of help to your son."

I hear so many children today _____, "I want" or "Buy me" or "Give me." I think
                                    8. say

it's important to teach children to think of others before they think of themselves. If they see their

parents _____ others, they might grow up to be charitable people.
            9. help

SUMMARY OF UNIT 8

Infinitives and Base Forms

EXAMPLES	EXPLANATION
Matel Dawson *wanted* **to help** others.	An infinitive is used after certain verbs.
His mother wanted *him* **to help** others.	An infinitive can follow an object noun or pronoun.
He was *happy* **to give away** his money.	An infinitive can follow certain adjectives.
We sell cards (**in order**) **to raise** money.	An infinitive is used to show purpose.
It's important **to help** others. **To help** others is our moral obligation.	INFORMAL: *It* introduces a delayed infinitive subject. FORMAL: The infinitive can be in the subject position.
It's good *for people* **to help** others. It's fun *for me* **to volunteer**.	*For* + noun or object pronoun is used to give the infinitive a subject.
I have *enough* time **to volunteer**. Dawson was *too* poor **to finish** school.	An infinitive can be used after a phrase with *too* and *enough*.
He often *heard* his mother **talk** about helping.	After sense perception verbs, a base form is used for a completed action.
It is important **to be loved**.	An infinitive can be used in the passive voice.
She *let* me **work**. She *made* me **work**. She *had* me **work**. She *got* me **to work**. She *convinced* me **to work**. She *persuaded* me **to work**.	After causative verbs *let, make,* and *have,* we use the base form. After causative verbs *get, convince,* and *persuade,* we use the infinitive.
He *helped* students **to get** an education. He *helped* them **pay** their tuition.	After *help,* either the infinitive or the base form can be used.

Gerunds

EXAMPLES	EXPLANATION
Going to college is expensive in the U.S.	A gerund can be the subject of the sentence.
Dawson *enjoyed* **giving** money away.	A gerund follows certain verbs.
He learned *about* **giving** from his parents.	A gerund can be used after a preposition.
He had a hard *time* **supporting** his family.	A gerund is used after certain nouns.
Those teenagers over there are volunteers. You can *see* them **cleaning** the park.	An *–ing* form is used after sense perception verbs to describe an action in progress.
He doesn't like to **go shopping**.	A gerund is used in many expressions with *go.*
I appreciate **being given** an education.	A gerund can be used in the passive voice.

Gerund or Infinitive—Differences in Meaning

EXAMPLES	EXPLANATION
I **used to spend** all my extra money. Now I save it.	Discontinued past habit
Patty **is used to working** in a poor neighborhood.	Present custom
Mimi always rode her bike on flat land. It was hard for her to **get used to riding** in the mountains.	Change of custom
Bicyclists can **stop to rest** when they get tired.	Stop one activity in order to do something else
When I was younger, I did the AIDS ride. I **stopped doing** it because it's too hard for me now.	Stop something completely
I **try to give** a little money to charity each year.	Make an attempt or effort
My old bike wasn't good enough for the ride. I **tried using** a mountain bike, and it was much better.	Experiment with a different method
Remember to help other people.	Remember and then do
Do you **remember reading** about Patty Stonesifer?	Remember something about the past

REVIEW

Fill in the blanks with the correct form of the verb given. Add prepositions, if necessary. In some cases, more than one answer is possible.

It's difficult for a college student ____to have____ time for anything else but studying. But when Charity
                                      1. have

Bell was a student at Harvard, she made time in her busy schedule _____ babies in need.
                                                                    2. help

When Bell was 23, she became interested _____ needy babies. She was volunteering at a
                                         3. help

children's hospital. The volunteer organization wanted her _____ to the kids and
                                                            4. read

_____ games with them. The parents of these very sick children were there, too, but they were
5. play

often too tired _____ or _____ with their kids. They were grateful to her
                 6. read   **7. play**

_____ them. One day she went to the hospital and heard a baby _____ loudly in
8. help   **9. cry**

the next room. She went into that room and picked up the baby; the baby immediately stopped

_____. She stayed with the baby for a few hours. When she began _____, the
10. cry   **11. leave**

baby started _____ again. Bell asked the nurse about this baby, and the nurse told her that the
              12. cry

baby was taken away from her parents and they couldn't find a temporary home for her.

The next day, Bell started _____ about how to be a foster parent. She made herself
                           13. learn

available to help on nights and weekends. Her phone started _____ immediately. She got used
                                                            14. ring

to _____ up the phone in the middle of the night. She became accustomed _____
   15. pick   **16. take**

in children all the time. Before she started taking care of babies, she used to _____ seven or
                                                                                17. sleep

eight hours a night. Then she had to get used to _____ only three or four hours a night.
                                                 18. sleep

By the time she was 28 years old and in graduate school, Bell had been a foster mother to 50 children.

_____ her studies, she had to take "her" babies to class with her. Her professors let her
19. complete

_____ this. They understood that it was necessary for her _____ and
20. do   **21. study**

_____ care of the babies at the same time. And her classmates didn't complain about
22. take

_____ a baby in the back of the class. Everyone understood how important it was for her
23. have

_____ these babies.
24. help

Even though Bell is sometimes tired, she is never too tired _____ in a child that needs her.
                                                            25. take

She gets very little money for _____ care of these children. However, she gets great satisfaction
                               26. take

_____ a baby _____. _____ her babies _____ is always
27. watch   **28. grow**   **29. see**   **30. leave**

a bit sad for her, but there are more babies who need her. _____ love to a child is her greatest joy.
                                                           31. bring

FROM GRAMMAR TO WRITING

PART 1 Editing Advice

1. Don't forget *to* when introducing an infinitive.

   He wants ∧*to* help other people.

   It's important ∧*to* be a charitable person.

2. Don't omit *it* when introducing a delayed infinitive.

   ~~Is~~ *It's* important for rich people to help others.

3. After *want, need*, and *expect*, use the object pronoun, not the subject pronoun, before the infinitive.

   My parents want ~~that I~~ *me to* donate money to charity.

4. Don't use *to* between *cost* or *take* and the indirect object.

   It costs ~~to~~ Leslie $5,000 to bring a girl to the U.S. from Niger.

   It took ~~to~~ him 20 hours to finish the bike ride.

5. Use *for*, not *to*, when you give a subject to the infinitive.

   It is easy ~~to~~ *for* me to ride my bike on flat land.

6. Use *to* + base form, not *for*, to show purpose.

   Carnegie worked hard ~~for~~ *to* build libraries.

7. Use a gerund or an infinitive, not a base form, as a subject.

   Help∧*ing* others makes me feel good. OR It makes me feel good to help others.

8. Don't confuse *used to* and *be used to*.

   I ~~am~~ used to drive to school. Now I ride my bike.

   I've lived in Alaska all my life and I love it. I∧*'m* used to ~~live~~ *living* in Alaska.

9. Be careful to use the correct form after *stop*.

   The story about Dawson was so interesting. I can't stop ~~to~~ think∧*ing* about it.

10. Use a gerund, not an infinitive, after a preposition.

    Have you ever thought about ~~to~~ volunteer∧*ing* with children?

11. Make sure to choose a gerund after certain verbs and an infinitive after others.

    I enjoy ~~to~~ help∧*ing* other people.

    He decided ~~volunteering~~ *to volunteer* in the public library.

12. Use a base form after a sense-perception verb that shows completion.

    I saw Mimi ~~to~~ finish her bike ride.

13. Use the base form, not the infinitive, after causative verbs *let, make*, and *have*.

    Bill Gates has billionaires ~~to~~ sign the Giving Pledge.

PART 2 Editing Practice

Some of the shaded words and phrases have mistakes. Find the mistakes and correct them. If the shaded words are correct, write *C*.

            C   *to*

It's important for everyone ∧ do something for others. I often thought about to help other
             1.   **2.**   **3.**

people. My parents wanted that I help in their business, but I saw my parents to work too hard,
                        4.   **5.**

and they had very little satisfaction from it or time for our family. I decided become a nurse
                                                         6.

instead. It took to me three years to complete the nursing program, and I'm happy I did it. First,
              7.   **8.**

find a job was easy because nurses are always in demand. Second, I enjoy working with sick
   9.   **10.**

people and make them to feel better. Some of my friends think is depressing to work with sick
          11.   **12.**   **13.**   **14.**

people all day, but it's easy for me to do it because I love helping people.
                15.   **16.**   **17.**

There's one thing I don't like about my job: I have to work nights, from 11 p.m. to 7 a.m. At
                                       18.

first, I couldn't get used to sleep in the day. My kids are home on Saturday and Sunday, and when
                19.

I was trying sleeping, they sometimes wouldn't stop to make noise. When they were younger,
          20.   **21.**

they're used to make a lot of noise, but now that they're older, they understand. My wife made
   22.

them understand that their dad needed his sleep and she needed them be quiet in the morning.
    23.   **24.**

My daughter is now thinking about become a nurse, too.
                       25.

People work for make money, but it's important for everyone finding a job that they love.
            26.   **27.**   **28.**

Working as a nurse has been wonderful for me. I get a lot of satisfaction helping other people.
   29.   **30.**

WRITING TIP

Often it's necessary for two or more actions to follow one of the words or phrases you studied in this unit. It's important that these actions are all in the same form. This is called *parallel structure*.

    *He continued to **earn** money and **help** people with it.*

    *I love **running** and **raising** money for good causes.*

PART 3 Write

Read the prompts. Choose one and write one or more paragraphs about it.

1. Andrew Carnegie wrote: "It is not good to have money if your spirit is poor." Describe what it means to have a rich spirit or a poor spirit. Give examples using people you know or have read about.
2. How does volunteering enrich the life of the volunteer?

PART 4 Edit

Reread the Summary of Unit 8 and the Editing Advice. Edit your writing from Part 3.

Adverbial Clauses and Phrases
Sentence Connectors
So . . . That/Such . . . That

New citizens at a U.S. Citizenship and Immigration
Services (USCIS) naturalization ceremony at the
New York Public Library in New York City

Once I thought to write a history of the immigrants in America. Then I discovered that the immigrants were American history.

OSCAR HANDLIN

COMING TO
AMERICA

Immigrants arrive at Ellis Island in the early 1900s.

A Nation of Immigrants

Read the following article. Pay special attention to the words in bold. 🎧 9.1

Ever since the United States became a country, it has been a nation of immigrants. The United States has taken in more foreigners than the rest of the world combined.

It is not uncommon for Americans to ask each other about their family background. Except for Native Americans, Americans have their roots in one or more countries. **Even though they are proud to be Americans,** many people often use two or more words to describe their national identity: "I'm Greek American," or "I'm an African American," or "I'm one-fourth English, one-fourth Irish, and one-half Polish."

Why have so many people chosen to leave everything behind **to come to a new land in spite of the hardships[1] they face?** The answer to that question is as diverse as the people who have come to the United States. In the 1600s, the first group of immigrants were the Pilgrims, who left England **to seek religious freedom in America.** Many other groups followed **to escape hardship** or **to find opportunity.**

In the 1800s, Germans came **because of political unrest and economic problems in Germany.** Irish and Chinese people came **because of famine in their countries.** At the beginning of the 20th century, many Jews came from Eastern Europe **in order to escape** religious persecution[2]. Many Italians came **for work.**

By 1910, almost 15 percent of the population was foreign born. Some people thought: **If immigration continues at this pace,** the United States will lose its "American" identity. In 1924, Congress passed a law limiting the number of immigrants. By 1970, less than 5 percent of the population was foreign born, an all-time low.

In 1965, Congress passed a bill allowing more immigrants to come, and the foreign-born population started to rise quickly. In the 1970s, Vietnamese and Cambodians came **because of war.** Immigration from

U.S. Foreign-Born Population and Percentage of Total 1850-2010

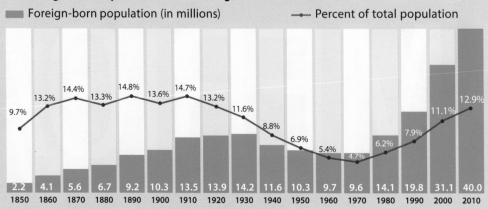

Foreign-born population (in millions) — Percent of total population

Year	1850	1860	1870	1880	1890	1900	1910	1920	1930	1940	1950	1960	1970	1980	1990	2000	2010
Population (millions)	2.2	4.1	5.6	6.7	9.2	10.3	13.5	13.9	14.2	11.6	10.3	9.7	9.6	14.1	19.8	31.1	40.0
Percent	9.7%	13.2%	14.4%	13.3%	14.8%	13.6%	14.7%	13.2%	11.6%	8.8%	6.9%	5.4%	4.7%	6.2%	7.9%	11.1%	12.9%

Source: U.S. Census Bureau, Census of Population, 1850 to 2000 and the American Community Survey, 2010

Asian countries quadrupled. Many others, such as Bosnians and Iraqis, came **because their countries were at war.** And, as always, people came **so that they could be reunited with family members who had come before.**

According to Pew Research Center, 13.6 percent of the population is foreign born, with most of the immigrants from South and East Asia and Mexico.

Since the U.S. has always been perceived as the land of freedom and opportunity, immigrants will continue to come and prosper, many achieving the American Dream.

_____

¹ hardship: difficulty
² persecution: unjust or cruel treatment because of differences in belief

COMPREHENSION Based on the reading, write T for *true* or F for *false.*

1. _____ The highest percentage of foreign-born Americans was in 1910.

2. _____ Americans often identify themselves with the nationality of their ancestors.

3. _____ Most of the immigrants coming to America today are from Europe.

THINK ABOUT IT Discuss the questions with a partner or in a small group.

1. How has the U.S. benefited from immigration? How has it faced challenges? Give examples.

2. What difficulties do immigrants experience when they first arrive in a new country? How can they deal with these problems? Share your ideas.

9.1 Adverbial Clauses and Phrases—Introduction

Some sentences have an adverbial clause or phrase and a main clause. We use adverbial clauses for a variety of reasons.

EXAMPLES	EXPLANATION
Before the 1960s, more than half of immigrants came from Europe.	To indicate time
Germans came to the U.S. **because of economic problems in Germany.**	To give reasons
Many immigrants come **so that they can be reunited with family members.**	To show purpose
Even though it's hard to be an immigrant, many people make that choice.	To show contrast
If the U.S. didn't have immigrants, it would be a less interesting place.	To state conditions

Note:

The adverbial clause or phrase can come before or after the main clause. If it comes before, it is usually separated from the main clause with a comma.

   I went to Canada before I came to the United States. (NO COMMA)

   Before I came to the United States, I went to Canada. (COMMA)

___

EXERCISE 1 Listen to the story about the author's family. Write T for *true* or F for *false.* 🎧 9.2

1. _____ The speaker's grandfather worked as a doctor in Chicago.

2. _____ The speaker's grandmother was used to traveling long distances.

3. _____ The family was not allowed into the United States at first because one of the children was sick.

EXERCISE 2 Listen again. Fill in the blanks with the words you hear. 🎧 9.2

I'm a Jewish American. My maternal grandfather came to the United States from Poland in 1911

_____because_____ he wanted a better life for his wife and children. Life was hard for them in Poland,
       1.

and they had heard stories of how you could better yourself in America _____ you were
                                                  2.

poor. _____ my grandfather was working as a tailor in Chicago, he saved money
         3.

_____ he could bring his family to join him. _____ 10 years of hard work,
        4.   **5.**

he had finally saved up enough money. _____ he had been in the United States for
                                      6.

10 years, he didn't learn much English _____ he had to go to work immediately.
                            7.

_____ my grandmother and her four children started their journey in 1921, they had
        8.

never left their village before. They arrived in New York _____ that was the entry point for
                                      9.

most immigrants at that time. They were tired and scared _____ they didn't speak one
                                  10.

word of English. They were afraid of what to do next, _____ finally, they saw my
                               11.

grandfather waiting for them. The immigration officials detained them in New York _____
                                              12.

my mother's youngest sister was sick. At that time, you couldn't enter the country _____
                                            13.

your health was good. She was taken to a hospital. _____ she was in the hospital for one
                                14.

week, she was released and the family was ready to start their new life. From New York, they took a train to

Chicago. _____ they arrived in Chicago, my mother, the oldest, was 16 years old. She went
            15.

to work in a factory _____ she could help her younger brother and sisters get an education.
               16.

EXERCISE 3 In Exercise 1, tell if the filled in words express time (T), reason (R), purpose (P), contrast (Ct), or condition (Cd).

1. __R__   5. _____   9. _____   13. _____

2. _____   6. _____   10. _____   14. _____

3. _____   7. _____   11. _____   15. _____

4. _____   8. _____   12. _____   16. _____

9.2 Reason and Purpose

EXAMPLES	EXPLANATION
My family left Poland **because they wanted to improve their lives.**	*Because* introduces a clause of reason.
My grandfather didn't have time to go to school **because of his job.**	*Because of* introduces a noun or noun phrase.
Since my grandparents were not wealthy, my father did not go to college.	*Since* means *because.* It is used to introduce a reason or cause. The main clause is the result.
The Pilgrims came **in order to seek religious freedom.** Vietnamese people came **to escape war.**	*In order to* shows purpose. The short form is *to.* We follow *to* with the base form of the verb.
My grandmother came **so that the family could be reunited.** He wants his wife to come next year **so they can be together again.**	*So that* shows purpose. The short form is *so.* The purpose clause usually contains a modal: *can, will,* or *may* for future; *could, would,* or *might* for past.
She came to the U.S. **for a better life.**	*For* shows purpose. *For* is followed by a noun (phrase).

Notes:

1. Remember: *Since* can also be used to show time. The context tells you the meaning of *since.*

    He has been in the U.S. **since** 2003. *(time)*

    Since my grandfather had to work hard, he didn't have time to study English. *(reason)*

2. *So* is also used to show result. The context tells you the meaning of *so.*

    I came to the U.S. alone, **so** I miss my family. *(result)*

    I came to the U.S. **so (that)** I could get an education. *(purpose)*

    Notice that a comma is used for result, but not for purpose.

EXERCISE 4 Fill in the blanks with *because, because of, since, for, (in order) to,* or *so (that).*

1. Many immigrants came to the U.S. ____(in order) to____ escape famine.

2. Many immigrants came _____ they didn't have enough to eat.

3. _____ they could give their children a good education, many immigrants came to the U.S.

4. _____ the political situation, many people left their countries.

5. Many immigrants came _____ they could escape war.

6. Many immigrants came _____ the poor economy in their countries.

7. Many immigrants came _____ be reunited with their relatives.

8. _____ war destroyed their homes, many people left their countries.

9. _____ escape poverty, many immigrants came to the U.S.

10. Often immigrants come _____ they want a better future for their children.

11. Immigrants come to the U.S. _____ a better life.

EXERCISE 5 Complete the conversation using *because, because of, for, since, so (that),* or *(in order) to.*
Answers may vary.

A: I heard you moved.

B: Yes. We moved last month. We bought a bigger house _____*so that*_____ we would have room for my
                                                         1.

parents. They're coming to the U.S. next month _____ they want to be near us.
                                                 2.

A: Don't you mind having your parents live with you?

B: Not at all. It'll be good for them and good for us. _____ our jobs, we don't get home until
                                               3.

after 6 p.m., and we don't want the kids to come home to an empty house.

A: Are your parents going to work?

B: No. They're not coming here _____ jobs. They're in their late 60s and are both retired. They're
                                          4.

coming here _____ they can help out. But they're not just coming _____ babysit.
                       5.   **6.**

We want the kids to spend time with my parents _____ they won't forget our language. Also, we
                                           7.

want them to learn about our culture _____ they've never been to our country. Our son is
                                       8.

starting to speak more English than Spanish. He prefers English _____ all his friends
                                               9.

speak English.

A: That's how many kids are in America. They prefer to speak English _____ they can be just like
                                          10.

their friends. Do your parents speak English?

B: Just a little. What about your parents? Where do they live?

A: They live a few blocks away from me, but we almost never see each other _____ our different
                                         11.

schedules. _____ they work in the day and I work in the evening, it's hard for us to get together.
         12.

ABOUT YOU Fill in the blank with a reason or purpose. Discuss your answers with a partner.

1. I came to the U.S. (or this town) _____.

2. I'm learning English grammar _____.

3. I plan/don't plan to go back to my country (home town) _____

    _____.

4. I love/don't love studying English _____.

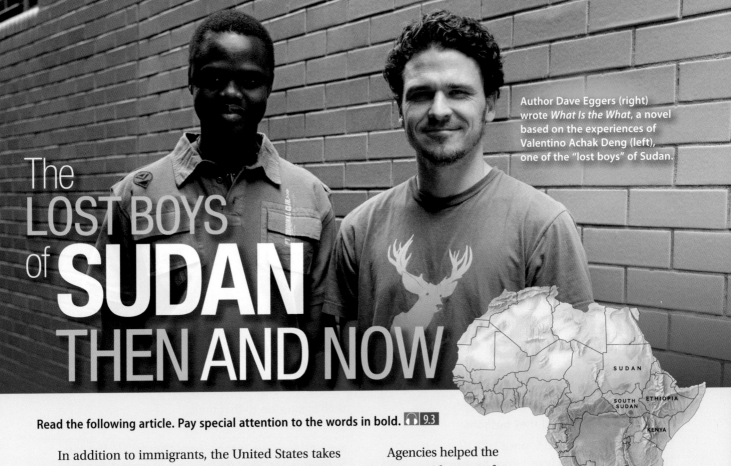

The LOST BOYS of SUDAN THEN AND NOW

Author Dave Eggers (right) wrote *What Is the What*, a novel based on the experiences of Valentino Achak Deng (left), one of the "lost boys" of Sudan.

SUDAN

SOUTH SUDAN   ETHIOPIA

KENYA

Read the following article. Pay special attention to the words in bold. 🎧 9.3

In addition to immigrants, the United States takes in thousands of refugees a year. One group of refugees that came in the 1980s were known as the Lost Boys of Sudan. They were a large number of children, mostly boys between the ages of 4 and 12, who were forced to leave their homes in South Sudan. One day, **while these young boys were in the field taking care of their cattle**[1], their villages were attacked. They ran for their lives. **For three months**, they walked hundreds of miles **until they reached Ethiopia.**

During their escape, many died. Those who reached Ethiopia stayed in refugee camps **until 1991, when a war started in Ethiopia and the camps were closed**. They ran again, back to Sudan and then to Kenya, where they stayed in refugee camps **for almost ten years**. Of the approximately 27,000 boys who fled Sudan, only 11,000 survived.

During their time in refugee camps, they got some schooling and learned basic English. In 1999, the United Nations and the U.S. government agreed to resettle 3,800 Lost Boys in the United States.

When they arrived in the United States, many challenges awaited them. They had to learn a completely new way of life. Many things were new for them: apartment living in a big city, strange foods, new technologies, and much more.

Agencies helped the Lost Boys with money for food and rent **until they found jobs. While they were working**, most of them enrolled in English classes. Many have now graduated from college and started projects to help their villages back home.

Valentino Achak Deng, who arrived in the U.S. in 2001 and settled in Atlanta, Georgia, is one of many refugees who have given back to their home countries after years of struggle. **When Deng and author Dave Eggers met in 2006**, they began collaborating on a story. The result was the novel *What Is the What?*, which tells of Deng's experience in Sudan and in the United States. With the money from the book, Deng opened a school in his hometown of Marial Bai, South Sudan. He also started a foundation, the Valentino Achak Deng Foundation, to help educate children in South Sudan.

When Deng reflected on his life experience, he said, "The lesson I can draw is that people can always learn, come through tough times, and persevere and grow."

---

[1] cattle: cows, bulls, and oxen as a group

Connecting Ideas 257

COMPREHENSION Based on the reading, write T for *true* or F for *false*.

1. _____ The Lost Boys were in a refugee camp in Ethiopia until they came to the U.S.

2. _____ When their villages were attacked, the Lost Boys ran back home.

3. _____ Some of the Lost Boys are helping their people in South Sudan.

THINK ABOUT IT Discuss the questions with a partner or in a small group.

1. How were the problems faced by the Lost Boys in the United States different from those facing other immigrants? Explain.

2. What do you think it would be like to be a refugee from your home country? Share your ideas.

9.3 Time Clauses and Phrases

EXAMPLES	EXPLANATION
When Deng and author Dave Eggers met in 2006, they began collaborating on a story.	*When* means "at that time" or "immediately after that time."
Whenever they tell their story, Americans are amazed.	*Whenever* means "any time" or "every time."
They walked **until they reached Ethiopia**. They received help **until they got jobs**.	*Until* means "up to that time."
Deng has been in the U.S. **since 2001**. He has been working **(ever) since he arrived**.	*Since* or *ever since* means "from that time in the past to the present." We use the present perfect or present perfect continuous in the main clause.
While they were taking care of their cattle, their villages were bombed. **As they were coming to the U.S.**, they were thinking about their new life ahead.	We use *while* or *as* with a continuous action.
They walked **for three months**. They stayed in a refugee camp **for many years**.	We use *for* with an amount of time.
During the day, they walked. **During their time in the refugee camp**, they studied English.	We use *during* with a time such as *the day* or *summer*, or with a specific time period (*their time in Ethiopia, the month of August*) or an event (*the flight to the U.S.*).

EXERCISE 6 Fill in the blanks with *since, until, while, when, as, during, for,* or *whenever*. In some cases, more than one answer is possible.

1. The Lost Boys were very young _____ when _____ they left Sudan.

2. The Lost Boys walked _____ many months.

3. _____ their march to Ethiopia, many of them died.

4. They lived in Ethiopia _____ about four years.

5. They crossed the river _____ the rainy season.

6. Some died _____ they were walking to Ethiopia.

7. They studied English _____ they were living in Kenya.

8. _____ they were traveling to the U.S., they were wondering about their future.

9. They had never seen a gas stove _____ they came to the U.S.

10. _____ they came to the U.S., they have had to learn many new things.

11. _____ they came to the U.S., they saw modern appliances for the first time.

12. They enrolled in English classes _____ they came to the U.S.

13. In the U.S., many of them worked _____ they were going to school.

14. Deng has been working on his project _____ 2007.

15. _____ they think about their terrible journey, they feel sad.

EXERCISE 7 Fill in the blanks with an appropriate time word. In some cases, more than one answer is possible.

_____When_____ I was a child, I heard many stories about life in America. _____
      1.   2.
I saw American movies, I dreamed about coming to the U.S. My uncle had lived in the U.S.

_____ many years, and he often came back to visit. _____ he came back,
      3.   4.
he used to tell me stories and show me pictures of the U.S. _____ I was a teenager, I
                                                                                          5.
asked my mother if she would let me visit my uncle _____ my summer vacation, but she
                                                                              6.
said I was too young and the trip was too expensive. _____ I was 20, I finally decided to
                                                                                  7.
come to the U.S. _____ I was traveling to the U.S., I thought about all the stories my
                          8.
uncle had told me.

But I really knew nothing about the U.S. _____ I came here. _____
                                                                    9.   10.
I came to the U.S., I've been working hard and trying to learn English. I haven't had time to meet

Americans or have much fun _____ I started my job. I've been here _____
                                            11.   12.
five months now, and I just work and go to school. _____ I'm at school, I talk to my
                                                                            13.
classmates _____ our break, but on the weekends I'm alone most of the time. I won't be
                  14.
able to make American friends _____ I learn more English.
                                              15.

ABOUT YOU Write sentences about leaving your country or hometown and traveling to the U.S. or another place. Use the words given. Share your answers with a partner.

1. for

   For many years I wanted to leave my country. But my parents thought I was too young,

   so they wouldn't let me.

2. whenever

3. before

4. since

5. while

9.4 Using the *-ing* Form after Time Words

EXAMPLES

subject   subject
The Lost Boys went to Ethiopia after **they left** Sudan.

The Lost Boys went to Ethiopia after **leaving** Sudan.

       subject   subject
While **they were living** in a refugee camp, the Lost Boys learned some English.

While **living** in a refugee camp, the Lost Boys learned some English.

EXPLANATION

If the subject of the main clause and the subject of the time clause are the same, the sentence can be shortened by deleting the subject of the time clause and changing the verb to a present participle (*-ing*).

EXERCISE 8 Change the time clause to a participial phrase.

1. While they were running from their homes, they saw many dangerous animals.

   While running from their homes, they saw many dangerous animals.

2. The Lost Boys went to Kenya before they came to the U.S.

3. While they were living in Kenya, they studied English.

4. Before they came to the U.S., the Lost Boys had never used electricity.

5. Deng learned how to use a computer after he came to the U.S.

6. Before he found a job, Deng got help from the U.S. government.

7. Deng went back to South Sudan after he graduated from college.

8. While he was studying for his degree, Deng raised money for a school in South Sudan.

SLAVERY—
An American Paradox[1]

Read the following article. Pay special attention to the words in bold. 🎧 9.4

A slave family picking cotton near Savannah, Georgia

Even though most immigrants have come to the United States with great hopes and dreams, one group of people came unwillingly. They were brought as slaves from Africa. Almost half a million Africans were brought to work in the agricultural South. African families were torn apart as slaves were treated like property to be bought and sold.

In 1776, when the thirteen American colonies declared their independence from England, Thomas Jefferson, one of the founding fathers of the United States, wrote, "All men are created equal" and that every person has a right to "life, liberty, and the pursuit of happiness." **In spite of these great words,** Jefferson owned 200 slaves. The newly formed U.S. Constitution considered each slave to be three-fifths of a person. In order to keep slaves divided from each other and dependent on their masters, they were prohibited from learning to read and write.

Since the main southern crop, tobacco, was exhausting the land at the end of the 18th century, it seemed that the need for slavery would come to an end. However, there was suddenly a big demand for cotton. Previously, the production of cotton had been very slow because it was very time-consuming to remove the seeds. But a new invention made the production of cotton much faster. Suddenly, southern farmers found a new area of wealth—and a new reason to keep slaves. **Even though the African slave trade ended in 1808,** domestic slave trade continued. The slave population continued to grow as children were born to slave mothers. By 1860, there were four million slaves in the United States.

The country became divided over the issue of slavery, and the Civil War, between the North and the South, was fought from 1861 to 1865. **In spite of the fact that the North won and African Americans were freed,** it took another hundred years for Congress to pass a law prohibiting discrimination because of race, color, religion, sex, or national origin.

Although many new arrivals see the United States as the land of opportunity for everyone, there are still many challenges and a lot of work to be done.

---

[1] paradox: a situation that has contradictory aspects

COMPREHENSION Based on the reading, write T for *true* or F for *false*.

1. _____ The U.S. Constitution did not count slaves as part of the population.

2. _____ Thomas Jefferson owned slaves.

3. _____ When the slaves were freed, they gained equality.

THINK ABOUT IT Discuss the questions with a partner or in a small group.

1. Does the information about Thomas Jefferson surprise you? Why or why not?

2. Can laws truly reduce discrimination? Give reasons for your opinion, and share some examples if possible.

9.5 Contrast

EXAMPLES	EXPLANATION
Even though I know slavery existed, I cannot believe it was possible. **Although the U.S. Constitution guaranteed freedom,** many African Americans weren't free. **In spite of the fact that Jefferson wrote about equality,** he owned slaves.	For an unexpected result or contrast of ideas, we use a clause beginning with *even though, although,* or *in spite of the fact that.*
In spite of the difficulties, the Lost Boys started a new life in the U.S.	We use *in spite of* + a noun (phrase) to show contrast.
Although the Lost Boys are happy in the U.S., they **still** miss their country. **Even though it's hard to start a new life in a different country,** many immigrants do it **anyway.**	In speech and informal writing, *still* and *anyway* can be used in the main clause to emphasize the contrast.

Notes:

1. Informally, *even though* and *although* can be shortened to *though.*

    ***Though** it was difficult, I adjusted to life in a new country.*

2. In speech, *though* is often used at the end of a statement to show contrast with the preceding statement. (We don't use *even though* and *although* at the end of a statement.)

    *I adjusted to life in a new country. It was difficult, **though**.*

3. *While* is also used to show contrast. (Remember: *While* can also be a time word. The context tells you whether it shows time or contrast.)

    ***While leaving your home can be difficult,** many are forced to do it.*

EXERCISE 9 Circle the correct words to complete the conversation. If both choices are possible, circle both of them.

A: Are you surprised by slavery in the U.S.?

B: (*Even though*/In spite of) I've read about it and seen movies about it, it's hard for me to understand. I've
           1.

   always thought of the U.S. as a land of freedom and opportunity, (*although/in spite of*) I know it's not perfect.
                                                       2.

   But slavery was so terrible. How could that have happened in the U.S.?

A: I rented a movie recently about an African American man in the North who was kidnapped in the 1800s and

   taken to the South. (*In spite of the fact that/Even though*) he was a free man, he was sold into slavery. The
                                         3.

   name of the movie is *12 Years a Slave.*

continued

B: (*Although/In spite of*) I saw it a few years ago, I remember it well. (*In spite of/In spite of the fact that*) it was a
wonderful movie, it was very hard to watch the cruel way slaves were treated.

A: Do you think it was a realistic movie?

B: Unfortunately, it was. In fact, the reality was probably even worse than what we saw in the movie.

EXERCISE 10 Fill in the blanks with *in spite of* or *in spite of the fact that*.

1. <u>In spite of the fact that</u> the law says everyone has equal rights, some people are still suffering.

2. _____<u>In spite of</u>_____ Thomas Jefferson's declaration of equality for all, he owned slaves.

3. _____ slavery ended in 1865, African Americans
   did not receive equal treatment under the law until 1964.

4. The slave population continued to grow _____
   Americans stopped importing slaves from Africa.

5. Many immigrants come to America _____ the difficulty of starting a new life.

6. The Lost Boys did not lose hope for a bright future _____ the challenges they faced.

7. _____ his busy schedule, Deng tries to help his village in South Sudan.

8. _____ everything in America was new for them,
   the Lost Boys have adapted well to life in the U.S.

9. Many people still believe in the American dream _____
   life is not perfect in the U.S.

EXERCISE 11 Circle the correct words to complete the paragraph. If both choices are possible, circle both
of them.

When I was 16 years old, I wanted to come to the U.S. (*Even/*(Even though)) I was very
                                                                                1.

young, my parents gave me permission to leave home and live with my uncle in New Jersey.

(*In spite of the fact that/In spite of*) I was only in high school, I worked part time and saved money for
                          2.

college. (*Although/In spite of*) it was hard, I managed to finish high school and start college. My uncle
                     3.

always encouraged me to go to college (*in spite of/even though*) he is not an educated man. A lot of my
                                                       4.

friends from high school didn't go to college (*even though/in spite of*) the opportunities they had. I decided
                                                        5.

to become an English teacher (*even though/although*) I still have a bit of an accent.
                                                 6.

U.S. POPULATION:
Past, Present, and Future

Read the following article. Pay special attention to the words in bold. 🎧 9.5

As of 2018, the U.S. population was over 327 million. This number is expected to rise to more than 438 million by 2050. Most of the population growth will be from recent immigrants and their descendants. **Unless there are changes in immigration patterns**, nearly one in five people will be an immigrant in 2050. This is even higher than the top figures between 1890 and 1910, when about 15 percent were foreign born. These numbers assume that the immigration policy in the U.S. will not change significantly.

For most of the 19th and 20th centuries, the majority of immigrants to the U.S. were Europeans. However, since 1970, this trend has changed. More than 50 percent of the immigrants who have arrived since 1970 are Spanish speakers. The Hispanic population increased more than 50 percent between 1990 and 2000. **If current patterns of immigration continue and if the birth rate remains the same**, Hispanics, who are now 18 percent of the total population, will be 29 percent of the population by 2050. Hispanics are already about 38 percent of the population of California and Texas.

Because of their increasing numbers, Hispanic voters are gaining political power. In 2008, President Barack Obama received 67 percent of the Hispanic vote. In 2012, when Hispanics made up 10 percent of the voting population, Obama received 71 percent of their vote. It is clear that Hispanics have the power to determine elections.

Even if immigration policy changes, Hispanics will continue to see their numbers—and influence—grow, as will others who make their homes here. America will continue to be thought of as a land of hope and opportunity.

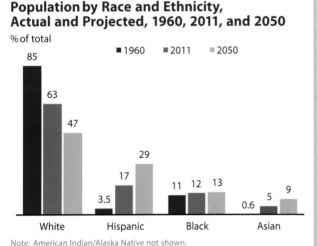

Population by Race and Ethnicity, Actual and Projected, 1960, 2011, and 2050

% of total

■ 1960 ■ 2011 ■ 2050

White: 85, 63, 47
Hispanic: 3.5, 17, 29
Black: 11, 12, 13
Asian: 0.6, 5, 9

Note: American Indian/Alaska Native not shown.
Source: Passel, Jeffrey, and D'Vera Cohn. 2008. "U.S. Population Projections: 2005–2050." Washington, D.C. Pew Hispanic Center February; Census Bureau 2011 population estimates.
PEW RESEARCH CENTER

Children marching in a 4th of July parade

COMPREHENSION Based on the reading, write T for *true* or F for *false*.

1. _____ African Americans are the largest minority in the U.S. today.

2. _____ By the middle of this century, 50 percent of the population will be Hispanic.

3. _____ Hispanics helped determine the presidential elections of 2008 and 2012.

THINK ABOUT IT Discuss the questions with a partner or in a small group.

1. What information in the text is new to you? Do the projections for the future of the United States surprise you? Why or why not?

2. How will politicians have to take changes in the population into account in the future? Explain.

9.6 Condition

EXAMPLES	EXPLANATION
If Hispanics vote together, they will have a lot of political power.	We use *if* to show that the condition affects the result.
Even if the immigration of Hispanics slows down, their number will probably increase.	We use *even if* to show that the condition doesn't affect the result.
You don't have political power **unless you vote**. (*unless you vote = if you don't vote*)	We use *unless* to mean *if not*.

Note:

If, even if, and *unless* can be used with present, past, and future sentences. In a future sentence, we use the simple present in the condition clause.

EXERCISE 12 Fill in the blanks with the correct form of the verb given.

1. If the Hispanic population ____continues____ to grow, 29 percent of the U.S. population

       continue

_____will be_____ Hispanic by the year 2050.

    be

2. Even if the number of immigrants _____ down, the general population _____.

                           go   increase

3. If more children _____ born in the next 50 years, more schools _____.

                be   passive: need

4. School classes _____ bigger if the number of school-age children _____.

                 get   increase

5. The U.S. population _____ almost 440 million by 2050 if immigration _____

                        be   continue

at the same rate.

6. Children of immigrants _____ their native language unless their parents

                      forget

_____ them to speak it.

    encourage

EXERCISE 13 Change the *if* clause in the sentences below to an *unless* clause.

1. Immigrants can't become American citizens if they don't pass a test.

   <u>Immigrants can't become American citizens unless they pass a test.</u>

2. Visitors can't enter the U.S. if they don't have a passport.

   _____

   _____

3. Immigrants will continue to come to the U.S. if conditions in their native countries don't improve.

   _____

   _____

4. In the 1800s, Southern farmers couldn't prosper if they didn't find a new crop to grow.

   _____

   _____

5. Foreigners cannot work in the U.S. if they don't have permission.

   _____

   _____

EXERCISE 14 Fill in the blanks in this conversation. Use *if* or *unless.*

A: My youngest daughter is seven years old, and she doesn't speak Spanish anymore. ____If____ I say
   _{1.}

   something to her in Spanish, she understands, but she answers in English.

B: _____ all her friends speak English, of course she's going to speak English.
   _{2.}

A: My mother can't understand what my daughter is saying _____ I translate it for her.
   _{3.}

B: I have the same problem. My son is 14, and he won't speak Spanish _____ he has to.
   _{4.}

   Last month my parents came to visit from Guatemala. My parents had a hard time understanding my son

   because he mixes Spanish and English. There are a lot of Spanish words he doesn't remember

   _____ I remind him.
   _{5.}

A: Maybe we should put our kids in a bilingual program at school. _____ they're in the
   _{6.}

   bilingual program, they'll have to speak Spanish.

B: I don't think the school will put them in a bilingual program _____ they're already
   _{7.}

   fluent in English.

A: I guess our kids won't speak Spanish well _____ we return to our native countries.
   _{8.}

ABOUT YOU Fill in the blanks and discuss your answers with a partner.

1. My English won't improve quickly unless _____

2. People understand my English even if _____

3. If _____, people don't understand me well.

EXERCISE 15 Fill in the blanks to complete this conversation between a Colombian woman who's going to immigrate to the U.S. and her friend. Use context clues to help you. Answers may vary.

A: I'm planning to go to Boston. I'm worried about the weather. They say it's very cold in the winter.

B: I'm sure people go out even if ___the weather is cold___.
                                          1.

A: What if people won't understand me? My accent isn't perfect.

B: Even if _____, people will probably understand you.
              2.

A: But I make so many grammar mistakes.

B: Don't worry. People will understand you even if _____.
                                                        3.

   Are you planning to get a job there?

A: I don't think I'm going to need one. I'm going to live with my relatives, and they said I can live

   there for free.

B: Even if _____, you'll need money for other things,
              4.

   like books, clothes, and transportation.

A: I know college is going to be expensive for me because I'm going to be an international student. I think

   college is free for American residents, isn't it?

B: No. Even if _____, you have to pay for college, but
                 5.

   it's cheaper for residents.

FUN WITH GRAMMAR

Create a story. Work with a partner. Use at least five of the following connectors in the story. When you are finished, check for errors and then read your story to your class. Vote on which pair has the best story. Begin the story like this:

   *Matilda ran to meet her friends at the 4th of July parade. She was late **because**...*

because	during	even if	even though	if
in order to	in spite of	so that	unless	whenever

Who Are the DREAMERS?

Parents all over the world want the same thing: a bright future for their children. Unfortunately, situations in many countries make this difficult. These situations have resulted in many families immigrating to the U.S., sometimes illegally.

In 2001, the Development, Relief, and Education for Alien Minors Act (DREAM) was introduced into Congress. **As a result**, the children of illegal immigrants became known as *Dreamers*. The act planned to offer them a route to legal residency in the United States. **However**, the act repeatedly failed to get the votes needed to pass, and **therefore,** it never became law.

The process of getting the act passed into law was taking **so long that** in June 2012, the government introduced DACA (Deferred Action for Childhood Arrivals). This federal program gave Dreamers certain temporary rights. They could legally live, work, and study in the U.S., but they did not have all the same rights as citizens. **Nevertheless**, they could get a driver's license, enroll in a college, or obtain a work permit. The future began to open up for the approximately 800,000 dreamers in the U.S.

Luz Divina, **for example,** was brought to the U.S. from Aguascalientes, Mexico, when she was just two months old: "I didn't know I was undocumented until my sophomore year of high school when I realized I couldn't get a drivers' permit, apply for jobs, and go to college programs like all my friends were doing." She says she felt depressed for years . . . "until I finally applied for DACA. I finally had a chance at the real world." Luz's dream is to become an educator and writer, and to help others with similar problems.

However, it is too soon to talk of a happy ending to the stories of young people such as Luz. There are those who feel that the children of illegal immigrants do not deserve any special treatment. It is **such a complex topic that** Congress cannot agree on what to do, and the continuation of DACA is in doubt. **Consequently,** at the time of writing, the future of Dreamers remains uncertain.

COMPREHENSION Based on the reading, write T for *true* or F for *false*.

1. _____ The name Dreamers comes from the high hopes new immigrants have.

2. _____ The children of illegal immigrants could not get basic documents before DACA.

3. _____ Before DACA, Luz Divina's situation caused her emotional stress.

THINK ABOUT IT Discuss the questions with a partner or in a small group.

1. How do you think it feels as a young person not to be able to do the same simple things as your friends?

2. Do you think that allowing Dreamers basic rights is a good thing? Why or why not?

9.7 Sentence Connectors

Sentence connectors, also called transitions, show the relationship between the ideas.

EXAMPLES	EXPLANATION
Everyone needs basic rights in order to live a normal life. **However,** this is not always easy for children of illegal immigrants. It is wonderful to see young people hopeful for the future. **Nevertheless,** there are people who oppose DACA.	Sentence connectors that show contrast are *however* and *nevertheless*. These words are similar in meaning to *but*.
Immigrating without the necessary paperwork is illegal. **In addition,** any child that accompanies an adult is illegal, too. **Furthermore,** these children may be adversely affected as they grow up.	Sentence connectors that add more information to the same idea are *in addition, furthermore, also,* and *moreover*. These words are similar in meaning to *and*.
Dreamers have to meet many conditions. **First,** they have to have been under 31 years old when DACA began. **Next,** they must have arrived in the U.S. before the age of 16. **In addition,** Dreamers must have lived in the U.S. continuously since June 2007.	Ideas can be ordered using *first, second, third, next, then,* etc. We can begin with *first* and continue with *furthermore, moreover, also, in addition*.
DACA introduced basic rights for Dreamers. **As a result,** many young immigrants could lead more normal lives. It is possible DACA will be terminated. **Therefore,** Dreamers face a very uncertain future.	Sentence connectors that show result or conclusion are *therefore, as a result,* and *for this reason*. These words are similar in meaning to *so*.
Life was very difficult for Dreamers before DACA. **For example,** they could not enroll in college. Dreamers are a very large group. **In fact,** there are more than 800,000 young people who are protected by DACA.	Other connectors are *for example* and *in fact*. *In fact* emphasizes the preceding statement. Sometimes it introduces something that might surprise the reader or listener.

Punctuation Notes:

1. We use either a period or a semicolon (;) before a sentence connector if it comes at the beginning of a sentence or clause. We use a comma after a sentence connector.

    My friend Carlos was accepted into the DACA program. **Therefore,** *he was able to attend college.*

    My friend Carlos was accepted into the DACA program; **therefore,** *he was able to attend college.*

2. Some sentence connectors can come in the middle of a sentence. We separate these from the sentence by putting a comma before and after the connector.

    Many people want to immigrate to America. The process, **however,** *can be long and complicated.*

Some connectors are used more in writing and formal speech than in everyday conversation. We generally use simpler connectors in informal speech.

Formal	Informal
Therefore, As a result, For this reason	so
Nevertheless, However	but
Moreover, Furthermore	and

EXERCISE 16 Choose the correct sentence connectors to fill in the blanks. In some cases both choices are possible, so circle both options.

1. The Lost Boys were happy living with their families in Sudan. (*However*/*In addition*), a war forced them to leave.

2. The Lost Boys faced many problems when they left Sudan. They didn't know where to go. (*Furthermore*/*Moreover*), they didn't have enough to eat.

3. Some of them couldn't swim. (*As a result*/*However*), some drowned when they had to cross a river in their escape.

4. Finally, they found safety in a refugee camp in Kenya. (*However*/*In fact*), conditions in the camp were very poor.

5. Many of the Lost Boys had never seen modern appliances before. (*Also*/*For example*), they had never used a gas stove.

6. They faced problems in the U.S. They had to find jobs quickly. (*For example*/*In addition*), they had to go to school to improve their English.

7. They are happy that they came to the U.S. (*In fact*/*Nevertheless*), they still miss their family and friends back home.

8. My grandfather immigrated to the U.S. for several reasons. (*First*/*In addition*), he needed to find a job to make more money. (*In fact*/*Furthermore*), he wanted to be reunited with his relatives who had come before him.

9. Most immigrants have come to the U.S. because they wanted to. (*However*/*Furthermore*), Africans were brought to America against their will to work as slaves.

10. In 1776, Thomas Jefferson wrote, "All men are created equal." (*Nevertheless*/*Therefore*), Jefferson had 200 slaves at that time.

11. Members of the same African family were sent to different areas to work as slaves. (*Therefore*/*As a result*), families were torn apart.

12. Slavery officially ended in 1865. (*However*/*Consequently*), many African American families continued to suffer.

13. African Americans had been the largest minority for many years. (*In fact*/*However*), this changed in 2003 when the Hispanic population became the largest minority.

14. DACA introduced basic rights for Dreamers and allowed them to accomplish ordinary goals like getting a driver's license. (*Moreover*/*Furthermore*), it allowed them to look toward the future with greater confidence.

15. The U.S. attracts more immigrants than any other country. (*In fact*/*For example*), one in five of the world's immigrants lives in the U.S.

EXERCISE 17 Complete each statement. Answers will vary.

1. The U.S. is a rich country. However, _it has many poor people. Many jobs do not pay enough_ _money for people to support their families._ _____

2. It is important for me to learn English. Therefore, _____

_____

_____

3. It is important for me to learn English. However, _____

_____

_____

4. Living in another country is difficult. Immigrants may have to adjust to a new language. In addition, _____

_____

_____

5. Some children speak one language at home and another at school. As a result, _____

_____

_____

6. To learn a new language, you must master the grammar. Furthermore, _____

_____

_____

7. I don't speak English perfectly. However, _____

_____

_____

8. English is not the only language of the U.S. In fact, _____

_____

_____

9. Life is hard for recent immigrants. First, _____

_____. Then, _____

_____

10. Children learn to speak English quickly. As a result, _____

_____

_____

9.8 So . . . That / Such . . . That

There are many patterns with *so* and *such . . . that*.

EXAMPLES	EXPLANATION
Dena was **such a hard working student that** her teachers recommended her to all the top colleges.	*such* + *a/an* + adjective + singular noun + *that*
The Lost Boys saw **such terrible things that** they will never forget them.	*such* + adjective + plural noun + *that*
Getting a driver's license is **so basic that** citizens do not even think of it as a right.	*so* + adjective + *that*
Children of immigrants learn English **so easily that** they become fluent in a short time.	*so* + adverb + *that*
In Miami, there are **so many Spanish speakers that** you can hear Spanish wherever you go.	*so many* + plural count noun + *that*
Before DACA, there were **so few opportunities** for Dreamers **that** their lives were very hard.	*so few* + plural count noun + *that*
There was **so much poverty** in Ireland in the 1800s **that** many people were forced to leave the country.	*so much* + noncount noun + *that*
There was **so little time** to change planes **that** we had to run.	*so little* + noncount noun + *that*

Note:

That is often omitted in informal speech.

> Peter works **so hard** *(that)* he doesn't have time to rest.

EXERCISE 18 Fill in the blanks with *so, so much, so many, so few, so little,* or *such (a/an)*.

1. We had _____ so many _____ problems in our country that we decided to leave.

2. I waited _____ long time that I thought I would never get permission.

3. When I got to the airport, the security lines were _____ long that I had to wait for two hours.

4. There were _____ people arriving at the same time that the process took a long time.

5. I was _____ happy when I got my green card that I started to cry.

6. The U.S. offers _____ freedom that people from all over the world want to come here.

7. Before I got my visa, I had to fill out _____ papers and give _____

    information that I thought I would never be able to do it.

8. We have been in the U.S. for _____ long time that we hardly speak our

    native language anymore.

9. My neighbor's daughter was _____ young when she arrived from China that she doesn't

    remember anything about China at all.

continued

10. Before DACA, there were _____ educational opportunities available to Dreamers that their

    job choices were very limited.

11. I spoke _____ English when I arrived in the U.S. that I always had to take my dictionary

    with me everywhere.

EXERCISE 19 Fill in the blanks with *so, so much, so many, so little, so few,* or *such a*. Then complete each
statement with a result. Answers will vary.

1. I was _____ happy when I got permission to come to the U.S. that _____

    _____ .

2. Many Dreamers were _____ young when they came to the U.S. that _____

    _____ .

3. Some people have _____ hard time learning English in the U.S. that _____

    _____ .

4. Some people had _____ hard life in their native countries that _____

    _____ .

5. In 1910, there were _____ foreign-born Americans that _____

    _____ .

6. I had _____ time to prepare for that trip that _____

    _____ .

SUMMARY OF UNIT 9

1. Words that connect a dependent clause or phrase to an independent clause:
   (Abbreviations: C = Clause; NP = Noun Phrase; VP = Verb Phrase; PP = Participial Phrase)

FUNCTION	CONNECTORS	EXAMPLES
Reason	*because* + C	**Because he studies hard**, his English is improving.
	since + C	**Since he studies hard**, his English is improving.
	because of + NP	**Because of his effort**, his English is improving.
Time	*when* + C	Many young people decide to go to college **when they obtain Dreamer status.**
	whenever + C	**Whenever people move to a new country**, they face difficulties.
	until + C or NP	Dreamers had a very hard life **until DACA was introduced.** Children who were brought into the U.S. illegally could not get a driver's license **until 2012.**
	while + C or PP	**While they were traveling to the U.S.**, the children's parents were hoping for a better future for their family.
	for + NP	Silvia lived in her native country **for** only **a few months** as a baby.
	during + NP	Dreamers have difficult lives because of something their parents **did during their childhood.**
	since + NP or C	Dreamers must have lived in the U.S. continuously **since June 2007.** Angelo has had a difficult time **since his family brought him to the U.S.**
Purpose	*(in order) to* + VP	He came to the U.S. **(in order) to have a better life.**
	so (that) + C	He came to the U.S. **so (that) he could improve his life.**
	for + NP	He came to the U.S. **for a better education.**
Contrast	*even though* + C	**Even though life was difficult for them**, the Lost Boys didn't lose hope.
	although + C	**Although life was difficult for them**, the Lost Boys didn't lose hope.
	in spite of the fact that + C	**In spite of the fact that life was difficult for them**, the Lost Boys didn't lose hope.
	in spite of + NP	**In spite of the difficulties**, the Lost Boys didn't lose hope.
Condition	*if* + C	**If population growth continues in the same way**, the U.S. will have 438 million people by 2050.
	even if + C	**Even if immigration slows**, the population will increase.
	unless + C	**Unless there are changes in population patterns**, one in five people in the U.S. will be an immigrant by 2050.

2. Words that connect two independent clauses:

FUNCTION	CONNECTORS	EXAMPLES
To add more to the same idea	*in addition* *furthermore* *moreover*	To become a Dreamer you must have arrived in the U.S. before your 16th birthday, and you must have lived in the U.S. continuously since June 2007. **In addition**, you must be a student, or have completed school or military service.
To add a contrasting idea	*however* *nevertheless*	The law says that everyone is equal. **However,** inequalities still exist.
To show a result	*therefore* *as a result* *for this reason* *consequently*	Some people suffer economic hardships. **Therefore,** they want to leave their countries.
To give an example	*for example*	Besides learning English, the Lost Boys faced many challenges when they arrived in the U.S. **For example**, they had to learn about city life.
To emphasize the truth of the preceding statement	*in fact*	The Lost Boys didn't see their parents for many years. **In fact**, they didn't even know if their parents were dead or alive.

3. Words that introduce result clauses:

CONNECTORS	EXAMPLES
so + adjective + *that*	She was **so happy that** she cried.
so + adverb + *that*	He speaks English **so fluently that** everyone thinks he's American.
so many + plural noun + *that*	The town has **so many** good **restaurants that** it's hard to choose one.
so few + plural noun + *that*	The city has **so few parks that** children play in the streets.
so much + noncount noun + *that*	There is **so much rain that** I cannot see the road.
so little + noncount noun + *that*	We have **so little time that** we should plan every step.
such a/an + adjective + singular noun + *that*	It was **such a difficult language that** few people tried to learn it.
such + adjective + plural noun + *that*	They were **such unusual stories that** no one could believe them.

REVIEW

Circle the correct words to complete this story. If both choices are correct, circle both.

Many people have come to America (*because*/*for*) freedom. But between the 1600s and the early 1800s,
1.

Africans were brought to America against their will (*for*/*to*)work in the fields of the South. Africans were
2.

taken from their homes and put on slave ships (*for*/*to*) cross the Atlantic. Conditions were (*so*/*such*) hard
3.   **4.**

that many died along the way.

Working conditions on the farms were terrible, too. (*For example*/*Also*), slaves had to pick cotton in the
5.

hot southern sun all day. They worked hard from morning till night (*so that*/*in order to*) plantation owners
6.

could become rich. These owners were often cruel to their slaves. (*In fact*/*However*), they often beat their
7.

slaves who didn't obey. (*In addition*/*Furthermore*), they provided only a minimum of food for survival.
8.

(*Although*/*Unless*) many people in the North were against slavery, slavery continued in the South
9.

(*because of*/*since*) Southern slave owners did not want to give up their cheap labor supply.
10.

(*Even though*/*However,*) an 1808 law prohibited the importation of slaves, slavery continued.
11.

(*In fact*/*In spite of*), by 1860, there were 4 million slaves in America. (*In spite of*/*In spite of the fact that*) the
12.   **13.**

difficulties of living under slavery, slaves formed strong communities. They tried to preserve their African

cultural practices, which included music and dance. (*Because*/*For*) people from the same regions in Africa
14.

were separated from each other, they lost their native languages, used English, and were given names by

their owners.

Most people of African descent in the North were free. (*In addition*/*However*), they didn't have an easy
15.

life. They couldn't attend public schools. (*Furthermore*/*However*), they weren't allowed to vote. Many slaves
16.

from the South tried to run away to the North. (*However,*/*Although*) some were caught and sent back to
17.

their owners.

(*Unless*/*Until*) the slaves were finally freed in 1865, they faced many difficulties.
18.

(*In spite of the fact that*/*In spite of*) the majority of Africans by that time were born in America, they
19.

suffered discrimination (*because*/*because of*) the color of their skin.
20.

Discrimination was still legal (*when*/*until*) 1964, when Congress passed a law prohibiting
21.

discrimination in jobs and education. (*Although*/*In spite of*) there has been progress toward equality for
22.

all, there are still many inequalities in American life.

FROM GRAMMAR TO WRITING

PART 1 Editing Advice

1. Use *to*, not *for*, with a verb when showing purpose.

    She came to the U.S. ~~for~~ *to* get a better education.

2. Don't combine *so* with *because*, or *but* with *even though*.

    Because his country was at war, ~~so~~ he left his country.

    Even though he speaks English well, ~~but~~ he can't find a job.

3. Use *because of* when a noun phrase follows.

    People don't understand me well because *of* my accent.

4. Don't use *even* without *though* or *if* to introduce a clause.

    Even *though* Peter misses his family, he's happy in the U.S.

5. Use the *-ing* form, not the base form, after a time word if the subject is deleted.

    Before ~~come~~ *coming* to the U.S., he studied English.

6. Don't confuse *so that* (purpose) with *so* (result).

    She wanted to have a better life, so ~~that~~ she came to the U.S.

7. After *so that*, use a modal before the verb.

    Farmers used slave labor so that they *could* become rich.

8. In a future sentence, use the simple present in the *if* clause or time clause.

    If I ~~will~~ go back to my hometown, I will tell my family about life in the U.S.

9. *However* connects two sentences. *Although* connects two parts of the same sentence.

    I studied English in my country. ~~Although~~ *However,* I didn't understand Americans when I arrived.

10. An adverbial clause or phrase must be attached to the main clause.

    She went to Canada because her parents were living there.
    ~~She went to Canada. Because her parents were living there.~~

11. Use *so* + adjective/adverb. Use *such* when you include a noun.

    It was ~~so~~ *such a* long and boring trip to the U.S. that I slept most of the way.   OR
    The trip to the U.S. was so long and boring that I slept most of the way.

12. Use correct punctuation with sentence connectors.

    She likes living here*. H*~~, however,~~ she misses her family back home.

PART 2 Editing Practice

Some of the shaded words and phrases have mistakes. Find the mistakes and correct them. If the shaded words are correct, write *C*.

    Life as an immigrant can be hard. I came to the U.S. five years ago ~~for~~ *to* study English. I chose to
1.

live in this city because my sister was living here. Even I had studied English in my country,
   C
2.   **3.**

I didn't have experience talking with native speakers. I wanted to prepare myself, therefore, I took private
                                                                     4.

lessons with an American in my country for learn American expressions. In addition, before come here, I
                                    5.   **6.**   **7.**

read a lot about life in the U.S. so that I was prepared. But I wasn't. There were many surprises.
                                      8.

For example, I was surprised by how cold it is in the winter in this city. Therefore, I couldn't believe that
9.   **10.**

some students call their teachers by their first names. Back home, we always call our teachers "Professor"

for show respect. I also miss getting together with friends after class. Now I'm at a city college, and most
11.

students have jobs and families. As a result, everyone leaves after class. Because they want to get home
                                    12.   **13.**

to their families. I gave my phone number to some classmates so that we get together on weekends, but
                                                      14.

no one ever calls me. I thought I wouldn't be lonely since I'd be with my sister and her family. But I was
                                                  15.

wrong. Because my sister has a busy life, so she doesn't have much time for me either.
                                          16.

    I had so hard time when I arrived here that I wanted to go back. Even though, little by little I got used
           17.   **18.**   **19.**

to life here. I discovered that church is a good place to meet people, so that I joined a church. When I
                                                         20.

will save more money, I'm going to get an apartment with one of my new friends from church. Even though
21.

life has become easier, but I still miss my family back home.
                    22.

WRITING TIP
The charts in this unit show many ways of combining ideas to make effective, well-organized points. Aim to include a selection of connectors in your writing. This will improve the focus and interest level of your work.

PART 3 Write
Read the prompts. Choose one and write one or more paragraphs about it.

1. Describe the problems or challenges immigrants or refugees can face when they arrive in the U.S.
2. Describe the challenges international students can face when they become students in the U.S.

PART 4 Edit
Reread the Summary of Unit 9 and the Editing Advice. Edit your writing from Part 3.

CHILDREN

We worry about what a child will become tomorrow, yet we forget that he is someone today.

STACIA TAUSCHE

Children joyfully posing for a photo in Shanti Niketan, Bengal, India

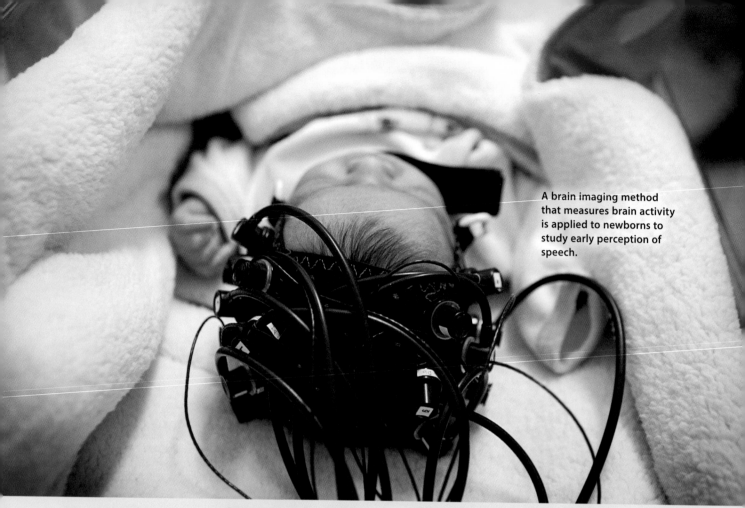

A brain imaging method that measures brain activity is applied to newborns to study early perception of speech.

EARLY **CHILD** DEVELOPMENT

Read the following article. Pay special attention to the words in bold. 🎧 10.1

Do you think **that babies can benefit from listening to classical music or seeing great works of art?** Some parents think **that these activities can increase a baby's intelligence.** While there is no scientific evidence to support this, research shows **that a baby's early experiences influence brain development.** The first three years of a baby's life affect his or her emotional development and learning abilities for the rest of his or her life. It is a well-known fact **that talking to infants increases their language ability** and **that reading to them is the most important thing parents can do to raise a good reader.** A recent study shows **that children from birth to eight years old are spending much more time with screens than books.**

Babies whose parents rarely talk to them or hold them may experience long-term damage. One study shows **that kids who hardly play or who aren't** touched very much develop brains 20 to 50 percent smaller than normal.

A study at the University of North Carolina followed children from preschool to young adulthood. The results showed **that children who got high-quality preschool education from the time they were infants benefited in later life.** In this study, 23 percent of children who had high-quality preschool education graduated from college, compared with only 6 percent of children who did not have preschool education.

While it is important to give babies stimulating activities, experts warn **that parents shouldn't overstimulate them.** Finding a balance between play, relaxation, and educational activities is beneficial for parents and children alike.

COMPREHENSION Based on the reading, write T for *true* or F for *false*.

1. _____ If a baby listens to classical music, this will help develop his or her brain.

2. _____ Reading to babies helps them become better readers.

3. _____ The first three years of children's lives affect their learning for the rest their lives.

THINK ABOUT IT Discuss the questions with a partner or in a small group.

1. In what other ways can parents help their children's early development? Give examples.

2. The fact that young children are spending "more time with screens than books" will have an effect on their later development? What effects might this have? Explain.

10.1 Noun Clauses

A noun clause functions as a noun in a sentence. Like all clauses, it has a subject and a verb.

EXAMPLES	EXPLANATION
Parents know **(that) kids need a lot of attention.** Studies show **(that) early childhood education is important.**	A noun clause can follow certain verbs. *That* introduces a noun clause. *That* is often omitted, especially in conversation.
I'm *sure* **(that) children need a lot of attention.** Some parents are *worried* **(that) they don't spend enough time with their kids.**	A noun clause can be the complement of the sentence after certain adjectives.
A: I hope **that our children will be successful.** **B:** I hope **so**, too. **A:** Do you think **that the children are learning in preschool?** **B:** Yes, I think **so.**	Noun clauses can be replaced by *so* after the verbs *think, hope, believe, suppose, expect,* and *know.*
I believe **that babies' brains are fascinating *and that* they can teach us a lot about learning.** I agree **that the study is important *but that* care must be given to the babies.**	We connect two noun clauses in the same sentence with *and that* or *but that.*

Notes:

1. A noun clause often follows one of these verbs:

believe	find out	predict	suppose
complain	forget	pretend	think
decide	hope	realize	understand
dream	know	regret	
expect	learn	remember	
feel*	notice	show	

   * *Feel* followed by a noun clause means "believe" or "think."

   I **feel** *that early education is important.*

2. A noun clause often follows *be* + the following adjectives:

afraid	clear	sure
amazed	disappointed	surprised
aware	glad	worried
certain	happy	

EXERCISE 1 Listen to the conversation. Write T for *true* or F for *false*. 🎧 10.2

1. _____ The man is not convinced that playing music to young children is useful.

2. _____ The two speakers agree that preschool education is important.

3. _____ The woman thinks play is more important than the man does.

EXERCISE 2 Listen again. Fill in the blanks with the words you hear. 🎧 10.2

A: _____Do you know that_____ it's good to read to children when they're very young?
                    1.

B: Yes, I do. But _____ playing music was important, too.
                              2.

A: _____ music is beneficial, but I suppose it can't hurt.
            3.

B: _____ it's good to give kids as much education as possible before they go to school.
            4.

A: I'm sure that's a good idea. But _____ they're just kids. They need to play, too.
                                              5.

B: Of course they do. _____ my children will be successful one day.
                                  6.

A: _____ they'll be very successful and happy.
            7.

B: _____ .
            8.

EXERCISE 3 Respond to each statistic about American families by beginning with *I'm surprised that . . .* or *I'm not surprised that . . .* Discuss your reactions with a partner.

1. The number of children in the U.S. is increasing rapidly.

   I'm surprised that the number of children in the U.S. is increasing rapidly.

2. About 7 million American children are home alone after school.

   _____

   _____

3. About 22 percent of American children live in poverty.

   _____

   _____

4. About 70 percent of married mothers work outside the home.

   _____

   _____

5. Sixty-nine percent of children live with two parents.

_____

_____

6. Twenty-three percent of American children live with at least one foreign-born parent.

_____

_____

7. Twenty-two percent of children ages 5 to 17 speak a language other than English at home.

_____

_____

8. By 2050, 39 percent of U.S. children are projected to be Hispanic.

_____

_____

ABOUT YOU Fill in the blanks with a noun clause to talk about families or raising children in the U.S. or your country. Discuss your answers with a partner.

1. I'm surprised _____

_____

2. I think _____

_____

3. It's unfortunate _____

_____

4. I've noticed _____

_____

EXERCISE 4 What's your opinion? Answer the questions using _I think_ and a noun clause. Discuss your answers with a partner.

1. Should the government help families pay for childcare while the parents work?

2. Can children get the care and attention they need in day care?

3. Should grandparents help more in raising their grandchildren?

4. Should employers give new mothers and fathers maternity leave? For how long?

5. Should parents read books to babies before they learn to talk?

6. Should parents buy a lot of toys for their children?

The
TEENAGE
BRAIN

Teenagers out for a ride in a rural area of France

Read the following article. Pay special attention to the words in bold. 🎧 10.3

For many American teenagers, 16 is the magic number—the age when they can get their driver's license. But this is also the time when parents worry the most about their kids.

In the United States, one in three teen deaths is from a car crash. Parents often wonder **if kids really understand the risks they are taking when they are behind the wheel.** They warn their kids **what to do and what not to do** while driving, but they really don't know **whether their kids will follow their advice or not.** They hand over the car keys—and hope for the best.

Studies show that when teens drive alone, they take risks at the same rate as adults. But when they drive with other teens, they take more risks.

Scientists have been using scans[1] to study the teenage brain. Even though the brain is almost full size by the time a child is six years old, scientists are finding that the brain makes great changes between the ages of 12 and 25. During this time, it is natural that young people seek thrills[2]. According to Laurence Steinberg, a developmental psychologist from Temple

University, "The teenage brain is like a car with a good accelerator but a weak brake . . . . Adolescents are more impulsive,[3] thrill-seeking, drawn to the rewards of a risky decision than adults."

While new technologies can make driving more dangerous, there are other technologies that help parents keep track of their teenagers' driving habits. There are phone apps that let parents know **what their kids are doing behind the wheel.** Parents can know **if their child is texting or tweeting while driving** or **how fast their teenager is driving.**

Risky behavior is a normal stage of development in teenagers. "I can't stand riding on a roller-coaster now," said Professor Steinberg. "I liked it as a teenager. I can't stand driving fast now. I liked driving fast when I was a teenager. What has changed? I'm not as driven today by this thrill-seeking sensation[4]."

---

[1] scan: an examination of an inside part of the body done with a special machine
[2] thrill: a feeling of strong excitement or pleasure
[3] impulsive: done with a sudden urge
[4] sensation: a physical feeling

COMPREHENSION Based on the reading, write T for *true* or F for *false*.

1. _____ When teenagers drive with other teenagers in the car, they take more risks.

2. _____ The brain is fully developed by the age of 12.

3. _____ The majority of teen deaths are the result of car crashes.

THINK ABOUT IT Discuss the questions with a partner or in a small group.

1. Do you recognize yourself in the description of teenagers presented in this article? How are or were you similar? Different? Give examples.

2. What is your opinion of parents using technology to track their teenage children's behavior? Explain.

10.2 Noun Clauses as Included Questions

A noun clause is used to include a question in a statement or another question.

DIRECT QUESTION	INCLUDED QUESTION
Wh- questions with auxiliaries or **be**	We use statement word order. We put the subject before the verb.
How fast is my daughter driving?	I'd like to know **how fast she is driving**.
What app can I use?	Please tell me **what app I can use**.
Wh- questions with auxiliaries or **do/does/did**	We remove *do/does/did*. The verb shows **-s** ending for *he, she,* or *it* in the present, or use the past form.
Why does a teenager take risks?	Scientists want to know **why a teenager takes risks**.
How did the car accident happen?	I'd like to know **how the car accident happened**.
Wh- questions about the subject	There is no change in word order.
Who bought the app?	I'd like to know **who bought the app**.
What makes the teenage brain different?	Scientists want to know **what makes the teenage brain different**.
Yes/No questions with auxiliaries or **be**	We add the word *if* or *whether*. We use statement word order. We put the subject before the verb.
Is the teenager driving too fast?	The app can tell you **if the teenager is driving too fast**.
Will my teenage brother follow my advice?	I wonder **whether my teenage brother will follow my advice**.
Yes/No questions with **do**	We remove *do/does/did*. We add *if* or *whether*. The verb shows the *-s* ending for *he, she,* or *it*, in the present, or uses the past form.
Does my teenager follow my advice?	I want to know **if my teenager follows my advice**.
Did you do the same thing when you were my age?	My son wants to know **whether I did the same thing when I was his age**.

continued

An included question can be used after phrases such as these:

I don't know	I'm not sure	Do you remember
Please tell me	Nobody knows	Can you tell me
I have no idea	I can't understand	Do you understand
I wonder	I'd like to know	Would you like to know
I don't remember	I can't tell you	Does anyone know
You need to decide	It's important to ask	Do you know

Notes:

1. We can add *or not* at the end of an included *yes/no* question.

    *I'm not sure if/whether my teenage sister follows my advice **or not**.*

2. We can add *or not* directly after *whether*, but not directly after *if*.

    *I'm not sure **whether or not** my teenage sister follows my advice.*

3. In an included question, sometimes the pronouns must be changed.

    *How old were **you** when **you** started to drive?*

    *My daughter wants to know how old **I** was when **I** started to drive.*

Punctuation Note:

We use a period at the end of the included question if the sentence is a statement. We use a question mark if the sentence begins with a question.

   *I don't know how fast she drives**.***

   *Do you know how fast she drives**?***

EXERCISE 5 Fill in the blanks with *who, what, where, when, why, how, how many, how much, if,* or *whether*. In some cases, more than one answer is possible.

1. I don't know _____*where*_____ my teenage son is.

2. Can you tell me ___*if OR whether*___ the app is useful or not?

3. I don't understand _____ teenagers take so many risks.

4. Do you know _____ I can buy the app online?

5. Do you know _____ the app costs?

6. I don't know _____ my teenage sister is a good driver or not.

7. Parents want to know _____ they can do to keep their teenagers safe.

8. Do you know _____ teenagers die in traffic accidents?

9. Professor Steinberg remembers _____ kind of behavior he had as a teenager.

10. He studies _____ the teenage brain works.

11. I wonder _____ teenagers understand how risky their behavior is.

12. Do you know _____ began the study of teenage brains? Was it Steinberg?

13. Do you know _____ Steinberg does his study? At what university?

14. I don't know _____ or not my cell phone has this app.

15. I'm 15 years old. Can you tell me _____ I'm old enough to get my driver's license?

EXERCISE 6 Write these questions as included questions after the words given. These are questions about the subject.

1. Who has an app to check their teenager's driving habits?

   I don't know _who has an app to check their teenager's driving habits._ _____

2. What happens if teenagers text while driving?

   Can you tell me _____

3. How many teenagers are involved in accidents each year?

   I don't know _____

4. Who invented this app?

   I wonder _____

5. Which parents use this app?

   I'd like to know _____

EXERCISE 7 Write these questions as included questions after the words given. These are *wh-* questions with *be* or an auxiliary verb.

1. When will your sister get her driver's license?

   I'd like to know _when your sister will get her driver's license._ _____

2. Why are teenagers so careless?

   Do you know _____

3. Why are scientists studying the teenage brain?

   I'd like to know _____

4. When can teenagers get their driver's license in this state?

   I don't know _____

5. When is the brain fully developed?

   Scientists want to know _____

In social situations where perhaps someone is at fault, an included question can be less direct and, therefore, more polite.

Direct question: *Who took the car keys?* (Maybe it was you!)

More polite: *Do you know who took the car keys?* (I'm not suggesting it was you, but it could be you.)

EXERCISE 8 Write these questions as included questions after the words given. These are *wh-* questions with *do, does,* or *did.*

1. How do scientists study the brain?

   I wonder ___how scientists study the brain.___

2. Why do teenagers take risks?

   I wonder _____

3. When did you get your driver's license?

   Please tell me _____

4. How do new technologies affect driving habits?

   It's interesting to know _____

5. How does Professor Steinberg study the teenage brain?

   I'd like to know _____

EXERCISE 9 Write these questions as included questions after the words given. These are *yes/no* questions with *do, does,* or *did.*

1. Do teenagers drive too fast?

   I'd like to know ___if teenagers drive too fast.___

2. Do teenagers understand the risk?

   I wonder _____

3. Does your son's cell phone have this app?

   Can you tell me _____

4. Did you drive carefully when you were a teenager?

   Do you remember _____

5. Does the brain develop completely by the age of 20?

   I'm not sure _____

EXERCISE 10 A mother is asking her teenage son some questions before giving him the car keys. Write these questions as included questions using the phrases given.

1. Where are you going?

   I want to know _____ *where you are going.* _____

2. Why do you need to use the car?

   You have to tell me _____

3. What time will you come back home?

   Please tell me _____

4. Is there going to be another teenager in the car?

   I'd like to know _____

5. Does your friend have permission from his parents?

   Do you know _____

6. Where does your friend live?

   I don't know _____

7. Did I ever meet this friend?

   I don't remember _____

10.3 Question Words Followed by an Infinitive

EXAMPLES	EXPLANATION
What should I do about my daughter? (a) I don't know **what I should do** about her. (b) I don't know **what to do** about her. How can I find a driving app? (a) Please tell me **how I can find one.** (b) Please tell me **how to find one.**	Some included *wh-* questions with *can, could,* and *should* can be shortened. Sentences (a) use a noun clause. Sentences (b) use an infinitive phrase.
Should I let my teenager use the car? (a) I can't decide **if I should let her use it.** (b) I can't decide **whether to let her use it.**	Some included *yes/no* questions can be shortened. Sentence (a) uses a noun clause. Sentence (b) uses an infinitive phrase. We use *whether,* not *if,* to introduce an infinitive phrase.

Notes:

An infinitive is commonly used after phrases such as these:

I don't know	I don't remember	I don't understand	Please tell me
I can't decide	I can show you	I forgot	I need to know

EXERCISE 11 Fill in the blanks with one of the words from the box below.

to begin	to chat	to compare	to do (*2 times*)	to get	to make	to write

A: I need to go to my friend Marek's house. Mom won't let me use the car. I don't know how

_____*to get*_____ there without a car. Can you drive me there?
    1.

B: I'm busy studying for a test. Why do you have to go to his house?

A: We have to work on a project together. We can't decide what _____.
                                                                    2.

B: What's your assignment?

A: We have to write about children in different countries. We can't decide what countries

_____ . We don't even know where _____ .
        3.   **4.**

B: Well, since we're from Russia, why don't you compare Russia with your friend's country?

A: He's from Poland. I'm not sure that our countries are so different.

B: I'm sure there are lots of differences.

A: We don't know whether _____ about small children or teenagers.
                              5.

B: Since you're a teenager, you know a lot about that subject already.

A: You're right. That's a good place to begin. But we don't know what kind of comparisons _____ .
                                                                                              6.

B: You could compare education, number of children in a typical family, the kinds of games or electronics

they have, or whether the family lets them use the car or not. There are a lot of things.

A: I'd really like to get together with my friend so we can brainstorm these ideas.

B: Why don't you just use a video chat?

A: I forgot how _____ online. I haven't done it in a long time.
                   7.

B: Don't worry. I'll show you what _____ .
                                        8.

ABOUT YOU Complete the statements and questions. You will use them to ask a partner about children or teenagers in his/her country. Then share the most interesting answer with the class.

1. Can you tell me what _____?

2. Do you know how _____?

3. I wonder why _____.

4. I'd like to know whether _____.

ALMA: Child Prodigy

Read the following article. Pay special attention to the words in bold. 🎧 10.4

Vienna, Austria, 2016

Alma Deutscher walks slowly to the piano, sits down, and makes herself comfortable. She raises her hands above the keys. What follows next is difficult to explain. Alma, a British musician and composer, is giving the first performance of her original opera, *Cinderella*. Why is this hard to explain? Because Alma is only 10 years old! If you closed your eyes, you would think the piece is being played by a mature professional musician. And, yes—she wrote every note being played by every instrument. Welcome to the world of child prodigies!

As Dr. Ellen Winner, a professor of psychology at Boston College, explains: **"A prodigy is . . . a more extreme version of a gifted child."** Experts agree that prodigies are **so gifted that they are able to perform at an expert adult level at an extraordinarily young age**.

Asked about her earliest musical memory in a TV interview, Alma said, **"I remember . . . when I was three, and I listened to this really beautiful lullaby by Richard Strauss, and that was when I really first realized how much I loved music."**

Composing her own music followed soon after. **"When I was four, I just had these melodies and ideas in my head,"** said Alma, **"and I would play them down at the piano."** As she talked, it was clear how natural this all felt to her. She said **that it was strange for her not to have melodies popping into her head.**

Such a high level of early achievement is not common. Dr. Joanne Ruthsatz, who researches child prodigies at Ohio State University, believes that the number of such children is as low as one in five million. These prodigies tend to specialize in just one area, unlike ordinarily gifted children, who may have a range of different skills and interests. Alma is a *musical* prodigy.

Dr. Ruthsatz's research has also led her to conclude that prodigies mainly use their intelligence to benefit society. **"They have this advanced moral development,"** says Dr. Ruthsatz. **"I don't have one that I am aware of . . . that doesn't help other people."**

Echoes of this can be heard in Alma's interview. **"I know that life is not always beautiful,"** she said. **"I want to write beautiful music because I want to make the world a better place."**

11-year-old composer and musician Alma Deutscher performing during the recording of a television show in Munich, Germany

COMPREHENSION Based on the reading, write T for *true* or F for *false*.

1. _____ When Alma plays the piano, it sounds like a performance by a professional adult.

2. _____ Alma realized she loved music when she composed her first piece.

3. _____ Dr. Ruthsatz thinks that child prodigies are mainly interested in themselves.

THINK ABOUT IT Discuss the questions with a partner or in a small group.

1. Would you like to be a prodigy? What are the advantages and disadvantages, in your opinion?

2. Do you think parents should treat prodigies differently than their other children? Why or why not?

10.4 Exact Quotes

EXAMPLES	EXPLANATION
Dr. Winner said, **"A prodigy is . . . a more extreme version of a gifted child."** Deutscher said, **"I know that life is not always beautiful."**	An exact quote is used when the exact words are worth repeating and are remembered because they have been recorded on video or audio or in print.
Alma said, "I want to write beautiful music." "I want to write beautiful music," **Alma said.** "I want to write beautiful music," **said Alma.**	The *said* or *asked* clause can come at the beginning or the end of a quote. If it comes at the end, the subject and the verb can be inverted.
"I just had these melodies and ideas in my head," **said Alma,** "and I would play them down at the piano."	An exact quote can be split, with the *said* or *asked* clause in the middle, separated from the quote by commas.

Punctuation Note:

Study the punctuation of sentences that contain an exact quote. Note that the first letter of an exact quote is a capital.

> The child psychologist said, "Your daughter is an extremely gifted musician."
>
> The mother asked, "How can we help her to develop her talent?"
>
> "Should we let her practice whenever she wants to?" asked the father.
>
> "I love to work with children," said the teacher, "because they teach me so much."

EXERCISE 12 Read these quotes. Add capital letters, quotation marks, and other punctuation.

1. The young pianist asked, "~~can~~ "Can I keep playing, Mom?"

2. His mother said don't practice too long or you'll give yourself a headache

3. The child said today I'm going to start writing an opera

4. That's a wonderful idea said his father

5. Parents can dramatically influence systems in their child's brain wrote child psychologist Margot Sunderland

6. Your son is doing well said the psychologist but should keep doing his exercises

10.5 Exact Quotes vs. Reported Speech

EXACT QUOTE	REPORTED SPEECH
Dr. Winner said, "A prodigy is . . . a more extreme version of a gifted child."	Dr. Ellen Winner said **that a prodigy was a more extreme version of a gifted child.**
Deutscher said, "I know that life is not always beautiful."	Alma Deutscher said **that she knew that life was not always beautiful.**
Alma said, "I listened to this really beautiful lullaby by Richard Strauss."	Alma said **that she had listened to a really beautiful lullaby by Richard Strauss.**

Notes:

1. We use an exact quote when we want to write exactly what someone has said.
   Exact quotes are common in stories and news reports.

2. We use reported speech when we want to report what someone has said.

EXERCISE 13 In the paragraph below, underline the noun clauses that show reported speech. Circle the verbs in the noun clauses.

Last week, my daughter's teacher called me at work and told me that my daughter had a fever and was resting in the nurse's office. I told my boss that I needed to leave work immediately. He said that it would be fine. As I was driving my car on the highway to the school, a police officer stopped me. She said that I was driving too fast. She said that I had been going 10 miles per hour over the limit. I told her that I was in a hurry because my daughter was sick. I said I needed to get to her school quickly. I told the police officer that I was sorry, that I hadn't realized I had been driving so fast. She said she wouldn't give me a ticket that time, but that I should be more careful in the future, whether my daughter was sick or not.

ABOUT YOU Complete the sentences with real things that people have said to you. Use exact quotes as far as you can remember them. Then tell a partner using reported speech.

*The bus driver today told me, **"Your card has expired."** (quotation)*

*The bus driver today **told me that my card had expired.** (reported)*

1. _____ told me _____
   _____.

2. _____ used to say _____
   _____.

3. _____ always says _____
   _____.

10.6 Reported Speech and the Sequence of Tenses

After a past tense verb in the main clause (such as *said, told, reported, wrote,* etc.), the tense of the verb in the noun clause moves back one tense. Notice the difference in verb tenses in the exact quotes on the left and the reported speech on the right.

EXACT QUOTE	REPORTED SPEECH
He said, "I **know** you." (present)	He said (that) he **knew** me. (simple past)
He said, "I **am studying**." (present continuous)	He said (that) he **was studying**. (past continuous)
He said, "She **saw** me yesterday." (simple past)	He said (that) she **had seen** him the day before. (past perfect)
He said, "She **was helping** me." (past continuous)	He said (that) she **had been helping** him. (past perfect continuous)
He said, "I **have taken** the test." (present perfect)	He said (that) he **had taken** the test. (past perfect)
He said, "I **had** never **done** that." (past perfect)	He said (that) he **had** never **done** that. *(No change)* (past perfect)
Modals	
She said, "I **can** help you tomorrow."	She said (that) she **could** help me the next day.
She said, "She **may** leave early." *(possibility)*	She said (that) she **might** leave early.
She said, "You **may** go." *(permission)*	She said (that) **I could** go.
She said, "I **must** go."	She said (that) she **had to** go.
She said, "I **will** stay."	She said (that) she **would** stay.
She said, "You **should** leave."	She said (that) **I should** leave. *(No change)*
She said, "You **must have** known."	She said (that) **I must have** known. *(No change)*

Notes:

1. Observe all the differences between a sentence that has an exact quote and a sentence that uses reported speech.

   EXACT QUOTE:
   She said, "I will help you tomorrow."
   - quotation marks
   - comma after *said*
   - doesn't contain *that*
   - pronouns = *I, you*
   - verb = *will help*
   - time = *tomorrow*

   REPORTED SPEECH:
   She said *(that) she would help me the next day.*
   - no quotation marks
   - no comma after *said*
   - contains *that* (optional)
   - pronouns = *she, me*
   - verb = *would help*
   - time = *the next day*

2. Other time word changes in reported speech:

   today → that day

   yesterday → the day before; the previous day

   tomorrow → the next day; the following day

   this morning → that morning

   tonight → that night

   now → at that time

3. We even change the tense in the following sentence:

   *The teacher asked me what my name **was**.*

   The tense shows that the conversation took place at a different time and place.

EXERCISE 14 An adult is talking about things her parents and grandparents used to tell her when she was a little girl. Change to reported speech. Follow the rule of sequence of tenses.

1. You are the love of my life.

   My grandmother told me that _I was the love of her life._

2. You will always be my baby.

   My mother said that _____

3. You have an easy life compared to mine.

   My father told me that _____

4. We had a much harder life.

   My grandparents told me that _____

5. We want you to be happy.

   My parents said that _____

6. You have to listen to your teacher.

   My father told me that _____

7. You can be anything you want if you study hard. *(Change all three verbs.)*

   My parents told me that _____

8. We don't want you to make poor choices.

   My parents told me that _____

9. I was always a good student.

   My father said that _____

10. We will always love you.

    My grandparents said that _____

11. You should follow your dreams.

    My mother told me that _____

12. You can get your driver's license when you're 16. *(Change both verbs.)*

    My parents told me that _____

13. You should have studied harder.

    My parents said that _____

10.7 Say vs. Tell

EXAMPLES	EXPLANATION
She **said that** her son was a good driver.	In reported speech, *say* is not followed by an indirect object.
She **told me that** her son was a good driver.	In reported speech, *tell* is followed by an indirect object.
She **said**, "I love you." She **said to her daughter**, "I love you."	In an exact quote, we use *say* or *say to someone*. We do not usually use *tell* in an exact quote.

Notes:

1. Other verbs used in reported speech that do not have an indirect object are: *add, answer, explain, reply.*

   She **explained that** she had never had an accident.

2. Other verbs used in reported speech that have an indirect object are: *inform, notify, remind, promise.*

   She **reminded her son that** he should drive safely.

EXERCISE 15 Fill in the blanks with *said* or *told*.

1. He _____told_____ his children that they should study hard.

2. I _____said_____ that I was a very happy child.

3. At the age of four, my son _____ that he wanted to learn the cello.

4. The music teacher _____ the parents that their daughter was very talented.

5. Dr. Ruthsatz _____ that child prodigies like to help other people.

6. Alma Deutscher _____, "I just had these melodies and ideas in my head."

7. The mother _____ to her son, "Eat your vegetables."

8. The mother _____ her son that she would pick him up after school.

9. My parents _____ me that they wanted me to get a good education.

10. I called my parents last week and _____ them about my new job.

11. The little girl _____ to her mother, "I want to grow up to be just like you."

12. Our parents _____ us to be honest.

EXERCISE 16 Change each sentence to reported speech. Follow the rule of sequence of tenses.

1. Lisa said, "I need to put the kids to bed."

   <u>Lisa said that she needed to put the kids to bed.</u>

2. Lisa said to her son, "I'll read you a story."

   <u>Lisa told her son that she would read him a story.</u>

3. Lisa and Paul said, "We will take our kids to the park tomorrow."

   _____

   _____

4. Lisa said, "The children went to bed early last night."

   _____

   _____

5. Lisa and Paul said, "Our son wants us to read him a story."

   _____

   _____

6. Lisa said to the teacher, "Our son's name is Tod."

   _____

   _____

7. Tod said to his mother, "I don't want to go to bed."

   _____

   _____

8. Tod said to his teacher, "I can write my name."

   _____

   _____

9. Tod said to his father, "I can't sleep."

   _____

   _____

continued

10. Tod said to his friend, "I love my new bicycle."

_____

_____

11. Tod said to his father, "I want to watch a program on TV."

_____

_____

10.8 Exceptions to the Rule of Sequence of Tenses

EXAMPLES	EXCEPTIONS TO THE RULE
Some parents **say** that this book **is** very helpful.	When the main verb is in the _present_ tense, we do not change tenses.
The mother told her child that the **Earth is round**.	In reporting a general truth, it is not necessary to follow the rule of sequence of tenses.
My brother has five children. He said that he **loves** children and that he **wants** to have more children.	In reporting something that is still true in the present, it is not necessary to follow the rule of sequence of tenses.
Our teacher said that she **will/would** pick up her kids after class. My kindergarten teacher said that she **would** teach me to tie my shoes.	When a future action has not happened yet, we can use _will_ or _would_. When the future reference is already past, we use _would_. (This is not an exception.)
A: Alma's musical ability is amazing. **B:** I didn't hear you. What did you say? **A:** I said that Alma's musical ability is amazing.	When repeating speech immediately after it was said, we do not usually follow the rule of sequence of tenses.
My mother said that she **was** born in 1948. My mother said that she **had** a difficult childhood.	In reporting a statement about the past, it is _not_ necessary to change the verbs if it is clear that the original verb was past.

EXERCISE 17 Circle the correct verb to complete this essay. In some cases, both choices are possible, so circle both options.

I have two daughters. When I was a child, I said that I (_want_/_wanted_) to have a large family. But
1.

now that I'm an adult, I see how hard it is to be married, work, and raise kids. Before we were

married, my husband said that we (_will_/_would_) share child-care responsibilities. Yesterday it was
2.

his turn to take care of the kids. I told him that I (_need_/_needed_) some time to be with my friends and
3.

that we (_are_/_were_) going out to lunch. After I left, he told the kids that they (_can_/_could_) watch TV all
4.   5.

day. I told him that our doctor always tells us that kids (_watch_/_watched_) too much TV. I told my
6.

husband that he (*needs/needed*) to take the kids out for exercise yesterday. But he told me that he
7.

(*wants/wanted*) to work on his car. He said that he (*will/would*) take them out next weekend. When I
8.   9.

asked him about the lunch he gave the kids, he said that they (*ate/had eaten*) a lot of popcorn while
10.

they were watching TV, so they weren't hungry for lunch. I always tell my husband that the kids

(*shouldn't eat/shouldn't have eaten*) snacks before they eat a meal. Sometimes I say that I really
11.

(*have/had*) three children: my two kids and my husband!
12.

10.9 Reporting an Imperative

EXAMPLES	EXPLANATION
"Take a break from practicing the piano." The parents told their daughter **to take** a break from practicing the piano. "Read me a story, please." My daughter **asked** me **to read** her a story.	To report an imperative, an infinitive is used. We use *ask* for an invitation or request. We use *tell* for a command or instruction. We don't use *say* to report an imperative.
"Don't watch TV." My father told me **not to watch** TV.	For a negative, we put *not* before the infinitive.

EXERCISE 18 Change these imperatives to reported speech. Use *asked* or *told* + an object pronoun.

1. The mother told her kids, "Study for your test."

   <u>The mother told her kids to study for their test.</u>

2. The son said to his mother, "Give me a cookie, please."

   _____

3. She told the babysitter, "Don't let the kids watch TV all day."

   _____

4. The girl said to her father, "Buy me a doll."

   _____

5. The mother said to her kids, "Eat your vegetables."

   _____

6. The father said to his daughter, "Help me in the garage."

   _____

continued

7. The girl said to her parents, "Take me to the zoo."

_____

8. The dentist said to the boy, "Brush your teeth after every meal."

_____

9. I said to my parents, "Don't spoil your grandchildren."

_____

10. The girl said to her mother, "Comb my hair."

_____

11. The father said to his daughter, "Do your homework."

_____

12. The father said to his teenage daughter, "Don't come home late."

_____

13. The father said to his teenage son, "Drive safely."

_____

10.10 Using Reported Speech to Paraphrase

We often use reported speech when we want to paraphrase what someone has said. The exact words are not important or not remembered. The idea is more important than the exact words.

EXACT QUOTE	REPORTED SPEECH
Dr. Winner wrote, **"A prodigy is a more extreme version of a gifted child."**	Dr. Winner said **that a prodigy was like a gifted child but even more so.**
Alma said, **"I know that life is not always beautiful."**	Alma told the interviewer **that she understood life wasn't perfect.**
Alma answered, **"I want to write beautiful music because I want to make the world a better place."**	Alma said **that she hoped her music could improve the world.**

EXERCISE 19 Circle the correct words to complete this story. In some cases, both answers are possible, so circle both options.

Last month, I babysat for a family that lives near me. It was my first babysitting job. They

(said/told) that the children (would/will) sleep through the night and not cause any problems.
  1.   2.

But Danielle, the three-year-old girl, woke up at 9:00 and (said/told) that (I/she) (can't/couldn't)
                                                              3.   4.   5.

sleep. I (*said/told*) her that I (*will/would*) read (*her/you*) a story. Every time I finished the story,
6. 7. 8.

she (*said/told*) me (*read/to read*) (*her/me*) another one. She finally fell asleep at 10:00. Then
9. 10. 11.

Estelle, the five-year-old, started crying. When I went to her room, she told me that (*I/she*)
12.

(*has seen/had seen*) a monster in the closet. I tried to (*tell/say*) her that monsters (*don't/didn't*)
13. 14. 15.

exist, but she didn't stop crying. I tried to call the parents and tell them that Estelle (*is/was*) upset
16.

and that she (*is/was*) crying. They told me (*call/to call*) (*them/us*) in case of any problem, but
17. 18. 19.

when I called, there was no answer. Later they told me that they (*must/had to*) turn off their cell
20.

phone because they were at a concert.

They said (*we/they*) (*would/will*) be home by 11:00 p.m. But they didn't come home till
21. 22.

1:00 a.m. They called and told me that the concert (*has started/had started*) an hour late. I called my
23.

mother and told her that I (*couldn't/can't*) leave because the parents hadn't come home. She told me
24.

(*don't/not to*) worry. She said that it (*is/was*) my responsibility to stay with the kids until the parents
25. 26.

came home. When they finally got home, they told me that (*we/they*) (*don't/didn't*) have any money to
27. 28.

pay (*me/you*) because they (*had forgotten/have forgotten*) to stop at an ATM. They said that (*they/we*)
29. 30. 31.

(*would/will*) pay (*you/me*) (*next/the following*) week.
32. 33. 34.

When I got home, my mother was waiting up for me. I told her that I (*don't/didn't*) ever want to
35.

have children. She laughed and told me that the children's behavior (*wasn't/isn't*) unusual. She told me
36.

that (*you/I*) (*will/would*) change (*my/your*) mind someday. I (*said/told*) her that I (*didn't/don't*) want to
37. 38. 39. 40. 41.

babysit ever again. She told me that I (*will/would*) get used to it.
42.

FUN WITH GRAMMAR

Race your classmates! Unscramble each sentence. Then put the sentences in order to form a story. Write
the finished story on a piece of paper and take it to your teacher. The first to write the story correctly wins.

1. I was / me / to / a child, / many / people / when / told / smile / more.

2. realize / I / smiling. / I / didn't / wasn't

3. people / down? / Why / also said, / " / " / are / you / looking / many

4. after / I / doing / these / why / I / wasn't / things. / wondered /awhile,

5. take me / I / discovered / doctor. / I / couldn't / well,/ so / I / asked / eye / my / that / to / soon / to the /
   see / parents

6. got / glasses, / I / right! / noticed / after / that / people / were / I

7. was / to / smile. / see / this / by / looking / and / made / there / a lot / me / up,

The creator of Sesame Street, Joan Ganz Cooney, with some of the characters at the 12th Annual Sesame Workshop Benefit Gala

An INNOVATION in KIDS' TV

Read the following article. Pay special attention to the words in bold. 🎧 10.5

It is one of the most watched TV shows in the world. It is seen in 120 countries and is translated into a number of different languages. At the beginning, the producers were not sure if this program **was going to be** successful or not. They never imagined that 50 years later it **would** still **be** here. Welcome to the world of *Sesame Street*.

In the 1960s, documentary television producer Joan Cooney realized that children **were watching** a lot of TV but **were learning** very little from it. Cooney wanted to investigate how television **could be used** to educate young children and entertain them at the same time. She thought that she **could help** prepare them better for school.

At first, TV producers didn't think that *Sesame Street* **would hold** the interest of young children. They thought that small children **didn't have** the attention span[1] to watch an hour of educational TV. Cooney thought otherwise. "What if it went down more like ice cream than spinach?"

Cooney brought in puppeteer[2] Jim Henson. Henson created the Muppets, with such characters as Big Bird and Elmo. Henson wanted to create characters that kids **could relate** to. Cooney realized that without these characters, learning the alphabet and learning to count **wouldn't be** as much fun.

The show was always excellent at helping kids learn the basics of numbers and letters, but it became clear that children's emotions **needed** to be addressed, too. After attacks on the World Trade Center on September 11, 2001, the producers realized that kids **had become** fearful and that they **needed** a way to express how they **were feeling**. So the show started dealing with children's fears. In 2002, the producers of the South African version of the program, *Takalani Sesame*, thought that it **would be** a good idea to deal with HIV.[3] They understood how frightening this disease **could be** for small children, so they brought in a five-year-old Muppet named Kami, who is HIV positive.

It is clear that *Sesame Street* has evolved over the years. But it is still a favorite TV show for preschool kids around the world.

---

[1] attention span: the time that a person can concentrate on something
[2] puppeteer: an artist who makes puppets behave like actors
[3] HIV: human immunodeficiency virus, or AIDS

COMPREHENSION Based on the reading, write T for *true* or F for *false*.

1. _____ Children don't have the attention span to watch an hour of educational TV.

2. _____ Not only does *Sesame Street* teach numbers and letters, it also deals with children's fears.

3. _____ The characters in *Sesame Street* are the same in all countries.

THINK ABOUT IT Discuss the questions with a partner or in a small group.

1. Did you watch *Sesame Street* or similar shows as a child? Did you enjoy them? What did you learn? Share your experience.

2. Do you agree that it is good for young children to be exposed to serious issues as part of their regular entertainment? Give your reasons.

10.11 Noun Clauses after Past-Tense Verbs

EXAMPLES	EXPLANATION
The producers thought **that small children *could learn* from TV.** They didn't imagine **that the show *would last*** over **50 years**.	If the verb in the main clause is in the past (for example: *thought, realized*), we follow the rule of sequence of tenses in Chart 10.6.

EXERCISE 20 Use the words under the blank to complete each statement.

1. No one imagined that _Sesame Street would be such a popular program._
   Sesame Street will be such a popular program.

2. Joan Cooney thought that _____
   Early education can be fun.

3. She realized that _____
   Small children are watching a lot of TV.

4. She thought that _____
   I can help kids prepare for school.

5. People believed that _____
   Kids don't have the attention span to watch a one-hour program.

   _____

6. The producers realized that _____
   Kids became fearful after September 11.

7. They thought that _____
   We should address kids' fears.

8. Parents were happy that _____
   Our kids can learn at home.

9. Alma's parents realized that _____
   Alma is gifted.

10. No one believed that _____
    A young girl can write and perform such complex music.

    _____

10.12 Noun Clauses as Reported Questions

A noun clause can be used to report a question. If the main verb is in the past tense (*asked, wanted to know, tried to understand,* etc.), we follow the rule of sequence of tenses. (See Chart 10.8 for exceptions.)

EXACT QUOTE	REPORTED SPEECH
Wh- Questions with auxiliaries or ***be***	
"How old are your kids?" "What are you watching on TV?"	She asked me **how old my kids were.** I wanted to know **what she was watching on TV.**
Wh- Questions with ***do/does/did***	
"How do kids learn?" "How did you get the idea for *Sesame Street*?"	She wanted to know **how kids learned.** Cooney was asked **how she had gotten the idea for *Sesame Street*.**
Wh- Questions about the subject	
"Which kids watched the show?" "Who saw the September 11 episode?"	She asked me **which kids had watched the show.** I wanted to know **who had seen the September 11 episode.**
Yes/No Questions with auxiliaries or ***be***	
"Will young kids watch a one-hour program?" "Can kids learn the alphabet from TV?"	She wanted to know **if young kids would watch a one-hour program (or not).** They asked her **whether (or not) kids could learn the alphabet from TV.**
Yes/No Questions with ***do/does/did***	
"Do small kids like *Sesame Street*?" "Did Jim Henson create the Muppets?"	She asked me **whether small kids liked** (*or* **like**) ***Sesame Street*.** I asked her **if Jim Henson had created the Muppets.**

Notes:

1. Remember: Reported speech is often a paraphrase of what someone has said.

    She asked me, "Do your kids spend a lot of time in front of the TV?"

    *She asked me **if my kids watched a lot of TV.***

2. The most common changes that are made are:

    will → would   can → could

GRAMMAR IN USE

When a statement is still true or it is reported soon after it is spoken, the verb in reported speech often does not follow the rule of sequence of tenses after *said, thought,* and so on. This is especially true in conversation.

*He said the post office **is** a big glass building.* ("It **is** a big glass building.")

A: What's wrong with Hernando?

B: He told me he's very tired today. ("**I'm** very tired today.")

EXERCISE 21 Change these exact questions to reported questions. Follow the rule of sequence of tenses. In some cases, it's not necessary to follow the rule of sequence of tenses.

1. Did you see the September 11 episode on *Sesame Street*?

   She asked me _if (or whether) I had seen the September 11 episode._

2. How much TV do your kids watch?

   She asked me _____

3. Do they like *Sesame Street*?

   She wanted to know _____

4. Why is this show so popular?

   At first I didn't understand _____

5. Have you ever seen the show?

   I asked my brother _____

6. How long has *Sesame Street* been on TV?

   I wanted to know _____

7. Do you like Big Bird?

   I asked my sister _____

8. Is Jim Henson still alive?

   He asked me _____

9. How does *Sesame Street* handle scary situations?

   We wanted to know _____

10. Has *Sesame Street* made any changes in the past 50 years?

    He asked me _____

11. Will the Muppets hold kids' attention?

    Cooney wanted to know _____

12. Was *Sesame Street* the first educational TV program for kids?

    I asked my teacher _____

13. How long will *Sesame Street* last?

    They had no idea _____

EXERCISE 22 Choose the correct option to complete this essay. In some cases, both choices are possible, so circle both options.

When I was 18 years old and living in my native Estonia, I didn't know where

(*I wanted/did I want*) to go in my life. I couldn't decide (*I should/if I should*) get a job or go to
   1.   2.

college. I didn't even know what I (*want/wanted*) to study. Then I read an article about an *au pair*
                                      3.

program in the U.S. This is a program where young people go to live with a family for a year to

take care of their small children.

I became very excited and asked my mother (*if I could/could I*) apply. At first she said,
                                                                4.

"Absolutely not." She asked me why (*did I want/I wanted*) to leave our family for a year. I told her
                                        5.

that it (*will/would*) be a good opportunity for me to improve my English and gain experience.
           6.

My mother said she would talk it over with Dad, and they finally agreed to let me go.

After filling out the application, I had an interview. The interviewer asked me what kind of

experience (*did I have/I had*) with small children. I told her that I had two younger brothers and
              7.

that I always helped my parents take care of them.

She also asked me (*whether/if*) I (*knew/had known*) how to drive. Sometimes an au pair has
                      8.   9.

to drive kids to school and to playdates. I told her that I (*had/have*) just gotten my license. I asked
                                                            10.

her how many hours a week I (*will/would*) have to work, and she said 45. I wanted to know
                                11.

(*if I would/would I*) get paid, and she said I would be paid about $200 a week. I also wanted to
   12.

know (*if/whether*) I (*would have/had had*) the opportunity to go to school in the U.S., and she
       13.   14.

said yes. I asked her (*if or not/whether or not*) I had to do housework, and she said that I only had
                          15.

to take care of the kids.

I was so happy when I was accepted. My year in the U.S. was wonderful. When I got back,

I knew what I (*wanted/had wanted*) to do. I majored in early childhood education and I am now
                  16.

a preschool teacher.

EXERCISE 23 Fill in the blanks to complete this story. Answers may vary.

I'm from Japan. I never imagined that I _____ would be _____ in the U.S. someday. But
                                                    1.

I heard about an au pair program and decided to apply. I didn't know

_____ my parents _____ me permission to come
            2.   3.

here, but they did. They thought that living in another country _____
                                                                      4.

me more independent and responsible. And they were right.

Before I came to the U.S., I wondered _____ my life _____
5.   6.

like. I thought that I _____ all the time and not have time for school and
7.

friends. But that's not true. I've made a lot of good friends in my English class. I didn't realize

that I _____ people of different ages in a college class, but the students are as
8.

young as 17 and as old as 75! I was also surprised by how many people of different nationalities I

_____ . I've met students from many countries, from Panama to Portugal to Peru!
9.

Before I came here, I thought that my English _____ almost perfect because I
10.

had been studying it since I was a child. But I realized that I _____ a lot of
11.

expressions, like "It's a piece of cake" (it's easy).

I wondered _____ the American family _____ me. They treat
12.   13.

me like a member of the family. I love their two preschool kids.

At first I made one big mistake. One afternoon, when the parents were working, the kids

asked me _____ they _____ watch TV. I thought that it
14.   15.

_____ OK. I let them watch whatever they wanted for as long as they wanted.
16.

I thought that I _____ study while the kids were watching TV. When their mom
17.

came home, she was upset. She said that the kids _____ allowed to watch only
18.

one program a day: *Sesame Street*. She thought that this program _____ very
19.

educational and that other programs _____ not so good for kids. She also told me
20.

that she _____ the kids to use electronic devices a lot. She thought that it
21.

_____ better for them to play with other kids than to play with electronics.
22.

ABOUT YOU Fill in the blanks to talk about yourself and your parents when you were a child or a
teenager. Follow the rule of sequence of tenses. Discuss your answers with a partner.

1. When I was a child, I dreamed that _I would be a movie star._____

2. When I was a child, I wondered _____

3. My parents told me that _____

4. My parents hoped that _____

5. My parents thought that _____

6. When I was a child, I thought that _____

7. When I was a child, I didn't understand _____

8. When I was a child, I never imagined _____

SUMMARY OF UNIT 10

DIRECT STATEMENT OR QUESTION	SENTENCE WITH AN INCLUDED STATEMENT OR QUESTION	EXPLANATION
She loves kids. She is patient.	I know **that she loves kids**. I'm sure **that she is patient**.	A noun clause is used as an included statement.
Is the baby sick? What does the baby need?	I don't know **if the baby is sick**. I'm not sure **what the baby needs**.	A noun clause is used as an included question.
What should I do with a crying baby? Where can I find a babysitter?	I don't know **what to do with a crying baby**. Can you tell me **where to find a babysitter**?	An infinitive can replace *should* or *can*.
I want to make the world a better place. Have you always loved music?	Alma said, **"I want to make the world a better place."** **"Have you always loved music?"** asked the reporter.	An exact quote is used to report what someone has said or asked.
Do your kids watch *Sesame Street*? I will teach my son to drive.	She asked me **if my kids watched** *Sesame Street*. She said **that she would teach her son to drive**.	A noun clause is used in reported speech after verbs such as *said, asked, knew,* etc.
Trust yourself. Don't give the baby candy.	He told us **to trust ourselves**. He told me **not to give the baby candy**.	An infinitive is used to report an imperative.

PUNCTUATION WITH NOUN CLAUSES	
I know where he lives.	Period at the end. No comma before the noun clause.
Do you know where he lives?	Question mark at the end. No comma before the noun clause.
He said, "I like you."	Comma after *said*. Quotation marks around the quote. Period before the final quotation mark.
"I like you," he said.	Quotation marks around the quote. Comma before the final quotation mark. Period at end.
He asked, "What do you want?"	Comma after *asked*. Quotation marks around the quote. Question mark before the final quotation mark.
"What do you want?" he asked.	Quotation marks around the quote. Question mark before the end of quote. Period at the end.

REVIEW

Use the sentence under each blank to form a noun clause. Answers may vary.

Two years ago, when I was 18, I didn't know ___*what to do*___ with my life. I had just graduated
1. What should I do?

from high school, and I couldn't decide _____.
2. Should I go to college or not?

A neighbor of mine told me _____ and decided to
3. I had the same problem when I was your age.

go to the U.S. for a year to work as an au pair. She asked me _____.
4. Have you ever heard of this program?

I told her _____. She told me _____, and
5. I haven't.   6. I lived with an American family for a year.

_____. I asked her _____. I was surprised to
7. My English has improved a lot.   8. How much will this program cost me?

find out _____. I asked her
9. You'll earn about $200 a week.

_____, and she said _____ but
10. Is the work very hard?   11. It is.

_____.
12. It is very rewarding.

When I told my parents _____, they told me
13. I am thinking about going to the U.S. for a year.

_____. They thought _____ and
14. Don't go.   15. You are too young.

_____. I reminded them
16. You don't have any experience.

_____. I didn't think
17. I have babysat our neighbors' kids many times.

_____, but to my surprise they did. When I filled out the application, I was afraid
18. Will they agree?

_____. But I was. My parents were worried. I told them
19. I won't be accepted.

_____. I promised them _____.
20. Don't worry.   21. I will e-mail you almost every day.

When I arrived, my American family explained to me _____. They had
22. What do I have to do?

two small kids, and I had to wake them, make them breakfast, and take them to school in the morning.

I asked them _____. They told me that
23. Do I have to wait for them at school?

_____. I told them
24. While the kids are in school, you can take English classes.

_____. They told me
25. I don't have enough money to pay for school.

_____. I was so happy to study English. When the year was
26. We will pay for your classes.

over, I was very sad to leave my new family, but we promised _____.
27. We will stay in touch.

Now I am back home and in college. My parents can see _____. I don't
28. I've become more mature.

know _____, but for me it was great.
29. Is this experience for everyone?

FROM GRAMMAR TO WRITING

PART 1 Editing Advice

1. Use *that* or nothing to introduce an included statement. Don't use *what*.

   that
   I know ~~what~~ she is a good driver.

2. Use statement word order in an included question.

   he is
   I don't know how fast ~~is he~~ driving.

3. We *say* something. We *tell* someone something.

   told
   He ~~said~~ me that he wanted to go home.

   said
   He ~~told~~, "I want to go home."

4. Use *tell* or *ask*, not *say*, to report an imperative. Follow *tell* and *ask* with an object.

   told
   She ~~said~~ her parents not to worry.

   me
   My son asked ∧ to give him the car keys.

5. Don't use *to* after *tell*.

   She told ~~to~~ me that she wanted to be a teacher.

6. Use *if* or *whether* to introduce an included *yes/no* question. Use statement word order.

   whether
   I don't know ∧ teenagers understand the risks while driving.

   if I should
   I can't decide ∧~~should I~~ let my daughter get her driver's license.

7. Follow the rule of sequence of tenses when the main verb is in the past.

   would
   Last year, my father said that he ~~will~~ teach me how to drive, but he didn't.

8. Don't use *so* before a noun clause.

   I think ~~so~~ raising children is the best job.

9. Use an infinitive to report an imperative.

   to
   My parents told me ∧ drive carefully.

   not to
   My parents told me ∧~~don't~~ text while driving.

PART 2 Editing Practice

Some of the shaded words and phrases have mistakes. Find the mistakes and correct them. If the shaded words are correct, write *C*.

that
When I was 14 years old, I told my parents ~~what~~ I wanted to work as a babysitter, but they
                                                              1.

C
told me that I was too young. At that time, they told me that they will pay me $1 an hour to help
2.   3.   4.

with my little brother. A few times they asked me could I watch him when they went out. They
                                          5.

always told me call them immediately in case of a problem. They told me don't watch TV or text
       6.   7.

my friends while I was working as a babysitter. They always told me that I have done a good job.
                                                                          8.

When I was 15, I got a few more responsibilities, like preparing small meals. They always

told that I should teach my brother about good nutrition. I asked them whether I could get more
9.   10.   11.

money because I had more responsibilities, and they agreed. I asked them if I can buy something
                                                                                          12.

new with my earnings. My parents said, "Of course."
                                   13.

When I turned 18, I started working for my neighbors, who have three children. The neighbors

asked me had I gotten my driver's license yet. When I said yes, they were pleased because I could
              14.   15.

drive the kids to different places. I never realized how hard was it to take care of so many kids. As
                                                                     16.

soon as we get in the car, they ask, "Are we there yet?" They think so we should arrive immediately.
                                           17.   18.

When they're thirsty, they ask me to buy them soda, but I tell them what it is healthier to drink
                                   19.   20.   21.

water. They always tell, "In our house, we drink soda." I don't understand why do their parents
                   22.   23.

give them soda instead of water. I didn't know whether to follow the rules of my house or theirs. So
                                               24.

I asked my parents what should I do. My parents told me not to say anything about their parents'
                         25.   26.

rules but that I should try to encourage healthy habits by example.
             27.

Little by little I'm learning how to take care of children. I hope that I will be as good a mom to
                                                                       28.

my kids as my mom has been to me.

WRITING TIP

Use exact quotes in your writing to bring life to your writing. However, using too many exact quotes can cause your own "voice" to be lost. If you need to include a lot of other people's ideas, reported speech can help you maintain a balance between other people's words and your own writing.

My father always said, "Lead by example."

*My father always **told me to lead by example**.*

PART 3 Write

Read the prompts. Choose one and write one or more paragraphs about it.

1. Write about some good advice your parents gave you when you were a child. Explain what the advice was and how this has helped you.
2. Write about how a teacher or another adult helped you or encouraged you when you were a child.

PART 4 Edit

Reread the Summary of Unit 10 and the Editing Advice. Edit your writing from Part 3.

Somewhere, something incredible
is waiting to be known.

CARL SAGAN

SCIENCE or SCIENCE FICTION?

The three telescopes at Deimos Sky Survey, based in Spain, watch for near-Earth space objects.

Time Travel

Scientists at the National Science Foundation released this first photo of a black hole on April 10, 2019. Some believe that time travel is possible through black holes.

Read the following article. Pay special attention to the words in bold. 🎧 11.1

If you **could travel** to the past or the future, **would** you **do** it? If you **could travel** to the past, **would** you **want** to visit anyone? If you **could travel** to the future, **would** you **come** back to the present and warn people about possible disasters?

Time travel, first presented in a novel called *The Time Machine,* written by H.G. Wells over 100 years ago, is the subject not only of fantasy but of serious scientific exploration.

About 100 years ago, Albert Einstein proved that the universe doesn't have three dimensions but it has four—three of space and one of time. He proved that time changes with motion. Einstein believed that, theoretically[1], time travel is possible. The time on a clock in motion moves more slowly than the time on a stationary clock. If you **wanted** to visit the Earth in the future, you **would have to get** on a rocket ship going at almost the speed of light[2], travel many light-years[3] away, turn around, and come back at that speed. While traveling, you **would age** more slowly.

Einstein came up with an example he called the "twin paradox." Suppose there is a set of 25-year-old twins, Nick and Rick. If Nick **decided** to travel fast and far on a rocket ship and Rick **decided** to stay at home, Nick **would be** younger than Rick when he returned.

Specifically, if Nick **traveled** 25 light-years away and back, the trip **would take** 50 "Earth years." Rick **would be** 75 years old, but Nick **would be** 25 and a half years old. If Nick **had** a five-year-old daughter when he left, his daughter **would be** 55 years old. So Nick **would be visiting** the future.

Using today's technologies, time travel is still impossible. If you **wanted** to travel to the nearest star, which is 4.3 light-years away, it **would take** 80 thousand years to get there. (This assumes the speed of today's rockets, which is 37 thousand miles per hour.) According to Einstein, you can't travel faster than the speed of light. While most physicists believe that travel to the future is possible, it is believed that travel to the past will never happen.

Although the idea of time travel seems the subject of science fiction, not science, many discoveries and explorations, such as traveling to the Moon, had their roots in science fiction novels and movies.

---

[1] theoretically: possible in theory but not proven
[2] speed of light: 299,792,458 meters per second (or 186,000 miles per second)
[3] light-year: the distance that light travels in a year through a vacuum (6 trillion miles or 9.46 trillion kilometers)

COMPREHENSION Based on the reading, write T for *true* or F for *false*.

1. _____ H.G. Wells' *The Time Machine* was a true story.

2. _____ Scientists believe that travel to the past is possible.

3. _____ Einstein showed that time is dependent on motion.

THINK ABOUT IT Discuss the questions with a partner or in a small group.

1. Review the questions in the first paragraph. Share your answers and give your reasons.

2. Do you think time travel will ever be possible? If it were, what would be the advantages and disadvantages? Explain.

11.1 Unreal Conditionals—Present

An unreal conditional is used to talk about an imagined situation. An unreal conditional in the present describes a situation that is not real now.

EXAMPLES	EXPLANATION
If we **had** a time machine, we **could travel** to the future. (Reality: We **don't have** a time machine.) I **would visit** my ancestors if I **could travel** to the past. (Reality: I **can't travel** to the past.)	We use a past form in the *if* clause and *would* or *could* + the base form of a verb in the main clause. When the *if* clause comes before the main clause, use a comma to separate the clauses. When the main clause is first, there is no comma.
If we **could travel** at the speed of light, we**'d be able** to go to the future.	All pronouns except *it* can contract with *would*: *I'd, you'd, he'd, she'd, we'd, they'd.*
If time travel **were** possible, some people **would do** it. If Einstein **were** here today, what **would** he **think** of today's world?	*Were* is the correct form of *be* in an unreal conditional clause for all subjects, singular and plural. However, it is common and less formal to use *was* with *I, he, she, it,* and singular nouns.
If I **were** in a time machine, I**'d be traveling** at the speed of light.	For a continuous time, we use *would + be +* verb *-ing*.
I wouldn't travel to the past **unless** I could return to the present. **Even if** I could know my future, I wouldn't want to know it.	A conditional can begin with *unless* or *even if*.
If I were you, I'd **study** more science.	We often give advice with the expression *"If I were you . . ."*
What if you **could travel** to the future? *What if* you **had** the brain of Einstein?	We use *what if* to propose a hypothetical situation.
If you **had** Einstein's brain, what **would** you **do**? If you **could fly** to another planet, where **would** you **go**?	When we make a question with conditionals, the *if* clause uses statement word order. The main clause uses question word order.

EXERCISE 1 Listen to the sentences about bringing back dinosaurs. Write T for *true* or F for *false*. 🎧 11.2

1. _____ Bringing back dinosaurs would change the world.

2. _____ Dinosaur DNA is not too old to allow scientists to bring them back.

3. _____ Most people agree that bringing back dinosaurs would be an exciting idea.

EXERCISE 2 Listen to the following sentences. Fill in the blanks with the words you hear. 🎧 11.3

1. If dinosaurs _____*were*_____ alive today, the world _____*would be*_____ very different.

2. Dinosaurs have been extinct for a long time. If dinosaur DNA _____ not so old, scientists

   _____ possibly bring them back.

3. The world _____ unsafe for humans if scientists _____ back the dinosaurs.

4. Some people say that if scientists _____ back extinct species, the world

   _____ interesting and exciting.

5. Other people say that scientists _____ the natural order of things if they

   _____ back an extinct species.

6. What do you think? _____ a good thing if scientists _____ to bring

   back extinct species?

EXERCISE 3 Complete the conversation with the correct form of the verb given and any
other words you see. Use *would* + the base form in the main clause. Use the past tense in the *if* clause.
Use contractions where possible.

A: If you _____*had*_____ the money to clone any animal, which animal
          <u>1. have</u>

   _____ ?
          <u>2. you/clone</u>

B: I _____ my dog.
          <u>3. clone</u>

A: Why?

B: Well, my dog is getting old, and I don't want to lose her. If I _____ clone her,
                                                                                    <u>4. can</u>

   I _____ the same great dog for many more years. What about you?
          <u>5. have</u>

A: I _____ my cat if I _____ afford it. My cat is awesome!
          <u>6. clone</u>   <u>7. able</u>

B: I read about cloning farm animals, but I don't understand why anyone would do that.

A: Well, if I _____ a cow that _____ high-quality milk or meat, it
                      <u>8. have</u>   <u>9. produce</u>

   _____ great if I _____ make many copies of this cow. I
          <u>10. be</u>   <u>11. can</u>

   _____ earn a lot of money!
          <u>12. can</u>

B: I hadn't thought about that. How about cloning people? If you _____ clone a good cow
                                                                                    <u>13. can</u>

   or sheep, why not clone a great person?

A: People have thought about cloning people. So far, it's never been done. Some people think that scientists

_____ with nature.
14. continuous form of interfere

B: But if you _____ clone a person, who _____?
15. can   16. you/clone

A: I think I _____ Albert Einstein. I read that his brain is preserved. If scientists
17. clone

_____ the DNA from his brain, they _____ make another
18. take   19. be able to

Einstein.

B: What if the "new" Einstein _____ any interest in science? What if he
20. not/show

_____ to become a musician or a carpenter?
21. decide

A: Hmm. I never thought of that. Also, the "new" Einstein _____ in a different
22. continuous form of live

world. He _____ access to computers and other new technologies.
23. have

B: And he _____ the same parents or friends. If he
24. not/have

_____ born today, I think he _____ a completely different person.
25. be   26. be

A: Well, it's fun to imagine.

Some owners and state agencies such as the
police pay to clone special dogs.

EXERCISE 4 Complete the conversations with the correct form of the verb given and any other words you see. Use *would* + the base form in the main clause. Use the past tense in the *if* clause. Use contractions where possible.

1. **A:** What ___would you do___ if you _____were_____ a scientist?
   a. you/do   b. be

   B: If I _____ a scientist, I _____ to find a cure for diseases.
   c. be   d. try

2. **A:** If you _____ make a copy of yourself, _____ it?
   a. can   b. you/do

   B: My mom says that one of me is enough. If she _____ two of me, it
   c. have

   _____ her crazy!
   d. drive

3. **A:** If you _____ come back to Earth in any form after you die, how
   a. can

   _____ back?
   b. you/come

   B: I _____ back as a dog. Dogs have such an easy life.
   c. come

   A: Not all dogs.

   B: I _____ as a dog in a good home.
   d. only/come back

4. **A:** If you _____ meet any person, dead or alive, who _____ to meet?
   a. can   b. you/want

   B: I _____ to meet Abraham Lincoln.
   c. want

5. **A:** If I _____ find a way to teach a person a foreign language in a week,
   a. can

   I _____ a million dollars.
   b. make

   B: You _____ a billion dollars. And I _____ your first customer!
   c. probably/make   d. be

6. **A:** If you _____ be invisible for a day, what _____?
   a. can   b. you/do

   B: I _____ to my teacher's house the day she writes the final exam.
   c. go

   A: That _____ cheating! You _____ get in trouble.
   d. be   e. can

   B: How _____ that I cheated?
   f. they/prove

7. **A:** What _____ if you _____ travel to the past or future?
   a. you/do   b. can

   B: I _____ to the past.
   c. go

   A: How far back _____?
   d. you/go

   B: I _____ back millions of years.
   e. go

   A: Why?

   B: So I _____ see dinosaurs.
   f. be able to

8. **A:** It _____ nice if people _____ live forever.
   a. be   b. can

   B: If people _____, the world _____ overpopulated. There
   c. not/die   d. be

   _____ enough resources for everybody.
   e. not/be

   A: I didn't think of that. If the world _____ overpopulated, I _____
   f. be   g. never/find

   a parking space!

ABOUT YOU Answer the following questions. Discuss your reasons with a partner.

1. If you could have the brain of another person, whose brain would you want?

   If I could have the brain of another person, I'd want Einstein's brain.

2. If you could travel to the past or the future, which would you do?

   _____

   _____

3. If you could make a clone of yourself, would you do it? Why or why not?

   _____

   _____

4. If you could change one thing about today's world, what would it be?

   _____

   _____

5. If you could travel anywhere in the world for free, where would you go?

   _____

   _____

6. If you could be a child again, what age would you be?

   _____

   _____

7. If you could change one thing about the town you live in, what would it be?

   _____

   _____

8. If you could meet any person from the past, who would it be?

   _____

   _____

EXERCISE 5 Fill in the blanks to tell what the following people are thinking. Use the correct unreal conditional and any other words you see.

1. One-year-old: If I _____could_____ walk, I ____would walk____ into the kitchen and take a cookie

canwalk

   out of the cookie jar.

2. Two-year-old: If I _____ talk, I _____ my mother that I hate peas.

cantell

3. Fourteen-year-old: I _____ happier if I _____ drive.

becan

4. Sixteen-year-old: If I _____ a car, my friends and I _____ out every night.

havego

5. Nineteen-year-old: I _____ a private university if I _____ a lot of money.

attendhave

6. Twenty-five-year-old: If I _____ married, my parents _____ about

benot/worry

   me so much.

7. Thirty-five-year-old mother: I _____ more time for myself if my kids

have

   _____ older.

be

8. Sixty-year-old grandmother: If I _____ grandchildren, my life

not/have

   _____ so interesting.

not/be

9. Ninety-year-old: If I _____ young today, I _____ learn all about

behave to

   computers and other high-tech devices.

10. One hundred-year-old: If I _____ you the story of my life, you

tell

    _____ it.

not/believe

EXERCISE 6 Give your opinion. Discuss your answers with a partner. Do you think the world would be better or worse if . . .

1. we could live to be 150 years old?
2. people didn't have to work?
3. every job paid the same salary?
4. there were no computers?
5. everyone spoke the same language?
6. we could predict the future?

11.2 Implied Conditionals

EXAMPLES	EXPLANATION
I'd love to meet my great-grandparents. I could ask them about their lives. Would you like to see a living dinosaur? I wouldn't want to know the future. Would you?	Sometimes the conditional (the *if* clause) is implied, and, therefore, not stated. In the examples, the implication is "if you had the opportunity" or "if the possibility presented itself."

EXERCISE 7 Fill in the blanks with the missing words to complete the conversations. Use context clues. Use contractions where possible. Answers may vary.

1. **A:** _____Would_____ you travel to the future if you could?
   a.

   B: I don't think so. _____ you?
   b.

   A: Yes. It would _____ very interesting.
   c.

   B: I _____ happy.
   d.

   A: Why not?

   B: I _____ miss my family and friends.
   e.

   A: But you could come back and tell them about the future. You _____ them about future
   f.

   disasters.

   B: Then I _____ changing the future. And it takes a long time to come back. By the time
   g.

   I came back, everyone I know _____ much older.
   h.

2. **A:** I _____ love to know more about the past.
   a.

   B: Then you should study more history.

   A: But I wouldn't learn about my ancestors. I _____ only _____ about famous people.
   b.   c.

3. **A:** _____ you want to live more than 100 years?
   a.

   B: Yes. But I _____ to be healthy. What about you?
   b.

   A: I _____ want to see my great-great-grandchildren.
   c.

4. **A:** I _____ love to meet a famous person from the past.
   a.

   B: Who _____ you want to meet and why?
   b.

   A: Maybe Michelangelo. I _____ to watch him paint the Sistine Chapel.
   c.

5. **A:** _____ you _____ to see a living dinosaur?
   a.   b.

   B: No, I _____ .
   c.

   A: I think it _____ interesting.
   d.

   B: I _____ afraid.
   e.

6. **A:** I _____ to travel into space.
   a.

   B: I wouldn't want to. Why would you?

   A: I _____ what Earth looks like from afar.
   b.

EXPLORING MARS

Read the following article. Pay special attention to the words in bold. 🎧 11.4

Mars, our closest planetary neighbor, has always fascinated people on Earth. **If** you **watch** a lot of science fiction movies, you **see** people from Earth meeting strange-looking "Martians." But**,** of course, this is just fantasy.

In 2004, the *Spirit* rover landed on Mars to study the climate and geology of the planet and to prepare for human exploration. In 2012, the *Curiosity* rover landed on Mars. Its mission is to find out if there was ever life on that planet. One of the jobs of *Curiosity* is to figure out where a future mission should look for life. **If** enough information is gathered, astronauts **will** probably **arrive** on Mars by the 2030s.

Travel to Mars will be much more difficult than landing on the Moon. When people landed on the Moon, they carried with them all the supplies they needed. But sending a spaceship with people and all the supplies they need for their time on Mars would make the spaceship too heavy. So **if** astronauts **go** to Mars, scientists **will send** supplies first. Many other problems **will have to** be solved, too.

Astronauts **will have** to return within a given time period. **If** they **don't come** back within this period of time, they **will miss** their chance of return. **If** astronauts **have** a problem with their equipment, they **will not be able** to rely on messages from Earth to help them. Because of the distance from Earth, it can take about 40 minutes from the time a message goes out from Earth until it is received on Mars. Also, a visitor to Mars **will be** gone for at least three years because of the distance and time necessary to travel there. But one of the biggest problems with traveling to Mars is the danger of radiation. Astronauts **will be** exposed to much more radiation than someone traveling to the Moon.

If you **had** the chance to go to Mars, **would** you **go**?

Curiosity, one of NASA's Mars rovers, took this selfie on May 12, 2019.

COMPREHENSION Based on the reading, write T for *true* or F for *false*.

1. _____ Scientists are looking for signs of life on Mars.

2. _____ One problem with traveling to Mars is exposure to radiation.

3. _____ Astronauts on Mars will have quick communication with scientists on Earth.

THINK ABOUT IT Discuss the questions with a partner or in a small group.

1. Are you interested in developments in space exploration? Give your reasons.

2. Do you think the benefits of astronauts traveling to Mars would be greater than the dangers and expense involved? Why or why not?

11.3 Real Conditionals vs. Unreal Conditionals

EXAMPLES	EXPLANATION
If astronauts **go** to Mars, they **will have** to return within a given time period. They **won't be able to** rely on scientists on Earth if they **have** a problem. **If** you're interested in Mars, you **should read** this article.	We can use *if* to describe a **real** future possibility. We use the present in the *if* clause and the future or a modal in the main clause.
If you **were** on Mars, you **would weigh** about one-third of what you weigh on Earth. If you **could** go to Mars, **would** you **go**?	We can use *if* to describe an **unreal** situation in the present. These examples are about hypothetical or imaginary situations. They are not plans for the future.

EXERCISE 8 Fill in the blanks with the correct form of the verb and other words given. Make real conditionals about the future. Use contractions where possible.

1. **A:** You're such a good science student.

   B: Thanks. If I _____*get*_____ a good grade point average in high school, I ___'ll apply___ to the best
                            a. get   **b.** apply

   universities. I want to major in chemistry.

2. **A:** I'm thinking about seeing the new science fiction movie this weekend.

   B: I love science fiction! If you _____, I _____ with you. What day?
                                       a. go   **b.** go

   A: I _____ on Saturday if I _____ work that day.
                  c. go   **d.** not/have to

3. **A:** I've just finished reading a great science fiction book. You can borrow it. But if you _____
                                                                           a. start

   it, you _____ it down. It's so good. Let me tell you about it.
                       b. not/be able to put

   B: If you _____ me about it, it _____ it for me. So please don't tell me.
                  c. tell   **d.** ruin

continued

4. A: Have you seen the latest *Jurassic Park* movie?

   B: No, but I want to see it. If I _____ time this weekend, I _____ it.
   a. have   b. watch

   A: I _____ it, too, if it _____ out on Netflix.
   c. watch   d. be

5. A: I need to write a paper about cloning. I don't know much about it.

   B: If you _____ "cloning," you _____ a lot of information.
   a. google   b. find

   A: If I _____ information about cloning humans, I _____ about that.
   c. find   d. write

EXERCISE 9 Fill in the blanks with the correct form of the verb given. Use both real conditionals and unreal conditionals.

A: Do you think that astronauts will travel to Mars soon?

B: Not so soon. I read that there's too much radiation. If a person _____*is*_____ exposed to too much

radiation, it can be harmful. It could damage the bones or even cause cancer. Scientists are trying to

build a spacecraft that can minimize radiation to the astronauts. If they _____ the radiation
2. solve

problem, probably travel to Mars _____ in our lifetime, possibly by the 2030s.
3. happen

B: What about radiation at the airport security point? My cousin travels for business all the time. If she

_____ through radiation at the airport frequently, _____ cancer?
4. pass   5. she/get

A: I don't think so. But if she _____ worried about it, she _____ for a pat
6. be   7. can/ask

down. I love to travel. If I _____ anywhere, I _____ into space.
8. can/go   9. go

A: Me, too. If I _____ to Mars today, I _____ back a rock as a souvenir.
10. can/go   11. bring

B: If you _____ for Mars today, you _____ back for at least
12. leave   13. not/come

three years.

A: Oh. I _____ my friends and family if I _____ them for three years.
14. miss   15. can/not/see

So maybe I'll take a more normal vacation. I'm thinking about going to Canada this summer. If I

_____ there, I _____ the Rocky Mountains.
16. go   17. visit

B: If you _____, you can bring me back a souvenir rock from there. By the way, are you
18. go

going to watch the TV program about Mars tonight?

A: I don't know. If I _____ time, I _____ it. If not, I _____ it
19. have   20. watch   21. record

on my DVR.

Two young children with a street vendor in Alton, Illinois, USA, circa 1912

LIFE One Hundred Years Ago

Read the following article. Pay special attention to the words in bold. 🔊 11.5

Most of us are amazed by the rapid pace of technology at the beginning of the 21st century. We often wonder what life will be like 20 or 50 or 100 years from now. But do you ever wonder what your life **would have been** like if you **had been** alive 100 years ago?

If you **had lived** around 1900 in the United States, you probably **wouldn't have graduated** from high school. Only six percent of Americans had a high school diploma at that time. If you **had been** a child living in a city, you **might have had** to work in a factory for 12 to 16 hours a day, six days a week. In 1900, six percent of American workers were between the ages of 10 and 15. If you **had worked** at a manufacturing job, you **would have had to work** about 53 hours a week and you **would have earned** about 20 cents an hour. (This is equivalent to about $5.00 an hour today.) Many of you **would have worked** on farms. About 38 percent of laborers were farm workers.

If you **had been** a woman in 1900, you probably **wouldn't have been** part of the labor force. Only 19 percent of women worked outside the home. If you **had gone** to a doctor, he probably **would not have had** a college education. And he **wouldn't have had** practical training before becoming a doctor. At that time, medical students learned only from textbooks.

If you **had had** a baby in 1900, it **would have been** born at home. If you **had gotten** an infection at that time, you **might have died** because antibiotics had not yet been discovered. The leading causes of death at that time were pneumonia, influenza, and tuberculosis.

What about your home? If you **had been living** 100 years ago, you probably **wouldn't have had** a bathtub or a telephone or electricity. You **would have been** living with a large number of people. Around 20 percent of homes had seven or more people.

Do you think you **would have been** happy with life 100 years ago?

COMPREHENSION Based on the reading, write T for *true* or F for *false*.

1. _____ Around 100 years ago, most children in the U.S. had to work.

2. _____ Around 100 years ago, most doctors in the U.S. had a college education.

3. _____ Around 100 years ago, most babies in the U.S. were born at home.

THINK ABOUT IT Discuss the questions with a partner or in a small group.

1. Review the question at the end of the text. Share your answer and give your reasons.

2. As the article suggests, many things have improved since 1900. What aspects of modern life, if any, may be worse, in your opinion? Explain.

11.4 Unreal Conditionals—Past

EXAMPLES	EXPLANATION
If you **had lived** 100 years ago, you probably **wouldn't have graduated** from high school. (Reality: You didn't live 100 years ago.)	An unreal conditional can describe a situation that was not real in the past.
You probably **would have been** born at home if you **had lived** in the U.S. around 1900. If you **had gotten** an infection, you **might have died**.	We use the past perfect in the *if* clause and *would/could/ might* + *have* + past participle in the main clause.
If my great-grandparents **had been able to** come to the U.S. 100 years ago, I **would have been** born here, and my life **would have been** different. (Reality: They couldn't come to the U.S. 100 years ago.)	In the *if* clause, we use *had been able to* to express the past perfect of *could*.
(a) If you **were** born 100 years ago, your life **would have been** different. OR (b) If you **had been** born 100 years ago, your life **would have been** different.	Sometimes we don't use the past perfect, especially with the verb *be*, if it is clear that the action is past. It is clear that you *were* born in the past. Sentences (a) and (b) have the same meaning.

Notes:

1. In relaxed speech, *have* after *could*, *would*, or *might* is pronounced /ə/.
2. We can use a continuous tense with unreal conditionals.

> If you **had been living** 100 years ago, you probably wouldn't have had a bathtub.

EXERCISE 10 Fill in the blanks with the correct form of the verb to complete this conversation about life in the U.S. 100 years ago. Answers may vary.

1. If you ___*had worked*___ in a factory, you ___*would have earned*___ about 20 cents an hour.

                 work   earn

2. If you _____ a baby 100 years ago, it probably _____ at home.

              have   be/born

3. If you _____ a child in a big city, you _____ all day in a factory.

             be   work

4. If you _____ around 1900, you probably _____ high school.

             live   not/finish

5. You _____ a car if you _____ at the beginning
                  not/have   live

    of the last century.

6. Your president _____ Theodore Roosevelt if you _____
                              be   live

    in the U.S. at the beginning of the last century.

7. If you _____ to travel to another city, you _____ by train.
                need   travel

EXERCISE 11 A woman is telling her daughter how life would have been if she had grown up in the late 1950s. Fill in the blanks with the correct form of the verb given to complete the story.

    It's great that you're thinking about becoming a doctor or astronaut. When I was your age, I didn't have the opportunities you have today. You can be anything you want, but if you ___*had been*___ a woman
                                                                      1. be

growing up in the fifties, your opportunities _____ limited. If you _____
                                            2. be   3. go

to college, you probably _____ in nursing or education,
                                      4. major

or you _____ a secretarial course. You probably
                            5. take

_____ married in your early twenties. If you _____ pregnant, you
               6. get   7. get

probably _____ your job. You probably _____ two or more
                   8. quit   9. have

children. Your husband _____ to support you and the children. Also, your house
                          10. work

_____ one TV and one phone. Because we had only one TV, the family spent more
          11. have

time together. You _____ a computer or a cell phone. If you _____
                12. not/have   13. grow

up in the fifties, your life _____ completely different.
                         14. be

ABOUT YOU Complete each statement. Discuss your answers with a partner.

1. If I had been born 200 years ago, _____

2. If I'd been alive in 1900, _____

3. If I had not gone to school as a child, _____

GRAMMAR IN USE

Sometimes we mix a past conditional with a present result.

    *If my mother **had** never **met** my father, I **wouldn't be** here today.*

Sometimes we mix a present conditional with a past result.

    *If I **were** an astronaut, I **would have gone** to the Moon.*

The SCIENCE of AGING

Read the following article. Pay special attention to the words in bold. 🎧 11.6

Do you **wish** you **could live** to be 100 years old or more? The answer to that question probably depends on how healthy you would be at that age, both physically and mentally. Does an elderly person **wish** he or she **had** the memory of a young person? Probably. As we age, most people's memories diminish[1].

How much of longevity[2] and health is determined by genetics[3]? How much by environment? To analyze why some people live a much longer, healthier life than others, scientists have been traveling to areas of the world where there are a number of centenarians, or people 100 or more years old. They have found certain groups in Japan, Italy, New York, and California who outlive others around them.

Women are more likely than men to live to be 100 by a ratio of four or five to one. However, scientists no longer think that this is genetic. Women take better advantage of diet and medical care than men do.

For years, scientists **have wished** they **could find** the genes for diseases. But now they have

changed their focus. They are looking for genes that can protect us from disease and aging. Scientists are looking at the genes of the "wellderly" (well + elderly). These are people over 80 who have no chronic[4] diseases, such as high blood pressure or diabetes. They have found that, besides genetics, there are many factors that influence longevity—diet, education, response to stress, and even luck.

Salvatore Caruso, a centenarian from Italy, broke his leg when he was a young man. As a result, he was unfit to serve in the Italian Army when his entire unit was called to serve during World War II. At the time, he **wished** he **could have served** with his unit. "They were all sent to the Russian front[5]," he said, "and not a single one of them came back." Whatever factors contribute to long life, a little luck doesn't hurt.

---

[1] to diminish: to lessen, reduce, or become limited
[2] longevity: the length of life
[3] genetics: the passing of physical characteristics from parents to children
[4] chronic: long lasting, persistent
[5] front: the area where two enemy forces meet in battle

Three generations of surfers

COMPREHENSION Based on the reading, write T for *true* or F for *false*.

1. _____ Some areas of the world have more centenarians than others.

2. _____ One factor that determines how long you will live is luck.

3. _____ Salvatore Caruso was wounded in World War II.

THINK ABOUT IT Discuss the questions with a partner or in a small group.

1. What is your answer to the question that begins the article? What factors other than health influence your choice?

2. More people now live to advanced ages than in the past. Is this good or bad for society? Give reasons for your opinion.

11.5 Wishes

EXAMPLES		EXPLANATION
Reality:	We get old.	To wish that a present or future situation were different, we use a past verb form for a wish about the present or future. After *wish*, we can use *that* to introduce the clause, but it is usually omitted.
Wish:	I wish (that) we **didn't get** old.	
Reality:	We **are learning** about Mars.	
Wish:	I wish (that) we **were learning** about other planets, too.	
Reality:	I **can't live** 150 years.	
Wish:	I wish (that) I **could live** 150 years.	
Wish:	I'm not young, but I wish (that) I **were**.	We can use an auxiliary verb (*were, did, could,* etc.) to shorten the wish clause.
Wish:	I don't have a good memory, but I wish (that) I **did**.	
Reality:	You don't want to study science.	Putting *would* after a wish shows that one person wants a change in another person or situation. Using *would* sometimes conveys a complaint.
Wish:	I wish (that) you **would study** more science.	
Reality:	Scientists haven't found a cure for diabetes.	
Wish:	I wish (that) scientists **would find** a cure for diabetes.	
Reality:	I **didn't know** my grandparents.	We can wish that a past situation were different. We use a past perfect verb for a wish about the past. If the real situation uses *could*, we use *could have* + past participle after *wish*.
Wish:	I wish (that) I **had known** them.	
Reality:	Salvatore Caruso **couldn't serve** in the military.	
Wish:	He wished (that) he **could have served**.	
Wish:	I never knew my great-grandparents, but I wish I **had**.	We can use the auxiliary verb *had* to shorten the *wish* clause.

EXERCISE 12 Fill in the blanks to complete this conversation about present or future wishes. Use context clues to help you.

A: I wish we ___*could stay*___ young forever. Don't you?
_{1.}

B: I just read a book about how to extend your life.

continued

A: Is it about some new scientific discovery?

B: Not at all. The authors are doctors. They write about things you can do to live a longer, healthier life.

A: Really? I wish I _____ to be at least 100 years old.

                                         2.

B: According to the book, there are a lot of things you could do to live longer.

A: Like what?

B: For one thing, the doctors recommend walking 30 minutes a day.

A: I wish I _____ time for a 30-minute walk. I work so many hours that I'm too tired to
                               3.

exercise when I get home.

B: Maybe you can walk to work.

A: No. I live too far. I wish I _____ closer to my job.
                                               4.

B: How about walking on the weekend?

A: I have too many other things to do on the weekends, like laundry and shopping. I wish I

_____ (*negative*) so many things to do. When it's Monday and I start work, I wish it
                       5.

_____ Friday. But when it's Friday and I have so many things to do on the weekend,
                       6.

sometimes I wish it _____ Monday. What other advice does this book give?
                                 7.

B: The authors recommend that we sleep seven to eight hours a night.

A: I wish I _____ so many hours, but I can't. I have too many things to do. It sounds
                       8.

like you have to work hard to live longer. There's no magic pill. I wish there _____
                                                             9.

a magic pill.

B: Me, too.

EXERCISE 13 Fill in the blanks to show that one person wishes for something different. Use *would* before the verb. Use contractions where possible.

1. Grandfather and grandson

    A: I wish I knew something about computers.

    B: Grandpa, you can still learn.

    A: I'm too old.

    B: I wish you ___*wouldn't say*___ that. You're never too old to learn.
                                    not/say

A: I wish you _____ me.

teach

B: I promise I'll give you some lessons.

A: You always say that. I wish you _____ a promise you can't keep.

not/make

2. Friends

A: Let's go to the science museum on Saturday.

B: I'd rather go to see a science fiction movie. There's a new movie I'd like to see. Let's go together.

A: I wish you _____ what I want to do for a change.

do

3. Cousins

A: I'd like to learn more about our ancestors.

B: What for? Why focus on the past?

A: I wish you _____ more interest in our family history. I'd love to know more about

show

our great-grandpa. I wish you _____ your DNA to a genealogy site so that we can learn

send

more about him.

B: Why me? Why not you?

A: Because I'm a woman. The DNA of a male gives more information about other males.

4. Friends

A: I wish scientists _____ a cure for AIDS.

find

B: Me, too. So many people have died of this disease. And I wish they _____ cancer

cure

and other diseases, too.

5. Wife and husband

A: I wish you _____ better care of yourself. You never go to the doctor.

take

B: I'm not sick.

A: I wish you _____ a checkup every year.

get

GRAMMAR IN USE

With *be*, the correct form is *were* for all subjects. However, this can sound formal. In conversation, we often use *was* with *I, he, she,* and *it*.

> *I wish I **were** younger.* (Formal)
> *I wish I **was** younger.* (Informal)

ABOUT YOU Fill in the blanks to complete each statement. Discuss your answers with a partner.

1. I wish I were _____

2. I wish I knew how to _____

3. I wish I didn't have to _____

4. I wish I had _____

5. I wish I could _____

6. My parents wish(ed) I would _____

7. I wish _____ *(person)* would _____

8. I wish the teacher would _____

EXERCISE 14 Fill in the blanks for a past wish.

1. When my dog died, I really missed him. I wish I ___had cloned___ him before he died.
   clone

2. I didn't pay much attention to science when I was younger. I wish I _____ more
   pay

   attention in my science class.

3. I'm so interested in dinosaurs. I wish they _____ extinct.
   not/become

4. I used to have pictures of my great-grandparents, but I left them in my country. I wish

   I _____ them here with me.
   bring

5. I wish I _____ in the 1800s, during the time of President Lincoln.
   live

6. My grandfather died before I was born. I wish I _____ him.
   can/know

7. I never asked my grandparents much about their lives. I wish I _____ them more
   ask

   about their childhood before they died.

ABOUT YOU Work with a partner and talk about something . . .

1. you wish you had done when you were younger.

2. you wish you had studied when you were younger.

3. your family wishes you had done differently.

4. you wish you had known before you came to this country.

5. you wish your parents had done or told you.

6. you wish had never happened.

EXERCISE 15 Fill in the blanks with the correct form of the verb given in each of the conversations. Some wishes are about the present; some are about the past. Some are wishes for a change.

1. **A:** I wish I _____had_____ good vision.
   a. have

   B: Why don't you try laser surgery? I had it two years ago, and I don't need glasses anymore. I had worn

   glasses since I was a child. I wish they _____ this surgery years ago.
   b. have

2. **A:** I wish I _____ thin.
   a. be

   B: Why don't you try a diet?

   A: I've tried every diet. Nothing works.

   B: You need to exercise every day.

   A: I'm too tired when I get home from work. I wish scientists _____ a pill that would make
   b. find

   me thin with no effort on my part.

3. **A:** I've been bald since I was 25 years old. I wish I _____ bald.
   a. not/be

   B: They say bald men are very attractive.

   A: I don't care what they say. I wish I _____ hair. I wish someone _____ a
   b. have   c. find

   solution for baldness.

4. **A:** I wish I _____ older.
   a. be

   B: Why? No one wants to get old.

   A: I didn't say "old." I just said "older." Older people have more experience and wisdom.

   B: I wish we _____ the wisdom of old people and the bodies of young people.
   b. have

5. **A:** I wish I _____ travel to the future.
   a. can

   B: Why?

   A: I would be able to see future problems and then come back and warn people about them.

   B: I wish I _____ go to the past.
   b. can

   A: Why?

   B: I would want to meet my grandparents. I never knew them. I wish I _____ them, but
   c. know

   they died before I was born.

continued

6. A: We saw a great movie last night about time travel. Too bad you didn't come with us.

   B: I wish I _____ with you, but I had to study for my biology test.
                                     can/go

7. A: I'm an only child. I wish I _____ a sister or brother.
                                   a. have

   B: Maybe you will someday.

   A: I don't think so. My parents are in their fifties. I wish they _____ another child when

                                                    b. have
      they were young.

8. A: We went to see a great movie last night. I wish you _____ with us.
                                           a. come

   B: You didn't tell me about it. I wish you _____ me. What was it about?
                                         b. tell

   A: It was about a man who wishes he _____ rich. And his wish comes true.
                                         c. be
      He's suddenly very rich, and he starts to have all kinds of problems.

   B: I wish I _____ those kinds of problems!
                         d. have

EXERCISE 16 A mother (A) is complaining to her adult son (B). Fill in the blanks with the correct form of the words given to express their wishes. Some wishes are about the present; some are about the past. Some are wishes for a change.

A: You never visit. I wish you _____would visit_____ me more often. I'm not going to live forever, you know.
                                   1. visit

B: I do visit you often. Isn't once a week often enough?

A: Someday I won't be here, and you'll say to yourself, "I wish I _____ my mom more often."
                                               2. visit

B: Mom, you're only 48 years old.

A: Who knows how long I'll be here? There are no guarantees in life. My own mother died when I was a

      teenager. I wish she _____ to see you and your sister.
                                  3. live

B: I do, too. But what can we do?

A: I wish you _____ married already.
                           4. be

B: Mom, I'm only 25 years old. There's plenty of time to get married.

A: Well, your sister's only 23, and she's already married. I wish you _____
                                                               5. be
      more like your sister. She finished college and then got married.

B: I wish you _____ comparing me to my sister. She has different goals in life.
                                 6. stop
      Besides, you don't like her husband.

A: You're right. I wish she _____ a different man.
                                      7. marry

B: There's nothing wrong with Paul. He's a good husband to her.

A: We'll see. You know, you're too thin. I wish you _____ more.
8. eat

B: I eat enough. When I was a teenager, you said I was too fat.

A: I'm still your mother. I wish you _____ to me.
9. listen

B: I do listen to you. But I've got to live my own life.

A: Sometimes you act like a child and tell me you're old enough to make your own decisions. Then you tell me you're too young to get married.

B: I'm not too young to get married. I just don't want to do it now. I'm happy being a rock musician.

A: I wish you _____ a real job.
10. have

B: I have a real job.

A: You didn't finish college. You left after your junior year. I wish you _____
11. get
your degree.

B: You don't need a college degree to be a rock musician.

A: Well, I hope I live long enough to see you married, with a good job.

B: With today's technologies, you'll probably live to be 150 years old. I'll be 127, and you'll probably still be telling me how to live my life.

FUN WITH GRAMMAR

Play a chain game using real and unreal conditionals! You can either practice by writing your answers on a shared piece of paper, or by speaking with your group.

Get into groups of three to five. The first student will complete the provided *if* clause. For example:

> *If I won a trip to Europe, **I would go** to France.*

The next student will take the main clause and form a new conditional sentence.

> *If I went to France, **I would visit** Paris.*

This chain continues until you are all out of logical ideas. Check each other's work and correct any errors. Use one or more of the following prompts. If you write your answers, read them to the class when you are done.

1. If we all live to be 100, _____.

2. If I were fluent in English, _____.

3. If I take a vacation this year, _____.

4. If I were very rich and famous, _____.

SUMMARY OF UNIT 11

Unreal Conditionals—Present

VERB → PAST	VERB → *WOULD/COULD/MIGHT* + BASE FORM
If I **were** an astronaut,	I **would go** to Mars.
If I **could** live to be 150 years old,	I **would know** my great-great-grandchildren.
If you **could** travel to the past,	you **could meet** your ancestors.
If we **didn't have** advanced technology,	we **wouldn't be** able to explore space.
If you **took** better care of yourself,	you **might live** to be 100 years old.

Unreal Conditionals—Past

VERB → PAST PERFECT	VERB → *WOULD/COULD/MIGHT* + HAVE + PAST PARTICIPLE
If you **had lived** 100 years ago,	you **wouldn't have had** a computer.
If you **had been** a doctor 100 years ago,	you **could have practiced** medicine without a college degree.
If my father **had** not **met** my mother,	I **wouldn't have been** born.
If you **had gotten** an infection 100 years ago,	you **might have died**.

Real Possibilities—Future

CONDITIONAL	RESULT
If we **explore** Mars,	we **will learn** a lot.
If you **eat** a healthy diet,	you**'ll live** longer.

Wishes

EXAMPLES	EXPLANATION
I wish my grandparents **were** here. I wish I **could go** to Mars. I wish we **were learning** about dinosaurs.	Wish about the present
I wish I **could live to be** 100.	Wish about the future
I wish my grandpa **would tell** me more about his childhood. My mother wishes my father **would take** better care of his health.	Wish for a change in another person or situation
I wish I **had studied** more science when I was younger.	Wish about the past

REVIEW

Circle the letter of the correct word(s) to fill in the blanks.

1. I _____ help you with your science project if I had more time.

   a. were   (c.) would

   b. will   d. would be

2. I might become a scientist. If I _____ one, I'll try to find a cure for diseases.

   a. will become   c. would become

   b. became   d. become

3. If I _____ you, I'd spend more time on science and less on science fiction.

   a. were   c. will be

   b. am   d. would be

4. I can't help you with your project. I would help you if I _____.

   a. can   c. would

   b. could   d. had

5. We can't travel at the speed of light. If we could travel at the speed of light, we _____ able to

   visit far away stars.

   a. would be   c. would have been

   b. will be   d. were

6. We would know more about Mars if it _____ so far away.

   a. weren't   c. wouldn't have been

   b. won't be   d. wouldn't be

7. Some people don't take good care of their health. If they _____ better care of their health,

   they would probably live longer.

   a. take   c. had taken

   b. would take   d. took

8. I wouldn't go to Mars even if you _____ me a million dollars.

   a. pay   c. will pay

   b. paid   d. would pay

continued

9. If I could visit any planet, I _____ Jupiter.

    a. will visit   c. would be visit

    b. would visit   d. would have visited

10. I don't know much about science. I wish I _____ more about it.

    a. knew   c. have known

    b. will know   d. know

11. We can't travel to the past. I wish we _____ travel to the past.

    a. could   c. can

    b. would   d. will

12. If I had known my great-grandparents, I _____ them about their childhood.

    a. would ask   c. could ask

    b. will ask   d. would have asked

13. My uncle never exercised and was overweight. He had a heart attack and died when he was 50 years old.

    If he _____ better care of himself, he might have lived much longer.

    a. would take   c. took

    b. had taken   d. will take

14. Salvatore Caruso broke his leg and couldn't serve in World War II. If he _____ in

    World War II, he might have been killed.

    a. were served   c. would serve

    b. has served   d. had served

15. My favorite dog died 10 years ago. I wish I _____ her.

    a. clone   c. had cloned

    b. will clone   d. would clone

16. I wish scientists _____ a cure for AIDS.

    a. find   c. would find

    b. found   d. will find

17. I didn't study physics in high school, but I wish I _____.

    a. have   c. were

    b. had   d. would

18. I don't know much about dinosaurs, but I wish I _____.

    a. had   c. would

    b. were   d. did

19. If you _____ the movie *Jurassic Park*, you would have been very scared.

    a. had seen   c. would have seen

    b. would see   d. will see

20. If scientists brought dinosaurs back from extinction today, the world _____ very

dangerous for humans.

    a. will be   c. would be

    b. would have been   d. were

FROM GRAMMAR TO WRITING

PART 1 Editing Advice

1. Don't use *will* with an unreal conditional.

    If I ~~will be~~ *were* on Mars, I would look for life forms.

2. Always use the base form after a modal.

    The teacher would ~~has~~ *have* helped you with your science project if you had asked her.

3. Use the past perfect, not the present perfect, for unreal conditionals and wishes.

    If you ~~have~~ *had* seen the movie, you would have understood more about dinosaurs.

    I wish you ~~have~~ *had* seen the movie.

4. For a real conditional about the future, use the simple present in the *if* clause.

    If I ~~will~~ have time tomorrow, I will help you with your science project.

5. In formal writing, use *were*, not *was*, in an unreal conditional.

    I wish I ~~was~~ *were* a better student in science.

PART 2 Editing Practice

Some of the shaded words and phrases have mistakes. Find the mistakes and correct them. If the shaded words are correct, write C.

There are a few things in my life that I wish were *C* different. First, I wish I ~~have~~ *had* a better job
                                                    1.   2.
and made more money. Unfortunately, I don't have the skills for a better job. When I was in high
    3.
school, I wasn't interested in college. My parents always said, "We wish you would continued
                                                                            4.
your education," but I was foolish and didn't listen to them. If I have gone to college, I will be
                                                                    5.   6.
making much more money now. And if I had more money, I could help my family back home.
                                7.   8.
And, if I will be better educated, my parents would be very proud of me. I wish I can convince
        9.   10.   11.
my younger brothers and sister about the importance of an education, but they'll have to make

their own decisions.

   Another thing I'm not happy about is my living situation. I have a roommate because I can't

afford to pay the rent alone. I wish I don't have a roommate. My roommate always watches TV,
                                    12.
and the TV is too loud. I wish he would turn off the TV at night and let me sleep. My parents have
                                    13.
told me, "If I were you, I will get a better roommate." But we signed a one-year lease together, and I
            14.   15.
can't do anything about it until next May. If I had known that he was going to be so inconsiderate,
                                                    16.
I never would had roomed with him. I wish it was May already! I prefer to live alone rather than
        17.   18.

live with a stranger. I'm saving my money now. If I will have enough money, I'll get my own
                                                    19.

apartment next May. Another possibility is to room with my cousin, who's planning to come here

soon. If he comes to the U.S. by May, I share an apartment with him. He's very responsible. I wish
         20.   21.

he has come to the U.S. with me last year, but he didn't get his visa at that time.
    22.

   I realize that we all make mistakes in life, but we learn from them. If I could give advice to
                                                               23.

every young person in the world, I'd say, "Look before you leap." And I will say, "Listen to your
                        24.   25.

parents. They've lived longer than you, and you can learn from their experience."

WRITING TIP

When writing several sentences about an unreal situation, it is important to use consistent verb forms for anything that is imaginary.

> If I had the opportunity to travel to Mars, I **would** definitely accept. I **wouldn't be** afraid because I **would trust** my equipment and the people I **was working** with. On Mars, I **would stay** in touch with my family as well as I **could**.

If you write I _will_ be afraid. . . . it suggests that the situation is real.

PART 3 Write

Read the prompts. Choose one and write one or more paragraphs about it.

1. What do you think would be the advantages or disadvantages of cloning human beings?
2. Write about an important decision you made in the past. What would your life be like if you hadn't made this decision?

PART 4 Edit

Reread the Summary of Unit 11 and the Editing Advice. Edit your writing from Part 3.

APPENDIX A

SUMMARY OF VERB TENSES

VERB TENSE	FORM	MEANING AND USE
SIMPLE PRESENT	I **have** class Mondays. He **doesn't have** class today. **Do** you **have** class today? **What do** you **do** every day?	• facts, general truths, habits, and customs • used with frequency adverbs, i.e., *always, usually, sometimes, never* • regular activities and repeated actions
PRESENT CONTINUOUS	I **am studying** biology this semester. He **isn't studying** now. **Are** you **studying** this weekend? **What** is she **studying** at college?	• actions that are currently in progress • future actions if a future time expression is used or understood
PRESENT PERFECT	I **have seen** the movie "Titanic." He **has seen** "Titanic" five times. **Have** you **seen** "Titanic?" **Why have** you never **seen** "Titanic?"	• action that started in the past and continues to the present • action that repeats during a period of time from the past to the present • repeated actions at indefinite times in the past
PRESENT PERFECT CONTINUOUS	She **has been working** there for years. I **haven't been working** regularly in awhile. **Have** you **been working** here long? **Where have** you **been working** lately?	• an action that started in the past and continues to the present
SIMPLE PAST	They **liked** the story. I **didn't like** the story. **Did** you **like** the story? **What did** you **like** about the story?	• recent or historical events • a narrative, or story, that is real or imagined • events in a person's life • the result of an experiment
PAST CONTINUOUS	She **was watching** TV when I called. I **wasn't watching** TV when you called. **Were** you **watching** TV around 10? **What were** you **watching**?	• an action in progress at a specific past time • often with the simple past in another clause to show the relationship of a longer past action to a shorter past action
PAST PERFECT	I **had just left** when she arrived. We **hadn't left** yet when she arrived. **Had** you already **left** the party when she arrived? **How** long **had** you **known** each other before you got married?	• used to indicate the first of two past events
PAST PERFECT CONTINUOUS	The movie **had been playing** for ten minutes when they arrived. The movie **hadn't been playing** for too long when they arrived. **How long had** the movie **been playing**?	• a continuous past action that was completed before another past action • used with action verbs, i.e., *arrive, ask, eat, enter*
FUTURE WITH *WILL*	I **will go** to the store He **won't go** to the store. **Will** you **go** to the store? **When will** you **go** to the store?	• future plans/decisions made in the moment • strong predictions • promises and offers to help

FUTURE WITH BE GOING TO	He's **going to study** all weekend. He **isn't going to study** Saturday. **Are** you **going to study** Saturday? **What are** you **going to study** Saturday?	• future plans that are already made • predictions
FUTURE CONTINUOUS	I **will be sleeping** at midnight. They'**re going to be attending** a concert at that time.	• actions that will occur in the future and continue for an expected period of time
FUTURE PERFECT	She **will have finished** by ten.	• actions that will be completed before another point in the future
FUTURE PERFECT CONTINUOUS	I **will have been standing** here for an hour when the train finally arrives.	• actions that will continue up until a point in the future

APPENDIX B

NONACTION VERBS

DESCRIPTION	FEELINGS	DESIRES	MEASUREMENTS	MENTAL STATES	SENSES
appear* be* consist of look* look like resemble seem	appreciate care dislike forgive hate like love mind miss	hope need prefer want wish	cost measure* weigh*	agree believe concern disagree doubt forget guess know imagine mean recognize remember* suppose surprise think* understand	belong contain have* own possess feel* hear* hurt notice see* smell* sound*

*Words that also have an active meaning.

APPENDIX C

IRREGULAR VERB FORMS

BASE FORM	PAST FORM	PAST PARTICIPLE	BASE FORM	PAST FORM	PAST PARTICIPLE
be	was/were	been	fight	fought	fought
bear	bore	born/borne	find	found	found
beat	beat	beaten	fit	fit	fit
become	became	become	flee	fled	fled
begin	began	begun	fly	flew	flown
bend	bent	bent	forbid	forbade	forbidden
bet	bet	bet	forget	forgot	forgotten
bid	bid	bid	forgive	forgave	forgiven
bind	bound	bound	freeze	froze	frozen
bite	bit	bitten	get	got	gotten
bleed	bled	bled	give	gave	given
blow	blew	blown	go	went	gone
break	broke	broken	grind	ground	ground
breed	bred	bred	grow	grew	grown
bring	brought	brought	hang	hung	hung
broadcast	broadcast	broadcast	have	had	had
build	built	built	hear	heard	heard
burst	burst	burst	hide	hid	hidden
buy	bought	bought	hit	hit	hit
cast	cast	cast	hold	held	held
catch	caught	caught	hurt	hurt	hurt
choose	chose	chosen	keep	kept	kept
cling	clung	clung	know	knew	known
come	came	come	lay	laid	laid
cost	cost	cost	lead	led	led
creep	crept	crept	leave	left	left
cut	cut	cut	lend	lent	lent
deal	dealt	dealt	let	let	let
dig	dug	dug	lie	lay	lain
dive	dove/dived	dove/dived	light	lit/lighted	lit/lighted
do	did	done	lose	lost	lost
draw	drew	drawn	make	made	made
drink	drank	drunk	mean	meant	meant
drive	drove	driven	meet	met	met
eat	ate	eaten	mistake	mistook	mistaken
fall	fell	fallen	overcome	overcame	overcome
feed	fed	fed	overdo	overdid	overdone
feel	felt	felt	overtake	overtook	overtaken

BASE FORM	PAST FORM	PAST PARTICIPLE	BASE FORM	PAST FORM	PAST PARTICIPLE
overthrow	overthrew	overthrown	stick	stuck	stuck
pay	paid	paid	sting	stung	stung
plead	pled/pleaded	pled/pleaded	stink	stank	stunk
prove	proved	proven/proved	strike	struck	struck/stricken
put	put	put	strive	strove	striven
quit	quit	quit	swear	swore	sworn
read	read	read	sweep	swept	swept
ride	rode	ridden	swell	swelled	swelled/swollen
ring	rang	rung	swim	swam	swum
rise	rose	risen	swing	swung	swung
run	ran	run	take	took	taken
say	said	said	teach	taught	taught
see	saw	seen	tear	tore	torn
seek	sought	sought	tell	told	told
sell	sold	sold	think	thought	thought
send	sent	sent	throw	threw	thrown
set	set	set	understand	understood	understood
sew	sewed	sewn/sewed	uphold	upheld	upheld
shake	shook	shaken	upset	upset	upset
shed	shed	shed	wake	woke	woken
shine	shone/shined	shone/shined	wear	wore	worn
shoot	shot	shot	weave	wove	woven
show	showed	shown/showed	wed	wedded/wed	wedded/wed
shrink	shrank/shrunk	shrunk/shrunken	weep	wept	wept
shut	shut	shut	win	won	won
sing	sang	sung	wind	wound	wound
sink	sank	sunk	withdraw	withdrew	withdrawn
sit	sat	sat	withhold	withheld	withheld
sleep	slept	slept	withstand	withstood	withstood
slide	slid	slid	wring	wrung	wrung
slit	slit	slit	write	wrote	written
speak	spoke	spoken			
speed	sped	sped			
spend	spent	spent			
spin	spun	spun			
spit	spit/spat	spit/spat			
split	split	split			
spread	spread	spread			
spring	sprang	sprung			
stand	stood	stood			
steal	stole	stolen			

Note:

The past and past participle of some verbs can end in -ed or -t.

burn	burned or burnt
dream	dreamed or dreamt
kneel	kneeled or knelt
learn	learned or learnt
leap	leaped or leapt
spill	spilled or spilt
spoil	spoiled or spoilt

APPENDIX D

GERUNDS AND INFINITIVES

VERBS FOLLOWED BY GERUNDS

admit	detest	miss	resent
advise	discuss	permit	resist
anticipate	dislike	postpone	risk
appreciate	enjoy	practice	stop
avoid	finish	put off	suggest
can't help	forbid	quit	tolerate
complete	imagine	recall	understand
consider	keep	recommend	
delay	mention	regret	
deny	mind	remember	

VERBS FOLLOWED BY INFINITIVES

agree	claim	know how	seem
appear	consent	learn	swear
arrange	decide	manage	tend
ask	demand	need	threaten
attempt	deserve	offer	try
be able	expect	plan	volunteer
beg	fail	prepare	want
can afford	forget	pretend	wish
care	hope	promise	would like
choose	intend	refuse	

VERBS FOLLOWED BY EITHER GERUNDS OR INFINITIVES

begin	love	start
continue	prefer	stop*
hate	remember*	try (in past form-*tried*)*
like	can (not) stand	

*The meaning is different in these; in others, the meaning is about the same.

ADJECTIVES FOLLOWED BY INFINITIVES

afraid	embarrassed	lucky	shocked
ashamed	excited	necessary pleased	sorry
careful	glad	proud	stupid
certain	good	ready	surprised
challenging	happy	relieved	upset
determined	hard	reluctant	useful
difficult	important	rewarding	willing
disappointed	impossible	right	wrong
easy	likely	sad	

APPENDIX E

VERBS AND ADJECTIVES FOLLOWED BY A PREPOSITION

accuse someone of
(be) accustomed to
adjust to
(be) afraid of
agree with
(be) amazed at/by
(be) angry about
(be) angry at/with
apologize for
approve of
argue about
argue with
(be) ashamed of
(be) aware of
believe in
blame someone for
(be) bored with/by
(be) capable of
care about
care for
compare to/with
complain about
concentrate on
(be) concerned about
consist of
count on
deal with
decide on
depend on/upon
(be) different from
disapprove of
(be) divorced from
dream about/of
(be) engaged to
(be) excited about

(be) familiar with
(be) famous for
(be) fond of
forget about
forgive someone for
(be) glad about
(be) good at
(be) grateful to someone for
(be) guilty of
(be) happy about
hear about
hear of
hope for
(be) incapable of
insist on/upon
(be) interested in
(be) involved in
(be) jealous of
(be) known for
(be) lazy about
listen to
look at
look for
look forward to
(be) mad about
(be) mad at
(be) made from/of
(be) married to
object to
(be) opposed to
participate in
plan on
pray to
pray for

(be) prepared for/to
prevent (someone) from
prohibit (someone) from
protect (someone) from
(be) proud of
recover from
(be) related to
rely on/upon
(be) responsible for
(be) sad about
(be) satisfied with
(be) scared of
(be) sick of
(be) sorry about
(be) sorry for
speak about
speak to/with
succeed in
(be) sure of/about
(be) surprised at
take care of
talk about
talk to/with
thank (someone) for
(be) thankful (to someone) for
think about/of
(be) tired of
(be) upset about
(be) upset with
(be) used to
wait for
warn (someone) about
(be) worried about
worry about

NONCOUNT AND COUNT NOUNS

NONCOUNT NOUNS

GROUP A	**Nouns that have no distinct, separate parts**			
	milk	yogurt	paper	cholesterol
	oil	poultry	rain	blood
	water	bread	air	
	coffee	meat	electricity	
	tea	soup	lightning	
	juice	butter	thunder	

GROUP B	**Nouns with parts too small or insignificant to count**		
	rice	hair	sand
	sugar	popcorn	corn
	salt	snow	grass

GROUP C	**Nouns that are classes or categories**	
	money or cash (nickels, dimes, dollars)	mail (letters, packages, postcards, flyers)
	furniture (chairs, tables, beds)	homework (compositions, exercises, readings)
	clothing (sweaters, pants, dresses)	jewelry (necklaces, bracelets, rings)

GROUP D	**Abstract nouns**					
	love	happiness	nutrition	patience	work	nature
	truth	education	intelligence	poverty	health	help
	beauty	advice	unemployment	music	fun	energy
	luck/fortune	knowledge	pollution	art	information	friendship

GROUP E	**Subjects of study**	
	history	grammar	biology
	chemistry	geometry	math (mathematics*)

*Even though *mathematics* ends with *s*, it is not plural.

QUANTITY WORDS WITH COUNT AND NONCOUNT NOUNS

SINGULAR COUNT	PLURAL COUNT	NONCOUNT
a tomato	tomatoes	coffee
one tomato	**two** tomatoes	**two cups of** coffee
	some tomatoes	**some** coffee
no tomato	**no** tomatoes	**no** coffee
	any tomatoes (with questions and negatives)	**any** coffee (with questions and negatives)
	a lot of tomatoes	**a lot of** coffee
	many tomatoes	**much** coffee (with questions and negatives)
	a few tomatoes	**a little** coffee
	several tomatoes	**several** cups of coffee
	How many tomatoes?	**How much** coffee?

COUNT OR NONCOUNT NOUNS WITH CHANGES IN MEANING

COUNT	NONCOUNT
Avocados and nuts are **foods** with healthy fats.	We have a lot of **food** at home.
He wrote a **paper** about hypnosis.	I need some **paper** to write my composition.
He committed three **crimes** last year.	There is a lot of **crime** in a big city.
I have two hundred **chickens** on my farm.	We ate some **chicken** for dinner.
I don't want to bore you with my **troubles**.	I have some **trouble** with my car.
She went to Puerto Rico three **times**.	She spent a lot of **time** on her project.
She drank three **glasses** of water.	The window is made of bulletproof **glass**.
I had a bad **experience** on my trip to Paris.	She has **experience** with computers.
I've learned about the **lives** of my grandparents.	**Life** is sometimes happy, sometimes sad.
I heard a **noise** outside my window.	Those children are making a lot of **noise**.
Some **fruits** have a lot of sugar.	I bought some **fruit** at the fruit store.

APPENDIX G

ARTICLES

THE INDEFINITE ARTICLE
A. To classify a subject

EXAMPLES	EXPLANATION
Chicago is **a** city. Illinois is **a** state. Abraham Lincoln was **an** American president.	• We use *a* before a consonant sound. • We use *an* before a vowel sound. • We can put an adjective before the noun.
Chicago and Los Angeles are cities. Lincoln and Washington were American presidents.	We do not use an article before a plural noun.

B. To make a generalization about a noun

EXAMPLES	EXPLANATION
A dog has sharp teeth. **Dogs** have sharp teeth.	We use an indefinite article *(a/an)* + a singular count noun or no article with a plural noun.
An elephant has big ears. **Elephants** have big ears.	Both the singular and plural forms have the same meaning.
Coffee contains caffeine. **Love** makes people happy.	We do not use an article to make a generalization about a noncount noun.

C. To introduce a new noun into the conversation

EXAMPLES	EXPLANATION
I have **a cell phone**. I have **an umbrella**.	We use the indefinite article *a/an* with singular count nouns.
I have **(some) dishes**. Do you have **(any) cups**? I don't have **(any) forks**. I have **(some) money** with me. Do you have **(any) cash** with you? I don't have **(any) time**.	We use *some* or *any* with plural nouns and noncount nouns. We use *any* in questions and negatives. *Some* and *any* can be omitted.
There's **an elevator** in the building. There isn't **any money** in my wallet.	*There* + a form of *be* can introduce an indefinite noun into a conversation.

THE DEFINITE ARTICLE

A. To refer to a previously mentioned noun

EXAMPLES	EXPLANATION
There's **a dog** in the next apartment. **The dog** barks all the time.	We start by saying *a dog*. We continue by saying *the dog*.
We bought **some grapes**. We ate **the grapes** this morning.	We start by saying *some grapes*. We continue by saying *the grapes*.
I need **some sugar**. I'm going to use **the sugar** to bake a cake.	We start by saying *some sugar*. We continue by saying *the sugar*.
Did you buy **any coffee**? Yes. **The coffee** is in the cabinet.	We start by saying *any coffee*. We continue by saying *the coffee*.

B. When the speaker and the listener have the same reference

EXAMPLES	EXPLANATION
The number on this page is AP5.	The object is present, so the speaker and listener have the same object in mind.
The president is talking about **the** economy.	People who live in the same country have things in common.
Please turn off **the lights** and shut **the door** before you leave **the house**.	People who live in the same house have things in common.
The house on the corner is beautiful. I spent **the money you gave me**.	The listener knows exactly which one because the speaker defines or specifies which one.

C. When there is only one in our experience

EXAMPLES	EXPLANATION
The sun is bigger than **the moon**. There are many problems in **the world**.	The *sun*, the *moon*, and the *world* are unique objects.
Write your name on **the top** of the page.	The page has only one top.
Alaska is **the biggest** state in the U.S.	A superlative indicates that there is only one.

D. With familiar places

EXAMPLES	EXPLANATION
I'm going to **the store** after work. Do you need anything? **The bank** is closed now. I'll go tomorrow.	We use *the* with certain familiar places and people—*the bank, the zoo, the park, the store, the movies, the beach, the post office, the bus, the train, the doctor, the dentist*—when we refer to the one that we habitually visit or use.

Language Notes:

1. Omit *the* after a preposition with the words *church, school, work,* and *bed*.

   He's **in church**.   They're **at work**.

   I'm going **to school**.   I'm going **to bed**.

2. Omit *to* and *the* with *home* and *downtown*.

   I'm going **home**.   Are you going **downtown** after class?

continued

E. To make a formal generalization

EXAMPLES	EXPLANATION
The shark is the oldest and most primitive fish.	To say that something is true of all members of a group, use *the* with singular count nouns.
The computer has changed the way people deal with information.	To talk about a class of inventions, use *the*.
The ear has three parts: outer, middle, and inner.	To talk about an organ of the body in a general sense, use *the*.

Language Note:

For informal generalizations, use *a* + a singular noun or no article with a plural noun.

    The computer has changed the way we deal with information. (Formal)

    A computer is expensive. (Informal)

    Computers are expensive. (Informal)

SPECIAL USES OF ARTICLES

NO ARTICLE	ARTICLE

Personal names:
  John Kennedy
	The whole family:
	  the Kennedys

Title and name:
  Queen Elizabeth
	Title without name:
	  the Queen

Cities, states, countries, continents:
  Cleveland
  Ohio
  Mexico
  South America
	Places that are considered a union:
	  the United States
	Place names: the _____ of _____
	  the District of Columbia

Mountains:
  Mount Everest
	Mountain ranges:
	  the Rocky Mountains

Islands:
  Staten Island
	Collectives of islands:
	  the Hawaiian Islands

Lakes:
  Lake Superior
	Collectives of lakes:
	  the Great Lakes

Beaches:
  Palm Beach
  Pebble Beach
	Rivers, oceans, seas:
	  the Mississippi River
	  the Atlantic Ocean
	  the Dead Sea

Streets and avenues:
  Madison Avenue
  Wall Street
	Well-known buildings:
	  the Willis Tower
	  the Empire State Building

Parks:
  Central Park
	Zoos:
	  the San Diego Zoo

NO ARTICLE	ARTICLE
Seasons: summer fall spring winter Summer is my favorite season. **Note:** After a preposition, *the* may be used. In (the) winter, my car runs badly.	Deserts: the Mojave Desert the Sahara Desert
Directions: north south east west	Sections of a piece of land: the West Side (of New York)
School subjects: history math	Unique geographical points: the North Pole the Vatican
Name + *college* or *university*: Northwestern University	The University/College of _____ the University of Michigan
Magazines: *Time* *Sports Illustrated*	Newspapers: the *Tribune* the *Wall Street Journal*
Months and days: September Monday	Ships: the *Titanic* the *Queen Elizabeth II*
Holidays and dates: Mother's Day July 4 (month + day)	The day of month: the fifth of May the Fourth of July
Diseases: cancer AIDS polio malaria	Ailments: a cold a toothache a headache the flu
Games and sports: poker soccer	Musical instruments, after *play*: the drums the piano **Note:** Sometimes *the* is omitted. She plays (the) drums.
Languages: English	The _____ language: the English language
Last month, year, week, etc. = the one before this one: I forgot to pay my rent last month. The teacher gave us a test last week.	The last month, the last year, the last week, etc. = the last in a series: December is the last month of the year. Vacation begins the last week in May.
In office = in an elected position: The president is in office for four years.	In the office = in a specific room: The teacher is in the office.

APPENDIX H

CAPITALIZATION AND PUNCTUATION RULES

CAPITALIZATION RULES

RULE	EXAMPLES
The first word in a sentence	**M**y friends are helpful.
The word *I*	My sister and **I** took a trip together.
Names of people	**A**braham **L**incoln; **G**eorge **W**ashington
Titles preceding names of people	**D**octor (**D**r.) **S**mith; **P**resident **L**incoln; **Q**ueen **E**lizabeth; **M**r. **R**ogers; **M**rs. **C**arter
Geographic names	the **U**nited **S**tates; **L**ake **S**uperior; **C**alifornia; the **R**ocky **M**ountains; the **M**ississippi **R**iver **Note:** The word *the* in a geographic name is not capitalized.
Street names	**P**ennsylvania **A**venue (**A**ve.); **W**all **S**treet (**S**t.); **A**bbey **R**oad (**R**d.)
Names of organizations, companies, colleges, buildings, stores, hotels	the **R**epublican **P**arty; **C**engage **L**earning; **D**artmouth **C**ollege; the **U**niversity of **W**isconsin; the **W**hite **H**ouse; **B**loomingdale's; the **H**ilton **H**otel
Nationalities and ethnic groups	**M**exicans; **C**anadians; **S**paniards; **A**mericans; **J**ews; **K**urds; **I**nuit
Languages	**E**nglish; **S**panish; **P**olish; **V**ietnamese; **R**ussian
Months	**J**anuary; **F**ebruary
Days	**S**unday; **M**onday
Holidays	**I**ndependence Day; **T**hanksgiving
Important words in a title	*Grammar in Context; The Old Man and the Sea; Romeo and Juliet; The Sound of Music* **Note:** Capitalize *the* as the first word of a title.

PUNCTUATION RULES

PUNCTUATION	EXAMPLES
A period (.) is used at the end of a declarative sentence.	This is a complete sentence.
A question mark (?) is used at the end of a question.	When does the movie start?
An exclamation point (!) is used at the end of an exclamation. It expresses a strong emotion.	This book is so interesting!

A comma (,) is used:
 	
• before the connectors *and*, *but*, *so*, and *or* in a compound sentence.
 	
• between three or more items in a list.
 	
• after a dependent clause at the beginning of a complex sentence. Dependent clauses include time clauses, *if* clauses, and reason clauses.
 	
• between the day and the date and between the date and the year.
 	
• between and after (if in the middle of a sentence) city, state, and country names that appear together.
 	
• after time words and phrases, prepositional phrases of time, and sequence words (except *then*) at the start of a sentence.
	
	• She gave Tomas a pen, but he wanted a pencil.
	
	• He needs a notebook, a pen, and a calculator.
	
	• If it's cold outside, you should wear a coat.
	
	• The test will be on Friday, May 20.
	
	  The school opened on September 3, 2010.
	
	• She lived and taught in Shanghai, China for five years.
	
	• Finally, the test was over and the student could leave.
	
	  After the movie, they decided to go out for coffee.

An apostrophe (') is used to indicate either a contraction or a possession:
 	
• Use an apostrophe in a contraction in place of the letter or letters that have been deleted.
 	
• Add an apostrophe and the letter -*s* after the word. If a plural word already ends in -*s*, just add an apostrophe.
	
	• I'm happy to see you.
	
	  You've read a lot of books this year.
	
	• That is Yusef's book.
	
	  The teachers' books include the answers.

Quotation marks (") are used to indicate: • the exact words that were spoken by someone. Notice that the punctuation at the end of a quote is inside the quotation marks. • language that a writer has borrowed from another source. • when a word or phrase is being used in a special way.	 • Albert Einstein said, "I have no special talent. I am only passionately curious." • The dictionary defines punctuation as, "the use of specific marks to make ideas within writing clear." • The paper was written by a "professional" writer.

APPENDIX I

SENTENCE TYPES

There are three basic sentences types: simple, compound, and complex.
Simple sentences usually have one subject and one verb:

        s   v

    Students love textbooks.

Simple sentences can have more than one subject and / or verb:

       s   s   v

    Children and adults like pizza.

Compound sentences are usually made up of two simple sentences (independent clauses) with a **connector** (a coordination conjunction such as *and*, *but*, *or*, *yet*, *so*, and *for*):

                              coord

    s   v   conj s   v

    They worked hard all semester, but they did not finish the project.

Complex sentences have one independent clause and at least one dependent clause. The dependent clause is often an adverb clause, which begins with a **connector** (a subordinating conjunction such as *while*, *although*, *because*, and *if*):

     sub

    conj dependent clause.   independent clause

    Although the test was very difficult, all the students received a passing grade.

APPENDIX J

CONNECTORS

COORDINATING CONJUNCTIONS

Coordinating conjunctions join two independent clauses to form a compound sentence. Use a comma before a coordinating conjunction in a compound sentence.

```
                                       coord
     independent clause                conj          independent clause
   ┌─────────────────────────┐        ┌───┐        ┌──────────────────────────────────┐
   The exam was extremely difficult,   but   all of the students received a passing score.
```

SUBORDINATING CONJUNCTIONS

Subordinating conjunctions introduce a dependent clause in a complex sentence.
When a dependent clause begins a sentence, use a comma to separate it from the independent clause.

```
          dependent clause                        independent clause
   ┌──────────────────────────────┐      ┌────────────────────────────────────────┐
   Although the exam was extremely difficult,   all of the students received a passing score.
```

When a dependent clause comes after an independent clause, no comma is used.

```
           independent clause                        dependent clause
   ┌──────────────────────────────┐      ┌────────────────────────────────────────┐
   All of the students received a passing score   although the exam was extremely difficult.
```

TRANSITION WORDS

Transition words **show the relationship between ideas in sentences.**
A transition followed by a comma can begin a sentence.

```
         independent clause          transition          independent clause
   ┌──────────────────────────┐      ┌──────┐        ┌──────────────────────────────────┐
   The exam was extremely difficult.   However,   all of the students received a passing score.
```

continued

CONNECTOR SUMMARY CHART

PURPOSE	COORDINATING CONJUNCTIONS	SUBORDINATING CONJUNCTIONS	TRANSITION WORDS
To give an example			For example, To illustrate, Specifically, In particular,
To add information	and		In addition, Moreover, Furthermore,
To signal a comparison			Similarly, Likewise, In the same way,
To signal a contrast	but yet	while, although	In contrast, However, On the other hand, Conversely, Instead
To signal a concession	yet	although, though, even though	Nevertheless, Even so, Admittedly, Despite this,
To emphasize			In fact, Actually,
To clarify			In other words, In simpler words, More simply,
To give a reason/cause	for	because, since	
To show a result	so	so	As a result, As a consequence, Consequently, Therefore, Thus,
To show time relationships		after, as soon as, before, when, while, until, since, whenever, as	Afterward, First, Second, Next, Then, Finally, Subsequently, Meanwhile, In the meantime,
To signal a condition		if, even if, unless, provided that, when	
To signal a purpose		so that, in order that	
To signal a choice	or		
To signal a conclusion			In conclusion, To summarize, As we have seen, In brief, In closing, To sum up, Finally,

GLOSSARY

- **Adjective** An adjective gives a description of a noun.

    It's a *tall* tree.   He's an *old* man.   My neighbors are *nice*.

- **Adverb** An adverb describes the action of a sentence or an adjective or another adverb.

    She speaks English *fluently*.   I drive *carefully*.

    She speaks English *extremely* well.   She is *very* intelligent.

- **Adverb of Frequency** An adverb of frequency tells how often an action happens.

    I *never* drink coffee.   They *usually* take the bus.

- **Affirmative** *Affirmative* means "yes."

    They *live* in Miami.

- **Apostrophe** ' We use the apostrophe for possession and contractions.

    My *sister's* friend is beautiful. (possession)

    Today *isn't* Sunday. (contraction)

- **Article** An article comes before a noun. It tells if the noun is definite or indefinite. The definite article is *the*. The indefinite articles are *a* and *an*.

    I have *a* cat.   I ate *an* apple.   *The* teacher came late.

- **Auxiliary Verb** An auxiliary verb is used in forming tense, mood, or aspect of the verb that follows it. Some verbs have two parts: an auxiliary verb and a main verb.

    You *didn't* eat lunch.   He *can't* study.   We *will* return.

- **Base Form** The base form of the verb has no tense. It has no ending (*-s* or *-ed*): *be, go, eat, take, write*.

    I didn't *go*.   We don't *know* you.   He can't *drive*.

- **Capital Letter** A B C D E F G . . .

- **Clause** A clause is a group of words that has a subject and a verb. Some sentences have only one clause.

    She speaks Spanish.

Some sentences have a **main clause** and a **dependent clause**.

MAIN CLAUSE	DEPENDENT CLAUSE (**reason clause**)
She found a good job	because she has computer skills.

MAIN CLAUSE	DEPENDENT CLAUSE (**time clause**)
She'll turn off the light	before she goes to bed.

MAIN CLAUSE	DEPENDENT CLAUSE (***if* clause**)
I'll take you to the doctor	if you don't have your car on Saturday.

- **Colon** :

- **Comma** ,

- **Comparative** The comparative form of an adjective or adverb is used to compare two things.

    My house is *bigger* than your house.

    Her husband drives *faster* than she does.

    My children speak English *more fluently* than I do.

- **Consonant** The following letters are consonants: *b, c, d, f, g, h, j, k, l, m, n, p, q, r, s, t, v, w, x, y, z.*

    NOTE: *Y* is sometimes considered a vowel, as in the world *syllable.*

- **Contraction** A contraction is two words joined with an apostrophe.

    He's my brother.   *You're* late.   They *won't* talk to me.

    (*He's* = *he is*)   (*You're* = *you are*)   (*won't* = *will not*)

- **Count Noun** Count nouns are nouns that we can count. They have a singular and a plural form.

    1 pen–3 pens   1 table–4 tables

- **Dependent Clause** See **Clause**.

- **Direct Object** A direct object is a noun (phrase) or pronoun that receives the action of the verb.

    We saw *the movie.*   You have *a nice car.*   I love *you.*

- **Exclamation Mark** !

- **Frequency Word** Frequency words (*always, usually, generally, often, sometimes, rarely, seldom, hardly ever, never.*) tell how often an action happens.

    I *never* drink coffee.   We *always* do our homework.

- **Hyphen** -

- **Imperative** An imperative sentence gives a command or instructions. An imperative sentence omits the subject pronoun *you.*

    Come here.   *Don't be* late.   Please *help* me.

- **Infinitive** An infinitive is *to* + the base form.

    I want *to leave.*   You need *to be* here on time.

- **Linking Verb** A linking verb is a verb that links the subject to the noun, adjective, or adverb after it. Linking verbs include *be, seem, feel, smell, sound, look, appear,* and *taste.*

    She *is* a doctor.   She *looks* tired.   You *are* late.

- **Main Clause** See **Clause**.

- **Modal** The modal verbs are *can, could, shall, should, will, would, may, might,* and *must.*

    They *should* leave.   I *must* go.

- **Negative** *Negative* means "no."

- **Nonaction Verb** A nonaction verb has no action. We do not use a continuous tense (*be* + verb *-ing*) with a nonaction verb. The nonaction verbs are: *believe, cost, care, have, hear, know, like, love, matter, mean, need, own, prefer, remember, see, seem, think, understand, want,* and sense-perception verbs.

    She *has* a laptop.   We *love* our mother.   You *look* great.

- **Noncount Noun** A noncount noun is a noun that we don't count. It has no plural form.

    She drank some *water.*   He prepared some *rice.*

    Do you need any *money?*   We had a lot of *homework.*

- **Noun** A noun is a person, a place, or a thing. Nouns can be either count or noncount.

    My *brother* lives in California.   My *sisters* live in New York.

    I get *advice* from them.   I drink *coffee* every day.

- **Noun Modifier** A noun modifier makes a noun more specific.

    fire department   *Independence* Day   *can* opener

- **Noun Phrase** A noun phrase is a group of words that form the subject or object of a sentence.

  A very nice woman helped me.　　I bought *a big box of cereal*.

- **Object** The object of a sentence follows the verb. It receives the action of the verb.

  He bought *a car*.　　I saw *a movie*.　　I met *your brother*.

- **Object Pronoun** We use object pronouns (*me, you, him, her, it, us, them*) after a verb or preposition.

  He likes *her*.　　I saw the movie. Let's talk about *it*.

- **Parentheses** ( )

- **Paragraph** A paragraph is a group of sentences about one topic.

- **Past Participle** The past participle of a verb is the third form of the verb.

  You have *written* a good essay.　　I was *told* about the concert.

- **Period** .

- **Phrasal Modal** Phrasal modals, such as *ought to, be able to,* are made up of two or more words.

  You *ought to* study more.　　We *have to* take a test.

- **Phrase** A group of words that go together.

  Last month my sister came to visit.　There is a strange car *in front of my house*.

- **Plural** *Plural* means "more than one." A plural noun usually ends with *-s*.

  She has beautiful *eyes*.　　My *feet* are big.

- **Possessive Form** Possessive forms show ownership or relationship.

  Mary's coat is in the closet.　　*My* brother lives in Miami.

- **Preposition** A preposition is a short connecting word. Some common prepositions are: *about, above, across, after, around, as, at, away, back, before, behind, below, by, down, for, from, in, into, like, of, off, on, out, over, to, under, up,* and *with*.

  The book is *on* the table.　　She studies *with* her friends.

- **Present Participle** The present participle of a verb is the base form + *-ing*.

  She is *sleeping*.　　They were *laughing*.

- **Pronoun** A pronoun takes the place of a noun.

  I have a new car. I bought *it* last week.

  John likes Mary, but *she* doesn't like *him*.

- **Punctuation** The use of specific marks, such as commas and periods, to make ideas within writing clear.

- **Question Mark** ?

- **Quotation Marks** " "

- **Regular Verb** A regular verb forms the simple past with *-ed*.

  He *worked* yesterday.　　I *laughed* at the joke.

- **-s Form** A present tense verb that ends in *-s* or *-es*.

  He *lives* in New York.　　She *watches* TV a lot.

- **Sense-Perception Verb** A sense-perception verb has no action. It describes a sense. The common sense-perception verbs are: *look, feel, taste, sound,* and *smell.*

    She *feels* fine.   The coffee *smells* fresh.   The milk *tastes* sour.

- **Sentence** A sentence is a group of words that contains a subject and a verb and gives a complete thought.

    SENTENCE: She came home.

    NOT A SENTENCE: When she came home

- **Singular** *Singular* means "one."

    She ate a *sandwich*.   I have one *television*.

- **Subject** The subject of the sentence tells who or what the sentence is about.

    My sister got married last April. *The wedding* was beautiful.

- **Subject Pronoun** We use a subject pronoun (*I, you, he, she, it, we, you, they*) before a verb.

    They speak Japanese.   *We* speak Spanish.

- **Superlative** The superlative form of an adjective or adverb shows the number one item in a group of three or more.

    January is the *coldest* month of the year.

    My brother speaks English the *best* in my family.

- **Syllable** A syllable is a part of a word. Each syllable has only one vowel sound. (Some words have only one syllable.)

    change (one syllable)   after (af·ter = two syllables)

    possible (pos-si-ble = three syllables)   responsible (re·spon·si·ble = four syllables)

- **Tag Question** A tag question is a short question at the end of a sentence. It is used in conversation.

    You speak Spanish, *don't you*?   He's not happy, *is he*?

- **Tense** Tense shows when the action of the sentence happened. Verbs have different tenses.

    SIMPLE PRESENT: She usually *works* hard.

    PRESENT CONTINUOUS: She *is working* now.

    SIMPLE PAST: She *worked* yesterday.

    FUTURE: She *will work* tomorrow.

- **Verb** A verb is the action of the sentence.

    He *runs* fast.   I *speak* English.

- **Vowel** The following letters are vowels: *a, e, i, o, u.*

    NOTE: *Y* is sometimes considered a vowel, as in the world *syllable.*

INDEX

NOTES

NOTES

NOTES

NOTES

NOTES